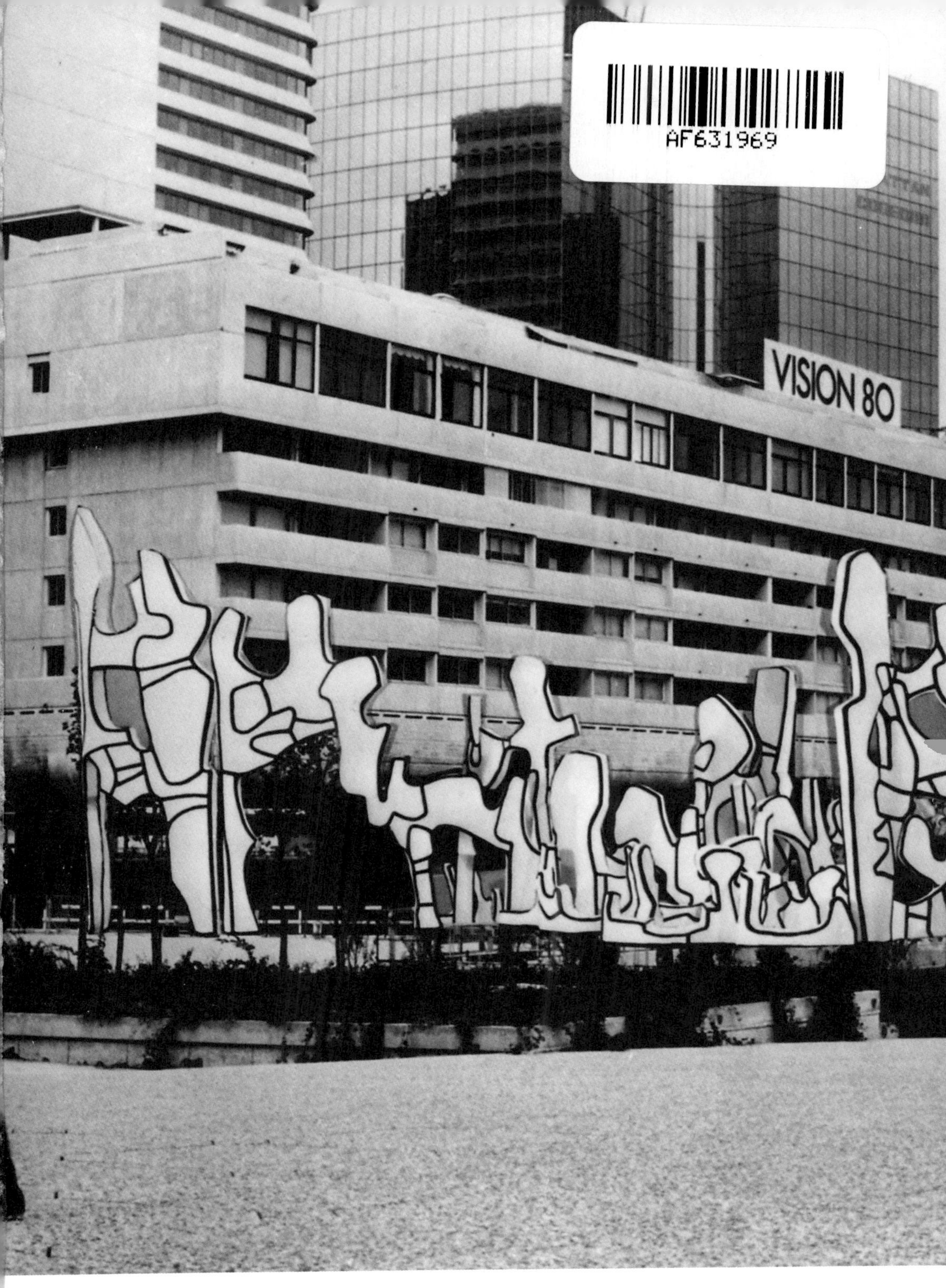
VISION 80

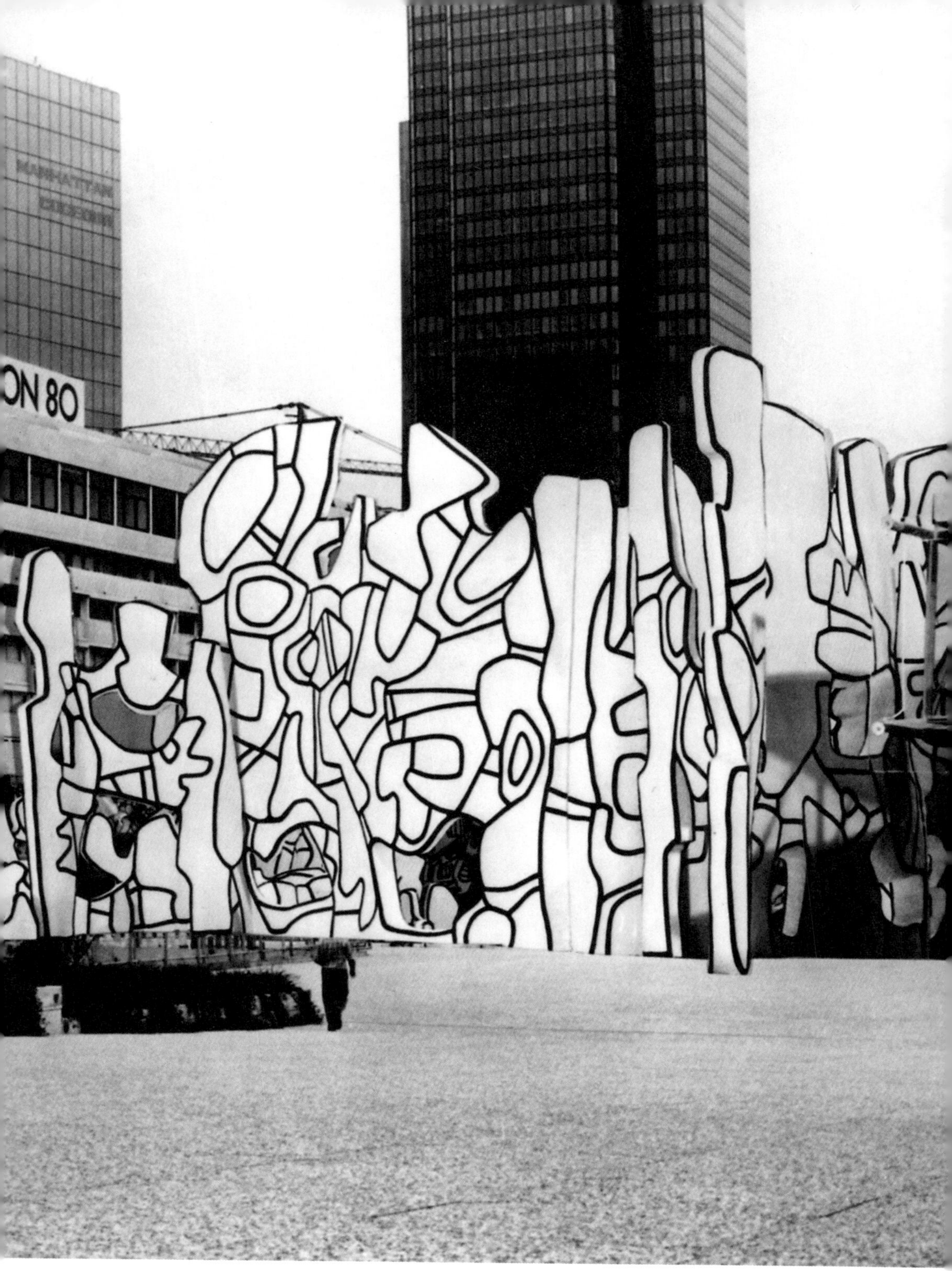
ON 80

Dubuffet and the City

People, Place, and Urban Space

Sophie Berrebi

Hauser & Wirth Publishers

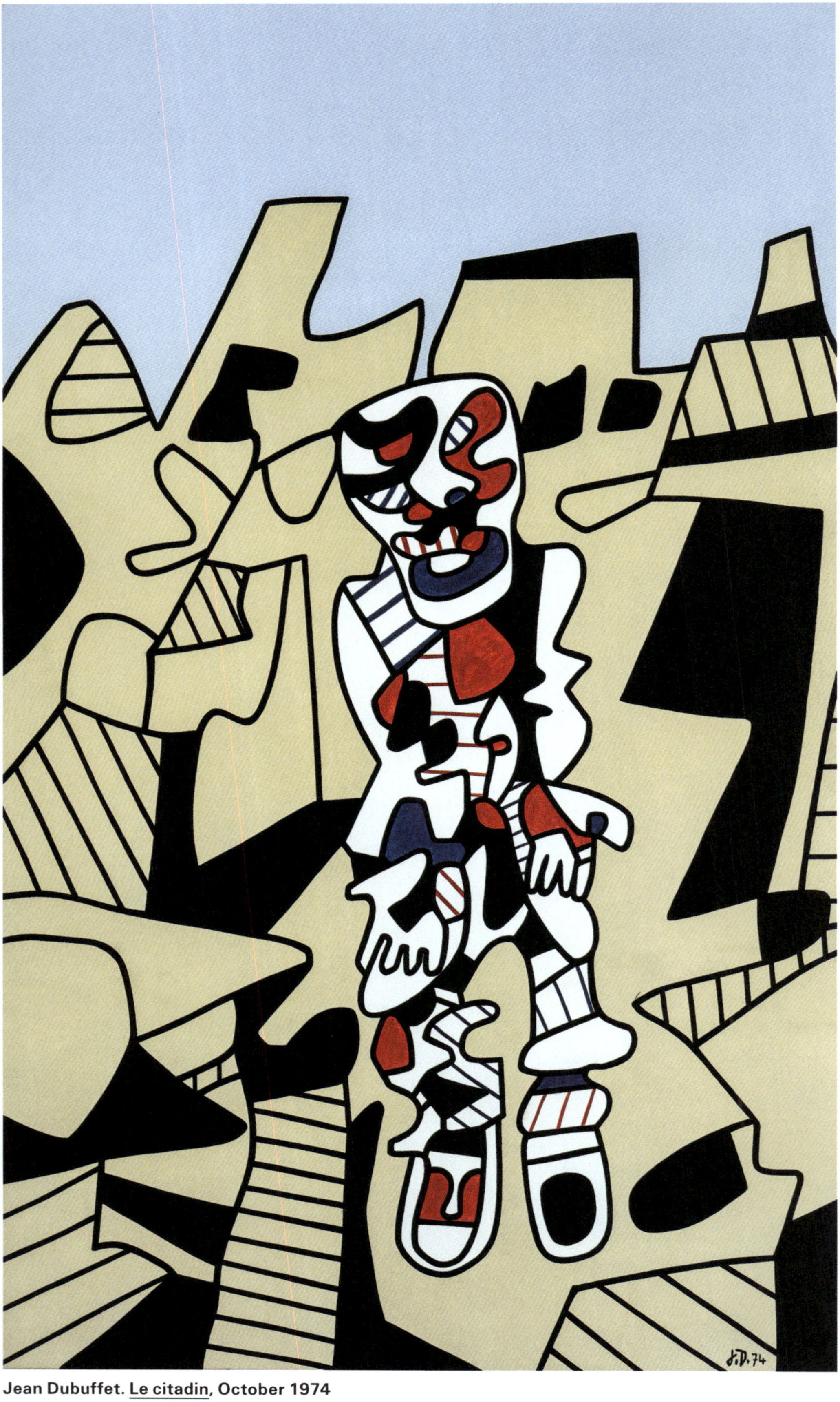

Jean Dubuffet. Le citadin, October 1974

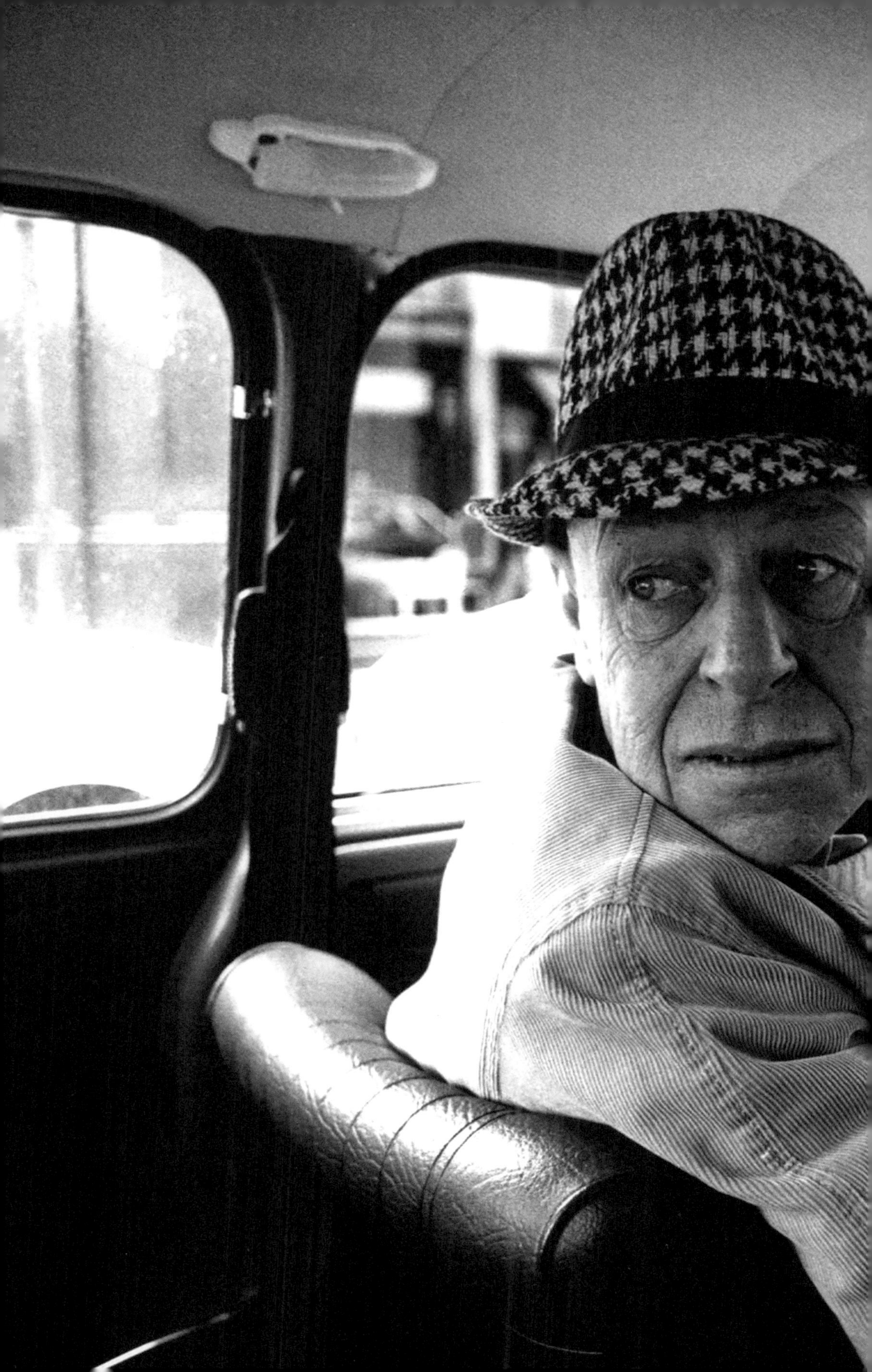

To Teri Wehn-Damisch
To Hubert Damisch, in memoriam

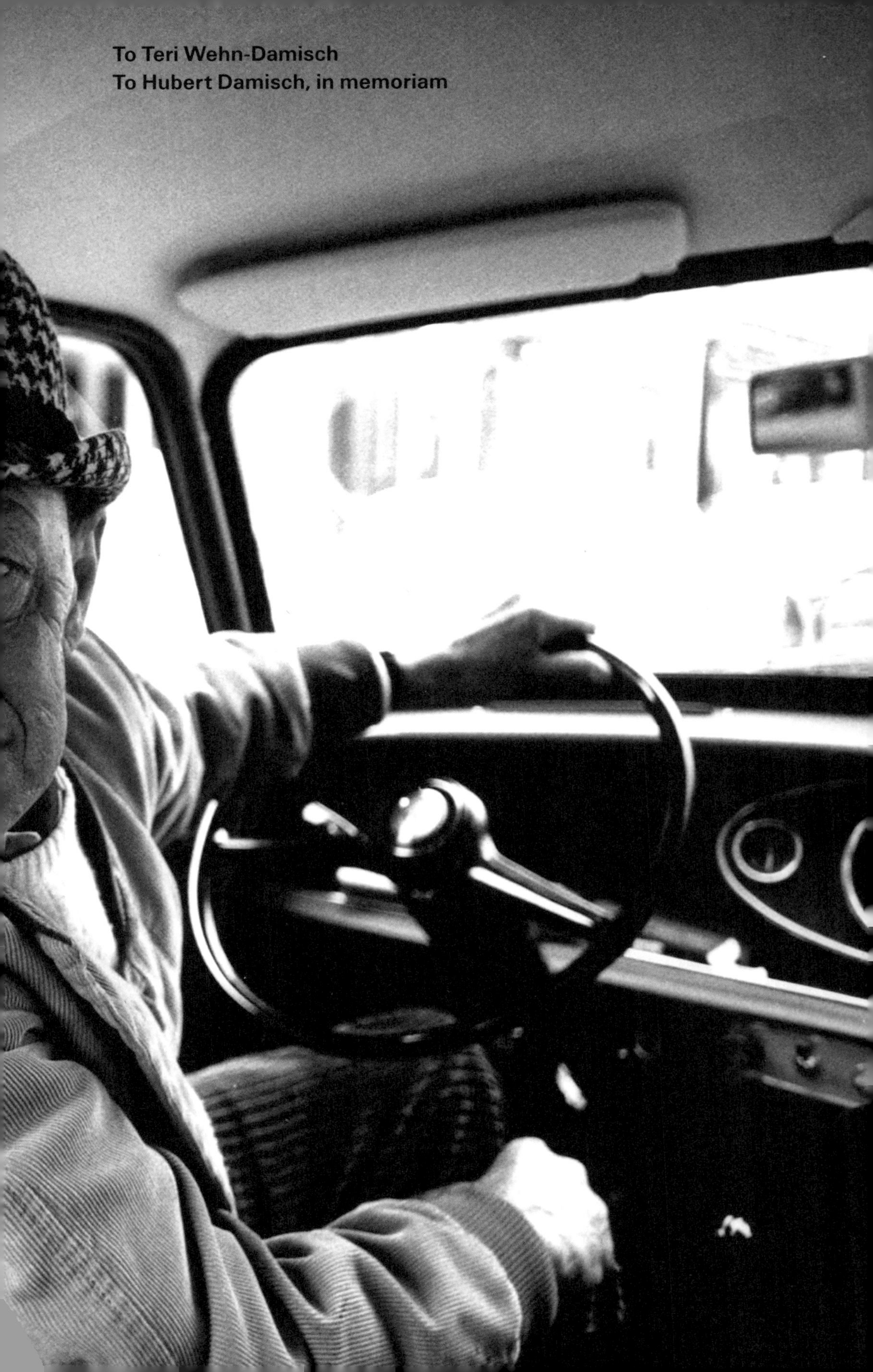

Contents

Editorial Note

Many of the titles Jean Dubuffet gave to his works of art are multivalent and/or incorporate wordplay in the original French. Thus, throughout the book, titles of works appear in the original language (very rarely, the artist titled a work in English himself), followed by an English translation at the first occurrence only in those cases in which the original title is purely descriptive and straightforward. The List of Illustrations on pages 277–83 also includes English translations, according to the same criteria. All works on view in the 2018 exhibition *Jean Dubuffet and the City*, Hauser & Wirth Zürich, are reproduced in the book and identified by asterisks in the List of Illustrations.

Quotations from unpublished correspondence conducted in French, from writings by Jean Dubuffet not previously translated into English, and from works of history and criticism written in French and not available in English are plentiful in this volume and have been translated by the author. Those responsible for all previously published translations of primary and secondary material quoted in the text are identified in the notes that appear after each chapter.

Furthermore, interspersed between the chapters are four longer texts by Dubuffet that the author has translated into English, three of them for the first time. "Plus modeste" (More Modest) was the first text by Dubuffet to make it into print. It appeared under the title "Notice commune" in the *Petit guide du visiteur* (*Small Guide for Visitors*), published on the occasion of Dubuffet's April 1945 exhibition of lithographs at Galerie André in Paris. Writing in a colloquial style, Dubuffet sketched his own biography through a series of vivid descriptions illustrating his fascination with everyday life in Paris and concluded with a plea addressed to the prospective gallery visitor to view his art as an unpretentious, modest endeavor.

"Saint-Ouen—le marché" (Saint-Ouen—The Market) narrates a Sunday stroll through the famous flea market at the Porte de Clignancourt, in the north of Paris. The short text was included in *Prospectus aux amateurs de tout genre* (*Prospectus for Amateurs of All Kinds*), the first anthology of Dubuffet's writings, compiled by Jean Paulhan and published by Gallimard in 1946. In the context of a 1967 reprint, in the collected writings of the artist, the editor, Hubert Damisch, explained that around the time this piece was composed, in 1944, Dubuffet was planning to write a "guide to Paris" that would include only unremarkable sites, devoid of any possible interest to tourists.

A third text, the assemblage poem *Trémolo sur l'œil* (Tremor on the Eye), is included here in facsimile as well as translation (running below the pages and following the typographic conventions adopted by Damisch in 1967). Written by the artist in October 1962 and published as a small book in 1963 in an edition of three hundred, the text is close in style and content to the inscriptions included in the paintings of the *Paris Circus* series. It "collages" bits of language found in public spaces, such as information on storefronts, handwritten messages on doors, names of places from signs, and common expressions heard on the street. Interwoven among these "found" phrases are nonsensical expressions and invented words. Dubuffet's scrawled handwriting covers the pages and surrounds sketches of figures drawn in styles that recall those of the various series with which he was then occupied: *Paris Circus*, *Légendes*, and *L'Hourloupe*.

Finally, "Réalisme radical" (Radical Realism), dated July 1983, is the latest text included here and offers a glimpse of the more drastic position regarding representation Dubuffet adopted in the closing years of his life. The first English translation appeared in the catalogue for an exhibition held at the Palazzo Martinengo in Brescia in 2002, *Dubuffet e l'arte dei graffiti*.

Introduction

Il est impossible de pas se contredire comme il est impossible d'éviter les télescopages sur les chemins à une seule pente mais il faut organiser la pensée sur le modèle de la circulation des véhicules à Tokyo avec des voies superposées à différents niveaux et dévolues à rouler en sens différents.

—Jean Dubuffet, 1978

More than ever, the city is all we have.

—Rem Koolhaas, 1994

Dubuffet and the City: People, Place, and Urban Space.

On the wall of the room in which I write this book, at the Fondation Dubuffet in Paris, hangs a large painting titled Dramatisation (fig. 1).[1] It depicts, in its center, a figure seated at a desk, in the same position as mine as I sit here writing. In the painting, by Jean Dubuffet, the figure lifts its head away from the table and looks out to the left, just as I, in an almost perfect mirror image, look up to the right to meet its gaze. But while I sit in a silent and empty room, the figure in the painting is surrounded by people and places: figures walking and talking in pairs, men alone, in suits and ties, looking worried, or perhaps just lost in their thoughts. They do not interact with the seated figure, however, because each is enclosed in its own space—a space that is delimited by a brushstroke or by the limits of the sheet of paper on which it is painted. The work, indeed, is an assemblage of smaller paintings on paper, combined by the artist onto a canvas support. No fewer than forty-two pieces are fitted together in the picture, which measures approximately three meters (well over ten feet) wide and over two meters (almost seven feet) high.

Between the scenes containing figures are areas covered in patterns, scrawls, and other drawings. In some of them, I can make out a pond, a parking lot, the façade of a modern building, and, seen from above, a dizzying network of highways stacked one above the other, with cars moving simultaneously in different directions. Or perhaps I am just imagining things, and it is the figure seated at the desk who is remembering experiences, moments, and places. Then again, maybe the scenes and places have nothing to do with one another or with the seated figure in the center of the picture. In the same way that cars on a highway enclose random lives and stories that happen to move briefly into view of one another, Dubuffet, here, may just have been inviting us to think about things that happen concurrently and independently from one another in different corners of a large, bustling place—a city, let's say. For although the series entitled Théâtres de mémoire (1975–79), which includes this painting of 1978, is not explicitly about the metropolis, the way in which the works in the cycle juxtapose heterogeneous scenes, moments, and patterns to create large pictures always seems to me to evoke a certain idea of the contemporary city: fragmented, busy, and discontinuous, yet interconnected through invisible networks.

My aim in this book is, first of all, to trace and identify signs of the city in Dubuffet's oeuvre. Some of them are self-evident, such as the figures of city dwellers that recur in countless works of all periods

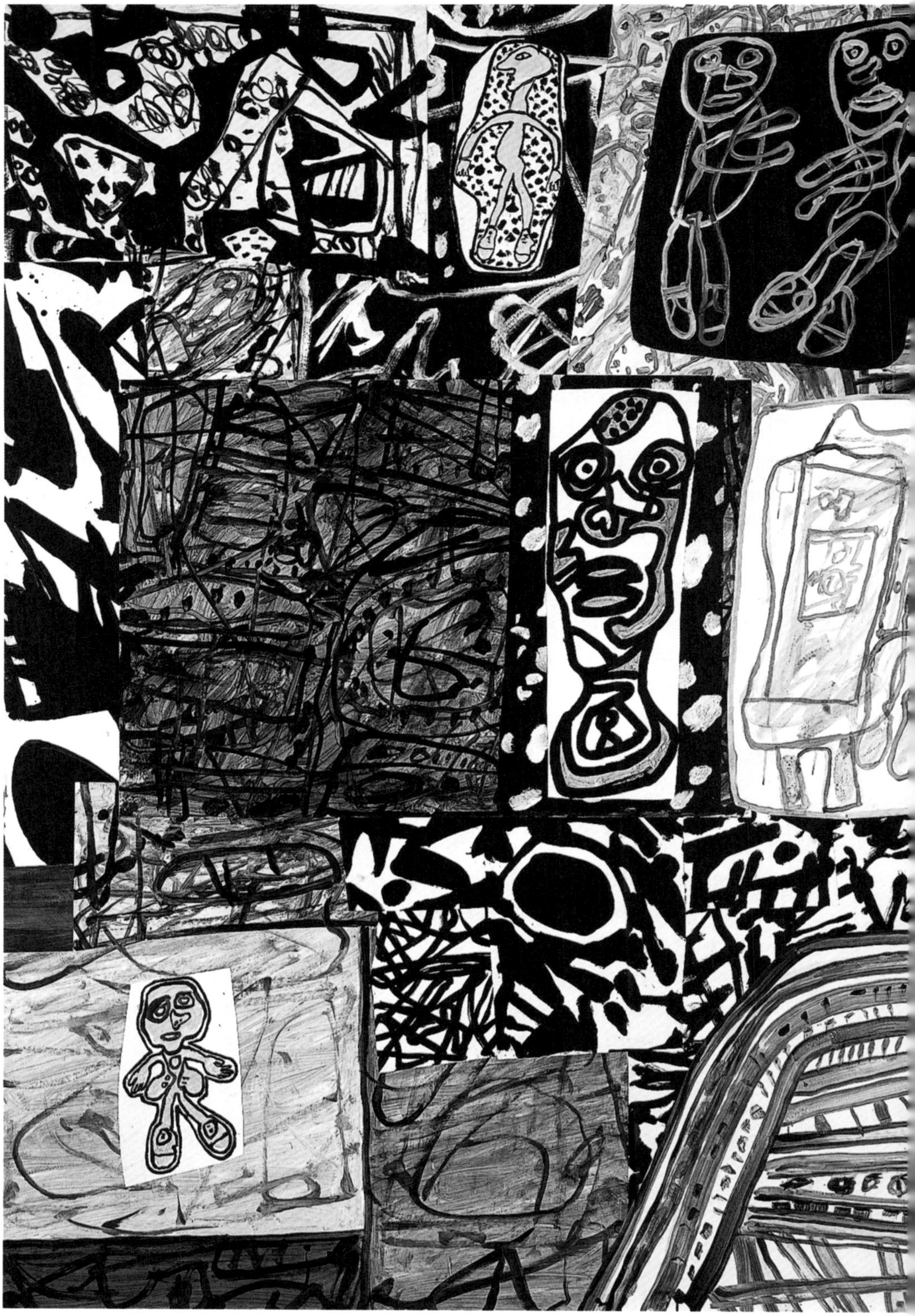

1. Jean Dubuffet. Dramatisation, January 12, 1978

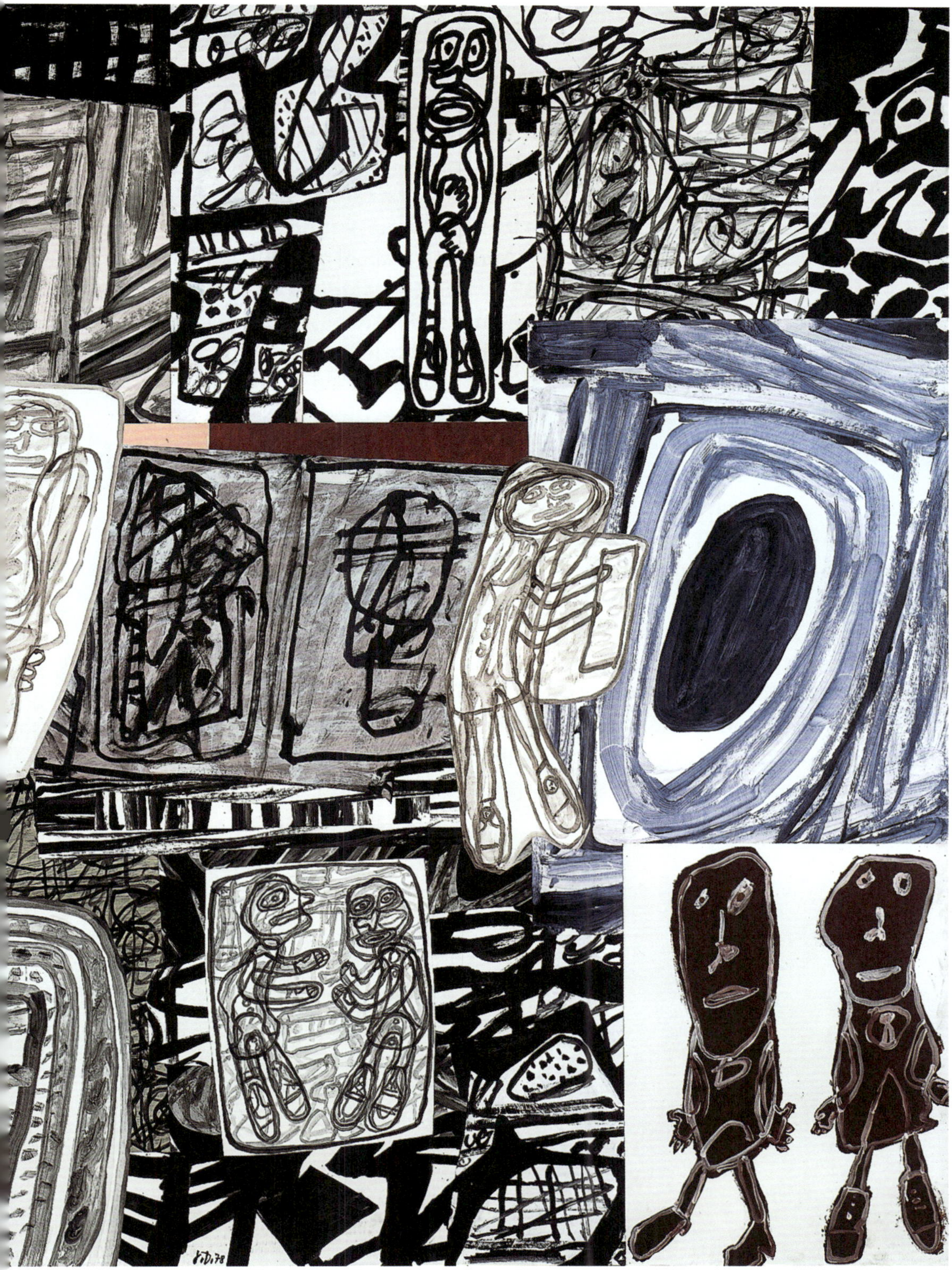

and the models for monuments he designed to be erected in the city. Further, the titles he gave to many of his paintings, drawings, and sculptures include the word *rue* (street), and several contain *Paris* or *ville* (city or town)—words that also show up in the titles of important series such as Marionnettes de la ville et de la campagne (Marionnettes of the City and the Country) of 1942–45 and Paris Circus of 1961–62. In other works, traces of the city are less obvious. Paintings on paper included in the series Lieux abrégés (Abridged Places) of 1975, Partitions of 1980–81, Psycho-sites of 1981–82, and Sites aléatoires (Random Sites; fig. 3) of 1982 claim to be about unspecified sites and places yet are filled with figures in business suits that Dubuffet sometimes called *passants*, or "passersby" (see figs. 60, 62). The connection with the city seems to be more tenuous here, as in the aforementioned Théâtres de mémoire, and yet I hope to show that these works were similarly produced by a mind in which the urban imaginary was deeply rooted. The sentence I have selected as an epigraph to this introduction (translated on p. 25) suggests as much. Taken from a letter addressed to the artist Pierre Carbonel, it dates to August 1978, a time when Dubuffet was fully immersed in making Théâtres de mémoire. The phrasing stuck with him, and he reiterated it years later in Bâtons rompus, the book-length essay presented in the form of questions and answers that was published shortly after his death, in 1985. There, he introduced a small change in the formulation: "I believe that thought obtains usable fruit only by constituting itself in a plural circulation, in layers, that are like the superimposed layers on the stacked highways of Tokyo."[2]

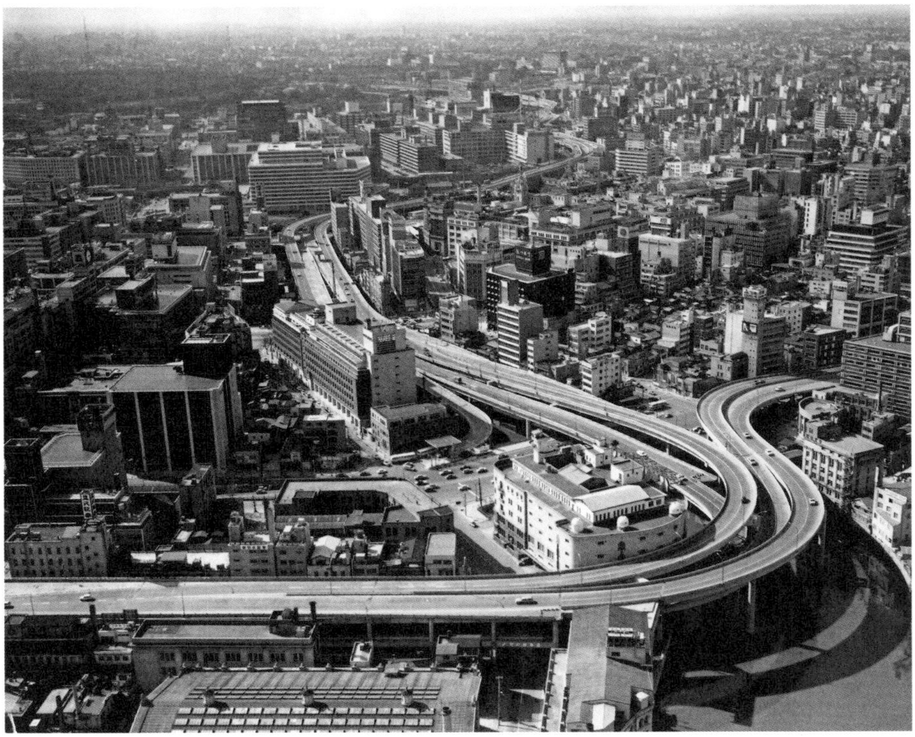

2. View of Tokyo, ca. 1960

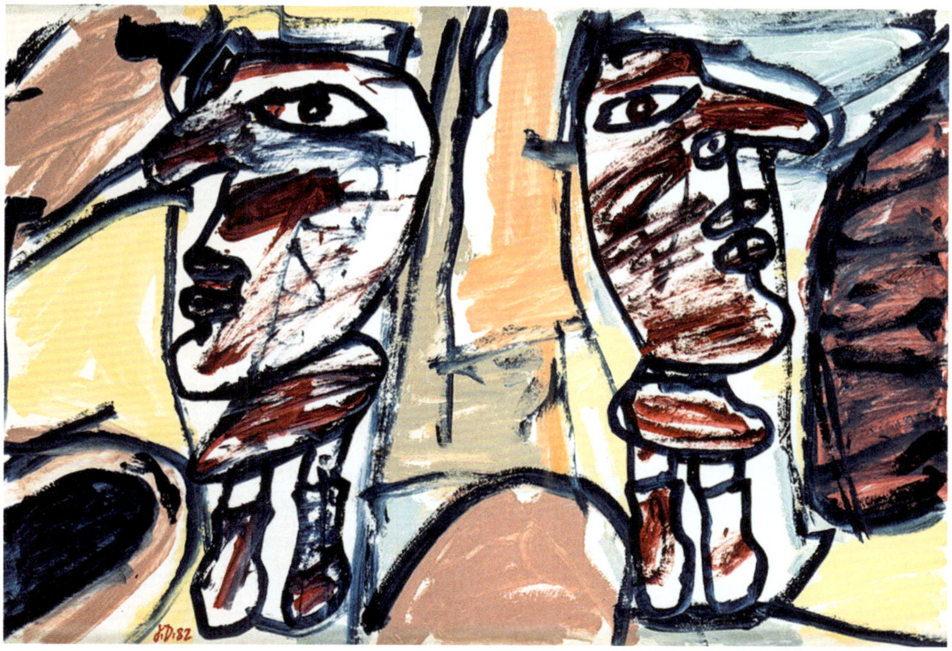

3. Jean Dubuffet. Site aléatoire avec deux personnages, June 24, 1982

In both versions of the metaphor, Dubuffet used the spectacular image of Tokyo's highway network to explain the workings of the mind. The image is both highly unusual and unmistakably Dubuffet. It is unexpected because the artist rarely evoked a specific urban feature; moreover, he never visited Tokyo in person. Images of its highway interchanges must have come to him through the press or perhaps television, and we can imagine that they appealed to him—a Parisian of the generation that had witnessed the beginnings of the automobile industry—both as an incongruous folly and as the apex of motorized urban modernity (fig. 2). I can imagine he may also have enjoyed mentioning so casually, as if it were familiar to him, a city that was so far away, just as, a few years later, in the paintings of the Mires series of 1983, he repeatedly referred to another place in Asia, equally unknown to him: Hong Kong's Kowloon.

And yet, such a sentence as my epigraph could be expected from Dubuffet, if only because "contradiction" is a term that has come to define both the artist and the man. Some critics have raised it, for example, when confronted with his claim to paint like ***l'homme du commun*** (Everyman) and the seemingly antipodal reality of an oeuvre that, in fact, resembles no one else's.[3] Other authors have been keen to point out that the artist repeatedly proclaimed his disdain of museums yet, over the years, exhibited his work in and entered the collections of some of the world's most eminent ones.

As for the idea of multiple streams of thought appearing simultaneously at different levels, as with cars converging and dispersing on a complicated highway interchange, this directly relates to what was perhaps Dubuffet's most consistent ambition throughout his career: to capture thoughts and mental images in his works and, even more intently, to convey the processes by which such thoughts form in the mind and then disappear. At the level of his artistic practice, this intention explains the speed at which he sometimes worked (as reflected in the dating of his pictures, often to the day) as well as the large number of works he produced overall (about 10,000 works are recorded in his catalogue raisonné). In letters, statements, and literary texts, Dubuffet frequently articulated the aim that his paintings, and painting in general, conjure thoughts and states of mind. In April 1944, shortly after completing the last of six paintings entitled Vue de Paris (View of Paris)—each bearing a different subtitle—he explained that wish to his friend Jean Paulhan: "It's as a joke that I title [them]: View of Paris. More exact title: 'view of the human mind at the moment when the thought of a View of Paris is in the process of forming itself there.'. . . Of course, it is a close fight, you have to implement all possible means, even tricks, it's true, to come upon this moment and fix it."[4] Statements from the very end of his career show how this idea of capturing and fixing a thought on canvas became more radical and transformed itself into a rejection of the so-called objective world, which he variously called "humanist vision" and a collection of "instituted images."[5] These he sought to reject in favor of a personal notion of reality that he described in several texts, nowhere as assertively as in the 1984 punctuation-free calligraphic artist's book Oriflammes (Banners): "I know that there is no reality outside that which thought institutes I celebrate my marriage with the world that my thought is pleased to project it will be from now on my god my food my bath and my theater."[6]

At this juncture, the first difficulties with dedicating a study to Dubuffet and the city appear. Dubuffet's rejection of the notion of an objective reality, and his desire to fix and depict something as impalpable as streams of thoughts, mean that his work escapes the old categories of abstraction and figuration. Moreover, in view of his notion of "instituted images" (in other words, representations of things that are widely identifiable), the very idea of representation becomes problematic, as the goal becomes to represent thoughts and mental images rather than the tangible objects that surround us. Looking for traces and images of the city might then run the risk of flattening out Dubuffet's work by selecting only those paintings and drawings that illustrate this theme most clearly by including streets, cars, buildings, and their inhabitants painted more or less recognizably, according to the very "humanist vision" the artist decried.

Compiling an iconography of the city is not, however, the purpose of this book. Rather—and the inclusion of series such as Théâtres de mémoire, Partitions, and others bearing no explicit connection to the city plays an important role in this—it is to understand how the city figured into the formation and unfolding of Dubuffet's practice and imaginary as a material, a source, and a vehicle for ideas and as the context in which his oeuvre developed over a period of more than forty years.

In turn, the issue of context poses additional difficulties with regard to Dubuffet's aesthetic posture, because it is something that Dubuffet consistently rejected. To be an artist of his time was not his concern, and instead, consciously or not, he devised strategies to extract himself from the time and place in which he worked.

The first of those strategies can be found in Dubuffet's having, to all intents and purposes, boxed up his youth and the works he produced during the first twenty years following his brief stint at art school. The works he thereby rejected include those he made during a period in 1920–22 when he socialized with the avant-garde artists grouped around André Masson, in Masson's studio on the rue Blomet, and the dealer Daniel-Henry Kahnweiler as well as a moment of experimenting with making masks in Montparnasse in the mid-1930s after meeting Emilie Carlu (Lili), who became his second wife in 1937 (fig. 4). Later, Dubuffet drew a veil over this period by calling it his "prehistory," a term that has been widely adopted by art historians. Dividing his career into "series" and "cycles" of works also contributed to his ability to construct a personal chronology that, to a large extent, eluded the historical context in which his ideas emerged and took form.

Another tactic, reiterated in public statements and interviews, consisted in professing a patent lack of interest in and knowledge of his artistic contemporaries. He extended this stance by refusing to be considered a part of any art movement, including, for example, Art Informel, in the early 1950s. His letter to Michel Tapié following the release of the critic's 1952 book on the subject, Un art autre (Art of Another Kind), which featured a detail of one of his paintings on the cover (fig. 5), was perfectly unambiguous: "I refuse with the greatest force to team up with all this. I do not subscribe to anything that is claimed in this book."[7]

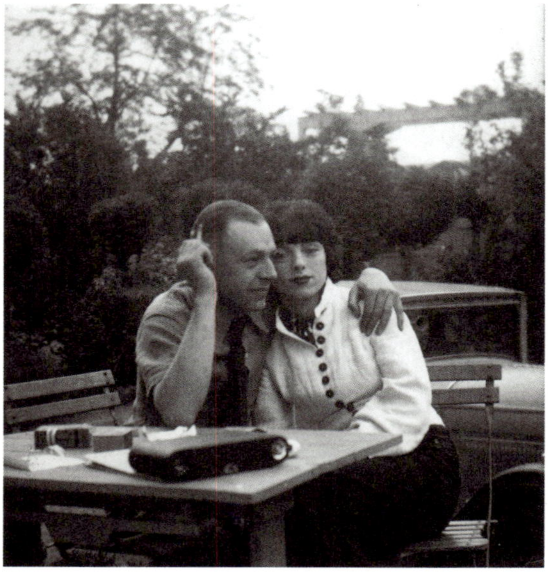

4. Jean Dubuffet and Emilie Carlu (Lili), 1935

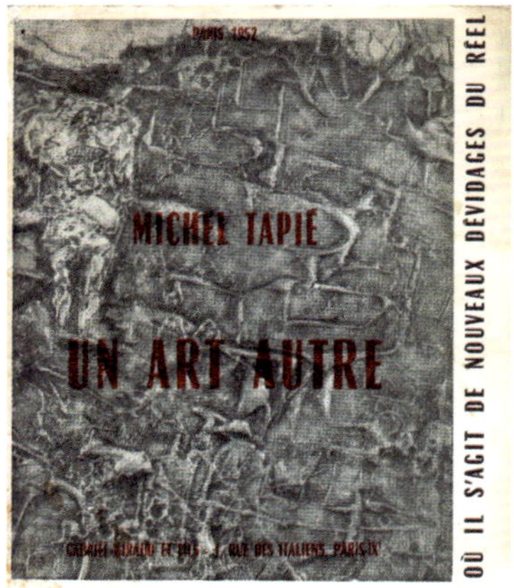

5. Cover of Michel Tapié's Un art autre (1952)

A third way Dubuffet constructed himself and his oeuvre as *hors contexte*—to borrow a phrase from the late philosopher and art historian Hubert Damisch—was by coining the term "Art Brut" in 1945 and fostering the study and collecting of art made by people living at the margins of society.[8] Art Brut supplied Dubuffet with an ersatz community of self-taught individuals, many of whom lived and worked in isolation from each other, from the world, and from the times in which they lived. Its success as a category meant that it could become—and, in some places, did become—the main, if not the only, aesthetic horizon against which Dubuffet's work was measured, casting him as a Robinson Crusoe—as Damisch called him—among other Crusoes.[9] During the artist's lifetime, these strategies were relayed in texts penned by authors who were close to him, such as Georges Limbour and Max Loreau. It is crucial, however, to move beyond the perception of Dubuffet as an artist working in isolation, disconnected from his surroundings, in order to propose new perspectives and create new understandings of his work.

The main context within which I intend to read Dubuffet's art is the historical, geographic, and conceptual framework of the city during a period of time—the second half of the twentieth century—that saw the megalopolis become a global phenomenon. While the city as a changing notion and experience is my primary focus, I devote much attention to the particular case of Paris, where Dubuffet lived and worked for the greater part of his life.

In "Biographie au pas de course" (Biography on the Run), the autobiographical text Dubuffet wrote in February–March 1985, shortly before bringing his life to a close, the artist suggested the importance of the geography of Parisian neighborhoods to the fledgling provincial artist he was in 1918, when he discovered France's capital city. Moving to Paris from his native Le Havre, in northern France, Dubuffet first settled in a room in the Quartier Latin. Soon after, "exhibitions of avant-garde paintings" and "modernist writings" convinced him that art should be "anchored in everyday life": "I took aversion to the Latin Quarter and student discussions. I took up residence in cheap rooms in outlying areas, enjoying the most miserable lodgings. I brought only a small amount of material: a box of paint tubes, canvas-covered boards that I propped up against the back of a chair."[10] A few pages and some time later, Dubuffet met Fernand and Jeanne Léger, and that new friendship led him to new neighborhoods: "I frequented in Montparnasse, in their company, restaurants for drivers and dance halls."[11] In this account, each part of town, with its particular social and economic characteristics, became the context of a different aesthetics, leading, in turn, to different attempts at painting, before Dubuffet left Paris altogether (after what may have been a romantic disappointment) for Buenos Aires, where an uncle of his lived. Aside from residing there for a few months in 1924, the artist also traveled several times to Algiers during the 1920s, where part of the family wine business was located. Over the

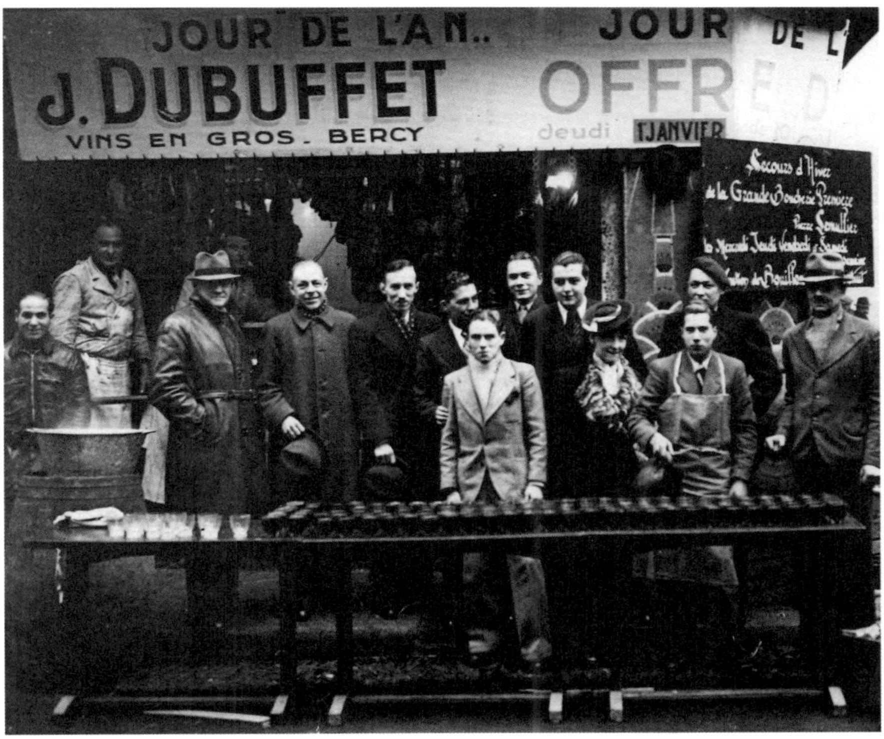

6. Les Halles, Paris (Dubuffet left of center, in buttoned-up overcoat), January 1, 1942

years, he also visited, among other cities, Brussels, Amsterdam, Copenhagen, London, Chicago, and Venice as well as New York, where he lived and worked for six months in 1951–52.[12]

In the 1930s, Dubuffet acquired an exhaustive knowledge of Paris, largely through his professional activities: just as the philosopher Henri Lefebvre, the artist's exact contemporary, gained primary knowledge of France's capital by working for a while in the 1920s as a taxi driver—an experience probably invaluable to becoming, as he did, the foremost theorist of urban space—Dubuffet's wine-dealing activities took him to all corners of Paris.[13] As a wholesale dealer in 1930–35, he worked in the Halle aux Vins in Bercy, a city within the city, selling wines to shops (fig. 6). A new attempt to rededicate himself to art was cut short in 1937, when he was forced to resume managing his business, which was close to bankruptcy. He changed his clientele from shops to cafés and restaurants and, in the essay "Plus modeste" (translated in full on pp. 53–56 as "More Modest"), he vividly evoked the daily efforts to keep the business afloat and make it profitable and described an everyday life made up of "anguished cavalcades through Paris! The crazed quest for orders! The jostling rounds of bill collection until ten o'clock at night ! Litigation! Dog days! Endless rotten luck!"[14]

Paris changed a great deal over Dubuffet's lifetime. The narrow, hilly streets behind the Panthéon where Dubuffet lived with Lili from 1935 to 1945 on the rue Lhomond, which appear in early paintings and drawings, remained relatively protected. But from the allée Maintenon, a small impasse off the rue de Vaugirard where he settled

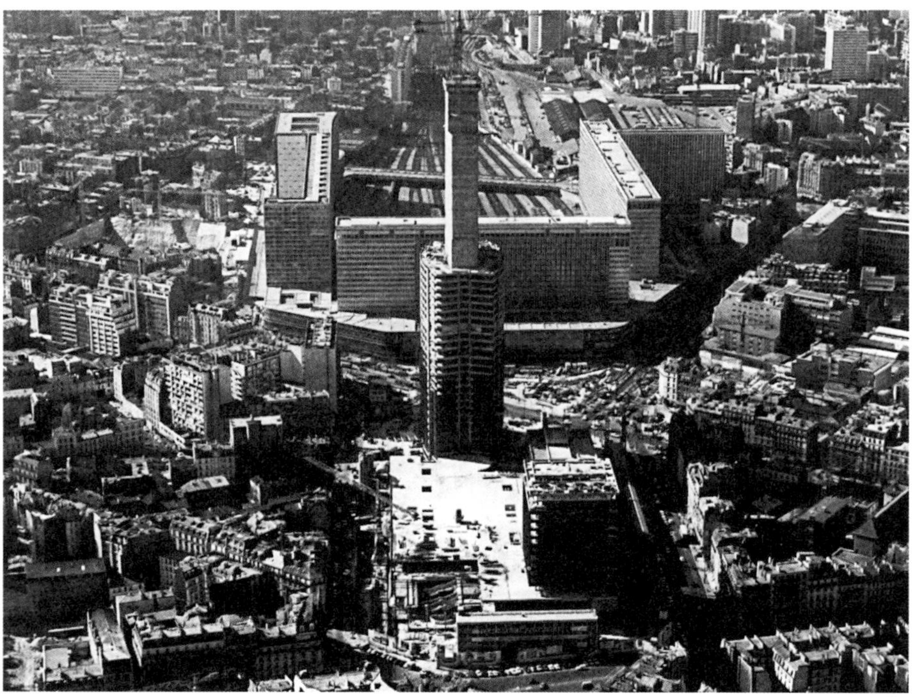

7. Tour Montparnasse under construction, Paris, March 14, 1972

in 1945, Dubuffet was only a stone's throw away from the Maine-Montparnasse development, one of the largest urban projects of the 1960s (see fig. 24). The Paris of the 1940s had altered comparatively little since the late nineteenth century, when the Seine Department prefect Baron Georges-Eugène Haussmann devised and implemented, under the lead of Napoléon III, a new master plan of the city and ordered extensive destruction and renovation of insalubrious areas. Haussmannian plans continued to be carried out into the 1920s. The Second World War and its immediate aftermath halted urban reforms devised in the 1930s, so it was only in the late 1950s that a flurry of new public plans and private developments of entire neighborhoods, including buildings, roadwork, and underground transportation, began to significantly modify the appearance of and everyday life in the city. Next to this, the emergence of new towns and so-called *grands ensembles*—huge housing estates—changed the landscape of Paris's rapidly extending suburbs. Within Paris, the most notable projects included the Maine-Montparnasse, Beaugrenelle, Belleville, and place d'Italie areas, the Réseau Express Régional (RER), the boulevard Périphérique, and the project that caused the greatest upset and lengthiest debates: Les Halles.[15] In the city's immediate outskirts, the development of the business neighborhood La Défense was of direct interest to Dubuffet, as he worked for several years, in the 1970s, on a commission for a large sculpture to be placed on the concrete esplanade, or deck, situated on axis with the Palais du Louvre and the Arc de Triomphe.

While these large-scale projects were needed to make the city safer and healthier, and were indeed presented as such, the planning and building boom of the 1960s was also ideologically triggered, by a spirit of modernization; historians have noted the ways in which space, circulation, and "urban fabric" became key notions promulgated by technocrats and urban developers. Moreover, as France lost its colonial empire and became a founding member of what is now the European Union, centralization, which had, for a moment in the postwar period, subsided—particularly following the publication, in 1947, of Jean-François Gravier's influential book Paris et le désert français—resumed in force.[16] The idea that Paris should be the new capital city of Europe (a title it eventually conceded to Brussels) spurred monumental plans for modernization of the city's infrastructure that, in time, turned Paris from a metropolis into a megalopolis.

As abundant literary and artistic production attests, writers and visual artists responded to these changes to the city. Dubuffet's answer was perhaps less immediately graspable than others'. He did not, like the writer and theorist Guy Debord, cut up maps of the city to create "psychogeographic" charts (fig. 8); yet, his Théâtres de mémoire and Tableaux d'assemblage create a similar effect of disorientation and singling out of particular "moments" (see fig. 45). Nor did Dubuffet gather fragments of everyday objects such as posters and handbills to integrate them into works of art, as the Nouveaux Réalistes did (fig. 9); instead, he embraced new materials such as Styrofoam and ballpoint pens. And while Jean-Luc Godard and Jacques Tati made, each in his own style, film essays and satires about the *grands ensembles* and the anonymous-looking high-rises mushrooming throughout the suburbs, Dubuffet, instead, designed outlandish architectural projects destined to be built in some of those new settings. The artist did not, as the novelist Georges Perec did in 1978, stand at the intersection of the rue Mabillon and the boulevard Saint-Germain to describe every single person and car that passed in front of him.[17] Instead, he compiled a list of names and words he saw on those streets and, adding a few imaginary ones, turned them into an urban poem of sorts in Trémolo sur l'œil (Tremor on the Eye),

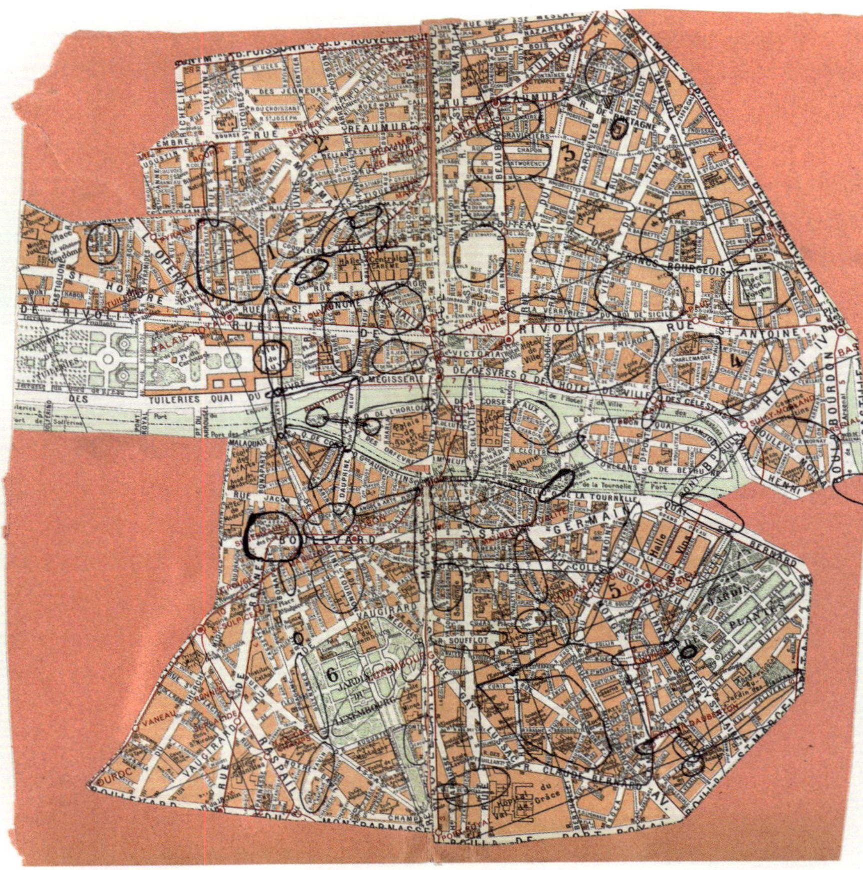

8. Guy Debord. Carte de Paris avant 1957, 1957

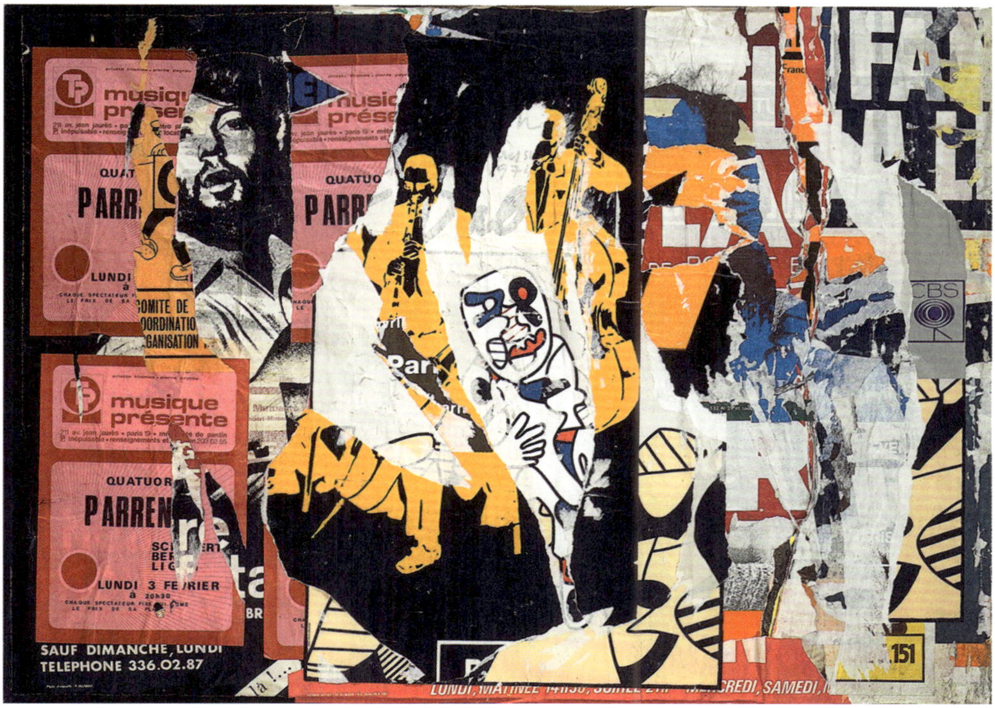

9. Jacques de la Villeglé. Ex-26, rue du Pont-Neuf, March 11, 1975

a wondrous little book that is reproduced in extenso and translated on pages 223–42 of this volume.

To analyze what Dubuffet did, how he did it, and to what effect, I propose to examine a number of works and series in the thematic chapters that follow. I first approach the city from a distance, from which it can be seen as a totality, before delving into its networks, looking at its inhabitants and its architecture, and, finally, in the concluding section, speculating about how it is possible to sense and represent place in a changing city.

Put differently, the first chapter deals with the ideas of "view" and "network" from Dubuffet's Vues de Paris of the 1940s, through the Paris Circus series of the early 1960s, and concluding with Théâtres de mémoire in the late 1970s. Following this, I turn to Dubuffet's conception of *l'homme du commun* and unpack the notion of the "man in the street" to review its various conceptual and formal incarnations throughout his oeuvre. The third chapter examines Dubuffet's architecture and sculpture projects. Starting with his 1968–69 exhibition Jean Dubuffet: Édifices, projets et maquettes d'architecture, which mimicked the genre of the architectural exhibition, I read his photomontages, architectural models, and monuments

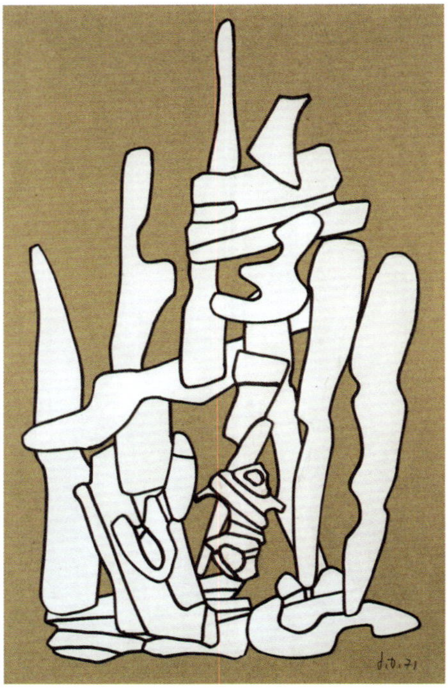

10. Jean Dubuffet. Monument, March 29, 1971

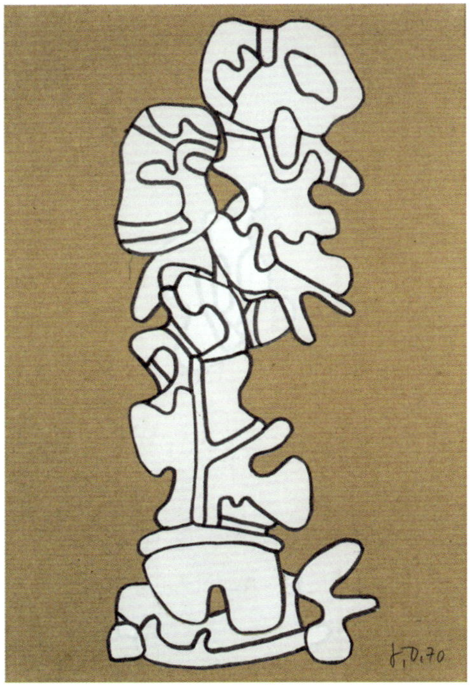

11. Jean Dubuffet. Monument à l'homme portant un lionceau, August 11, 1970

of the late 1960s and 1970s against the backdrop of the postwar International Style (and its offshoot, corporate modernism) in order to assess, through the artist's exchanges with scholars, journalists, and architects, his ambitions and their reception. Finally, in the concluding chapter, I narrow the focus of my investigation to the concept of place, which is evoked in multiple titles of works, including the monument project for La Défense, Site scripturaire, designed in 1973–74. Discussing the philosophical and geographic implications of these terms, I argue for their importance in Dubuffet's oeuvre and its relation to the city.

As this outline makes clear, the book deliberately moves back and forth within Dubuffet's chronology. To some extent, this is in keeping with the artist's own practice: his career is more easily summed up visually as a spiral than as a straight line, and he frequently looked back to older work when attempting to take his investigations "in a new direction."[18] Hence, Paris Circus reprises Marionnettes de la ville et de la campagne, while Théâtres de mémoire seems to recapitulate his entire oeuvre. In cutting through series and decades, I follow in the footsteps of the artist's own spiral-shaped trajectory.

Epigraphs: Jean Dubuffet to Pierre Carbonel, August 15, 1978, in Jean Dubuffet, Prospectus et tous écrits suivants, ed. Hubert Damisch, 4 vols. (Paris: Gallimard, 1967–95), vol. 3 (1995), 469. "It is impossible not to contradict oneself, just as it is impossible to avoid collisions on paths that have only one slope, but one must organize thoughts following the model of the circulation of cars in Tokyo, with lanes that are superimposed onto one another and on which traffic is organized in different directions." This translation from the French, and all others in the present volume, unless otherwise indicated, are my own. In the notes to all chapters, these four volumes of Dubuffet's writing are abbreviated as PES, followed by volume and page number.

Rem Koolhaas, "What Ever Happened to Urbanism?" (1994), in Office for Metropolitan Architecture, Rem Koolhaas, and Bruce Mau, S, M, L, XL, ed. Jennifer Sigler (Rotterdam: 010, 1995), 971.

Dubuffet's catalogue raisonné, Catalogue des travaux de Jean Dubuffet, begun by the artist himself in 1964, was issued in thirty-eight volumes between 1966 and 1991 by several different publishers. The first twenty-eight volumes have introductions by the Belgian philosopher and art critic Max Loreau (1928–1990), and the last ten, by Dubuffet himself. Several volumes have been reprinted or republished in the intervening years. In the notes to all chapters, the catalogue raisonné is abbreviated as CTJD, followed by the volume number, title, and publication details.

1 I am grateful to the Fondation Dubuffet for welcoming me during the research and writing of this book in the summer of 2017.

2 Jean Dubuffet, Bâtons rompus (1985), PES, vol. 3 (1995), 143.

3 On this point, see Hubert Damisch, "Dubuffet ou la lecture du monde" (1962), reprinted in Hubert Damisch, Entrée en matière: Correspondance 1961–1985, Textes 1961–2014, ed. Sophie Berrebi (Paris: La Maison Rouge–Fondation Antoine de Galbert; Zürich: JRP Ringier, 2016), 87.

4 Dubuffet to Jean Paulhan, [April 1944], in Jean Dubuffet and Jean Paulhan, Correspondance 1944–1968, ed. Julien Dieudonné and Marianne Jakobi (Paris: Gallimard, 2003), 66. Of the six paintings bearing this title, five have survived.

5 These phrases appear in "Une image de la réalité pour les heures philosophiques" (1984) and "Réalisme radical" (1983), in PES, vol. 3 (1995), 444–45 and 446–47, respectively. The latter appears in its entirety on p. 183 of the present volume, translated into English.

6 Jean Dubuffet, Oriflammes (1984), PES, vol. 3 (1995), 233.

7 Dubuffet to Michel Tapié, December 21, 1952, PES, vol. 2 (1967), 308.

8 Hubert Damisch, "Dubuffet, un mémoire (1985–2014)," in Damisch, Entrée en matière, 19.

9 This is how Hubert Damisch referred to Dubuffet in the preface to the volumes of the artist's writings that he edited. In one or two letters written to Damisch toward the end of his life, Dubuffet appropriated the image of Robinson Crusoe. See Hubert Damisch, "Le veritable Robinson," PES, vol. 1 (1967), 9–22.

10 Jean Dubuffet, "Biographie au pas de course" (1985), PES, vol. 4 (1995), 467.

11 Ibid., 469.

12 On Dubuffet's sojourn in New York and trip to Chicago, see Sophie Berrebi, The Insider as Outsider: Dubuffet and the United States, 1945–1962, PhD diss., Courtauld Institute of Art, 2003, ch. 2, "The Geologist and the Dripper: Dubuffet and the New York School."

13 See Rémi Hess, Henri Lefebvre et l'aventure du siècle (Paris: Métailié, 1991).

14 Jean Dubuffet, "Plus modeste" (1945), PES, vol. 1 (1967), 92.

15 See André Fermigier, La bataille de Paris: Des Halles à la Pyramide; Chroniques d'urbanisme (Paris: Gallimard, 1991), and Marcel Cornu, La conquête de Paris (Paris: Mercure de France, 1972).

16 Jean-François Gravier, Paris et le désert français, 2nd ed. (Paris: Flammarion, 1958).

17 Georges Perec, Tentative de description de choses vues au carrefour Mabillon le 19 mai 1978 (radio essay), available online at France Culture website as part of "Création on air," podcast by Irène Omélianenko, February 3, 2016, https://www.franceculture.fr/emissions/creation-air/tentative-de-description-de-choses-vues-au-carrefour-mabillon-le-19-mai-1978.

18 Dubuffet to Geneviève Bonnefoi, August 4, 1961, PES, vol. 2 (1967), 479.

It is not a chronicle of the changing Paris that we are after, then, when we look at this artist's work but rather unstable indications of an intertwined process of thinking about and undoing the city and its representation.

Gambadeuse d'asphalte and Élégante aux escarpins both suggest snapshots of people in a crowd in movement, dressed up and celebrating the city's liberation. Here, the nondescript browns and blacks and faded colors of the clothing serve as a reminder of the wearers' intimate connection with the street.

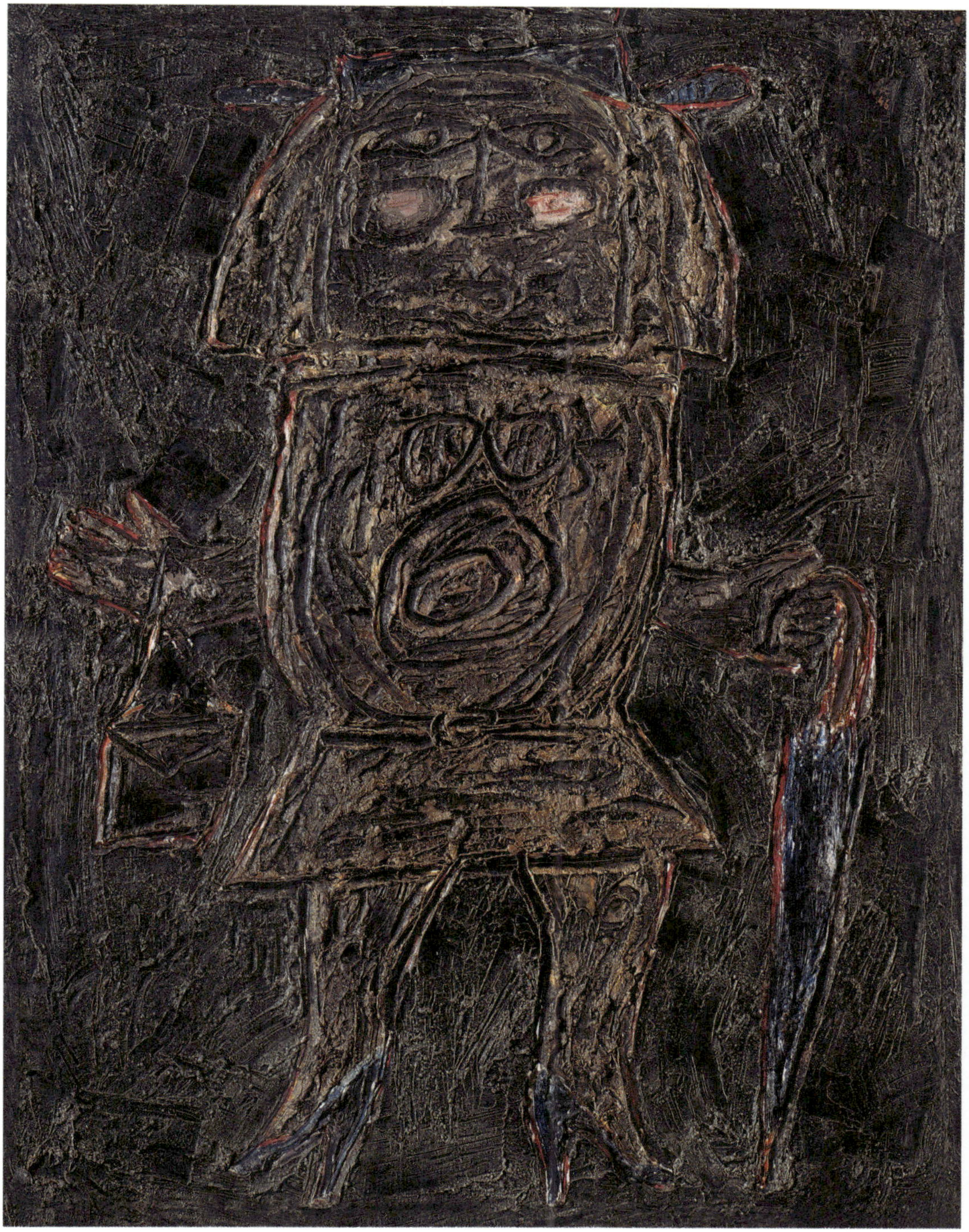

12. Jean Dubuffet. Élégante aux escarpins, January 1946

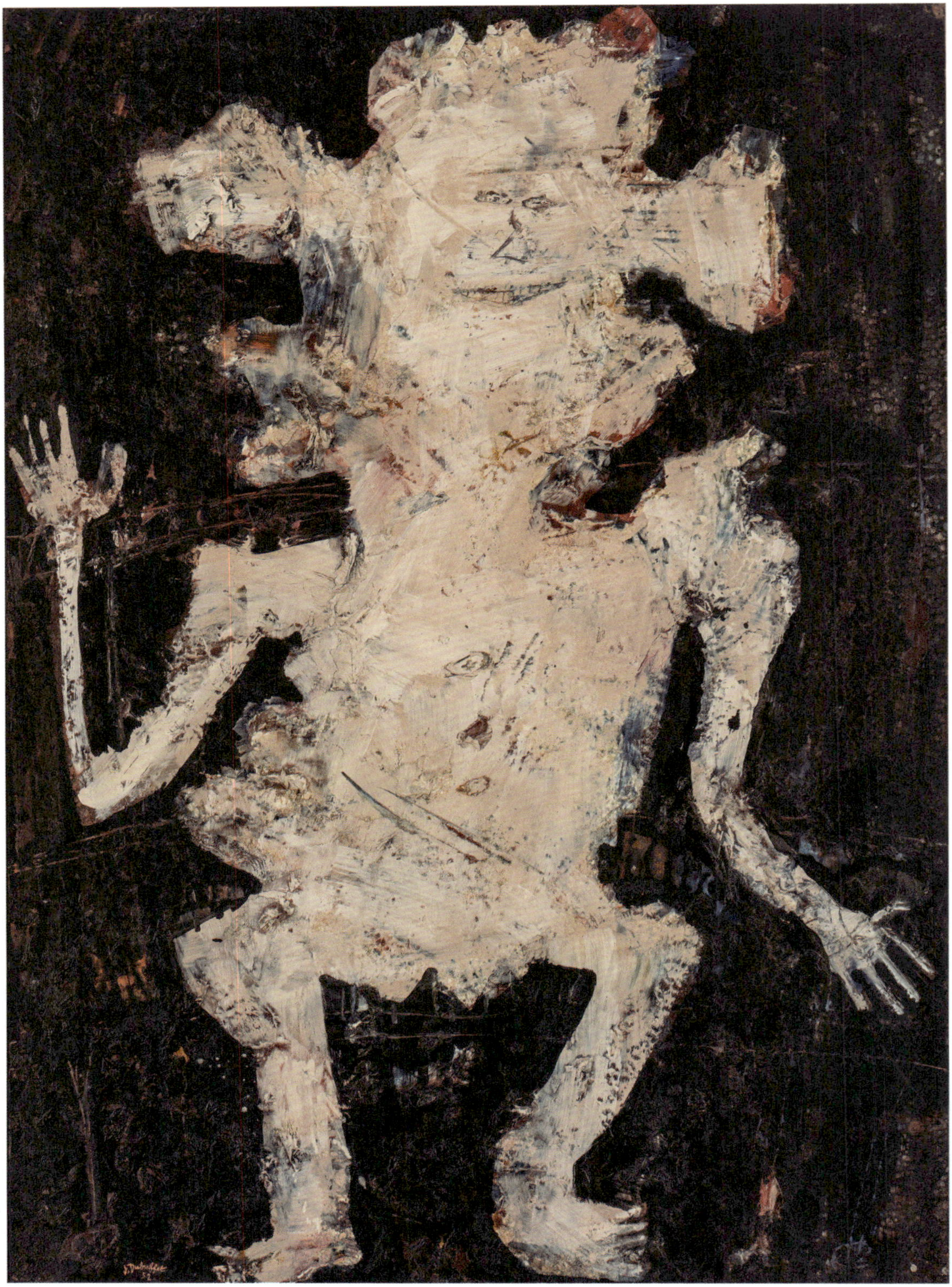

13. Jean Dubuffet. L'homme aux cocardes, October [n.d.]–November 4, 1952

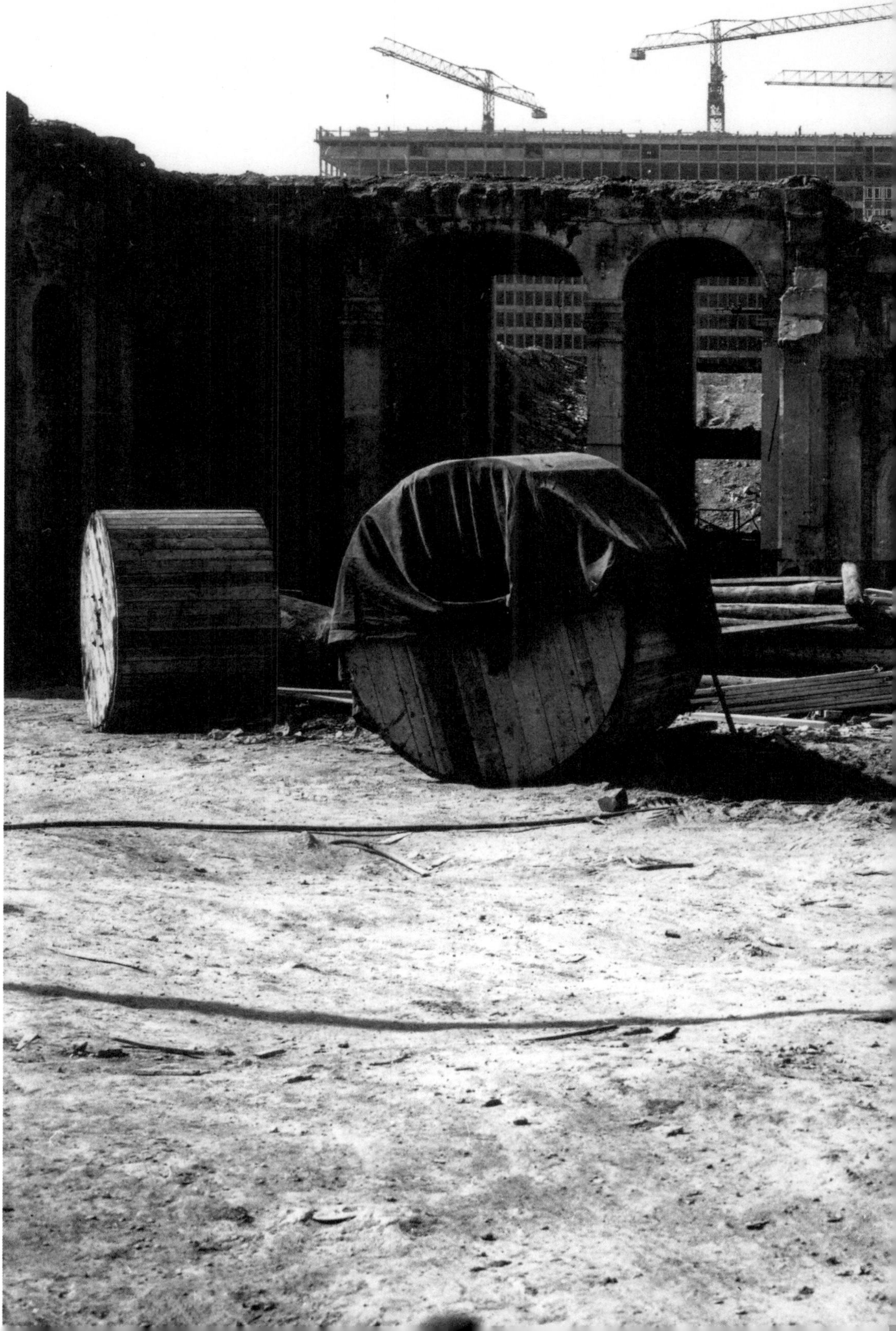

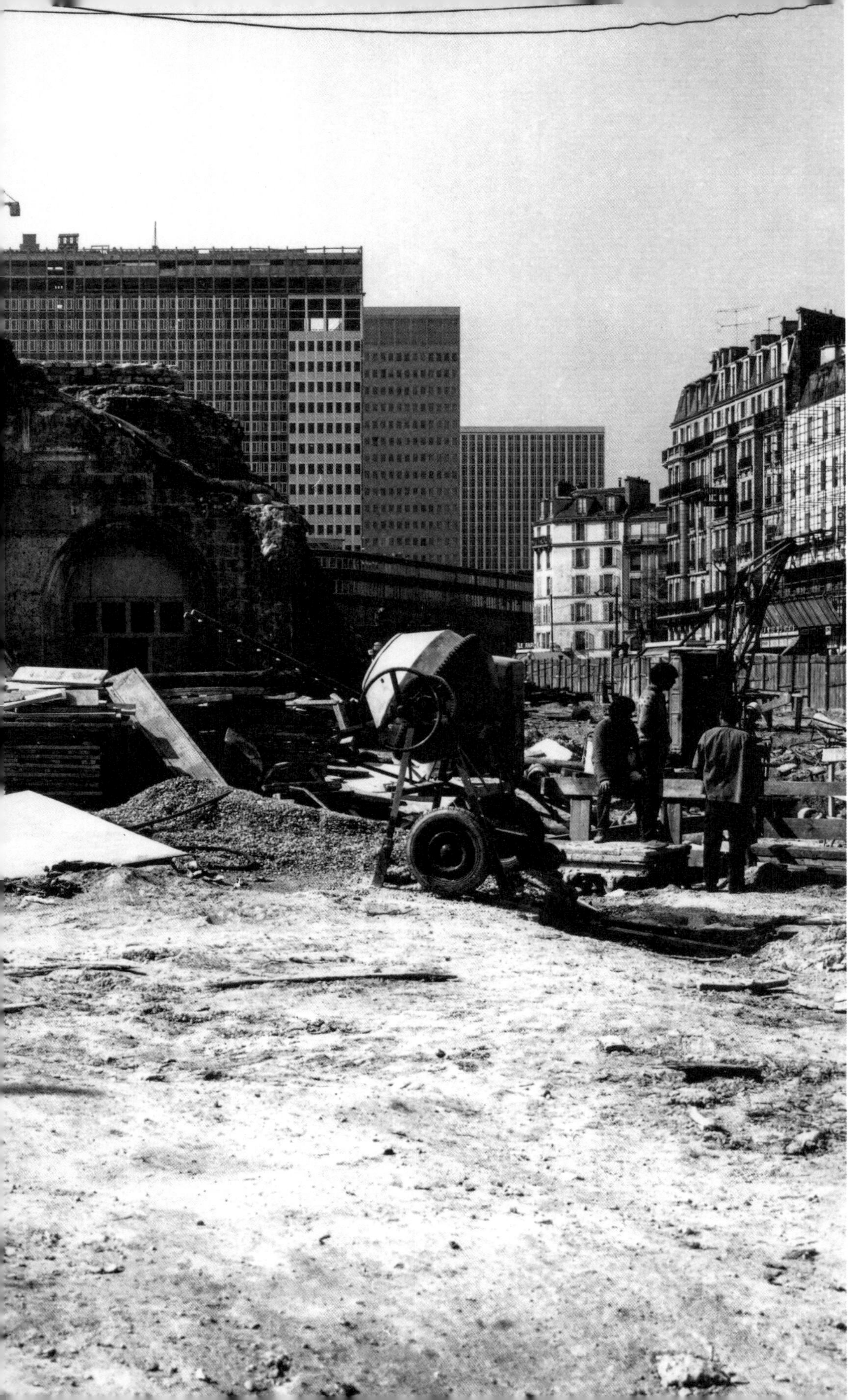

14. Place du 18 juin 1940, Paris, March 12, 1971

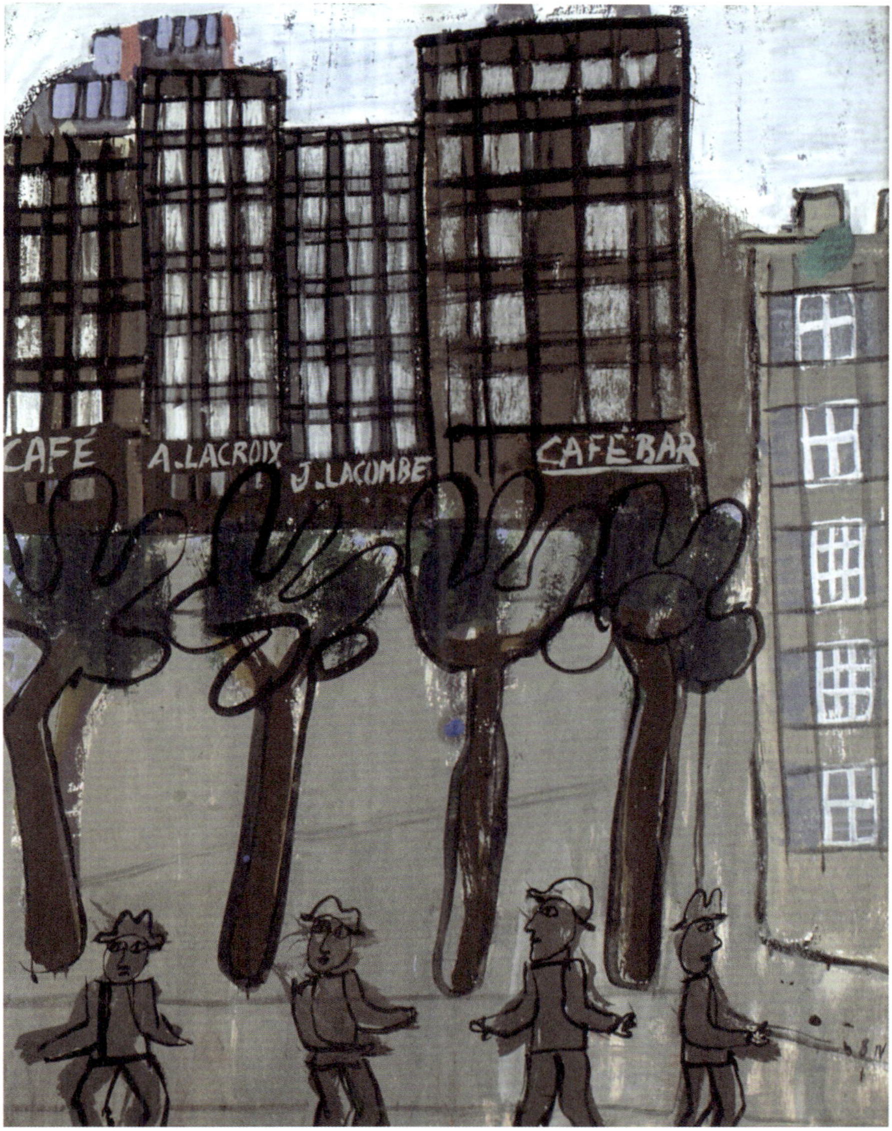

15. Jean Dubuffet. Vue de Paris, April 8, 1943

In <u>Trinité Champs-Elysées</u>, the monumental bus that occupies the largest portion of the painting assumes the scale of a building rooted in the middle of the street. There are figures on the bus but also behind it, standing on the sidewalk in front of shops, and each view appears to us in sequence, as perception-in-movement.

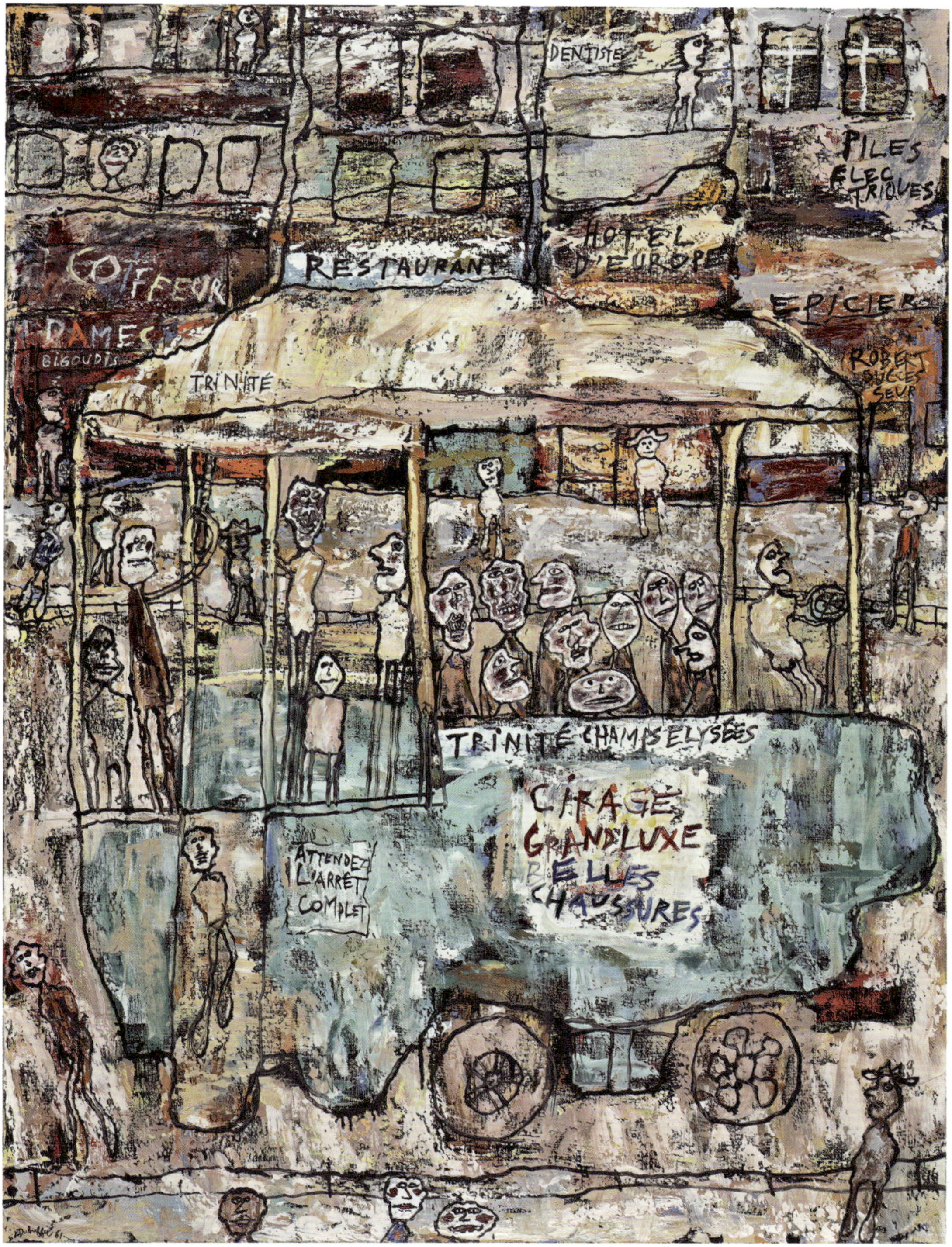

16. Jean Dubuffet. Trinité Champs-Élysées**, March 25–26, 1961**

The Paris of the 1940s had altered comparatively little since the late nineteenth century.

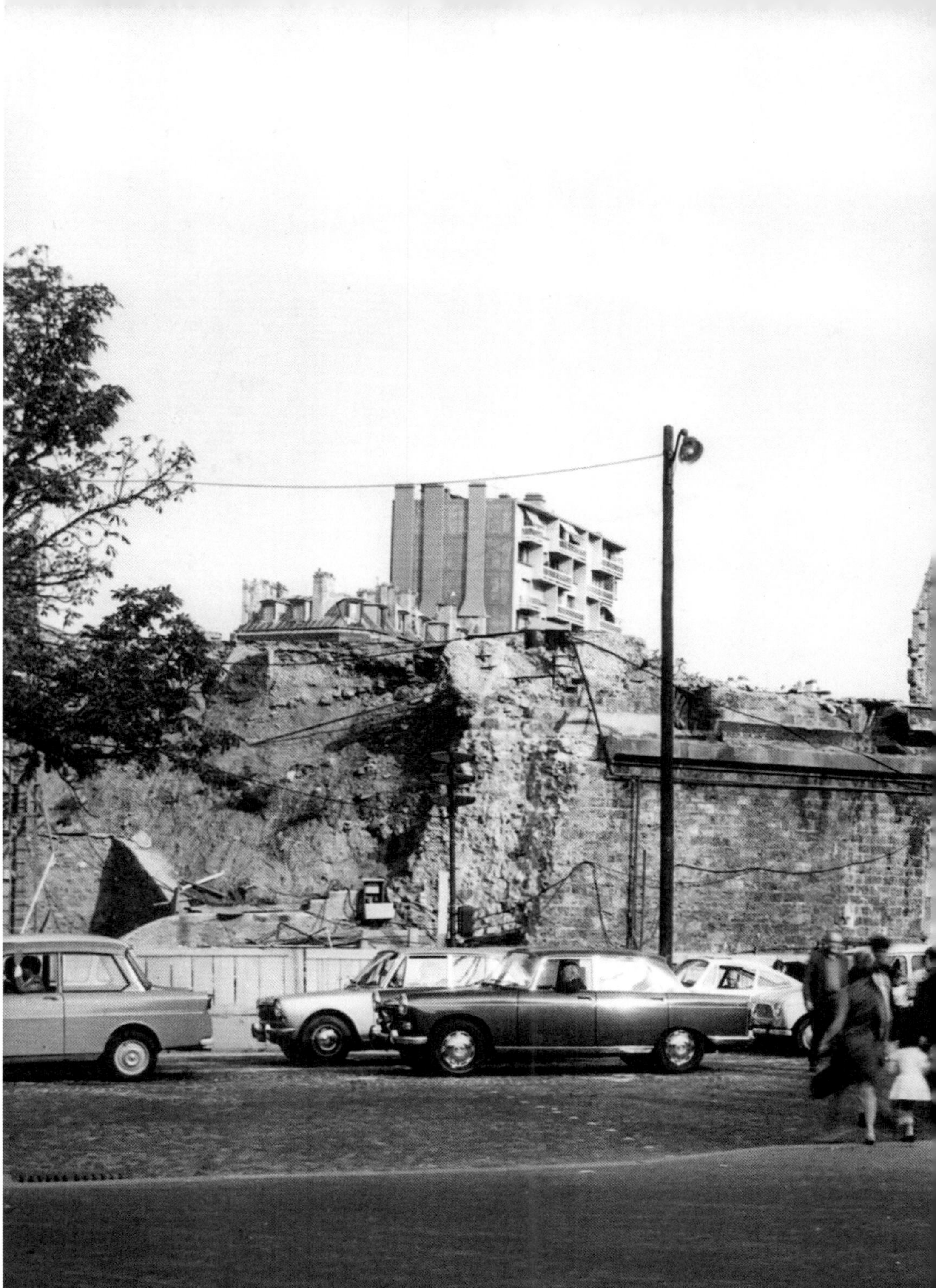

17. Avenue du Maine, Paris, September 1967

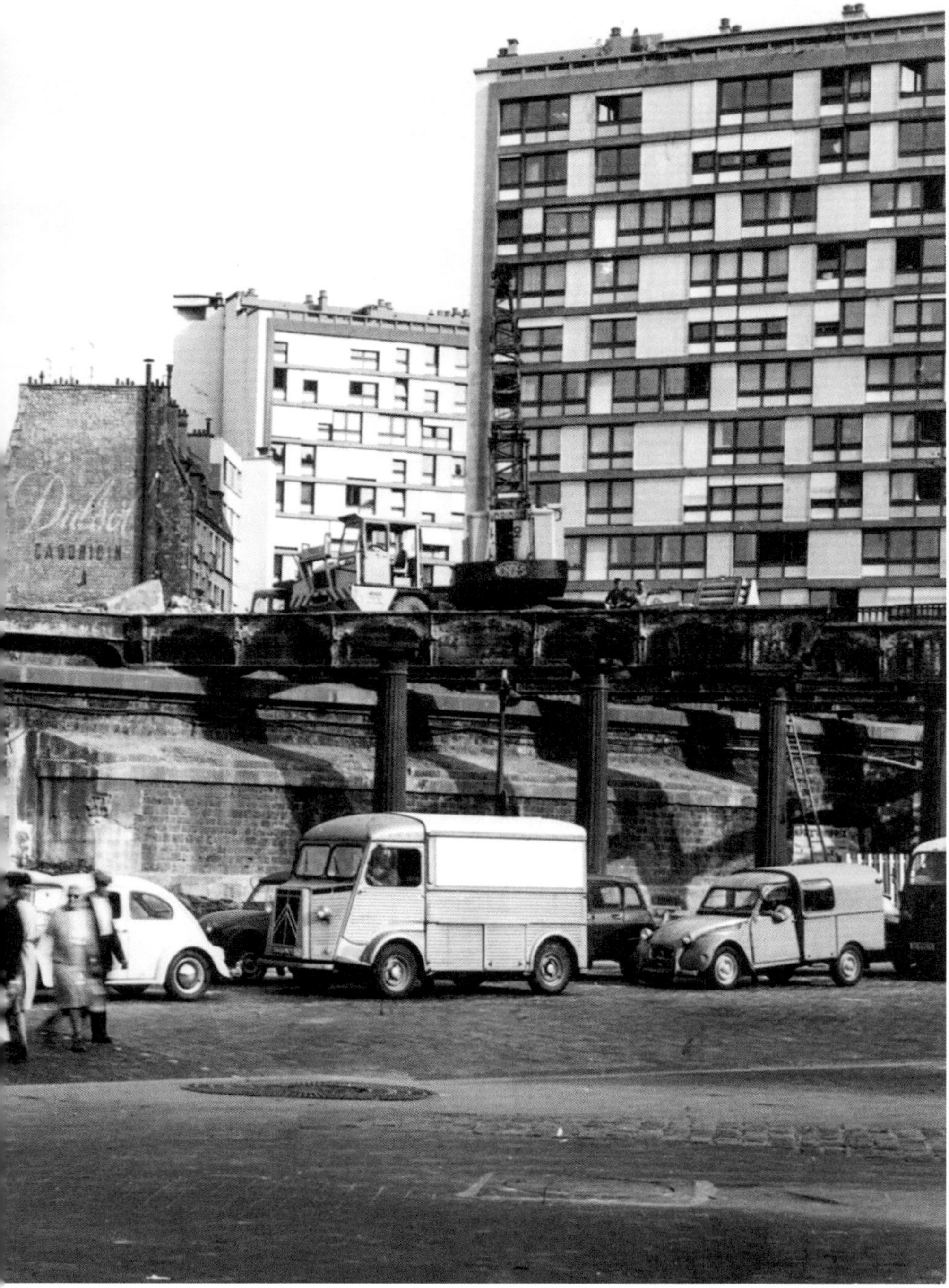

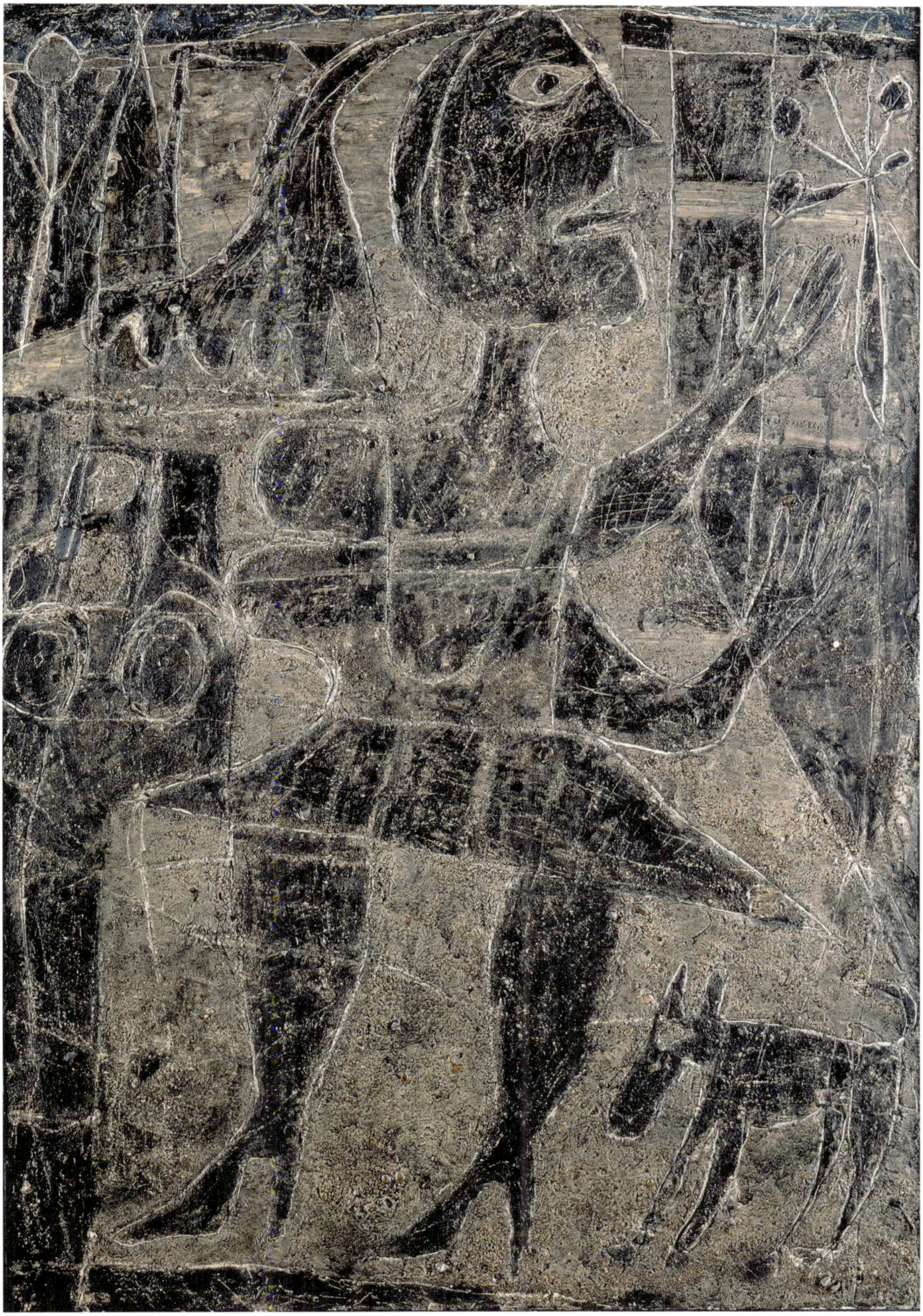

18. Jean Dubuffet. Gambadeuse d'asphalte, November 1945

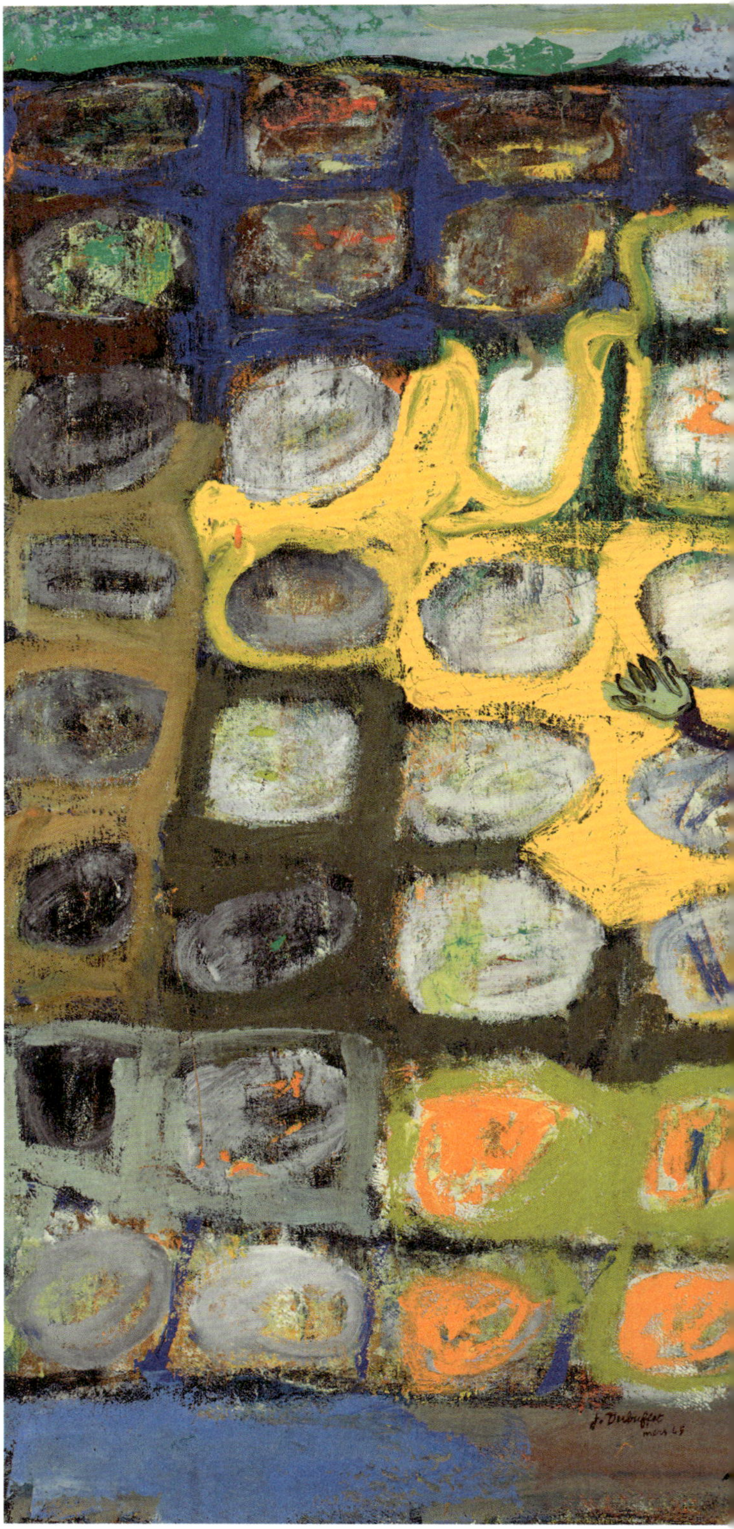

19. Jean Dubuffet. Rhéteur au mur, March 1945

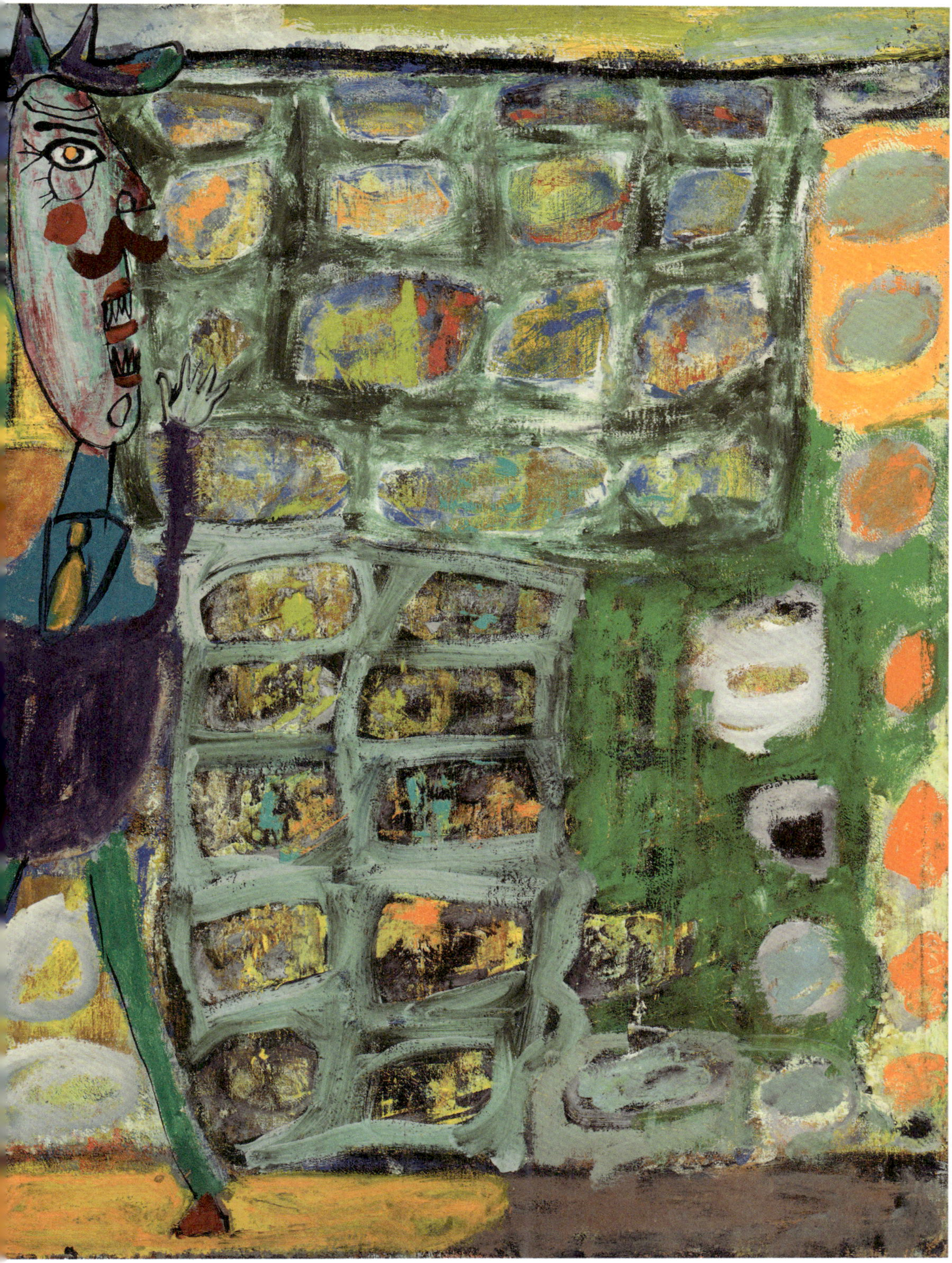

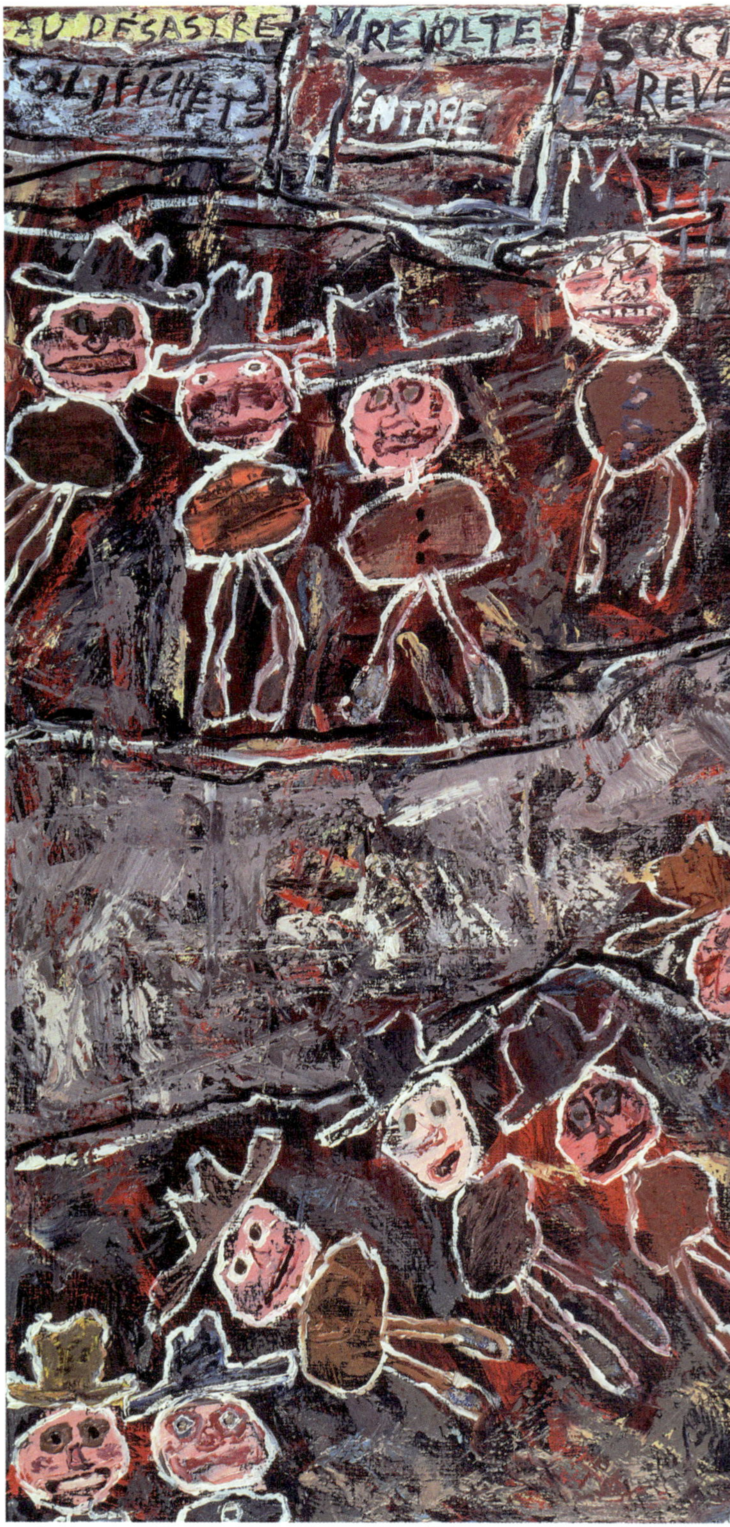

20. Jean Dubuffet. *Vire-volte*, May 31, 1961

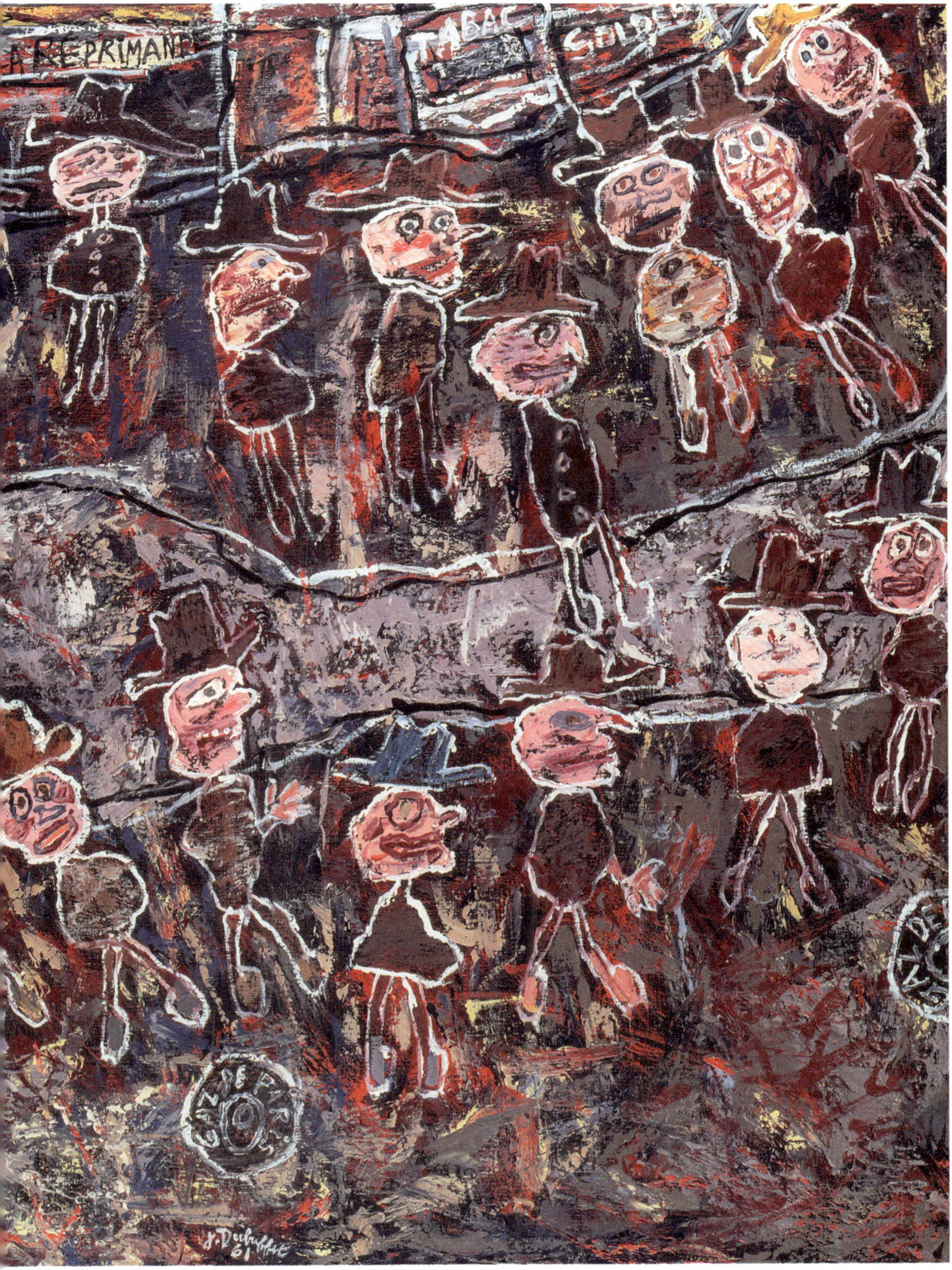
TABAC
J. Dubuffet 61

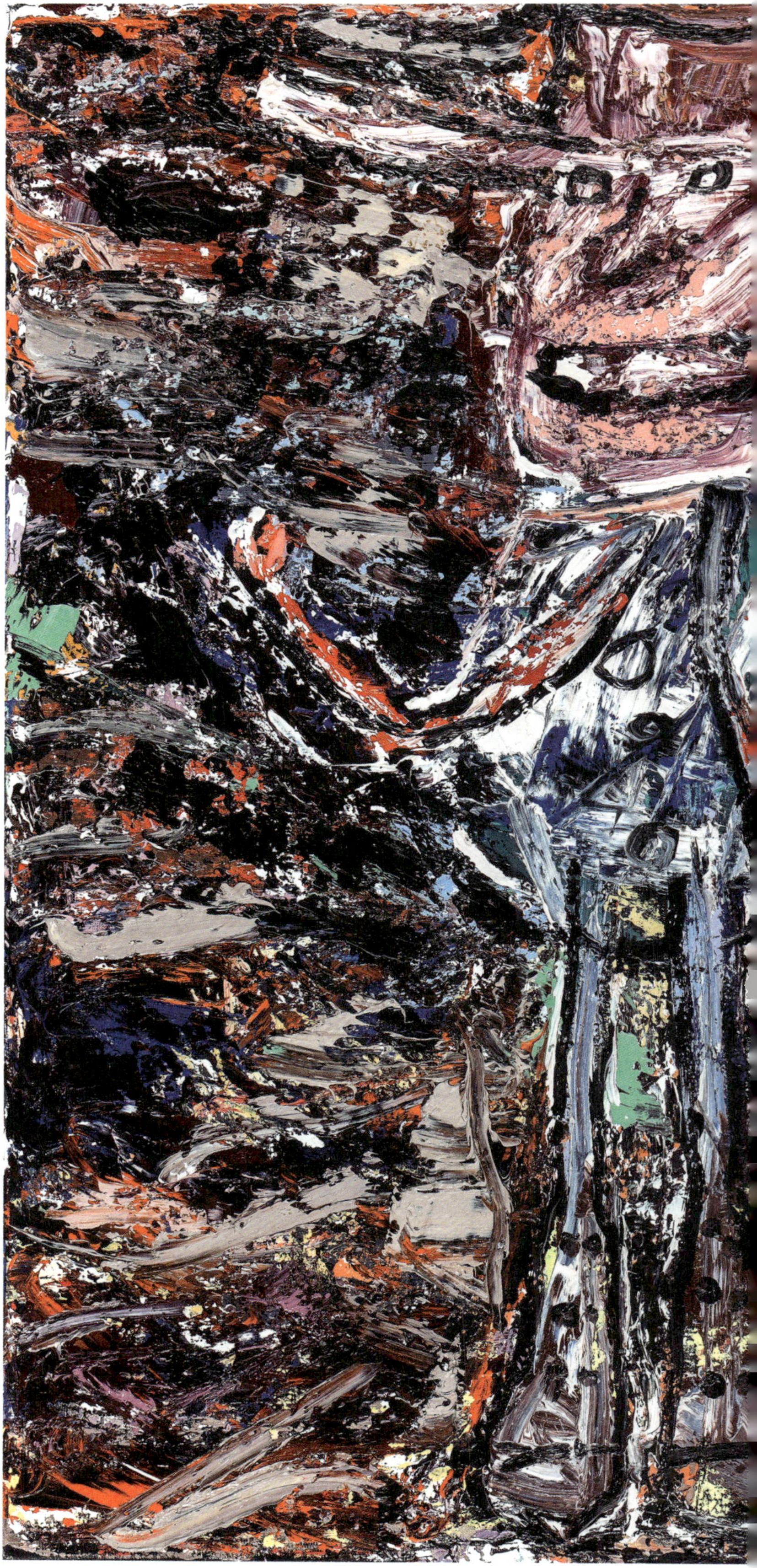

21. Jean Dubuffet. Deviseurs au journal, July 22–23, 1961

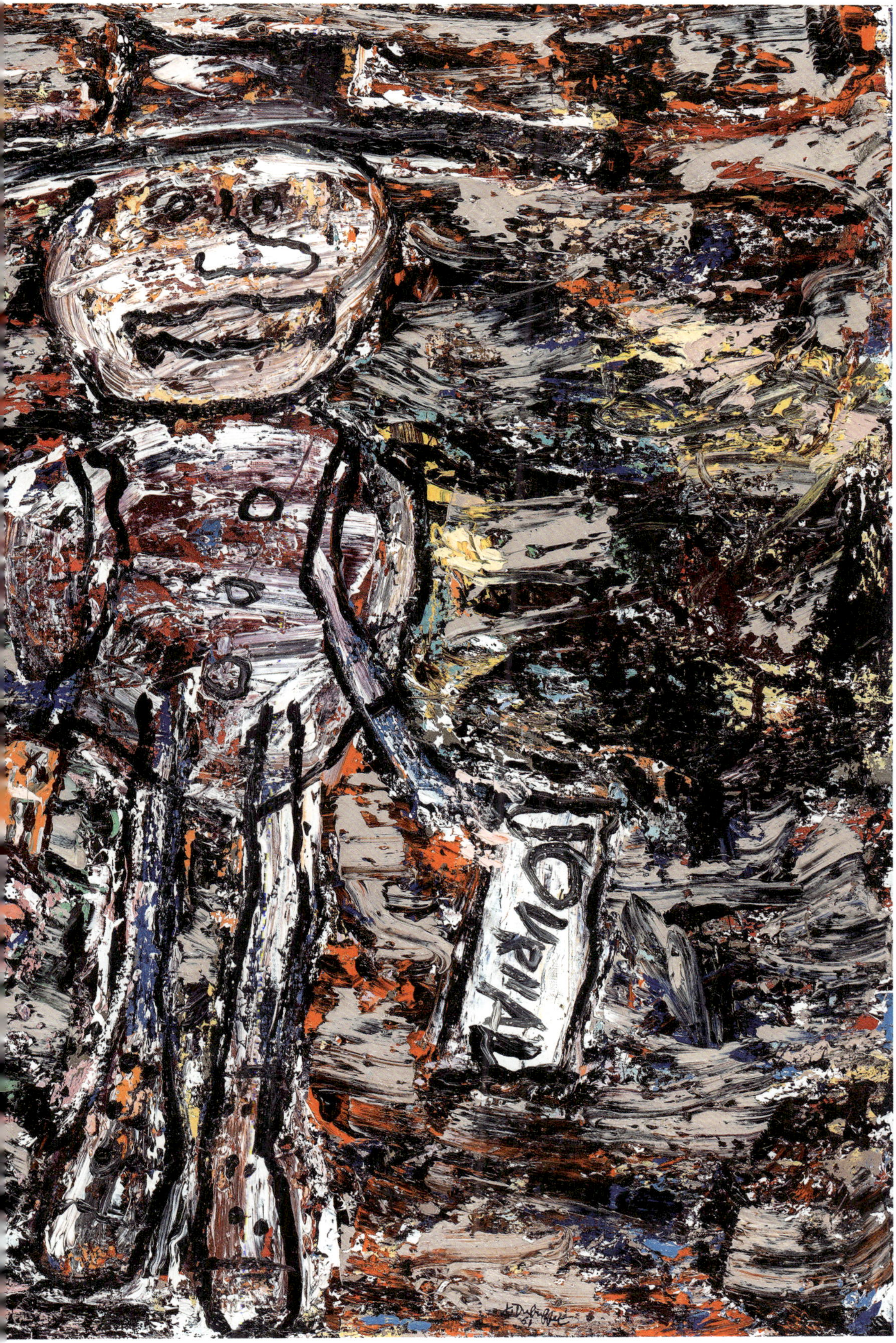

It was only in the late 1950s that a flurry of new public plans and private developments of entire neighborhoods, including buildings, roadwork, and underground transportation, began to significantly modify the appearance of and everyday life in the city.

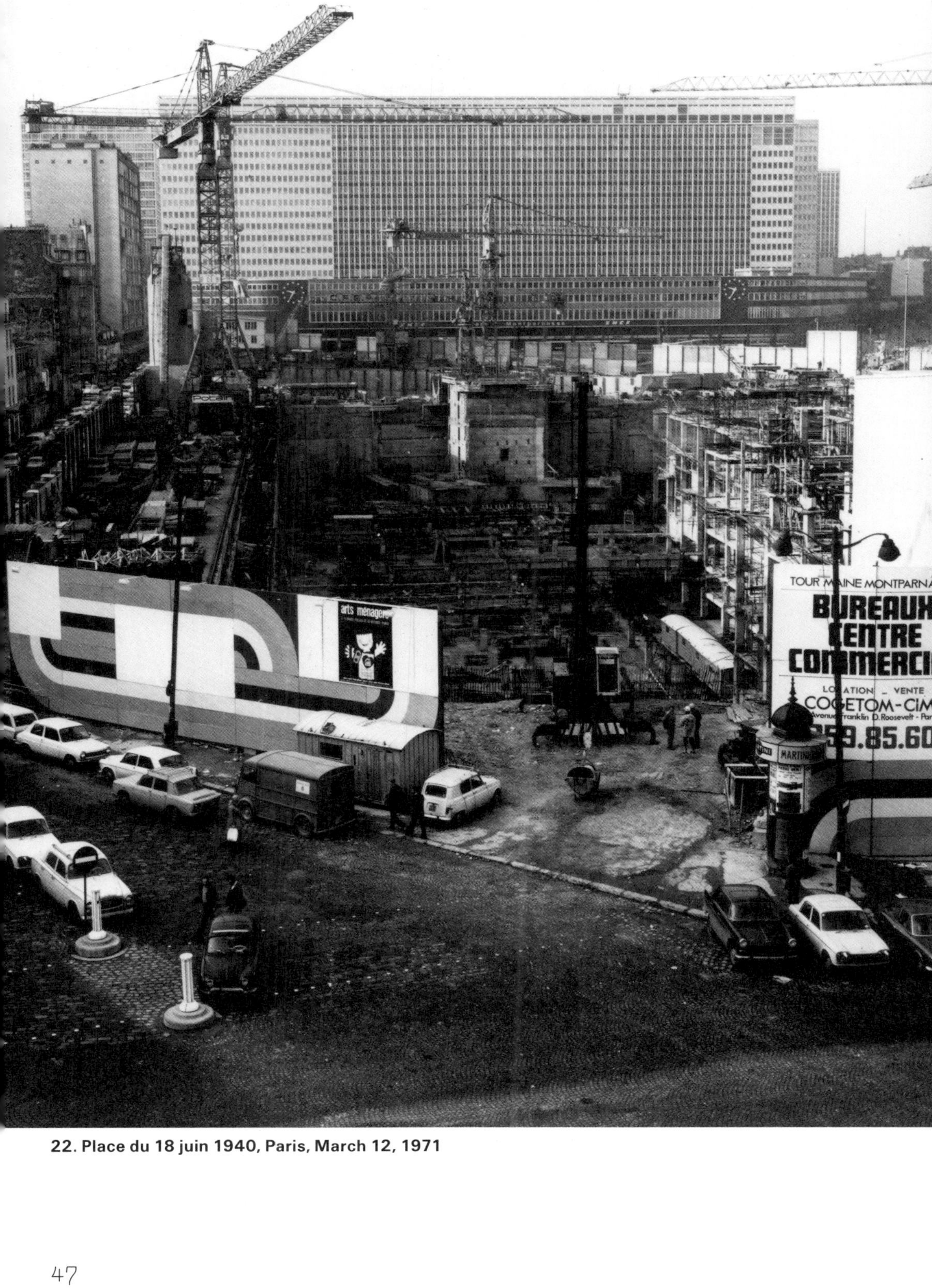

22. Place du 18 juin 1940, Paris, March 12, 1971

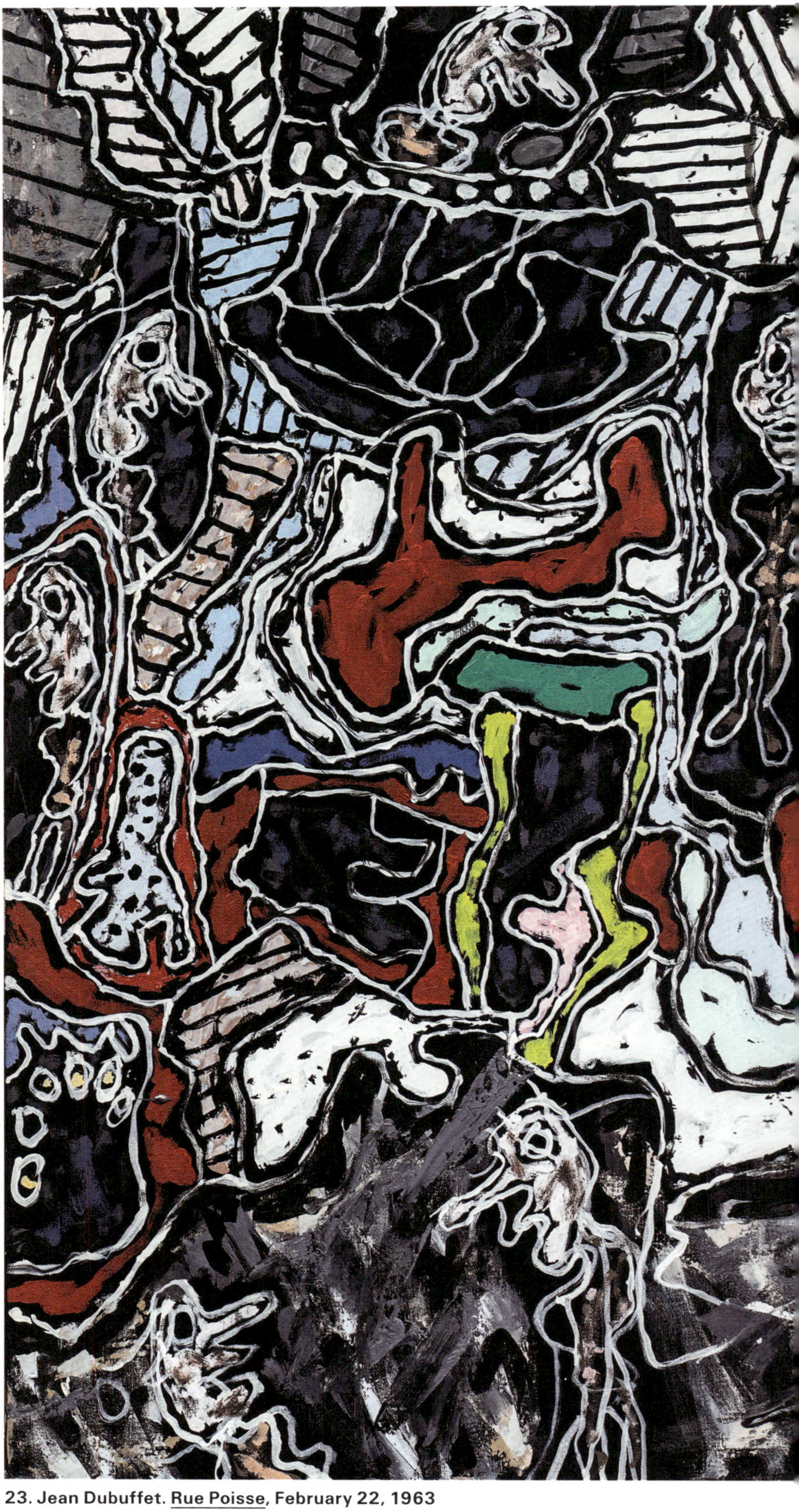

23. Jean Dubuffet. Rue Poisse, February 22, 1963

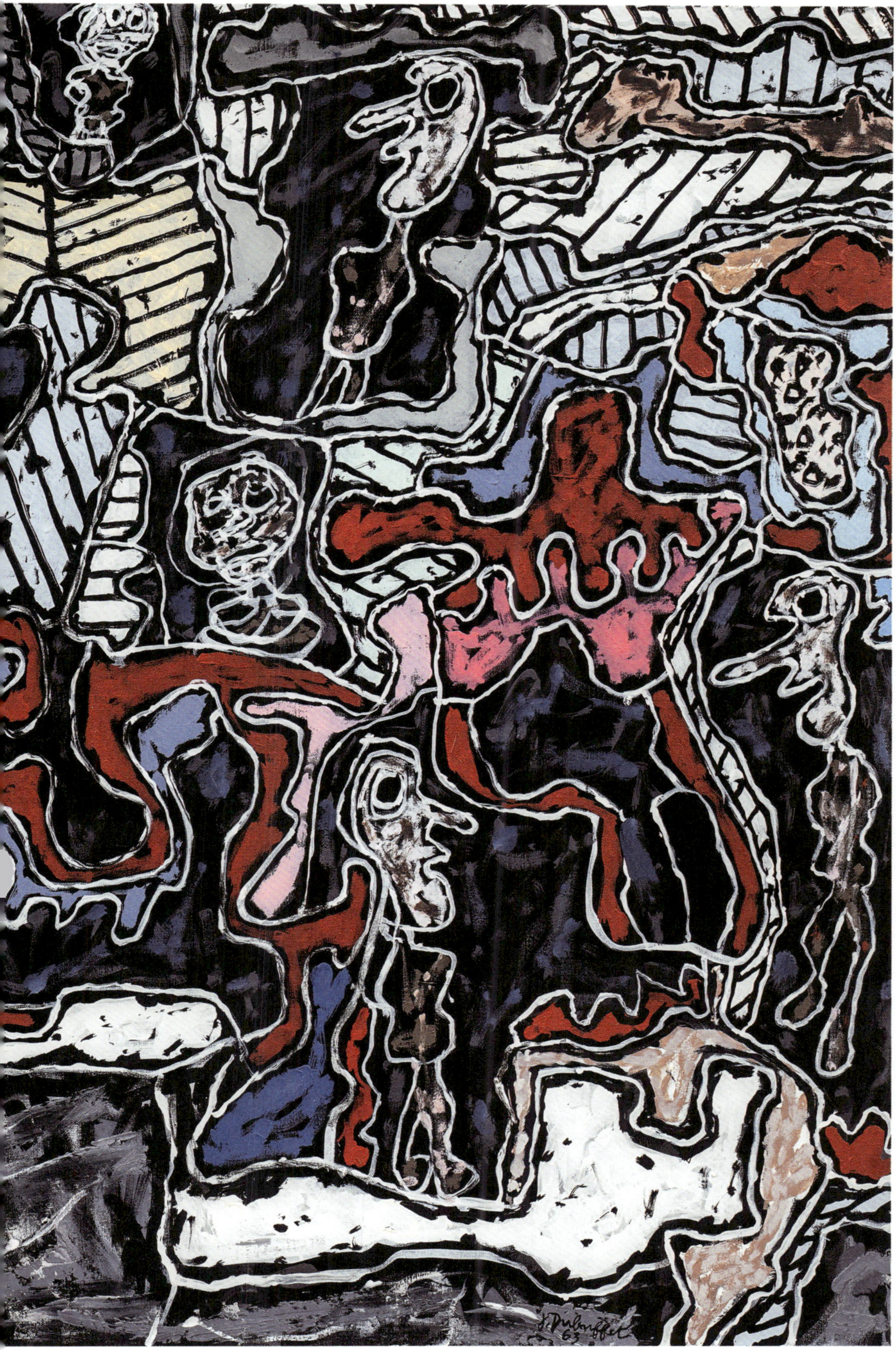
J. Dubuffet
63

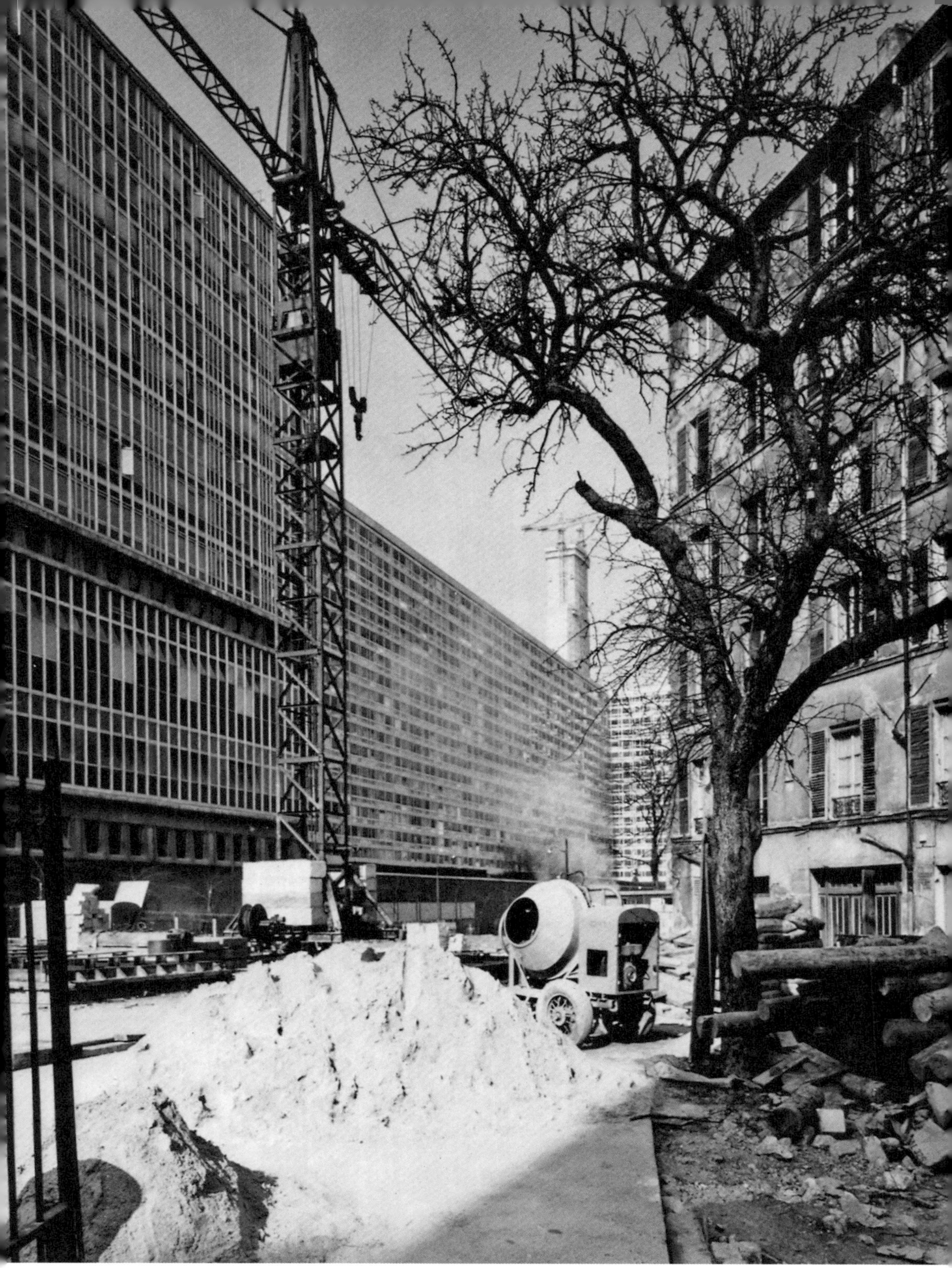

24. Maine-Montparnasse complex under construction, Paris, 1972

But from the allée Maintenon, a small impasse off the rue de Vaugirard where he settled in 1945, Dubuffet was only a stone's throw away from the Maine-Montparnasse development, one of the largest urban projects of the 1960s.

More Modest (1945)

Jean Dubuffet

The Saint-Sulpice fair gives some idea of what it's like, it's good but it's too small. Outside it's much better! This fair that is outside is so large that one never gets to the end of exploring it and nothing there is dolled up, everything is authentic, functional, consistent, living characters, speaks the language of the time (this exciting time of 1945 that will appear so attractive to people in 2945 and 3945, but it is even more so for us who find ourselves living it!). Quickly take a ticket. Of course you must first put on the suit of our time. There is already a joke there from the very beginning, a rather full-bodied joke of excellently dubious taste (let me here affirm my sympathies for dubious taste). Very practical trousers (an old Persian fashion) (this women's garment curiously worn by men). Cowhide shoes, shirts made of silkworm drool (there are also some made of cottonseed hair) and on the head: a lid (felt-hare). Adorned so gaily, you can roam about and enter any place, and if you know the language—it can be learned quickly—you can talk to anyone who passes by: he will answer you, he also wants to play, he has a ticket just like you. It will be a fabulous investigation, I assure you, a fascinating *folie bergère*. Interesting! It is unimaginable that some might be bored (poorly informed people) (not you, I hope?). Who would be there in these most outrageous rides and attractions—the bus, for example—or in front of these carnivalesque percolators, cash registers, irons, taxi-cars, sewing machines, typewriters, slot machines, with their bi-tubular trousers around the legs and their beautiful caps on the head and who would be bored? Exciting games are organized, complex and interesting. Why, if you get involved, you have to know how to lose. You do not have to play, though. Sometimes you are pressingly prompted to and it is not a bad thing, because otherwise there would be shy, hesitant people who would not dare to take part: but actually it is useful to take part.

*

When you are too young you are tormented by a thousand problems, you get bogged down: what to do, what not to do, what is good to do, or bad, how to live, how not to live, well, young friends, I want to tell you this: when we reach the age of forty, everything falls into place, you start to see things clearly, to understand how to navigate. When I left high school I studied painting for six or seven years and many other subjects at the same time: poetry, literature, avant-garde, rear guard, metaphysics, paleography, ethnography, foreign languages, ancient languages, well, you understand, I was looking for the Entrée. But it was not working out; I felt I was not adapted to my human condition; I was skidding, the clutch wasn't engaged. All these studies (woolly), all this knowledge (that I forgot as I studied it), and my systems (which I often changed) left me with a kind of anxiety that all of it was not substantial and did not, ultimately, amount to very much—that it was not worth living alone as I did, as an outcast, that at the root of all this there was some serious mistake, a perverted way of approaching things, and I felt ashamed in my corner, dehydrated, de-salted, lacking in vitamins, when I saw my pallid face in the reflection of a storefront I told myself it cannot go on like this, it cannot go on. Essentially I was there stupidly alone, with no place, no axis, no roots, no connections, part of nothing, no odors of anything, in short, I had missed the boat. I was like the kids watching from the sidewalk the cart being pulled by goats, but that's not fun at all, it's way more fun to be in the cart. I did have friends, but just like myself, they were not in the cart, either. Our discussions, well, they were always made up of idle comments, little niceties, little tricks, little attitudes, basically always the same constant harping, and that was not cheerful, not cheerful. Not substantial, not sustaining. When I used to see the firefighter with the butcher and the postman chatting among themselves at the hairdresser in Chaville, I felt that they looked pretty settled, those guys, they seemed to be doing pretty well, they exuded a joy and self-reliance that made me envious, and on top of that came the idea that there was, in their disconnected remarks, more sap, more unexpectedness and invention and, in short, more flavor. Let's say the word: more art—yes, more art, and more poetry, in the words of the barber boy—in his life—in his head—than among art specialists. That's the idea I had. That these guys beat me even on my own field. Of course their occupations and skills, they seemed absurd to me, I thought, poor guy, who sells ties at the Samar, well, what candor in this one! Ties! Yes, but actually it's better to sell ties than nothing at all, like me.

Here I am in the tram. Still my idea. Still feeling like a band of outsiders, like the one who does not take part in anything, who is not a local, who does not speak the language. I look at the person facing me. Quiet figure, peace, serenity. Does not make up problems. Is delighted to live. Is happy to have a seat and new shoes. The conductor tells a joke, he answers without thinking, with just the right tone. Ah, that's what cannot be imitated, the right tone. The woman next to him, peaceful. Has a good, intelligent and laughing face. Happy to wear earrings, happy that her man just got out of the hospital, that he got a raise. Such faces full of the picturesque and of character, full of animation and at the same time full of depth, complexity, humanism. In the end I cannot stand it, I put my brushes aside, I become a clerk, then a wine merchant. I was starting to feel better, I was getting a foothold. To spice things up, I needed a wife, furniture, a maid, a brother-in-law, a car, children. I get myself all that. Swiftly and without choosing, no need to be oversubtle, we'll see! I like to quickly put into practice the ideas that come to me; if we waste time weighing the pros and cons, nothing is ever done, life gallops by, we need to hurry.

I did not speak too much about my obsession with painting and other things because in these circles it's seen as a bit daft, a bit dippy. Disaster! here it goes again! I rent a small studio in boulevard Saint-Michel, I lock myself in. My wife does not accept it, that is understandable, she disappears into a hatch, dissolves. Bon voyage! The brother-in-law falls into the hatch, too, the whole family does. (The maid, the car had disintegrated ages ago). Me, I did not want to hear about anything, I was doing my painting: everything around me could scream, catch on fire, collapse! What a breather! What joy! Three good years. I knew it wouldn't last long, but I was determined to go to the extreme limits of what was possible. What you've got, you've got. You only live once. To have had three good years in one's life is already a prodigious achievement.

Inevitably at the end time was up. Out with the good life! In with the dirty jobs, the dirty canvassing, the swallowing of insults! The anguished cavalcades through Paris! The crazed quest for orders! The jostling rounds of bill collecting until ten o'clock at night! Litigation! Dog days! Endless rotten luck! Which make your stomach churn, your reproductive capacities completely shriveled because you are so anxious, you shit blood, you don't want to go on. Annoying! Very annoying! Five years like this. And then all of a sudden things get better! A real stroke of luck! A third dive into painting! A good little wife I have now (called Lili). A good nest egg (enough to live for almost a year). After that, we'll see.

*

Closeness with so many disparate sorts of people! Friendships formed in so many places! My head is full of memories! I have traveled around and seen many people! Big, very small, pretty, ugly, bankers, clerks, truckers, shifty brokers, coal merchants, some with a heart of gold, some a little dishonest, some a little boorish. So nice! So endearing! They all continually talk through their hats! They are off their heads, gushing! I wish that something of my amazement at all this, at all this extravagant and senseless treasure of the world, could be sensed in my works, that their simple presence on my wall could keep me in ecstasy, or rush me back into it, or even, who knows, communicate to others something of this ecstasy. But if it's a failure, if looking at these works does not communicate anything to you, dear visitor of the Galerie André, if you refuse to recognize art such as you conceive it, if you are convinced that art is something else, and that, as art, this is worthless and valueless—but as something else, perhaps, is it not attractive, effective, exciting, no? It's complete hogwash? It's all cock and bull? Well, never mind, I'm having fun, what do you want, to each his own, it doesn't make me a wicked man, let's hug anyway. My thing, you know, it's just low-key entertainment, it's not pretentious, you can see it, it's not grand tragedy, or high intellect. I also believe that if I thought it was, I wouldn't tell you. I wouldn't even dare think it. I'd fear spoiling it. You know those little gods of fairy tales that are annihilated as soon as their names are called out . . . what if art were like them? What if it were art that was too substantial, too self-conscious of its existence, Art, with its college of doctors, prelates, jurisconsults, their wrinkled brows, their serious views, that was hogwash (what real hair is to wigs) and that true art was

MORE MODEST?

Chapter One

Views and Networks of the City

J'aime que les rues tournent pour que le regard se trouve par là limité et les sites à tout moment renouvelés. Des longues avenues rectilignes j'éprouve qu'elles rapetissent la ville. Il faut augmenter la multiplicité des lieux dans une ville pour l'agrandir. . . . J'éprouve que c'est applicable aussi à l'univers philosophique. Il y a tout à gagner à caractériser et à multiplier les lieux de la pensée. À l'opposé donc de l'aspiration rationaliste à la constituer en un système univoque à partir d'un axe central (qui a le rôle de la grande avenue rectiligne).

—Jean Dubuffet, 1985

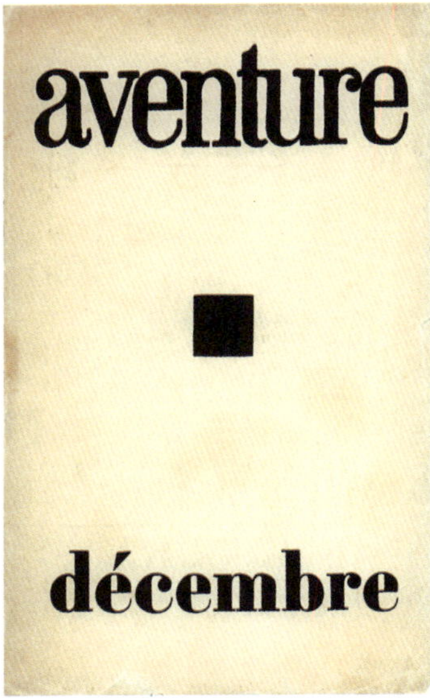
aventure

décembre

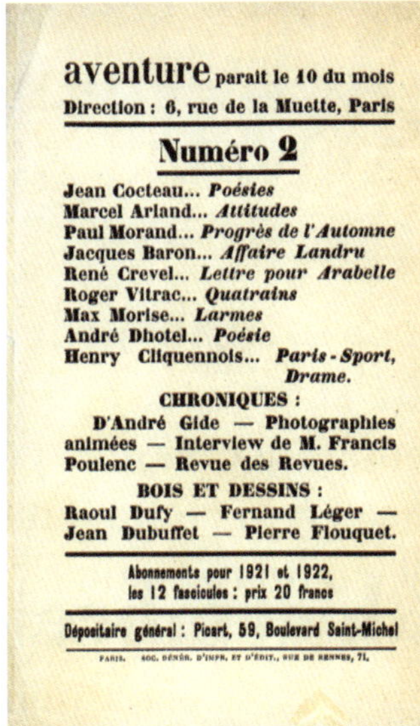
aventure parait le 10 du mois
Direction : 6, rue de la Muette, Paris

Numéro 2

Jean Cocteau... *Poésies*
Marcel Arland... *Attitudes*
Paul Morand... *Progrès de l'Automne*
Jacques Baron... *Affaire Landru*
René Crevel... *Lettre pour Arabelle*
Roger Vitrac... *Quatrains*
Max Morise... *Larmes*
André Dhotel... *Poésie*
Henry Cliquennois... *Paris-Sport, Drame.*

CHRONIQUES :
D'André Gide — Photographies animées — Interview de M. Francis Poulenc — Revue des Revues.

BOIS ET DESSINS :
Raoul Dufy — Fernand Léger — Jean Dubuffet — Pierre Flouquet.

Abonnements pour 1921 et 1922, les 12 fascicules : prix 20 francs

Dépositaire général : Picart, 59, Boulevard Saint-Michel

PARIS. SOC. GÉNÉR. D'IMPR. ET D'ÉDIT., RUE DE RENNES, 71.

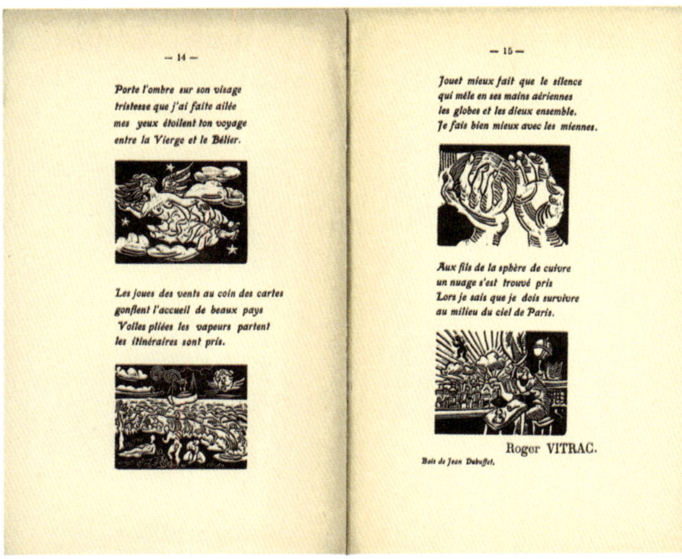
— 14 —

Porte l'ombre sur son visage
tristesse que j'ai faite ailée
mes yeux étoilent ton voyage
entre la Vierge et le Bélier.

Les joues des vents au coin des cartes
gonflent l'accueil de beaux pays
Voiles pliées les vapeurs partent
les itinéraires sont pris.

— 15 —

Jouet mieux fait que le silence
qui mêle en ses mains aériennes
les globes et les dieux ensemble.
Je fais bien mieux avec les miennes.

Aux fils de la sphère de cuivre
un nuage s'est trouvé pris
Lors je sais que je dois survivre
au milieu du ciel de Paris.

Roger VITRAC.

Bois de Jean Dubuffet.

25. Aventure, December 1921. Interior spread: Roger Vitrac's "Quatrains" with four woodcuts by Dubuffet

In 1921, the poet Georges Limbour invited Jean Dubuffet, his high-school friend from Le Havre, to contribute to the second issue of a small literary journal called Aventure, run by the twenty-year-old Dada-affiliated poets (and future Surrealists) Roger Vitrac and René Crevel. Dubuffet's contribution consisted in five small woodcut prints, each illustrating a quatrain by Vitrac (fig. 25). One of those prints is of particular interest to this story. It shows a figure caught in the rays of the sun and floating precariously above Paris. Evoking the ambitious Icarus of Greek mythology, whose wax-assembled wings melted when he flew too close to the sun, the wingless puppet seems to warn of the perils of artistic ambition. The verses that the print accompanies suggest as much: "Aux fils de la sphère de cuivre / un nuage s'est trouvé pris / Lors je sais que je dois survivre / au milieu du ciel de Paris" (In the threads of the copper sphere / a cloud has been caught / Whence I know that I must survive / in the middle of the Paris sky).[1]

The aspiring poet hovering in the Paris sky is not, however, the only subject of the print. That scene is inserted, by means of a window frame, into an interior, a room filled with the classic paraphernalia of a scholar. Here, we find a second figure, this one seated at a table with his hands covering his face. Personnage méditant devant une vue de Paris (Figure Meditating in Front of a View of Paris) (fig. 26), the title later given to the print, emphasizes the importance of this "second" scene to the detriment of the one that illustrates Vitrac's poem.[2]

There is much to speculate about and interpret in this scene. It evokes the process of artistic creation, with its moments of anxiety, reflection, and elation, and it should be remembered that Dubuffet, at that time, was living in Paris amid a constellation of poets, artists, and writers of different generations. Alongside Raymond Queneau and Armand Salacrou, Dubuffet was part of a loose group of contemporaries who shared Le Havre as a birthplace, of which Limbour, who was often compared to Arthur Rimbaud, was the rising star.[3] These men would meet in André Masson's studio, located at 45, rue Blomet, in the 15th arrondissement, with others including Michel Leiris and Max Jacob, Picasso's friend from his Bateau-Lavoir days in Montmartre.[4] Several of them were also regular guests at the Sunday receptions hosted by the dealer Daniel-Henry Kahnweiler at his home in Boulogne-Billancourt, where they mingled with other artists and writers such as Juan Gris, Antonin Artaud, Tristan Tzara, and Robert

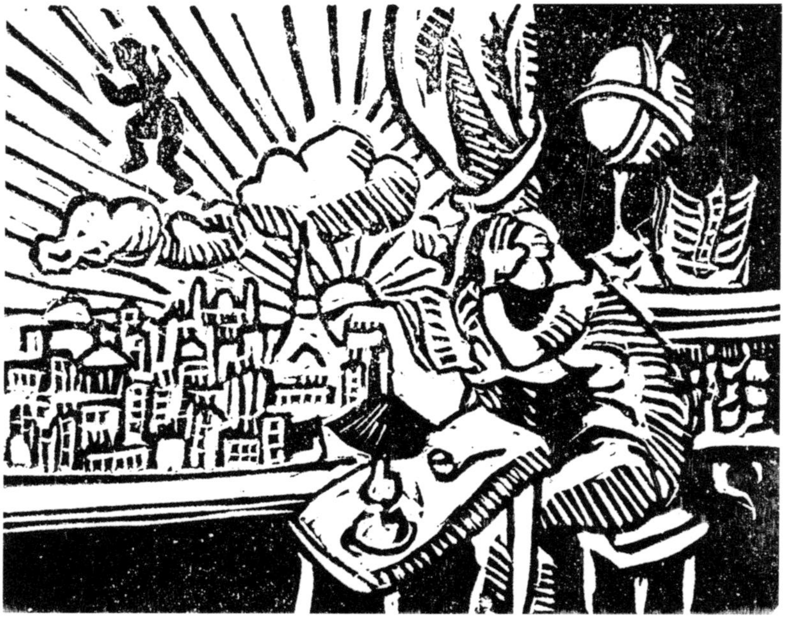

26. Jean Dubuffet. Personnage méditant devant une vue de Paris, 1921

Desnos.[5] It was from among these figures and those involved with ephemeral journals such as Aventure that André Breton would soon recruit the first members of the Surrealist movement—and where he would also encounter its dissidents. In later recollections of this period by its protagonists, Dubuffet is often mentioned merely in passing, as a discreet sidekick of the handsome and flamboyant Limbour (Limbour's literary career later somehow dwindled, and he became one of Dubuffet's closest exegetes). The lack of information surrounding Dubuffet during these years makes it tempting to identify the introspective figure sitting at the table in the woodcut with the young man he was then: the bound volumes and globe surrounding the figure recall the diversity of the artist's interests at the time.[6] Those elements, furnishing the room like props, conjure an atmosphere that recalls something of Johannes Vermeer's paintings of humanist scientists, such as The Geographer of 1669 (fig. 27). And while it is unlikely that Dubuffet would have seen that work in the flesh, he may well have been interested in another painting by Vermeer that was the subject of much attention in Paris in the spring of 1921: View of Delft (fig. 28), one of only three paintings by the recently rediscovered painter that were included in the large exhibition of Dutch art that took place at the Jeu de Paume in March and April and the one took the lion's share of attention in the show's reception. The critic Louis Gillet praised it as *peut-être le plus beau paysage du monde* (perhaps the most beautiful landscape in the world)—a phrase that was famously reiterated by Marcel Proust in La prisonnière (1923), the posthumously published fifth book of À la recherche du temps perdu (In Search of Lost Time)—while Proust's friend the critic Jean-Louis Vaudoyer wrote an extensive

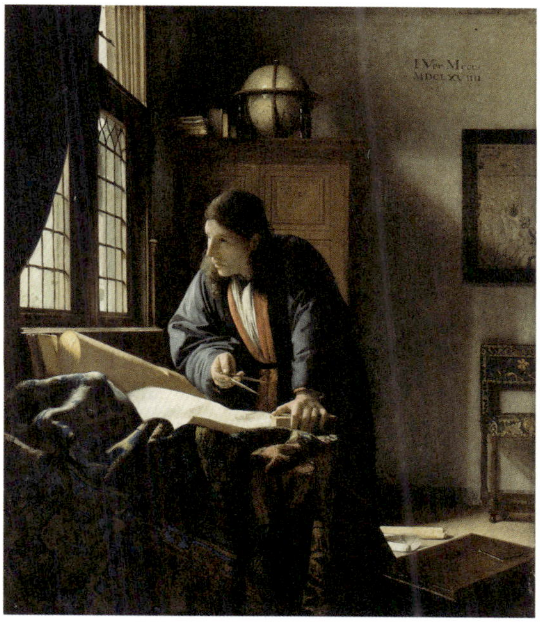

27. Johannes Vermeer. The Geographer, 1669

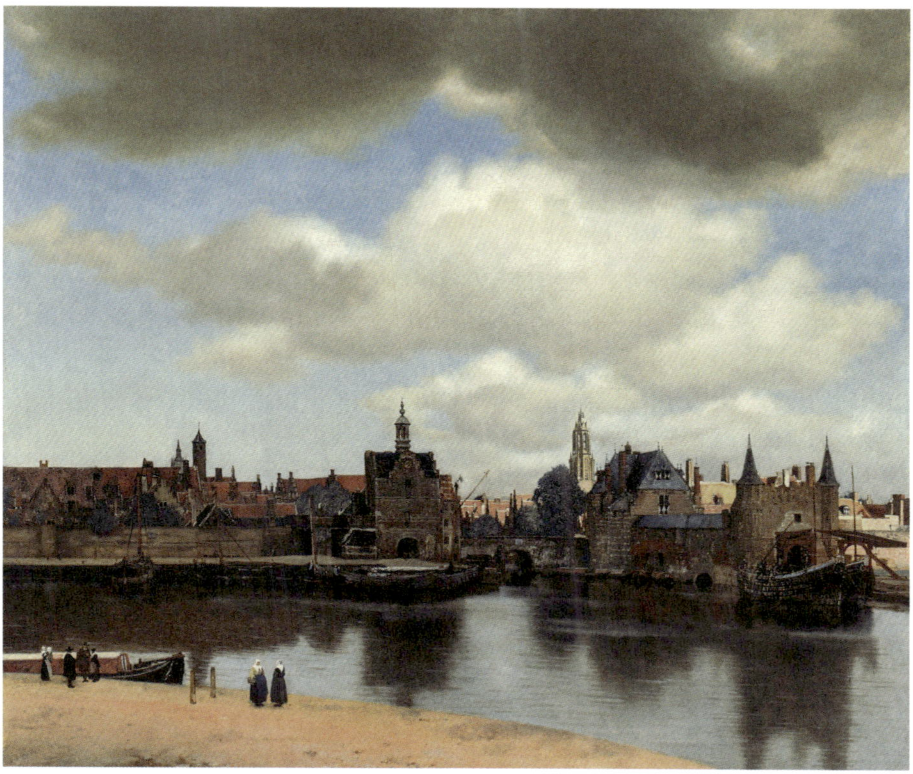

28. Johannes Vermeer. View of Delft, 1660–61

analysis of the painter and his work that was serialized in the newspaper L'Opinion.[7]

Whether or not Dubuffet saw Vermeer's View of Delft at the Jeu de Paume—I like to imagine that he did, and if I were writing fiction, I would place him there at the same time as Proust for the sake of an unlikely collision of two worlds—his own view of Paris demonstrates an awareness of and desire to engage with the history of landscape painting, of which View of Delft was a part. The way Dubuffet inserted his "view of Paris" into a window framed by a curtain directly recalls the *veduta*—a painting or print of a particular place, composed with single-point perspective—that is at the origin of Western landscape painting.[8] Vermeer's View of Delft, in 1660–61, was an important work within the relatively recent tradition of the *veduta*, presenting, through a rigorous perspective that possibly owed something to the use of a camera obscura, a topographically exact sight of the town of Delft rather than an idealized cityscape. As such, View of Delft and other paintings of its ilk updated a tradition that, as Henri Lefebvre contended in 1974 in La production de l'espace (The Production of Space), put towns and cities "into perspective" literally as well as metaphorically.[9] When "maps and bird's eye views" appeared in the sixteenth century, Lefebvre wrote, they broke with the "metaphysical character" of the medieval town conceived as "*imago mundi*, centre and epitome of the Cosmos."[10] Triggered by economic growth, towns built the infrastructure necessary for commercial exchange and, as a corollary to that development, "assumed [their] own identity and began to represent [themselves] graphically."[11]

It would be overkill to read a small woodcut by a fledgling artist through the lens of the ideological and philosophical implications of landscape painting, as can be done with Vermeer's painting—and yet, for all its anecdotal character within Dubuffet's oeuvre, Personnage méditant devant une vue de Paris is a good starting point to investigate the ways in which Dubuffet approached the representation of the city throughout his career. To sum things up so far: the woodcut depicts a perspectival view, a *veduta*, that confirms Dubuffet's knowledge of the history of art. The painter/protagonist sitting in the room beholds the city of Paris, with its Eiffel Tower dominating a shallow mountain of small cubes. But while the figure can visually embrace the city as a totality, he is also clearly removed from it.

This standpoint changes in Dubuffet's later evocations of the city, in 1943–44, in 1961–62, and in the Théâtres de mémoire series of 1975–79. Those dates encompass, respectively, the years of the Occupation, during World War II; the period of economic expansion after the immediate postwar period, known in France as the "Trente Glorieuses," or the "three glorious decades"; and the emerging "postindustrial society" that came on the heels of the first oil crisis of 1973.[12] Some of the impact of economic development could be directly measured in the radical infrastructure changes and spates of urban planning and building that transformed Paris in the 1960s and 1970s, durably affecting the very idea of the city. The philosopher Jean-Luc Nancy has reflected that the understanding of the city as an identifiable and graspable entity collapsed over the course of the twentieth century: "Neighborhood of the unknown, the city opens on all sides onto the expansion of a disassembled universe in which the shape of the city disappears or changes."[13] As a consequence, the coherent image of the city vanished. The time of the *veduta*, along with that of the eloquent analyses of Paris by Balzac, Baudelaire, and even Benjamin, is behind us, contended Nancy, writing in 1998, and those images have become obsolete—just as the "aesthetic, political and industrial *ideal cities*, which were so numerous in the past (Piero, Boullée, Tony Garnier . . .), have been deserted, and the literary topos of the city belongs rather to the past. Today we see the images, the ideas and the forms of the city unravel."[14] Dubuffet's artistic practice and incessant questioning of representation undoubtedly place him within this context of the collapse of the city both as entity and as representation, in which, wrote Nancy, what remains of the city is the "fragile energy of a novel meaning, rebellious to all stability."[15] It is not a chronicle of the changing Paris that we are after, then, when we look at this artist's work but rather unstable indications of an intertwined process of thinking about and undoing the city and its representation.

Views of Paris: Façades and Maps

Fast forward twenty or so years from the woodcut of 1921. In the midst of the war, in Occupied Paris, in 1942, Dubuffet makes a third attempt at starting a career as a painter. Then, in July 1943, he takes a bicycle trip across France to Villefranche-sur-Saône, and in September, another to Sin-le-Noble, near Douai. His sketchbooks from those months are filled with drawings of cows, horses, ravens, and farmers working in the fields. In Paris, he sketches the buildings and squares in the small, winding streets around his house behind the Panthéon. In the fall, Limbour brings the editor and writer Jean Paulhan to Dubuffet's studio. The two begin a close friendship, prolonged by an extensive correspondence.[16] Paulhan invites many of his writer friends, as well as the dealer René Drouin, to discover the artist and his work (at some point, Dubuffet makes a habit of reserving Thursday afternoons to cluster such visits together). In October 1944, less than two months after the Liberation of Paris, Dubuffet's first solo exhibition opens at Galerie René Drouin, on place Vendôme.[17] In this curtain raiser, Dubuffet foregrounds the theme of the city alongside that of the countryside. The phrase *vue de Paris* appears in several instances of the artist's work of these years, notably on the gray cardboard cover of a sketchbook dated 1943 and as the title of several drawings inside it (fig. 29) but also as the title of several gouaches and five large oil paintings made in the winter and spring of 1944, of which four are exhibited at René Drouin (fig. 30). Each of the latter depicts a variation on the same subject: a row of building façades, viewed frontally, occupying almost the entire canvas, with occasional narrow areas of open space to the sides and above through which the sky

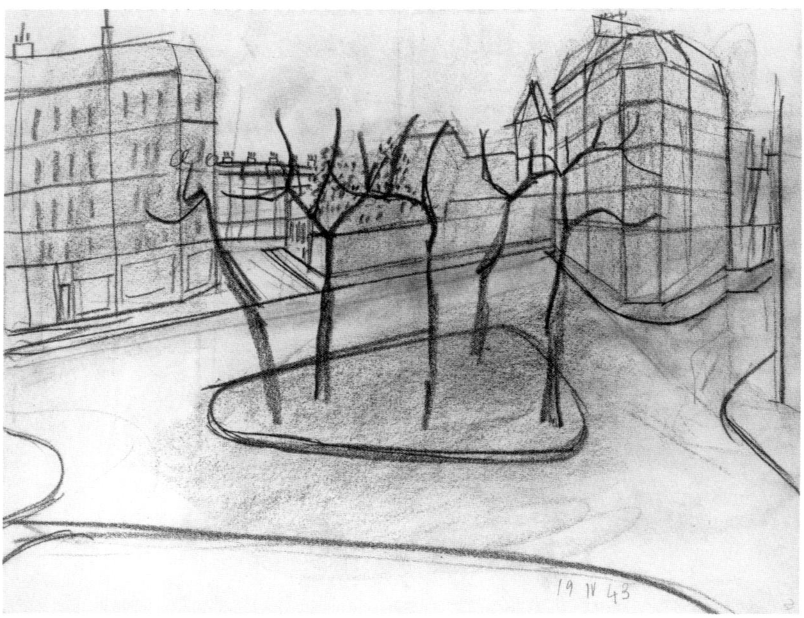

29. Jean Dubuffet. Vue de Paris (Église Saint-Médard), April 1943

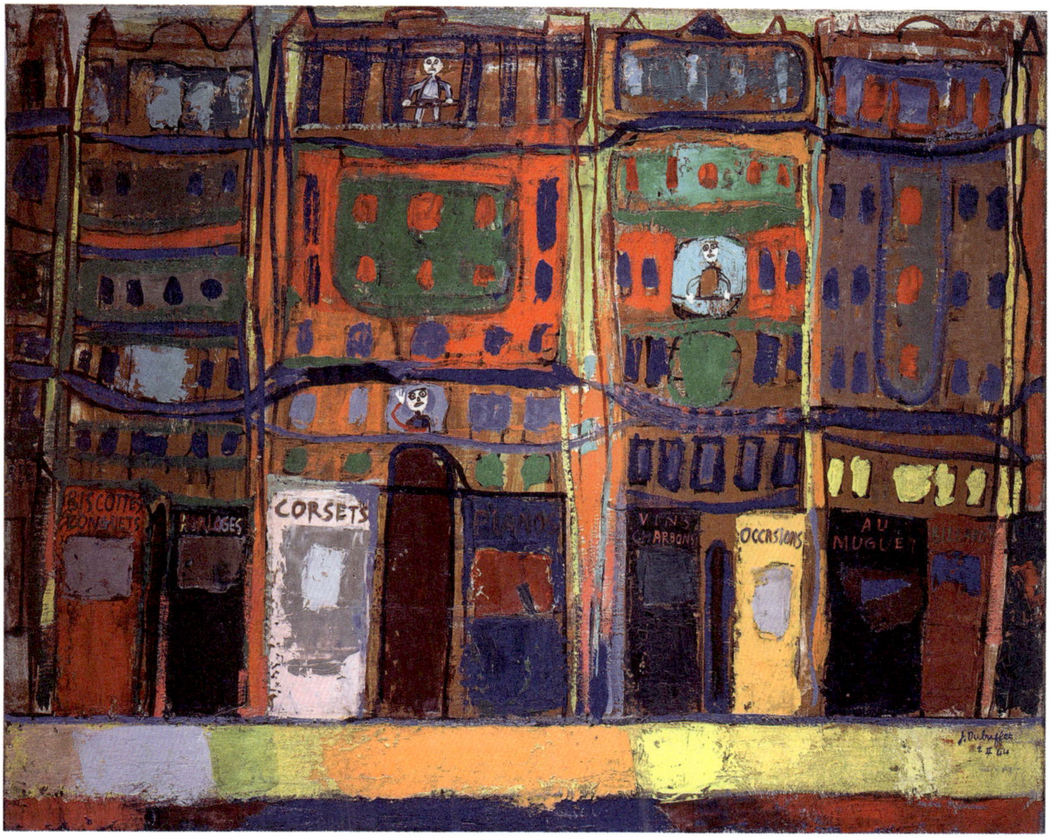

30. Jean Dubuffet. *Vue de Paris, le petit commerce*, February 2, 1944

appears. Here and there, sketchy figures peer from balconies and windows on the upper floors of the dwellings, while the ground floors are occupied by storefronts whose specialties are scrawled above their doors in capital letters.

These paintings, the largest Dubuffet had made so far, were, without a doubt, a statement of intent on the part of the artist: an intention to reprise the classic theme of the urban view, whose modern tradition, continued from Vermeer and such eighteenth-century practitioners as Canaletto, had manifested itself in nineteenth-century Paris with the Impressionists' paintings of fashionable boulevards. In the 1920s, the city became a topos for avant-garde painters. In France, Fernand Léger and Robert Delaunay foregrounded a modernity of industry, leisure, and commerce by reducing the city to dynamic geometric shapes and daring aerial views (fig. 32). But the genre of the cityscape, it should be remembered, also has a history in the popular realm of tourist postcards, obsolete forms of entertainment such as

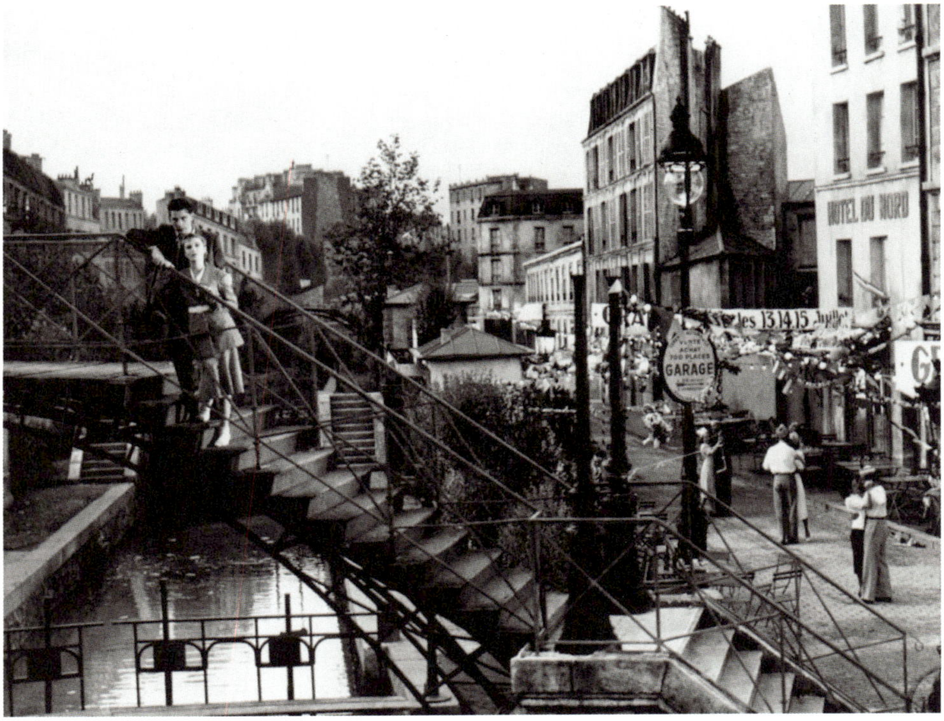

31. Still from Marcel Carné's <u>Hôtel du Nord</u>, 1938

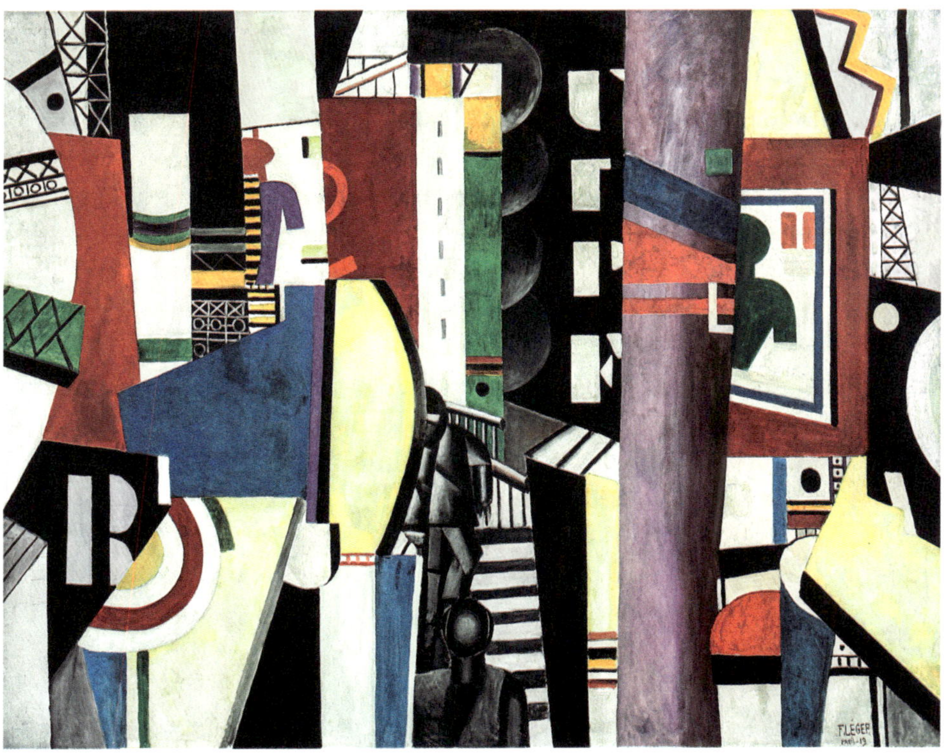

32. Fernand Léger. <u>La ville</u>, 1919

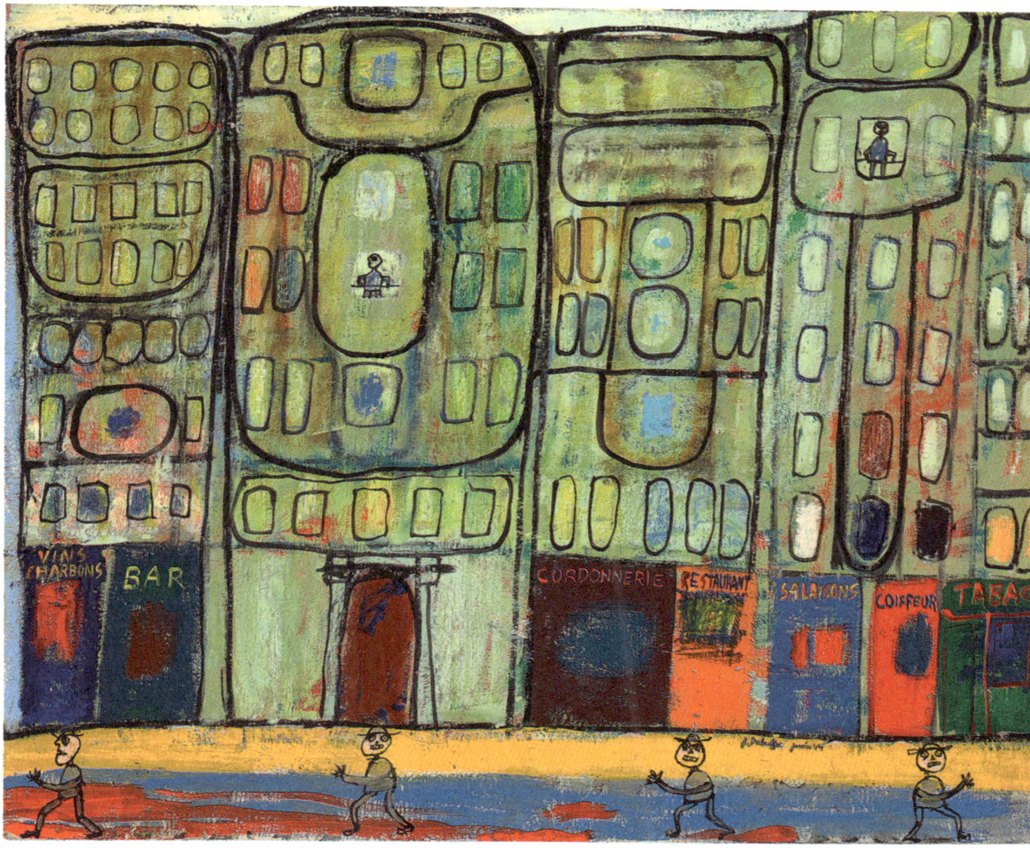

33. Jean Dubuffet. <u>Vue de Paris, quartiers résidentiels</u>**, February 1944**

panoramas and dioramas, and, of course, cinema. In the 1930s and 1940s, the poetic realists Marcel Carné and Jacques Prévert invented a bleak but sweet imagery of Paris in films such as *Hôtel du Nord* (1938), *Le jour se lève* (1939), and *Les enfants du paradis* (1945), in which the city was entirely reconstructed on film sets (fig. 31). Dubuffet undoubtedly had all these different histories in mind, however much he wanted to ignore some and acknowledge others.[18] His own "views of Paris" of 1944 are brightly colored and do not represent any specific location. Whereas perspective, in the drawings of 1943 bearing the same title, is classically, if rudimentarily, indicated through shading and foreshortening, the paintings made a year later are decidedly flat. All parts of the picture are brought unapologetically onto the same plane, thanks to linear drawing and flat brushwork. I write "unapologetically" because everything in these designs, including the façades stretching from one edge of the frame to the other, provocatively negates the idea of a "view" by obstructing the possibility of seeing beyond the buildings.

In abandoning perspective, Dubuffet was throwing us viewers—like the little figures on the sidewalk in *Vue de Paris, quartiers résidentiels* (fig. 33)—straight into the middle of the city, without a glimpse of a virtual getaway. The construction of these paintings was not only a matter of form and perspective; Dubuffet was rejecting an intellectual distance as well—*le regard éloigné* (the view from afar), as Claude Lévi-Strauss economically put it.[19] That is the distance from which a problem—like a city—can be "objectively" appraised and examined. Encircling the viewer in this manner was a deliberately iconoclastic gesture on the artist's part. It short-circuited the history of urban representation, mixing the popular, flat images of the panorama with the highbrow idea of a "view" and then pressing our noses against the high façades.

Nevertheless, the artist did introduce a visual trick into these paintings, by which an escape route for the eye becomes available. The image of the massive buildings can be mentally flipped ninety degrees to the horizontal to let a new picture appear that is different altogether. This new image—look again, for example, at *Vue de Paris, quartiers résidentiels*—shows a map or perhaps an aerial view (but with nothing of the drama of Delaunay's vertiginous paintings), in which the windows become fields of crops and the pipes and architectural details running across the façades become paths meandering through the countryside.

The double orientation of these pictures is more than a visual puzzle along the lines of the duck/rabbit discussed by (among others) the art historian Ernst H. Gombrich in his classic study *Art and Illusion*.[20] Rather, it disorients the viewer because the pictures resulting from this mental flipping closely resemble certain rural

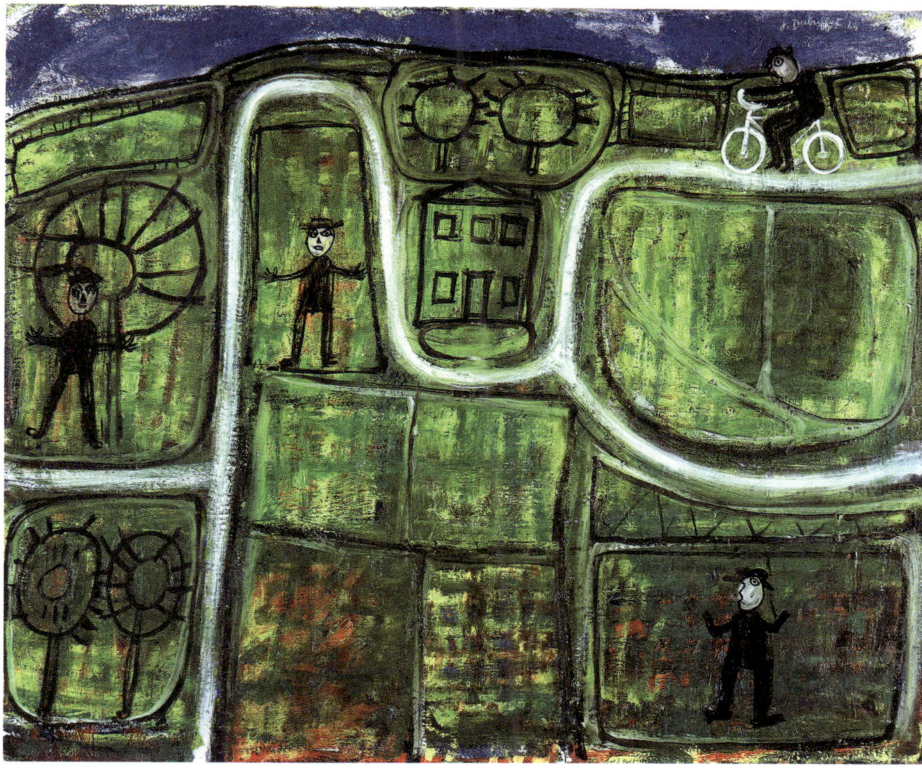

34. Jean Dubuffet. Paysage vert, January 1944

landscapes, such as Paysage vert (fig. 34), that Dubuffet painted during the same months as the city views. The double orientation and the visual similarities with these other works essentially abolish the rural/urban dichotomy with which—Lefebvre reminds us—the concept of the city originated and which stands at the root of the visual imaginary of the city.[21] This is why the *et* (and) in Marionnettes de la ville et de la campagne—the title given to the series in the first volume of the catalogue raisonné—was important to the artist: neither color nor brushwork distinguishes Vue de Paris, la vie de plaisir (View of Paris, the Life of Pleasure) from Le pépiniériste (The Nurseryman), painted during the same months of 1944 and both depicting networks of lines surrounding coarsely shaped rectangles.[22] Although the overall suggestion of an aerial view is combined with figures depicted frontally, the sense of surprise and double viewing is less strong in the rural landscapes, which never quite assume the shape of building façades. The flipping between the two viewpoints enabled Dubuffet to preserve a certain sense of depth within the pictures while giving up classical perspective, but it

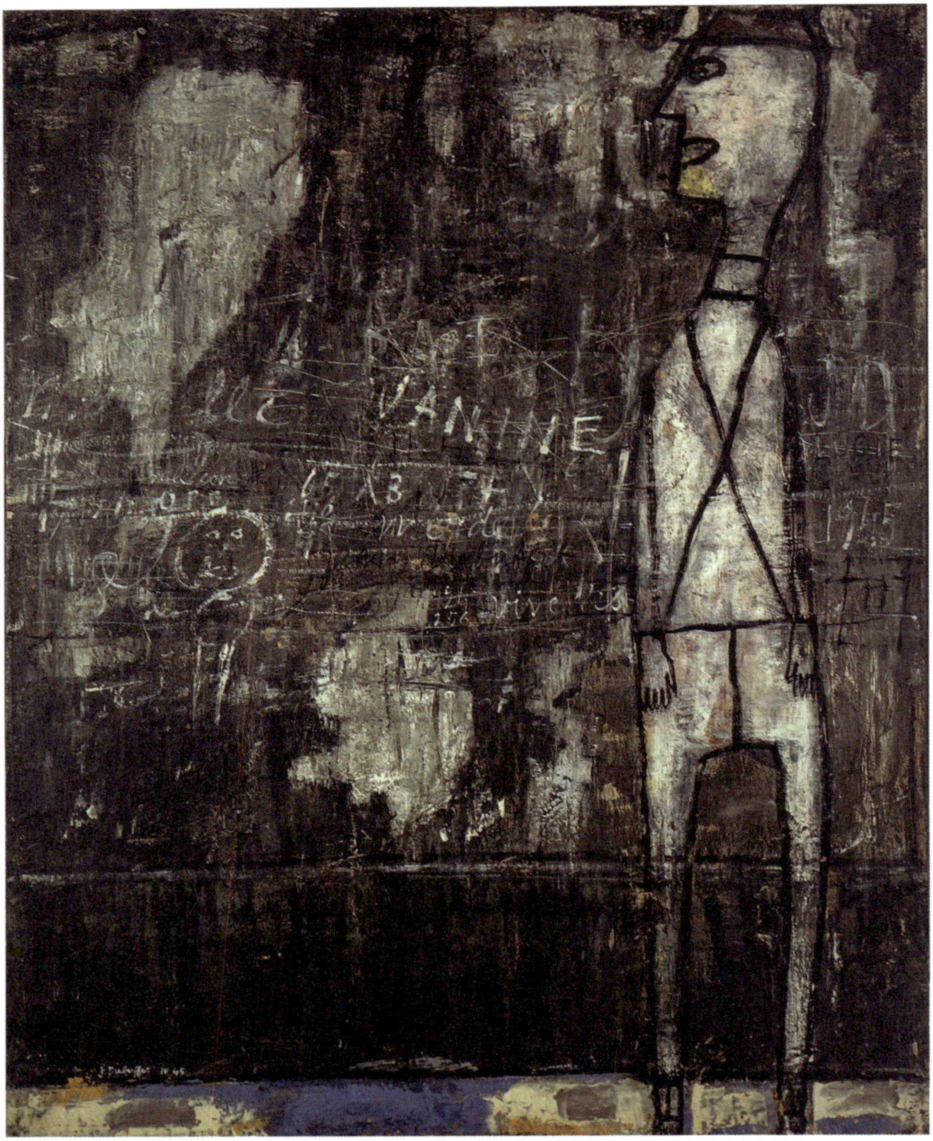

35. Jean Dubuffet. *Mur aux inscriptions*, April 1945

also allowed him to experiment playfully with two representational modes derived from technical apparatuses, each of which was identified with a "way of seeing" in a particular epoch. Panoramas, with their extended and detailed city views, had been a popular form of entertainment in the mid-nineteenth century, while the aerial views disseminated through wartime aerial reconnaissance photography had become, by the 1920s, strongly associated with the look of modernity.[23]

In his *Vues de Paris*, Dubuffet provoked viewers by giving the genre of landscape painting a rough treatment. He extended this provocation in a series of works prominently featuring walls and similarly rejecting depth and distance in favor of closeup views in which small details can be scrutinized. In the haunting lithographic series

Les murs (The Walls; see fig. 79) and the paintings Rhéteur au mur and Mur aux inscriptions (figs. 19, 35), all of 1945, a single male figure stands before or walks by a high wall whose rough surface is marked by anonymous graffiti and, perhaps, bullet holes like the ones captured by American military cameramen in footage of the Sorbonne and the Panthéon shot at the time of the Liberation.[24] The inscriptions, as if embedded in the bottom layer of a magic slate toy, suggest the passing of time and the accumulation of secret, defamatory, or anonymous messages, while the wall obstructing the view activates the imagination as to what might lie beyond it. Several years later, in Dubuffet's oeuvre, this attraction to the closeup detail and the idea of obstructing the view would transform themselves into a wholesale rejection of the sense of sight. In 1951, he argued to a Chicago audience composed of artists, collectors, and journalists, in a sentence that reads like a slogan: "Art addresses the mind and not the eyes."[25]

Meanwhile, it is the artist's walking figures that powerfully represent the denigration of vision that is the mark of the true

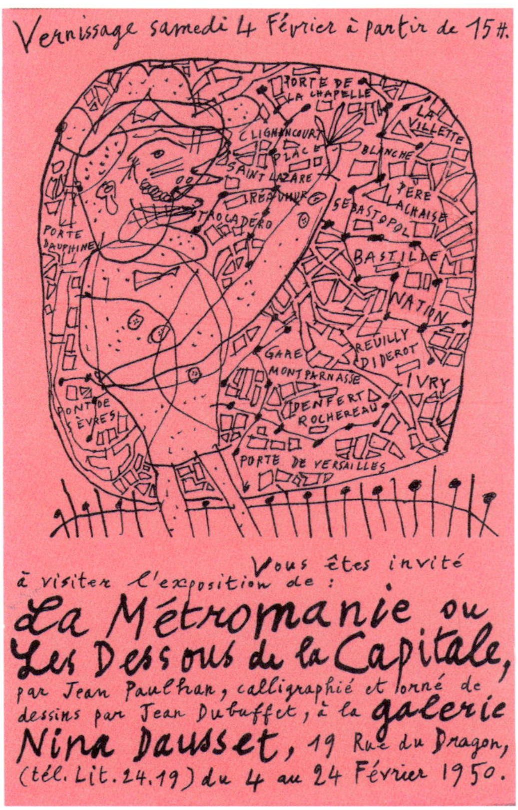

36. Flyer for La Métromanie ou Les dessous de la capitale exhibition, 1950

experience of the city, as Michel de Certeau compellingly argued in 1980 in his L'invention du quotidien (The Practice of Everyday Life): "The panorama-city is a 'theoretical' (that is, a visual) simulacrum, in short, a picture whose condition of possibility is an oblivion and a misunderstanding of practices." Contrary to this, "The ordinary practitioners of the city live 'down below,' below the threshold at which visibility begins. They walk—an elementary form of this experience of the city, they are walkers."[26] Dubuffet's passersby wander along old walls attempting to decipher coded communications and messages scribbled on old newspapers. The artist had previously alluded to such mundane or coded communications in the striking drawings featuring messages painted on and scratched into the texture of newspaper backgrounds entitled Messages (1944).[27]

It was also during these years that Dubuffet stepped down into the subway to uncover, physically and metaphorically, the underground of the city in a series of gouaches, one large painting, and, in 1949, a series of lithographs published as an artist's book, La Métromanie ou les dessous de la capitale (fig. 36).[28] Moving in closer from his distant, encompassing view of the city of 1921 through the façades of its buildings, the enigmatic language of its walls, and the tunnels and cars of the Métro, Dubuffet gives us Paris as a complex accumulation of layers, a city that cannot be beheld or grasped as a totality but only as different intersecting views, subtexts, and riddles.

Paris Circus: The World Seen through the Eyes of a Car

When Dubuffet returned, at the beginning of 1961, to the theme of Paris in a series of paintings and works on paper, the image of a secretive city seems to have all but vanished. The title of this new cycle, *Paris Circus*, suggests as much, with its reference to a theatrical structure with a stage offering a 360-degree view. Indeed, in these works, painted between February 1961 and the summer of 1962, the city seems to have been split open, like an apricot revealing a worm-filled pit. In several letters to friends and critics penned as he was working on this new series, Dubuffet explained that he had turned the clock back and was revisiting his work of the 1940s: "I live locked up in my studios, doing, guess what? Paintings in the spirit and manner of those I was making in 1943. I have reversed steam after closing off the *Matériologies* and decided to start all over again from the beginning."[29] But what does it mean to start all over again from the beginning? Presumably, he meant to return to his views of Paris of the 1940s and perhaps to the spirit of defiance toward both the history of art and its avant-garde manifestations. But Dubuffet, in 1961, was in a very different place than he had been twenty years before—that is, a late beginner supported by Jean Paulhan and a small coterie of writers. At the beginning of the 1960s, his work was the subject of museum retrospectives in Paris and Zürich, before New York, Chicago, and Los Angeles followed suit.[30] A new dealer, Daniel Cordier, now represented the artist's work in Europe and in the United States.[31] Throughout the 1950s, Dubuffet had been to other places and painted different things; he had intensified his experimentation with materials and techniques, leading to the speckled surfaces of the *Texturologies* series and the mineralogical-looking planes of the *Matériologies* paintings. He had visited the Algerian desert and lived in New York for half a year, but most significantly, he had settled in Vence, in the South of France, in 1955 and made it his main residence for over five years. When he moved back to Paris at the beginning of 1961, he was returning to a city in the midst of profound change, and to see it with the eyes of 1943 would have been an anachronism in relation not only to his own work but to the city itself. The population of Paris had increased since the war years, along with its economy and the size of its suburbs, which were now dotted with large, low-rise housing complexes hastily built to remedy the endemic housing shortage. Unlike Occupied Paris in the

1940s, it was a city projecting itself into the future, and Dubuffet's Paris Circus was very much a response to that atmosphere.

An emblem of this shift was a large exhibition that took place in March and April 1961 at the Grand Palais.[32] Entitled Demain Paris (Tomorrow Paris), it presented in-progress and future urban projects aimed at modernizing and sanitizing Paris, illustrated by a wealth of statistics, architectural models, and panoramic views (fig. 37). Analyses of traffic flow and the rhythm of life in the city were visualized with diagrams and figures on large placards. New infrastructure and architectural developments, such as the Pont de Neuilly and the Maine-Montparnasse complex (for which work began in August 1961), among dozens of others, were introduced through maps and models.[33] Most spectacular in the exhibition was a huge architectural model of Paris animated by sound and light effects that could be observed from an elevated walkway (see fig. 53). As the architecture critic Marcel Cornu argued in his critical 1972 study, La conquête de Paris (The Conquest of Paris), urban planning in the 1960s was marked by increased centralization of decision making, emblematized by the figure of Paul Delouvrier, delegate general of the district of the region of Paris, and by an increase in private-public real estate partnerships. In 1965, a *schéma directeur* (grand plan) for the Paris region was rolled out, which, for Cornu, marked the victory of the "prospectivist" discourse and announced the triumph of the gentrification of Paris. Along with the very real problems of housing shortages and antiquated infrastructure, it was the necessity to counterbalance the loss of colonial power and reduction of France to

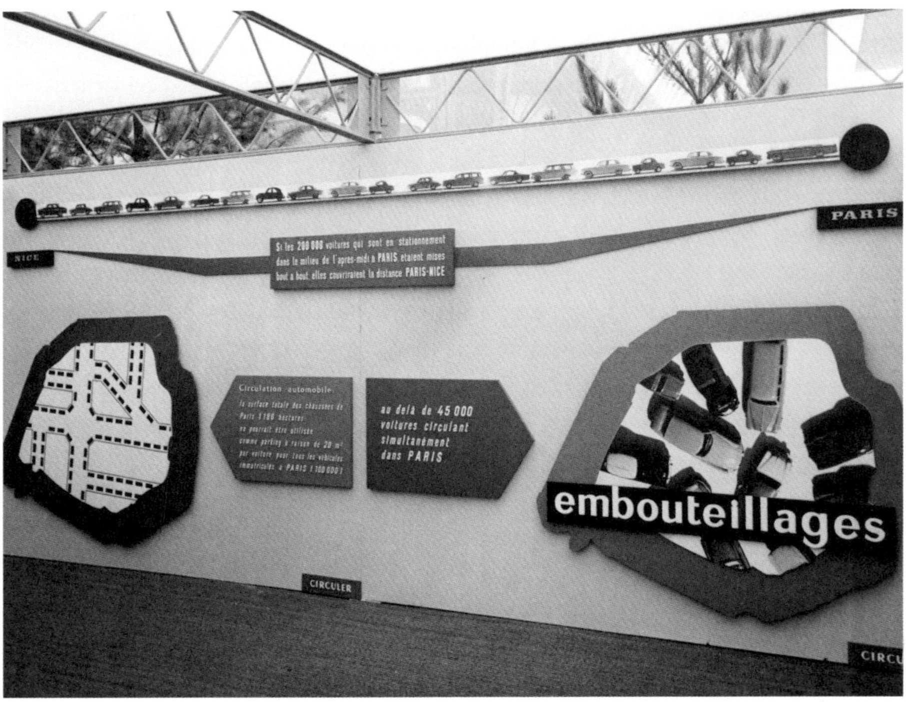

37. Demain Paris exhibition, Grand Palais, Paris, March–April 1961

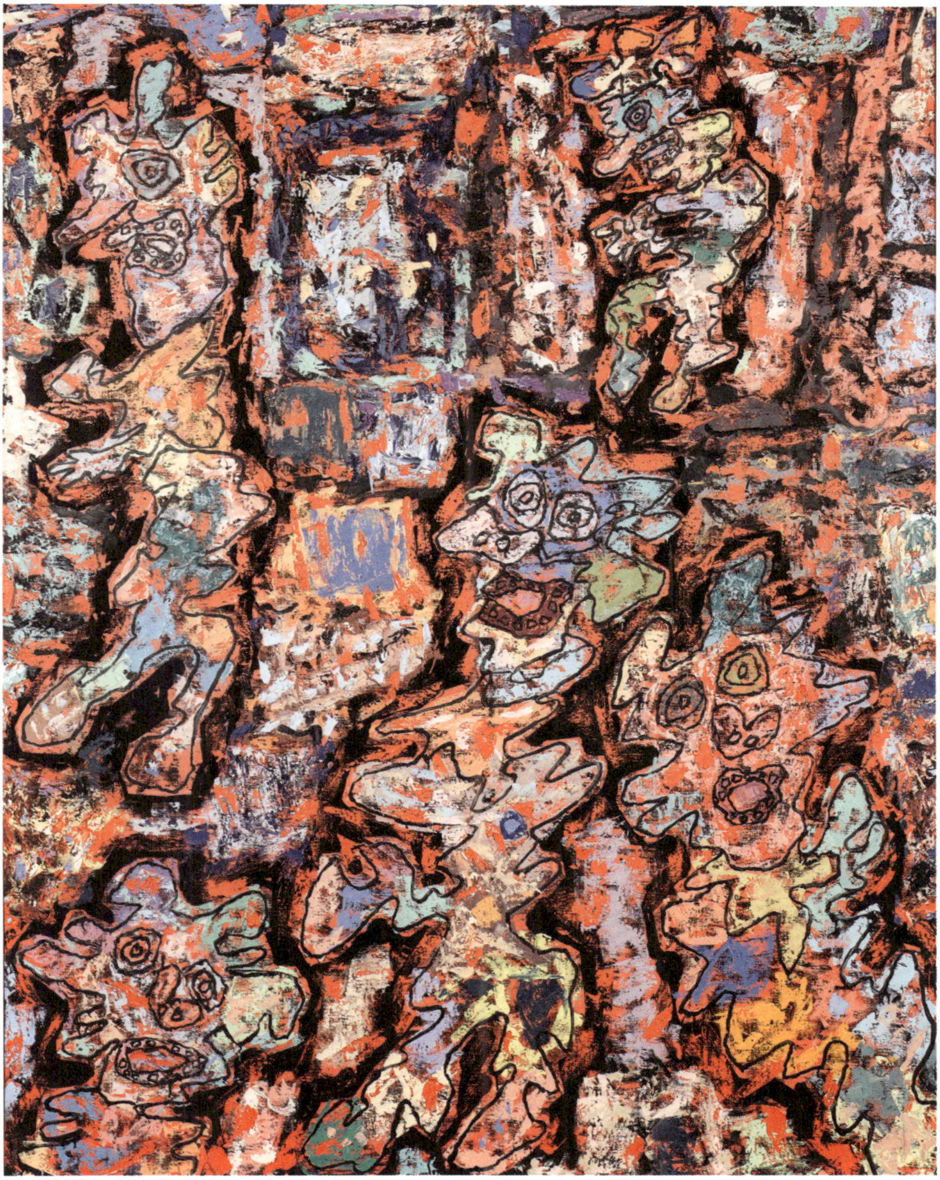

38. Jean Dubuffet. Théâtre de la rue, January 8–9, 1962

its mainland borders (mostly) that, in his view, explained the political need for the government to promote an expanded and modernized capital city. In contrast, the France of the *hexagone*—a metaphor that gained currency after 1962—aimed to play a central role in the building of the European Union (then the European Economic Community, or EEC) after the signing of the Rome Treaty in 1957.[34] Some French artists were taken by this idea of modernity and technical progress: in 1958–61, in collaboration with the architect Claude Parent, Yves Klein developed rough sketches and plans of an "air architecture," with climate-controlled spaces and glass walls, while, over several years in the 1960s, Nicolas Schöffer conceived a cybernetic city built around a computer that would control living conditions and maintain a "constant but dynamic equilibrium" of sensations.[35]

In contrast with the inspiration those artists and others drew from the possibilities of modern technology, Dubuffet's paintings of the period seem, at first glance, to be embedded in an outmoded perception of the city, in line with his own desire to return to his earlier views of Paris. Despite the appearance of automobiles in a painting such as Maison fondée of 1961 (fig. 54), it otherwise replicates the grid-like structure of those 1940s views, with their residential façades and storefronts on the ground floor. What had changed in the new work was the palette and the brushwork. Instead of the flat, bright colors of the earlier pictures, these paintings are more subdued; the colors are mixed, muddied, and molten. As Dubuffet continued to work over the following months, the paintings became busier, and the rectilinear or orthogonal grid-like structure disappeared, giving way to a distorted space, alternately concave and convex. Rue Turlupet of April 1961 (fig. 39), Rue passagère (Busy Street) of July–August 1961, and Les dames aux fenêtres (Ladies at the Windows) of July–August 1961 all depict a tightly woven space in which buildings not only are placed closely together but are opened up and flattened out, divided into cell-like shapes joined together like cloisonné, while figures marching on sidewalks enter the frame from all directions. Read in terms of urban space, these paintings are a far cry from the open, fluid, and rectilinear spaces promoted by the planners and architects whose projects were exhibited in Demain Paris (fig. 40).

Instead, if a model of urbanism could be called up, it would be the medieval "space of contact" described by the historian of urbanism Françoise Choay a few years later in her concise history of urban space in France: an enclosed urban environment in which houses, each with its own architectural idiosyncrasies, are places of both work and residence.[36] Huddled closely together, they created a lively environment in which street and buildings were indissociable

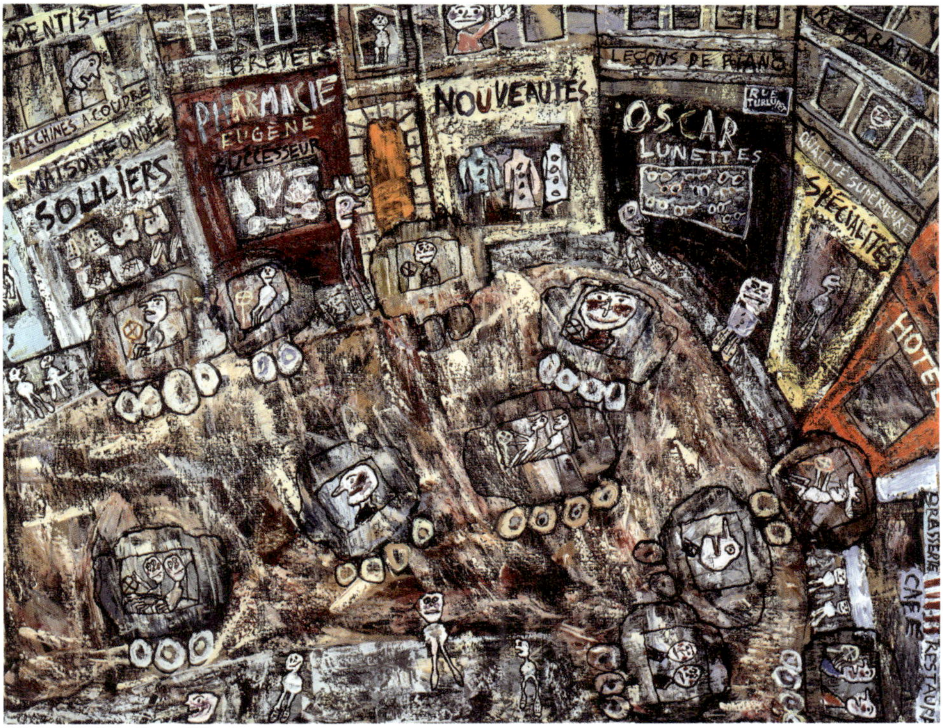

39. Jean Dubuffet. Rue Turlupet, April 5, 1961

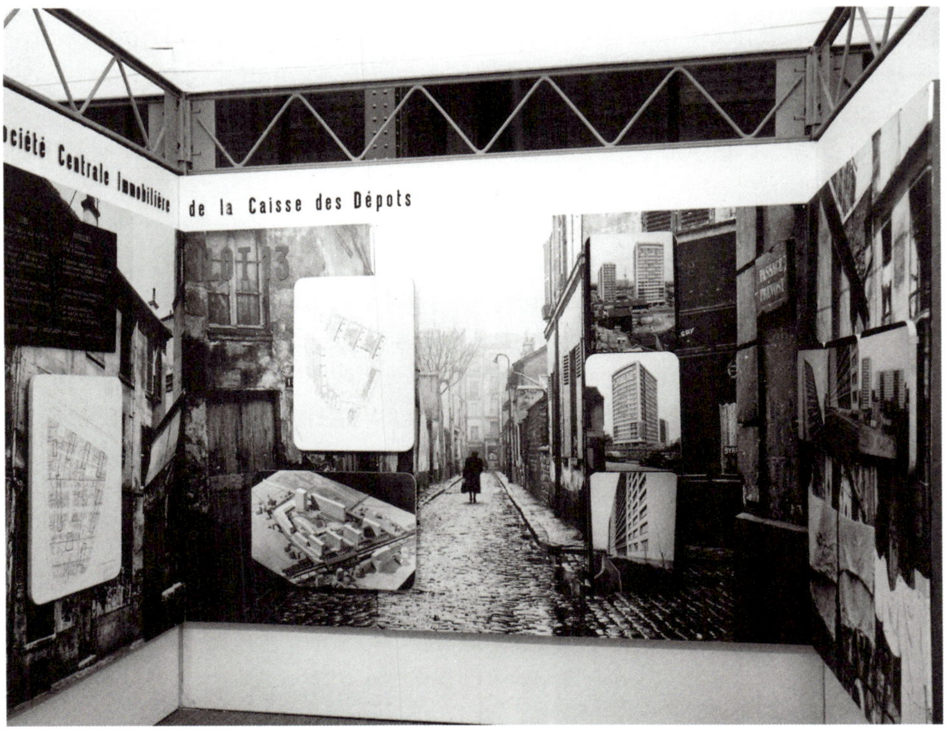

40. Demain Paris exhibition, Grand Palais, Paris, March–April 1961

from one another. While modern attempts to reinvent a medieval-like "space of contact" had only resulted in pastiche, argued Choay, citing holiday villages and suburban housing complexes as examples, she nevertheless contended that the city must be radically rethought, the very word "urbanism" abandoned in the face of the "disintegration of the *urbs*" ("city," in Latin) and modes of contact redefined within the new networks of "connected space." Choay's conclusions are somewhat rhetorical and vague, and yet they express a damning critique of urban planning that was voiced elsewhere in more specific and concrete ways, most forcefully by the writer and activist Jane Jacobs in her book The Death and Life of Great American Cities (1961). Against the then-dominant trends of city planning, Jacobs eloquently praised the large city and produced close readings of everyday life on city streets that showed how parks, sidewalks, and mixed-purpose neighborhoods worked and how they contributed to the quality of life in the city. Her focus on the everyday, her clear and sensitive analysis, opened up a gap within established urban policy. Reading Jacobs's book, which very quickly became a classic—an emblem of resistance to centralized town planning, and an inspiration to generations of architects and thinkers about the city—I am struck by its powerfully descriptive, optimistically prosaic tone and by the way the author's intimate knowledge of the city, her almost performative descriptions of seemingly insignificant everyday rituals, matched a number of contemporary artistic practices. Claes Oldenburg's environments The Street (1960) and The Store (1961), Guy Debord's psychogeographic maps, and the torn posters collected by the Affichistes Raymond Hains, François Dufrêne, and Jacques de la Villeglé (fig. 9) were the result of intimate readings of life on city streets and an experience of the urban environment not unlike Jacobs's.[37] For Dubuffet, the experience of city space was one of disruption, which, in the works of Paris Circus, appeared as much in the melting of strident colors as in the use of words inside the paintings. "Rien sous la dent" (no food on the plate), "rabais" (discount), "banque véreuse" (corrupt bank) "la maffia" [*sic*], "Au crapuleux" (The Villainous's [*sic*]), "Au chèque bidon" (Fake Checks & Co.), "gredin père et fils" (rascal father and son), Rue Poisse, Rue de l'Entourloupe, La main dans le sac (Caught Red-Handed): dozens of inscriptions on the works and some of their titles speak unambiguously of a corrupt and overpowering capitalism and point to the city as an economic space in which commerce and exchange value have come to overshadow production. In the words of Henri Lefebvre, "Retail is becoming more important than production, exchange more important than activity, intermediaries more important than makers, means more important than ends."[38]

If one object, more than any other during these years, symbolized consumption, economic growth, and the spirit of modernization, it was the automobile.[39] The number of cars in France increased wildly over the second half of the twentieth century, growing from 1.5 million in 1950 to 5 million in 1960 and 15 million in 1970.[40] Roland Barthes had compared cars to Gothic cathedrals in an essay on the Citroën DS published in Mythologies (1957).[41] In popular culture, the car was in equal degrees an object of admiration and of satire, an emblem of individual wealth and a sign of unruly urban growth, as traffic became an increasing problem in large cities and suburbs.[42] In the United States, Walker Evans pointed to the issue of rapid obsolescence of even this thriving technology in his 1962 photo essay "The Auto Junkyard," gleefully captioning an image of smashed-up cars "the fashionable colors of last year."[43] In France, the 1962 comedy La belle américaine ridiculed conspicuous consumption, tracking a massive, shiny American car that earns its purchasers various misfortunes as they attempt to maneuver it around the narrow streets of a village-like Paris.

Such humor is not absent from Paris Circus. In L'automobile, fleur de l'industrie (fig. 42), Dubuffet painted two splayed-out, junky-looking cars that would not be out of place in Evans's photo essay. The artist returned frequently to this subject not only in paintings but also in gouaches and drawings. More than a subject matter, however,

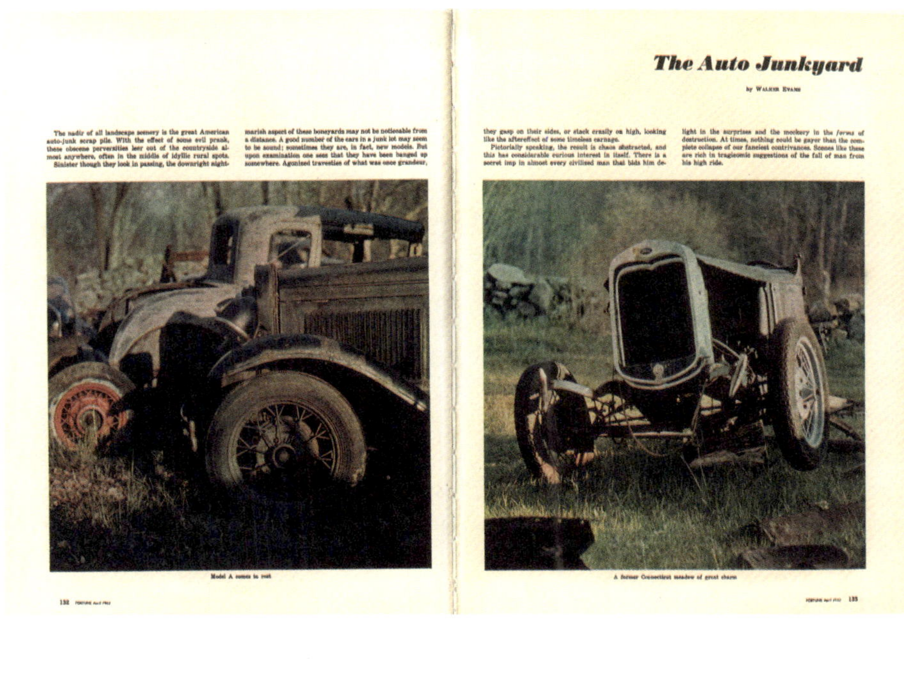

The Auto Junkyard

by Walker Evans

The nadir of all landscape scenery is the great American auto-junk scrap pile. With the effect of some evil prank, these obscene perversities leer out of the countryside almost anywhere, often in the middle of idyllic rural spots.

Sinister though they look in passing, the downright nightmarish aspect of these boneyards may not be noticeable from a distance. A good number of the cars in a junk lot may seem to be sound; sometimes they are, in fact, new models. But upon examination one sees that they have been banged up somewhere. Agonized travesties of what was once grandeur, they gasp on their sides, or stack crazily on high, looking like the aftereffect of some timeless carnage.

Pictorially speaking, the result is chaos abstracted, and this has considerable curious interest in itself. There is a secret imp in almost every civilized man that bids him delight in the surprises and the mockery in the *forms* of destruction. At times, nothing could be gayer than the complete collapse of our fanciest contrivances. Scenes like these are rich in tragicomic suggestions of the fall of man from his high ride.

Model A comes to rest

A former Connecticut meadow of great charm

132 FORTUNE April 1962

FORTUNE April 1962 133

41. First spread of Walker Evans's "The Auto Junkyard," Fortune, April 1962

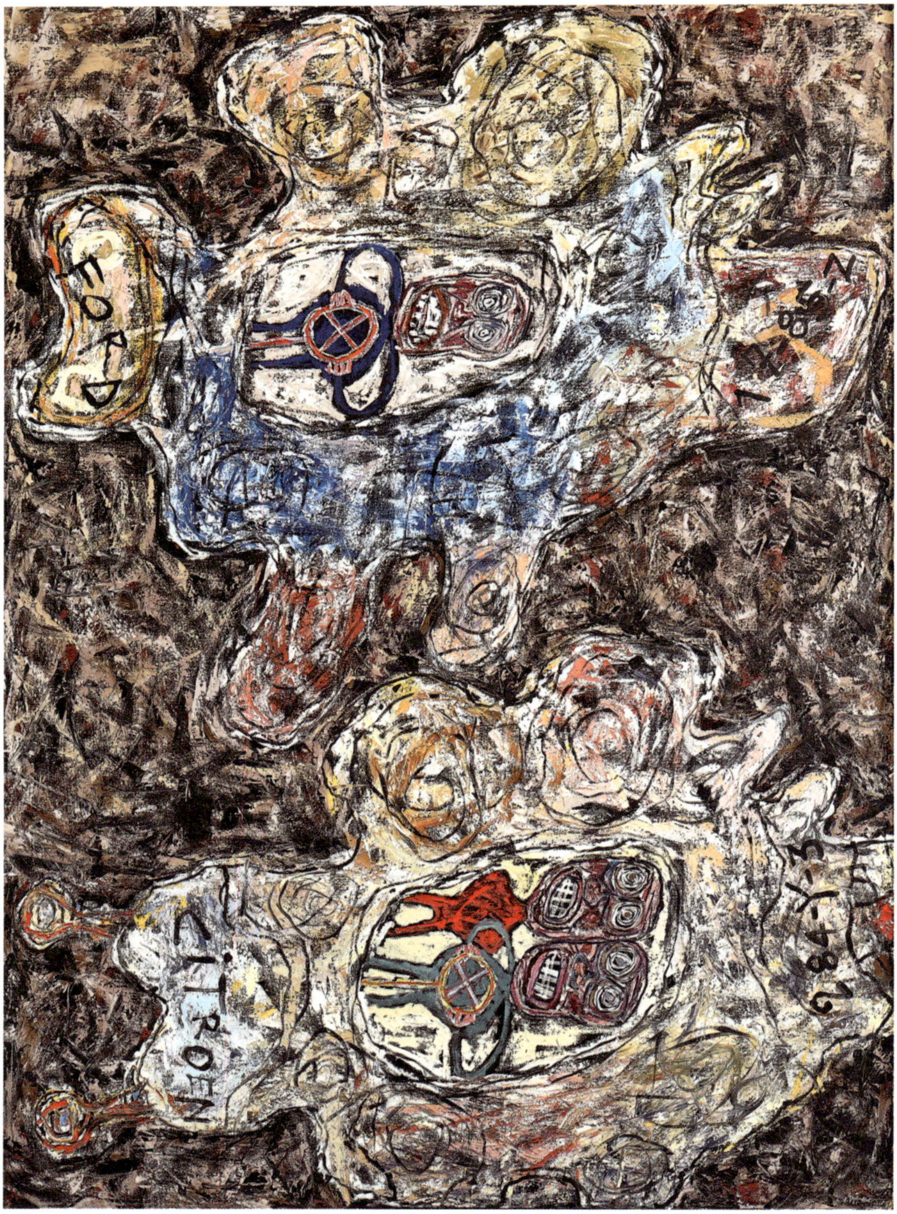

42. Jean Dubuffet. L'automobile, fleur de l'industrie, June 19–20, 1961

cars, even when absent from the paintings themselves, played a key role in the construction of pictorial space in the works of Paris Circus. In Vire-volte of May 1961 (fig. 20), for example, figures' bodies and the street itself are abruptly cut off by the frame, and the muddy-bright colors of buildings appear to be seen in a blur. The implicit presence of the automobile is conveyed in the impression of movement depicted through the distortion of space. As the literary scholar Kristin Ross reminds us, cars have come to modify the way we perceive our environment, as trains did earlier in history, creating "perception-in-movement."[44] This impression of movement is suggested in most of the paintings of Paris Circus, in which buildings, shop windows, streets, and figures twist and turn as if sucked toward an invisible vortex, not only simulating movement but also evoking the rounded edges of the view through an automobile window. Indeed, the curving of space and the cellular structure so characteristic of paintings such as *Rue Turlupet* and *Rue passagère* are reminiscent of windshields and passenger windows that possess, as Barthes described in "La nouvelle Citroën," "the curvature, the spread and the brilliance of soap-bubbles."[45] In front of these works, I have the impression that the entire city waltzes (or, perhaps more aptly for the period, twists) by the windshields behind which drivers, stuck in traffic, sit.

In some paintings, such as *Le passage clouté* (The Crosswalk) and *Trinité Champs-Elysées* (fig. 16), both of 1961, the point of view is clearly taken from the middle of the street, and it is easy to imagine Dubuffet behind the wheel of one of the little Simca cars he owned throughout his life—in an example of which he was photographed years later (see pp. 5–6). In *Trinité Champs-Elysées*, the monumental bus that occupies the largest portion of the painting assumes the scale of a building rooted in the middle of the street. There are figures on the bus but also behind it, standing on the sidewalk in front of shops, and each view appears to us in sequence, as perception-in-movement. In several paintings, such sequences are presented on top of one another, like layers of glass that confuse and endlessly shift the urban landscape. Whereas Jacques Tati, a few years later, in *Playtime* (1967; fig. 43), would place his camera so as to observe streets and office spaces from above, thereby adopting the viewpoint

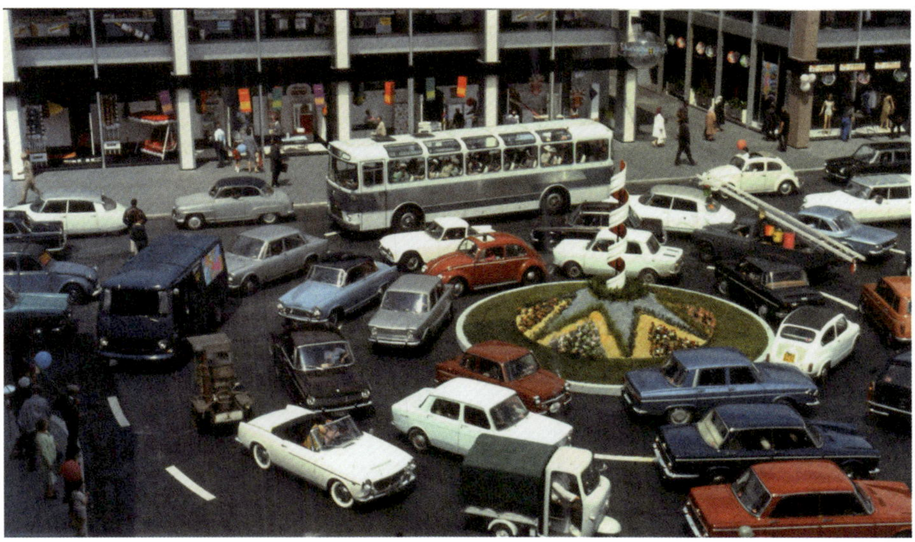

43. Still from Jacques Tati's *Playtime*, 1967

of the technocratic urban planner, Dubuffet settled right in the middle of the hubbub of the street. Showing us Paris through a windshield, through the eyes of the car, as it were, his view of the city is not anachronistic but, rather, is poised at the level of the street. Not unlike Jane Jacobs, he looked at the city in close-up, while the inscriptions on the storefronts—places of circulation and exchange—conjure the mental state of the city and its crowds.

Dubuffet here gives us a Paris balancing between the old world of small, intimate neighborhoods and the Paris that was to come, on the cusp of change brought about by the kind of urban planning lavishly presented in the exhibition Demain Paris, which would create, in the following decades, a radically other image of the city.

Théâtres de mémoire: Unraveling the Urban Fabric

Almost fifteen years separate the end of Paris Circus from the beginning of the series of large assemblage paintings to which Dubuffet gave, although not immediately, the title Théâtres de mémoire.[46] In the intervening years, he mostly worked on L'Hourloupe, the cycle within which he invented a new visual language, or, rather, a "logos"—a term that he used "at the opposite of its meaning," he explained, "as it usually designates the operation of the mind that names and classifies, whereas my own operation is rather instead to erase categories and regress toward an undifferentiated continuum."[47] In the course of L'Hourloupe, recognizable by its pared-down palette of black, white, and primary colors, his painting began to slide off the wall and turn into sculpture and then, eventually, to move outdoors. No longer content with evoking the city in painting, he made architectural models and designed monuments destined to be built in the city. Several photomontages (figs. 97, 98, 104, 105) exemplify the ways in which these structures were projected to work with—and against—their urban setting. I discuss these at length, along with Dubuffet's architectural experiments and projects, in chapters 3 and 4 of this book. In contrast with the monumental structures on which he worked in large studio spaces surrounded by assistants and in close contact with commissioners and architects, the works dating to the aftermath of L'Hourloupe were made with a strict economy of means. Paper, pencils, and paint were all he needed to make the small drawings of 1973–74 called Crayonnages as well as the paintings of the 1974 series Parachiffres and Mondanités (see figs. 59, 84, 85) and the 1975 cycle Lieux abrégés.

And then things became more complicated again. Combining some works from Lieux abrégés with others that were new and purpose-made, Dubuffet began to create assemblages in which he superimposed and juxtaposed cut-out pieces and leftover bits from the paintings (often 30 to 40 pieces but up to 90 for the largest assemblage) and mounted them on canvas. These Théâtres de mémoire are as monumental as they are elusive, escaping any easy analysis, as they effortlessly absorb the viewer who delves into their layers, fragments, and enigmatic scenes. Although I sense the city, or, rather, something of "the urban" in them, only fragments here and there can confirm this impression, in contrast, for example, to the Vues de Paris and Paris Circus, in which Dubuffet clearly took the city as a starting point in order to dismantle traditions and invent new ways of seeing.

My fascination with Théâtres de mémoire was one of the starting points for this book, even though the relationship with the theme of the city is far from explicit. In his writings, Dubuffet was quite firm about one thing: these works are about memory. It would be hard, in any case, to shake off the series's title. Differently from L'Hourloupe, which is an invented word, and differently as well from the purely descriptive Célébrations du sol (Celebrations of the Sun) or witty Plus beaux qu'ils croient (More Beautiful Than They Think—a series of portraits), the title Theâtres de mémoire has a scholarly source. It reprises the interpretation developed by the historian Frances Yates of what she called the "memory theater" of the sixteenth-century Italian philosopher Giulio Camillo.[48] The memory theater was, in Yates's visualization of Camillo's concept, a semicircular theater in which the benches for the audience were compartmentalized so as to assign specific knowledge to each section (fig. 44).[49] Camillo's theater (accounts are contradictory as to whether or not it was ever actually built) was one of the primary sources for Yates's classic study The Art of Memory (1966), which investigated the mnemotechnics used by public speakers in classical Greece and Rome to organize and remember discourses along with subsequent forms of the "art of memory," up until the Renaissance.[50] Dubuffet read Yates's book when it was published in French in 1975, and the techniques it described gave him something of an a posteriori understanding of his own artistic process and aims. And yet, as Hubert Damisch argued, the "art of memory" Dubuffet depicted in his paintings went very much against the grain of classical rhetoric.[51] Instead of choosing well-defined spaces and individuals, as encouraged by the propagators of classical memory techniques, Dubuffet made his figures generic and banal and his locations unspecific and ill-defined. The process by which they were brought into contact with one another appears to have been as disordered as the association of place and discourse in classical rhetoric was ordered. In a letter to the writer Ferit Edgü dated February 1979, a few months after completing the series, Dubuffet elucidated the reference to Yates and Camillo as a countermodel for his own practice, explaining how the title of the series, and the works it contained, called up the "grouping that constantly occurs in the memories of each one of us that, within a single moment, mixes together memories of different scenes and different events into some kind of composite soup."[52] The title of one work in the series, Les réminiscences associées (fig. 45), reiterates, in a more literary manner, this idea of "composite soup." Two figures facing the viewer are placed on either side of the painting, one cut off just below the throat and the other full length. Their bland expressions contrast with the

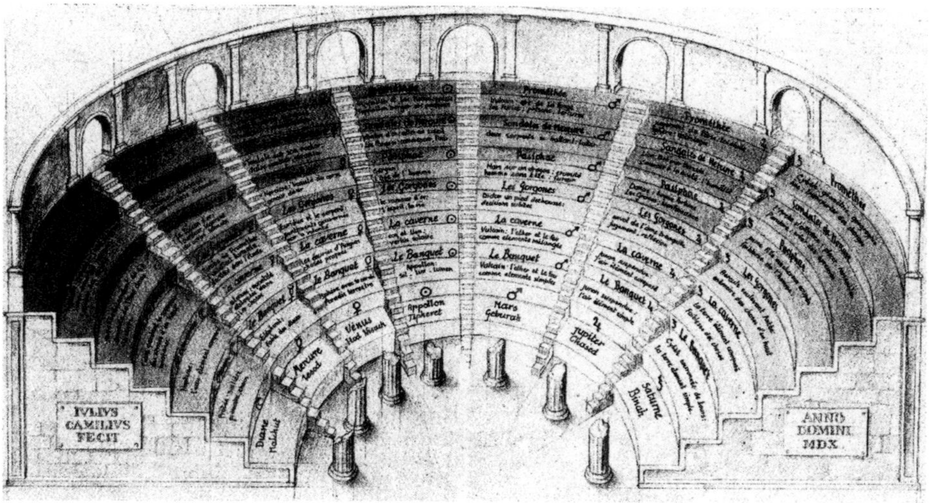

44. Rendition of Giulio Camillo's "memory theater," published in Frances Yates's *Art of Memory* (1966)

jittery alternation of different segments, each painted in a singular style and palette, that cover the entirety of the canvas: a black square in one corner, a pile of rocks to the left, a winding path at the top right, a milky white composition evoking Picasso's organic abstractions of the late 1920s and early 1930s, and, next to that, an area of white and red marks on black that prefigures Dubuffet's *Non-lieux* paintings of 1984. These images, and other more and less definable ones, appear as if popping up from the confines of the painting. They push me to search for memories that make sense of them but also, of course, to use my imagination to interpret them, for they are vague enough to be anyone's thoughts—those of the blank faces in the picture, or one's own. That is perhaps the role Dubuffet meant to assign to the figures in *Les réminiscences associées* and other works in *Théâtres de mémoire*. Facing viewers, those figures act as our doubles, as our surrogates. They show us precisely how imagination closely connects to memory through stimulation and association. Dubuffet suggested something of the sort when, in the book *Bâtons rompus*, he described working on these pictures with paintings, cut-out forms, and leftover fragments piled up on his studio floor: "Many of those, I have a memory of; I rummage through the piles to look for them" (see fig. 50).[53] Then comes the moment of assembling them: "I experiment, of course, with changing their positions, or replacing them with other pieces. But the assemblage then happens very quickly."[54] To Damisch, there was something very cinematic in the resulting works, as if the artist wanted to play back, in fast motion, the "entire film of his oeuvre."[55]

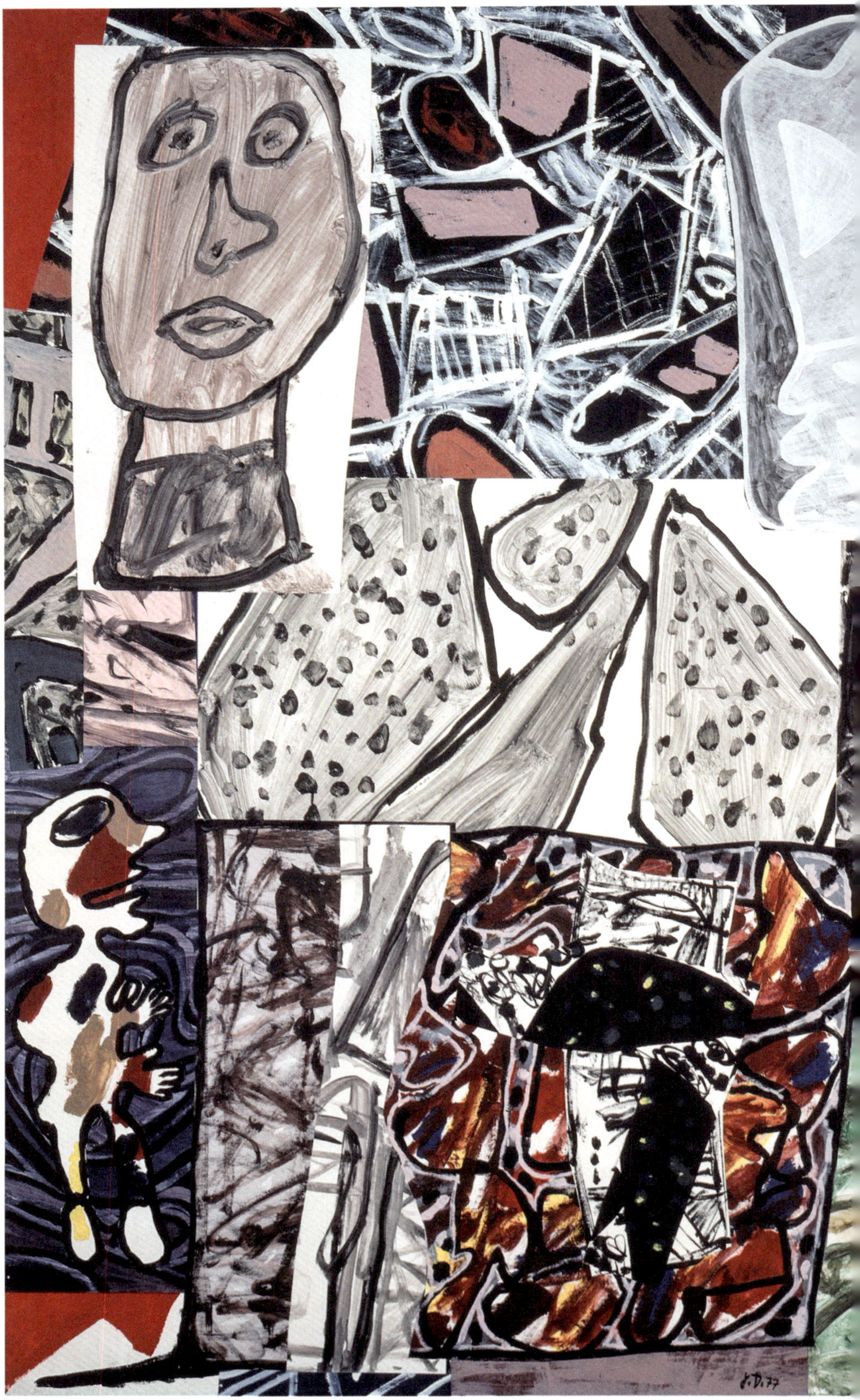

45. Jean Dubuffet. Les réminiscences associées, September 14, 1977

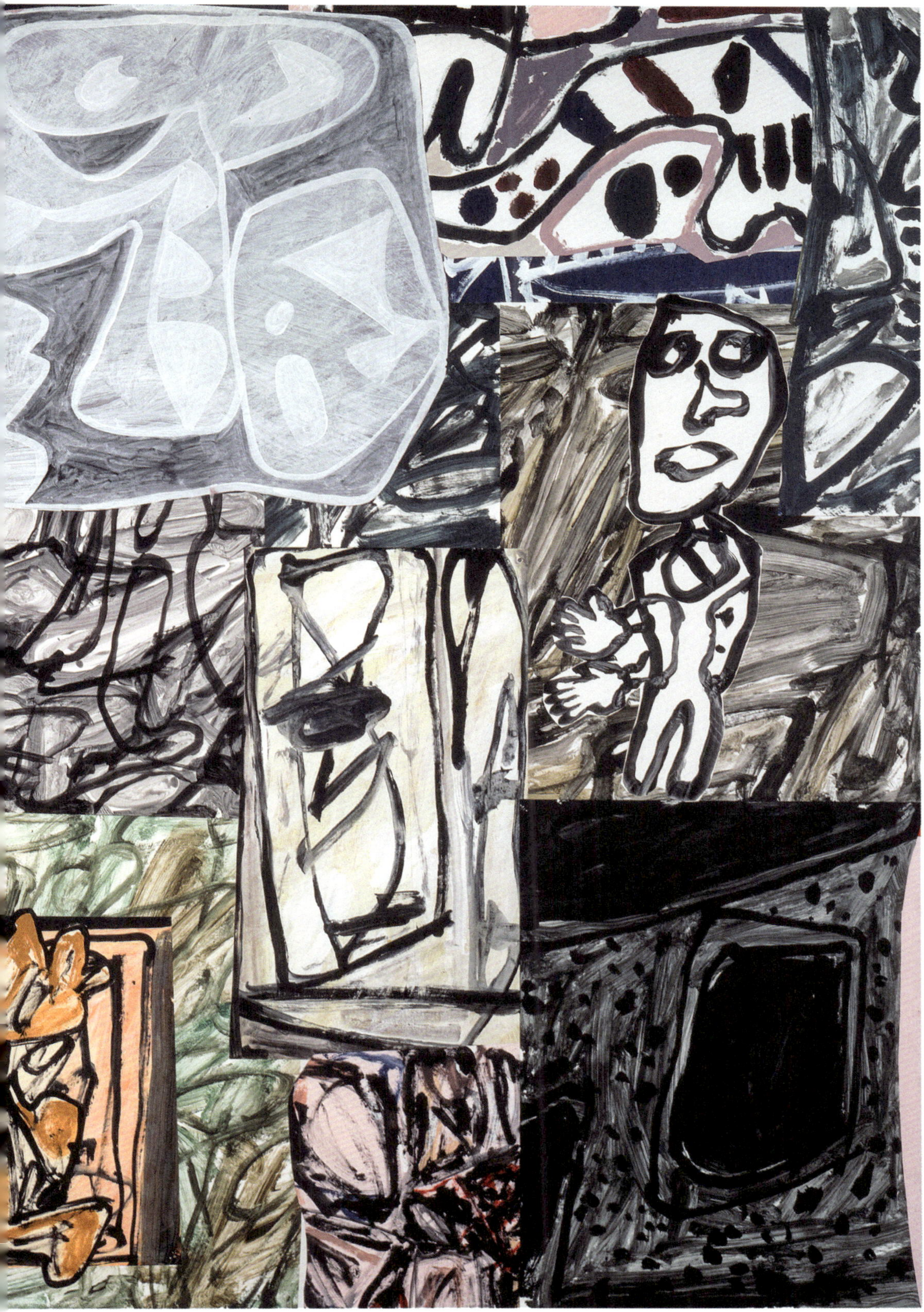

Browsing through the titles of the works and taking into account the number of segments in the final pictures that are suggestive of rooms, buildings, paths, or maps, it is clear that in these large tableaux, memory is projected into space. Dramatisation (fig. 1), thanks to its format and composition, organized around a central figure seated at a table, suggests a theatrical stage, while the titles of many other works, including Argument et contexte and Carnet de voyage (figs. 56, 101), make reference to actions and to space. Of course, as Georges Perec put it, "There isn't one space, a beautiful space, a beautiful space round about, a beautiful space all around us, there's a whole lot of small bits of space, and one of these bits is a Métro corridor, and another of them is a public park."[56]

Indeed, it is hard to escape the words of Dubuffet's contemporaries when looking at Theâtres de mémoire. The previous passage, from the first pages of Perec's Espèces d'espaces (Species of Spaces), a 1974 book of fragments and short evocations of what space might be, how it changes over time, and how it feels for a person who has been displaced, reads as a description of Dubuffet's paintings that are still to come: a prophetic ekphrasis. And some years earlier, this is Henri Lefebvre: "We are offered the 'world' as though it were a Meccano set, broken up into thousands of little 'worlds.'"[57] In his very literary text, Lefebvre was describing Mourenx, the first *ville nouvelle* to be built in France, twenty kilometers (twelve miles) or so from the medieval village of Navarrenx, his long-term summer residence in the Pyrénées region. Writing in April 1960, as the new town was swiftly emerging from the ground (3,000 residences were built between 1957 and 1961), Lefebvre pondered the difference between the experience of space in the medieval town and in the new, industrially manufactured "machines for living," introducing ideas that he would develop in 1974 in La production de l'espace. In that work, Lefebvre theorized ways in which space had been actively shaped by ideological, political, economic, and social forces throughout history and ultimately appropriated by capitalism. Perec's and Lefebvre's books stood beside those of many other philosophers, writers, and social scientists who, often drawing on the legacy of the École des annales,[58] paid particular attention to questions of space and spatial politics in envisioning politics, history, and philosophy anew. Michel Foucault's 1975 Surveiller et punir (Discipline and Punish), which theorized the shift from spectacular punishments to generalized state surveillance in the modern age through a particular ordering of social space, was exactly contemporary with this turn, as was Gilles Deleuze and Félix Guattari's small book Rhizome, which appeared in 1976.[59]

To varying degrees, the thinking of these and other authors was permeated by the reshaping of urban space in France and the

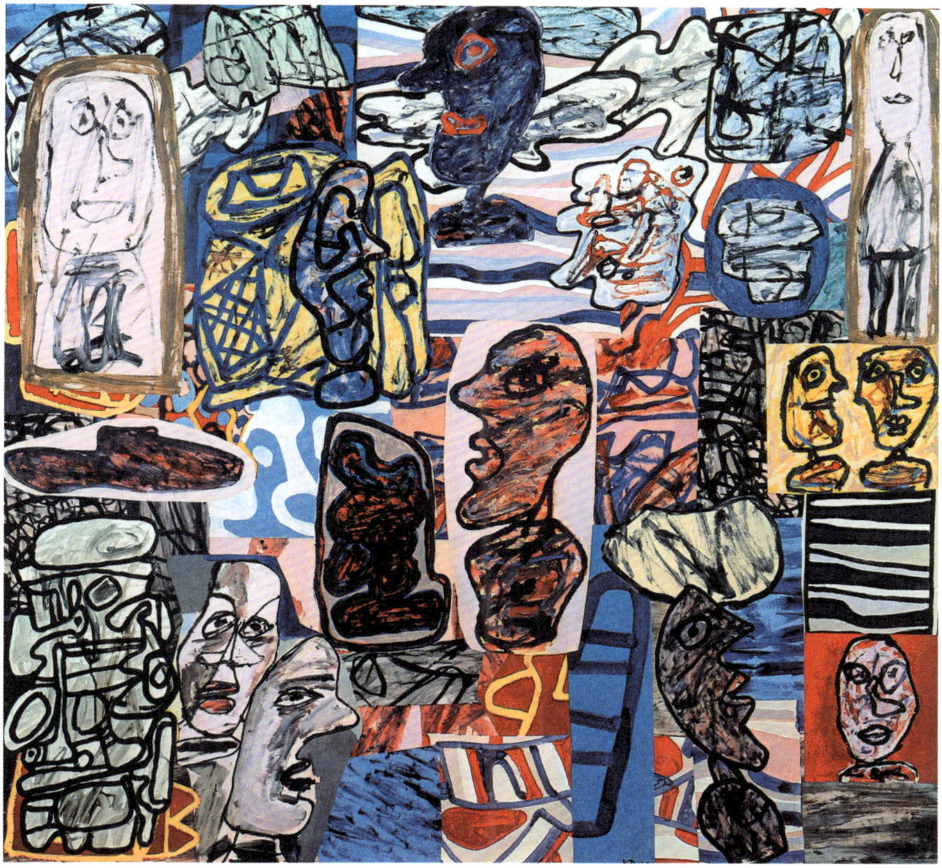

46. Jean Dubuffet. *Gens et lieux*, February 2, 1976

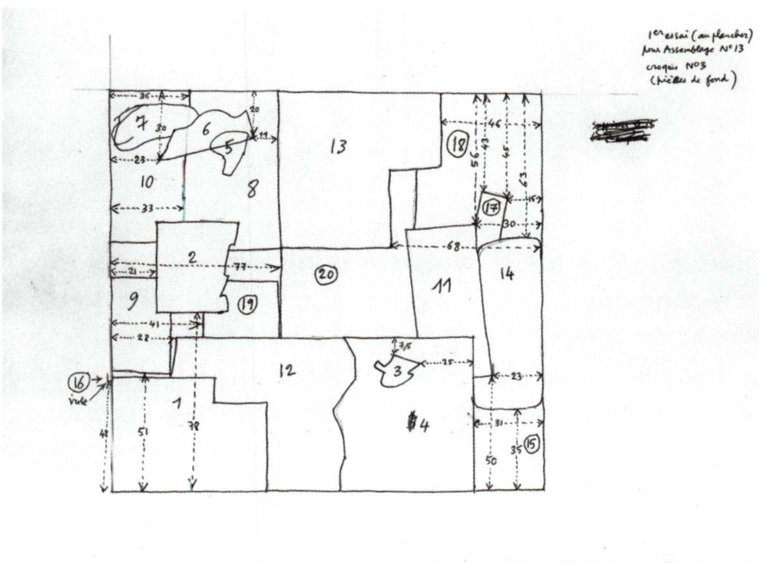

47. Jean Dubuffet. Sketch for assembling *Gens et lieux*, February 2, 1976

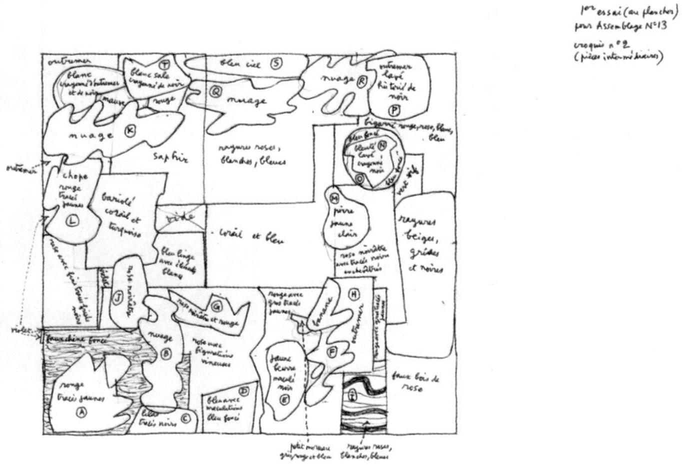

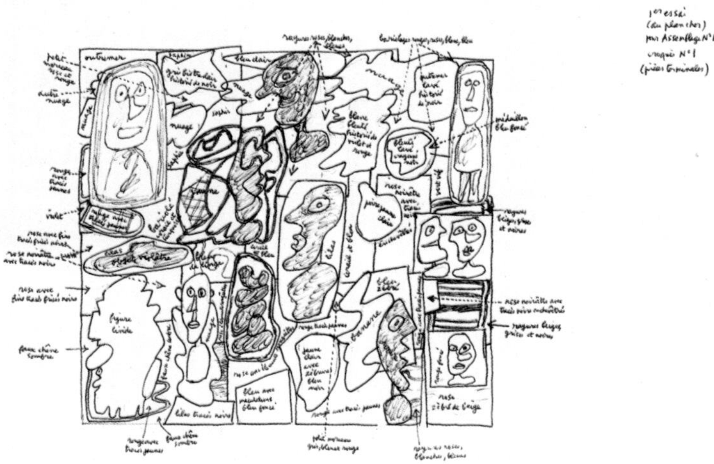

48, 49. Jean Dubuffet. Sketches for assembling Gens et lieux, February 2, 1976

new experiences brought about through the development of information technologies and the proliferation of infrastructure as the country became covered with highways and fast trains, airports, and new towns. The sociologist Alain Touraine, in his Production de la société (1974), showed how such a vocabulary contaminated his reading of society: "Society acknowledges itself as a network of actions and relations."[60] Deleuze and Guattari's concept of the "rhizome," a sprawling, antihierarchical network with multiple roots, had no direct relationship to architecture or urbanism and yet it reads today, within that context, as a philosophical position completely antagonistic to the authoritarian and highly centralized powers responsible for building the country's infrastructure.

In the case of Dubuffet, the issues of urbanism and architecture came through occasionally and indirectly. They appeared, for example, in a letter in which he described working on Théâtres de mémoire: "My work . . . is beginning to look like the attempt of an architect who, in drawing a map, would assemble elements whose scale is not indicated and that differ from one element to the next."[61] But they appeared also, more diffusely, in his use of the word *tissu* (fabric) and variations on the metaphors of sewing and weaving. For a start, the very process of making the assemblages suggests something of a patchwork. Arranging pieces of paintings, first on the ground and then on a large metal wall with the aid of magnets, required much toing and froing between the piles of material on the floor and the wall as the artist mounted a sequence, broke it up, and built it all over again.[62] Weaving—in French, *tisser*—and textiles provided a number of titles in the series from 1976 to 1979: Le tissu social, Le tissu de mémoire, La vision tisserande, Le fil des jours (The Thread of Days, or Day by Day), Tissu d'épisodes, La trame des heures (The Fabric of the Hours). Multifaceted associations of textiles with time and memory, from Penelope in Homer's Odyssey to the Maori verb *kanoi*, which means both "weave the main thread of a garment" and "trace one's ancestry," were certainly one of the attractions of the terminology for Dubuffet.[63]

But the word "fabric" is also commonly used in urbanism to describe a combination of infrastructure and buildings. As a metaphor in 1970s France, it was not neutral. In his short book published in March 1968, Le droit à la ville (The Right to the City)—a key text for the May 1968 movement—Lefebvre denounced the ideological implications of the phrase *tissu urbain* (urban fabric). "This metaphor is unclear," he wrote, arguing that it served a process of homogenizing society: "Carried by the urban fabric, urban society and life penetrate the countryside."[64] Lefebvre critiqued this wholesale reshaping of territory and what it leaves to the side: "Latent conflicts are accentuated, and then what was hidden under the urban fabric appears in the open."[65] This disintegration of social space was echoed in other terms by Touraine in his book-length essay La société post-industrielle (1969): "Our type of society is more 'mobilized' by economic growth than any other. The particularities of private life, of local societies, of types of life are invaded and destroyed by a growing geographic and social mobility, by the circulation of advertising and propaganda."[66]

A title such as Le tissu social reads ironically in this context of the disintegration of society and unraveling of the urban fabric, and yet, if Choay was right in arguing, in the introduction to her 1965 anthology of urbanism, that the city remains the "horizon" of industrial, urban society, then Dubuffet's textile metaphor in the Théâtres de mémoire addresses the dynamic process of disintegration and transformation of urban and social space both in its material reality and in our sensitive and imaginary experience of the city.[67]

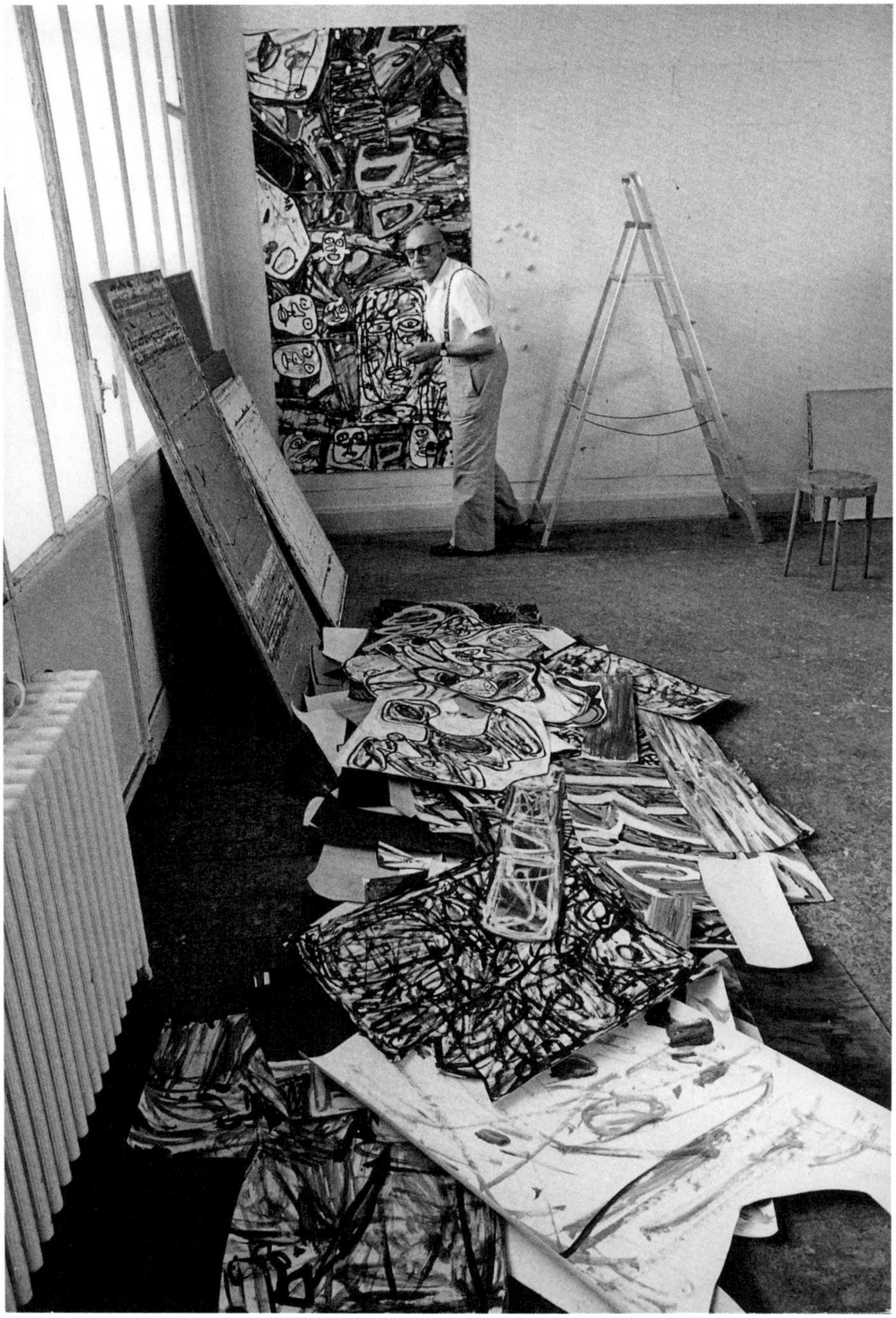

50. Kurt Wyss (photographer). Jean Dubuffet working on Garden Party, part of the series Théâtres de mémoire, Paris, June 30, 1976

Epigraph: Jean Dubuffet, Bâtons rompus (1985), PES, vol. 3, 124–25. "I like that the streets turn so that the gaze becomes limited and sites are constantly renewed. I feel that long, straight avenues shrink the city. It is necessary to increase the multiplicity of places in a city in order to enlarge it. . . . I feel that this is also applicable to philosophy. There is much to be gained by defining and multiplying places of thought. This is in contrast, then, to the rationalist aspiration to organize thought in a univocal system constituted around a central axis (which plays the role of the large, rectilinear avenue)."

1 Roger Vitrac, "Quatrains," Aventure, no. 2 (December 1921), 15.

2 The print appears in CTJD, vol. 1, Marionnettes de la ville et de la campagne, 1917–1945 (Paris: Minuit, 1993), 24 (no. 15).

3 See André Masson, Le rebelle du Surréalisme: Écrits, ed. Françoise Will-Levaillant (Paris: Hermann, 1968), 76–84, and Max Jacob to Michel Leiris, January 28, 1923, in Max Jacob, Correspondance, ed. François Garnier (Paris: Éditions de Paris, 1953–55), vol. 2 (1955), Saint-Benoît-sur-Loire 1921–1924, 141.

4 Several writers and artists have reminisced about this loose group of friends during the early 1920s. See, in particular, Michel Leiris, "45, rue Blomet," Revue de musicologie 68, no. 1 (1982), 57–63, and Armand Salacrou, "Rue Plélo, rue de Casablanca," La Nouvelle Revue française 249 (1973), 9–12.

5 Isabelle Monod-Fontaine, "Chronologie et documents," in Isabelle Monod-Fontaine, ed., Daniel-Henry Kahnweiler: Marchand, éditeur, écrivain, exh. cat. (Paris: Centre Georges Pompidou, 1984), 137.

6 See "More Modest" on pp. 53–56 of the present volume and "Biographie au pas de course," PES, vol. 4 (1995), 466–70.

7 Louis Gillet, "L'exposition d'art hollandais au Jeu de Paume," Revue des deux mondes, May 1921, 448, http://www.revuedesdeuxmondes.fr/article-revue/lexposition-dart-hollandais-au-jeu-de-paume/. Marcel Proust's famous passage discussing the fragment of yellow wall in View of Delft appears in La prisonnière, vol. 5 of À la recherche du temps perdu (Paris: Gallimard, 1923). See also Jean-Louis Vaudoyer, "Le mystérieux Vermeer," L'Opinion, March–April 1921.

8 See Alain Roger, Court traité du paysage (Paris: Gallimard, 1997), 73.

9 Henri Lefebvre, The Production of Space, trans. Donald Nicholson-Smith (London: Blackwell, 1991), 269.

10 Ibid., 278.

11 Ibid.

12 The phrase *les Trente Glorieuses* was coined by the economist Jean Fourastié in his eponymous book and became a classic term to describe the period. See Jean Fourastié, Les Trente Glorieuses (Paris: Fayard, 1979). Recent reassessments of the term have pointed out the shortcomings of Fourastié's analysis, particularly regarding social issues, ecology, and colonialism. See Céline Pessis, Sezin Topçu, and Christophe Bonneuil, eds., Une autre histoire des "Trentes Glorieuses" (Paris: La Découverte, 2016). On the postindustrial society, see Alain Touraine, La société post-industrielle (Paris: Denoël, 1969), and Daniel Bell, The Coming of Post-Industrial Society (New York: Basic Books, 1973).

13 Jean-Luc Nancy, La ville au loin (Paris: Mille et une nuits, 1999), 60.

14 Ibid., 61.

15 Ibid.

16 See Jean Dubuffet and Jean Paulhan, Correspondance 1944–1986, ed. Julien Dieudonné and Marianne Jakobi (Paris: Gallimard, 2003). It is mostly Dubuffet's letters to Paulhan that have survived, as Dubuffet destroyed the latter's letters following the rupture of their friendship.

17 Tableaux et dessins de Jean Dubuffet, Galerie René Drouin, Paris, October 20–November 18, 1944.

18 In a lecture about art destined for a broad audience, written around this time, Dubuffet made a provocative case for rethinking the idea of art as eternal. He took as his example not cinema or dioramas but painted decorative panels in buildings and cafés that were regularly replaced according to the taste of the day. See Jean Dubuffet, "Avant-projet pour une conférence populaire sur la peinture" (January 1945), PES, vol. 1 (1967), 50. Translated into English in Peter Selz, The Work of Jean Dubuffet (New York: The Museum of Modern Art, 1962), 10.

19 Claude Lévi-Strauss, Le regard éloigné (Paris: Plon, 1983).

20 E. H. Gombrich, Art and Illusion: A Study in the Psychology of Pictorial Representation, 5th ed. (1977; repr., London: Phaidon, 1992), 4–5.

21 Lefebvre, Production of Space, 268.

22 It is difficult to ascertain whether or not Dubuffet borrowed the subtitle La vie de plaisir from the film directed by Albert Valentin, shot in 1943 and released in May 1944, whose plot centers around a nightclub called La vie de plaisir. Yet, the title of the film, produced by German-controlled Continental Films, was perceived both then and later as offensive in the context of the Occupation. This gives us some idea of how provocatively Dubuffet's approach could be perceived.

23 On the aerial view and its aesthetic and ideological development in visual culture, see Jeanne Haffner, The View from Above: The Science of Social Space (Cambridge, MA: MIT Press, 2013), and Angela Lampe, "Une modernité en survol," in Angela Lampe, ed., Vues d'en haut, exh. cat. (Metz: Centre Pompidou-Metz, 2013), 32–47.

24 Rosemary Wakeman, The Heroic City: Paris, 1946–1958 (Chicago: University of Chicago Press, 2009), 28–29.

25 Jean Dubuffet, "Anticultural Positions," lecture delivered in English at Chicago Arts Club, December 1951. Translated into French and published in PES, vol. 1 (1967), 94–100. Published in English in Dubuffet and the Anticulture, exh. cat. (New York: R. L. Feigen, 1969), 8–9.

26 Michel de Certeau, The Practice of Everyday Life, trans. Steven F. Rendall (Berkeley: University of California Press, 1984), 93.

27 On this series of ink drawings, see Rachel E. Perry, "Les messages de Jean Dubuffet," Les Cahiers du MNAM, no. 140 (Summer 2017), 3–33.

28 On the multiple meanings of the underground and the theme of the Métro in Dubuffet's work, see Sophie Berrebi, "Métromania or the Undersides of Painting," in Christoph Lindner and Andrew Hussey, eds., Paris–Amsterdam Underground: Essays on Cultural Resistance, Subversion, and Diversion (Amsterdam: Amsterdam University Press, 2013), 24–36.

29 Dubuffet to Geneviève Bonnefoi, August 4, 1961, PES, vol. 2 (1967), 479.

30 Musée des arts décoratifs, Paris, December 16, 1960–February 25, 1961; Kunsthaus, Zürich, December 18, 1960–January 15, 1961; The Museum of Modern Art, New York, February 19–April 8, 1962. The last also traveled to Chicago and Los Angeles.

31 Daniel Cordier, who, during World War II, had served as secretary to the Resistance figure Jean Moulin, opened an art gallery in Paris in 1956 and, for a few years, also co-ran galleries in New York and Frankfurt.

32 A description of the exhibition and several installation views can be found in Ministère de la Cohésion des territoires, "Les rendez-vous du patrimoine—1961: L'exposition 'Demain Paris,' January 14, 2015, http://www.cohesion-territoires .gouv.fr/spip.php?page=album_patrimoine&album=36.

33 On the building of the Maine-Montparnasse complex, see Virginie Picon-Lefèbvre, Paris—Ville moderne: Maine-Montparnasse et la Défense, 1950–1975 (Paris: Norma, 2003), 158.

34 On the popularization of the term *l'hexagone* to describe France after 1962, see Eugen Weber, "L'Hexagone," in Pierre Nora, ed., Les lieux de mémoire, 3 vols. (Paris: Gallimard, 1984–92), vol. 3, Les France (1992), 1171–90. On the relationship between the use of this term and the decolonization of France, see Todd Shepard, "The Birth of the Hexagon: 1962 and the Erasure of France's Supranational History," in Manuel Borutta and Jan C. Jansen, eds., Vertriebene and Pieds-Noirs in Postwar Germany and France: Comparative Perspectives (London: Palgrave Macmillan, 2016), 53–69.

35 See Nicolas Schöffer, La ville cybernétique (Paris: Tchou, 1969), 126. See also the discussion of Schöffer's project in Larry Busbea, Topologies: The Urban Utopia in France, 1960–1970 (Cambridge, MA: MIT Press, 2007), ch. 2, "Spatial Urbanism and Mobile Architecture," 32–79.

36 Françoise Choay, Espacements: L'évolution de l'espace urbain en France (Paris: Skira, 1969), 18–47.

37 In France, Françoise Choay introduced Jacobs's ideas in the anthology of urbanism she published in 1965; see Françoise Choay, ed., L'urbanisme, utopies et réalités: Une anthologie (Paris: Seuil, 1965). The Death and Life of Great American Cities was not published in French until 1991, as Déclin et survie des grandes villes américaines (Liège: Mardaga, 1991).

38 Henri Lefebvre, "Notes on the New Town," in Henri Lefebvre, Introduction to Modernity: Twelve Preludes, September 1959–May 1961, trans. John Moore (London: Verso, 1995), 121.

39 On the symbolic value of the automobile and the literary and cinematic imagery developed during the 1960s, see Kristin Ross's fascinating book Fast Cars, Clean Bodies: Decolonization and the Reordering of French Culture (Cambridge, MA: MIT Press, 1995), especially, in this context, ch. 1, "La Belle Américaine."

40 See Marcel Roncayolo, "Vivre en ville," in Marcel Roncayolo, ed., La ville aujourd'hui: Croissance urbaine et crise du citadin (Paris: Seuil, 1985), vol. 4 of Histoire de la France urbaine, 530.

41 Roland Barthes, Mythologies (Paris: Seuil, 1957), 140.

42 See Choay, "L'urbanisme en question," introduction to Choay, L'urbanisme, utopies et réalités, 36.

43 Walker Evans, "The Auto Junkyard," Fortune, April 1962, 132–37, reprinted in Walker Evans, The Magazine Work, ed. David Campany (Göttingen: Steidl, 2014), 192–97.

44 Ross, Fast Cars, Clean Bodies, 39.

45 Barthes, Mythologies, 141. Translated into English at http://www.citroenet.org.uk/passenger-cars/michelin/ds/32.html.

46 See Jean Dubuffet, "Présentation" (February 1980), CTJD, vol. 32, Théâtres de Mémoire, 1975–1979 (Paris: Minuit, 1982), 7.

47 Dubuffet to Arnold Glimcher, September 15, 1969, PES, vol. 3 (1995), 354–55. See also note 19 on p. 219 of this volume.

48 Frances Yates, The Art of Memory (London: Routledge, 1966), chs. 6 and 7.

49 Ibid., 144–45.

50 Ibid., 134–35.

51 Hubert Damisch, "Dubuffet, un mémoire," in Hubert Damisch, Entrée en matière: Correspondance 1961–1985, Textes 1961–2014, ed. Sophie Berrebi (Paris: La Maison Rouge–Fondation Antoine de Galbert; Zürich: JRP Ringier, 2016), 51.

52 Dubuffet to Ferit Edgü, February 3, 1979, cited in Alfred Pacquement, ed., Jean Dubuffet: Les dernières années, exh. cat. (Paris: Réunion des musées nationaux, 1991), 86.

53 Jean Dubuffet, Bâtons rompus, PES, vol. 3 (1995), 130.

54 Ibid.

55 Damisch, Entrée en matière, 62.

56 Georges Perec, "Species of Spaces" (1974), in Georges Perec, Species of Spaces and Other Pieces, trans. John Sturrock (London: Penguin Books, 1997), 5–6.

57 Henri Lefebvre, Introduction to Modernity: Twelve Preludes, 1960–1961, trans. John Moore (London: Verso, 1995), 121. A "Meccano set" is a child's building toy known in the United States before 2015 as an Erector set, consisting of flat metal plates and girders pierced with holes and fitted together with nuts and bolts.

58 The École des annales, named after the journal Les Annales d'histoire économique et sociale, founded by the historians Lucien Febvre and Marc Bloch in 1929, pioneered a rethinking of history and its methods, notably by taking extensive geographic areas and periods of time (referred to as *longue durée*) as an object of study and working closely with other disciplines, such as economics and sociology.

59 Gilles Deleuze and Félix Guattari, Rhizome (Paris: Minuit, 1976), republished as the introduction to Gilles Deleuze and Félix Guattari, Mille plateaux (Paris: Minuit, 1980), 9–37. On the "spatial turn" in French theory as interpreted through

postmodernist Marxist thought in the United States, see Fredric Jameson, Postmodernism or the Cultural Logic of Late Capitalism (London and New York: Verso, 1991), ch. 6, "Space: Utopianism after the End of Utopia," and 364–67.

60 Alain Touraine, Production de la société (1974), quoted in a book review by Jean-Dominique Robert, Revue philosophique de Louvain, 4th ser., 74, no. 23 (1976), 488, http://www.persee.fr/doc/phlou_0035-3841_1976_num_74_23_5901_t1_0487_0000_2.

61 Dubuffet to Wolfgang Welsch, August 24, 1976. Archives Fondation Dubuffet, Paris.

62 On the process of making Théâtres de mémoire, see Dubuffet, "Présentation" (February 1980), 7–8, and Dubuffet, Bâtons rompus, 130.

63 Amiria Henare, "*Nga Aho Tipuna* (Ancestral Threads): Maori Cloaks from New Zealand," in Susanne Küchler and Daniel Miller, eds., Clothing as Material Culture (Oxford: Berg, 2005), 121–38. My thanks to Haidy Geismar for pointing out this reference.

64 Henri Lefebvre, The Right to the City, in Henri Lefebvre, Writings on Cities, ed. and trans. Eleanor Kofman and Elizabeth Lebas (London: Blackwell, 1996), 71–72.

65 Ibid., 72–73.

66 Touraine, La société post-industrielle, 10.

67 Choay, "L'urbanisme en question," 7.

The city seems to have been split open, like an apricot revealing a worm-filled pit.

Whereas Jacques Tati, a few years later, in Playtime (1967), would place his camera so as to observe streets and office spaces from above, thereby adopting the viewpoint of the technocratic urban planner, Dubuffet settled right in the middle of the hubbub of the street.

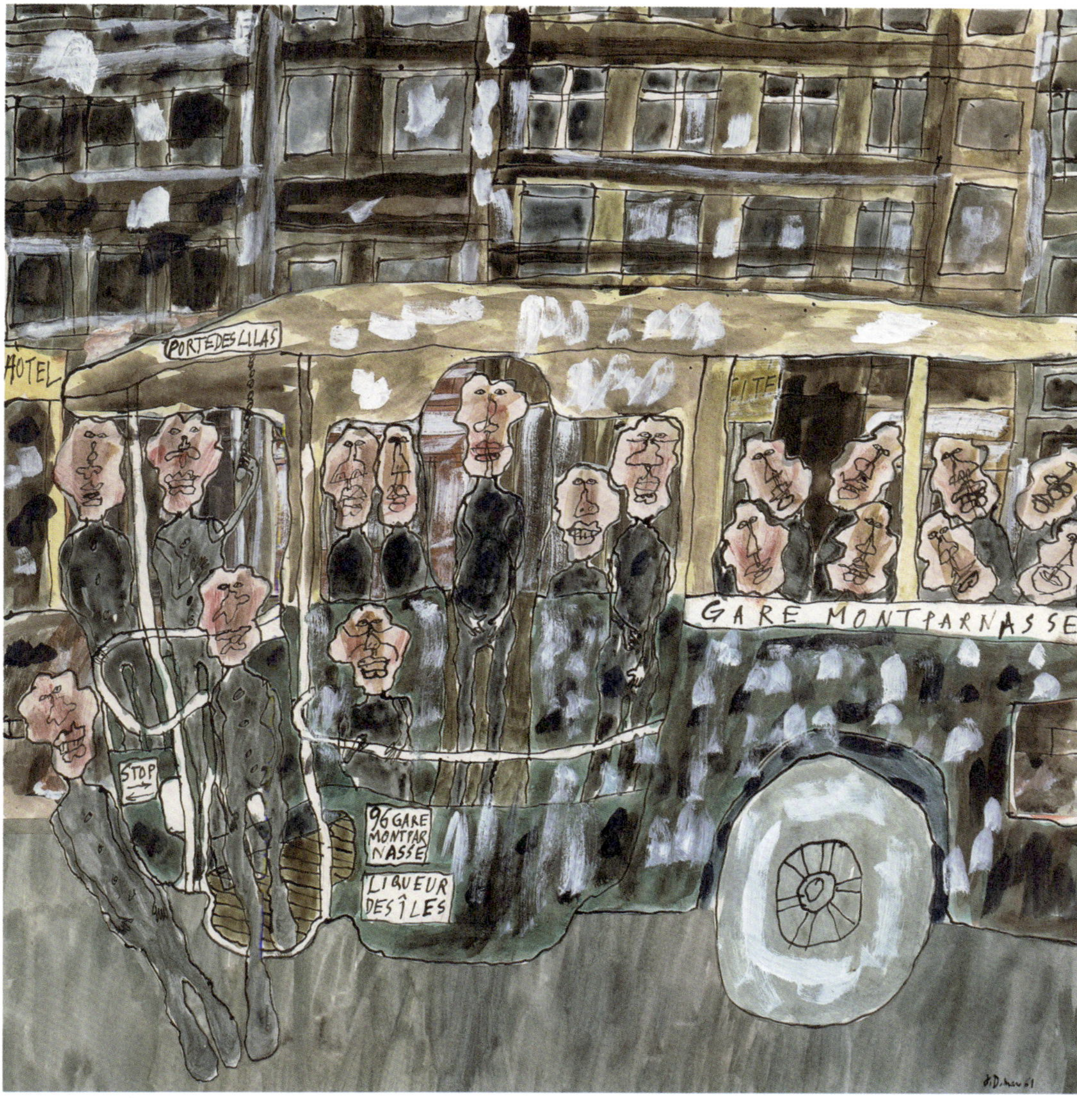

51. Jean Dubuffet. Autobus Gare Montparnasse (Liqueur des îles), early March 1961

New habits of circulation were determined by urban planners who built mass housing developments and decided on systematic divisions of activities and rational flows of people across Paris and its suburbs—but, of course, mental maps and ways of moving around the city were determined by everyone.

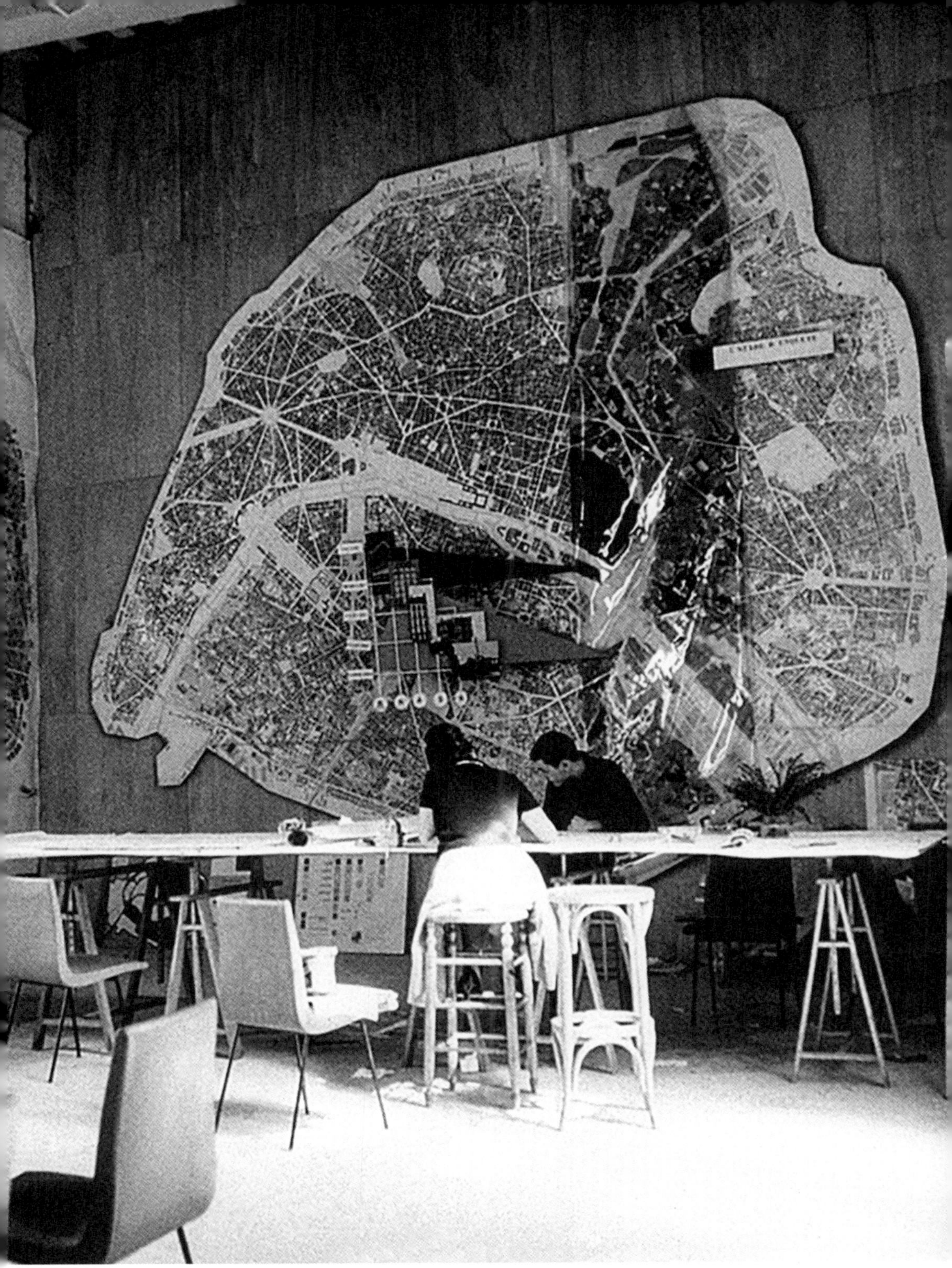

52. Architects at work on the urban master plan for Paris, early 1960s

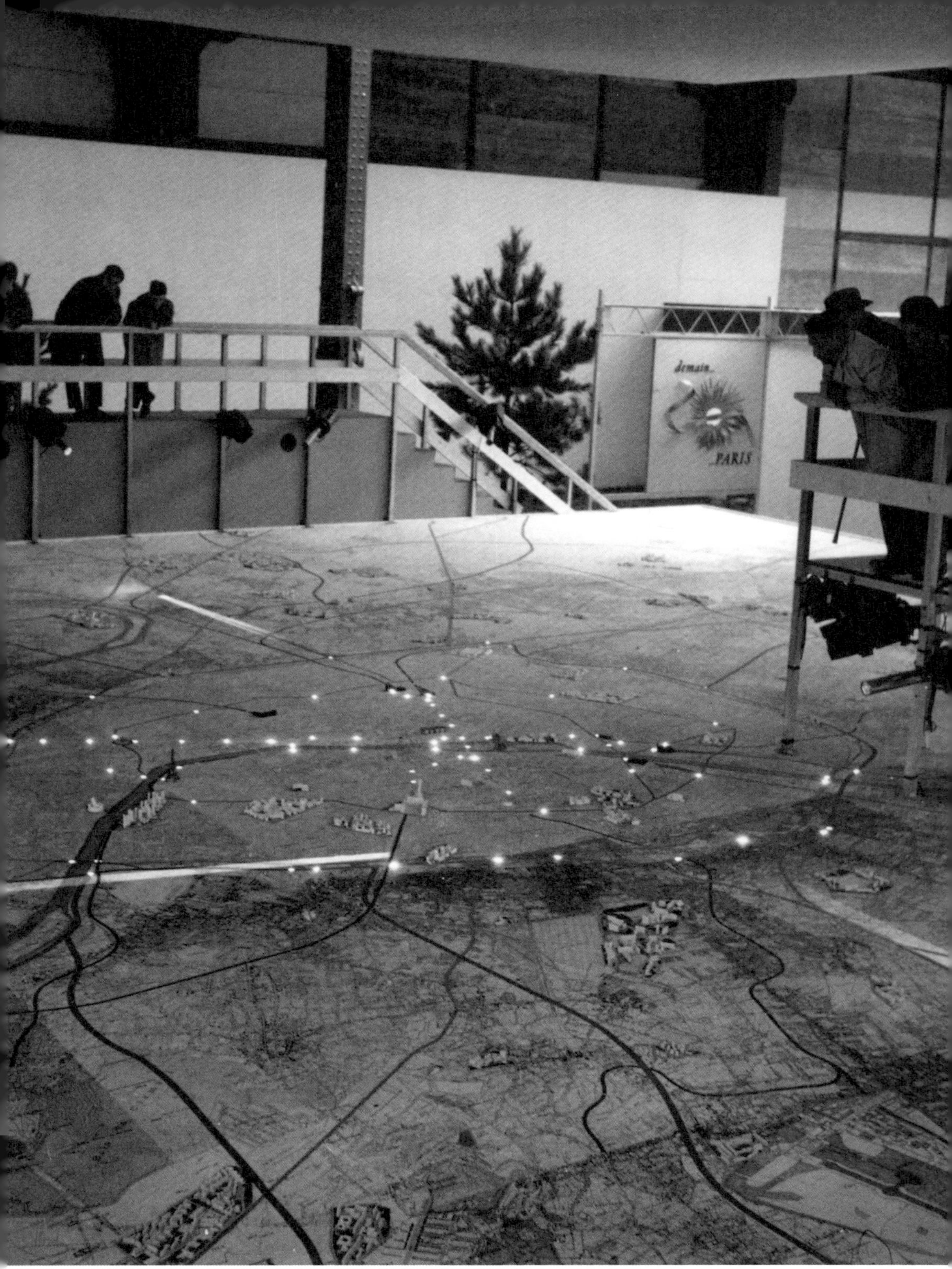

53. Demain Paris exhibition, Grand Palais, Paris, March–April 1961

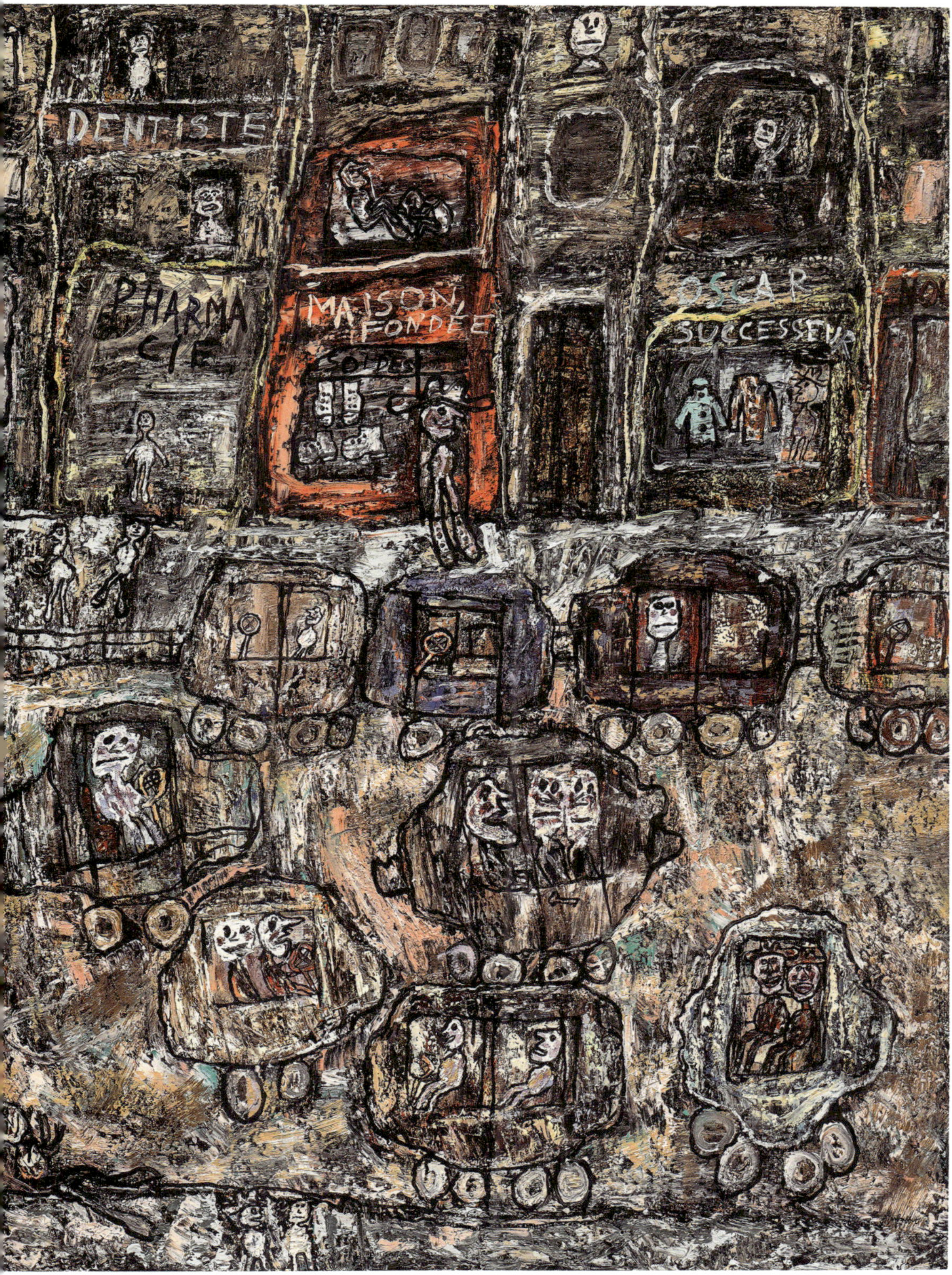

54. Jean Dubuffet. Maison fondée, March 27–April 5, 1961

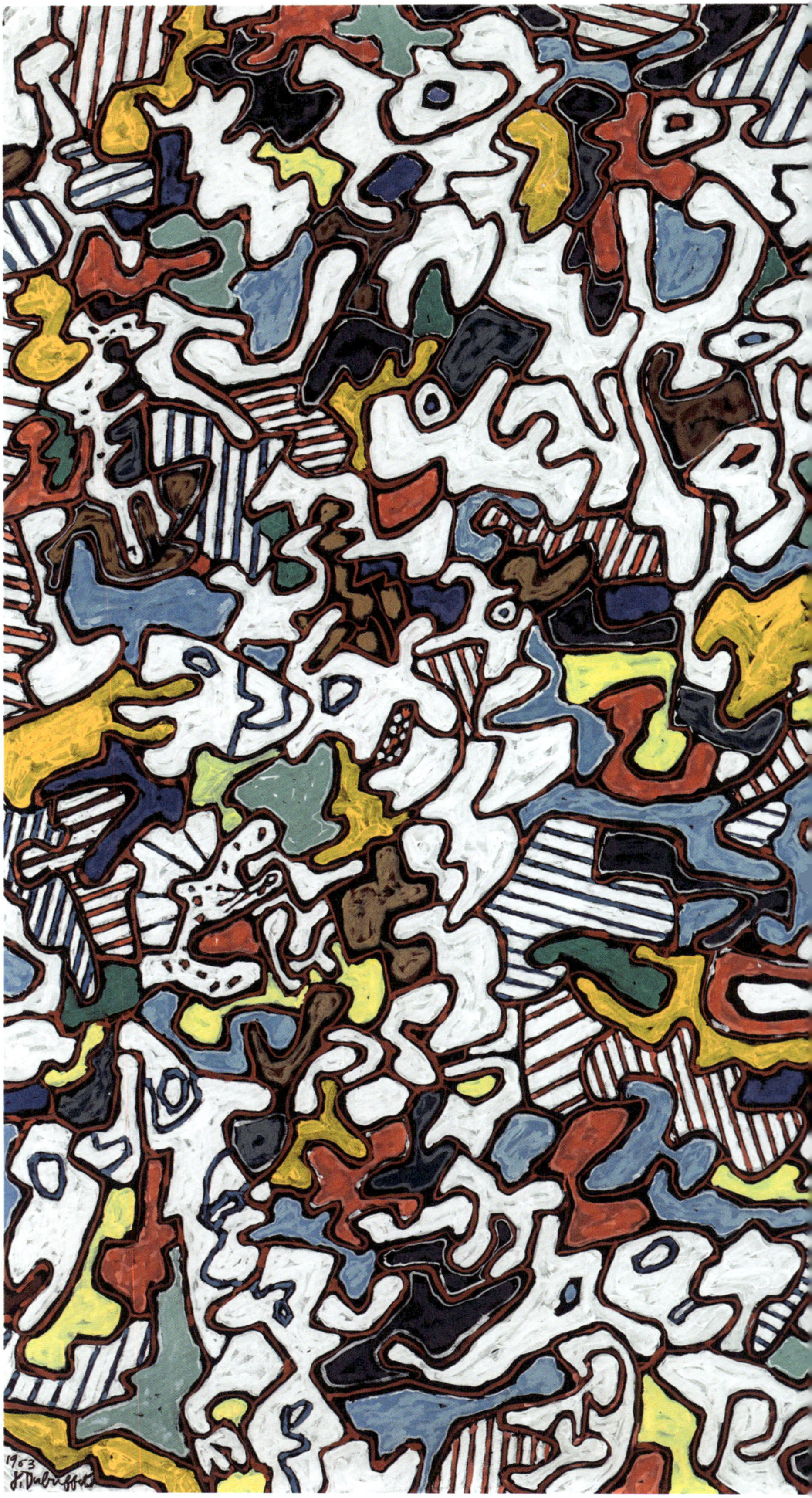

55. Jean Dubuffet. Être et paraître, July 25, 1963

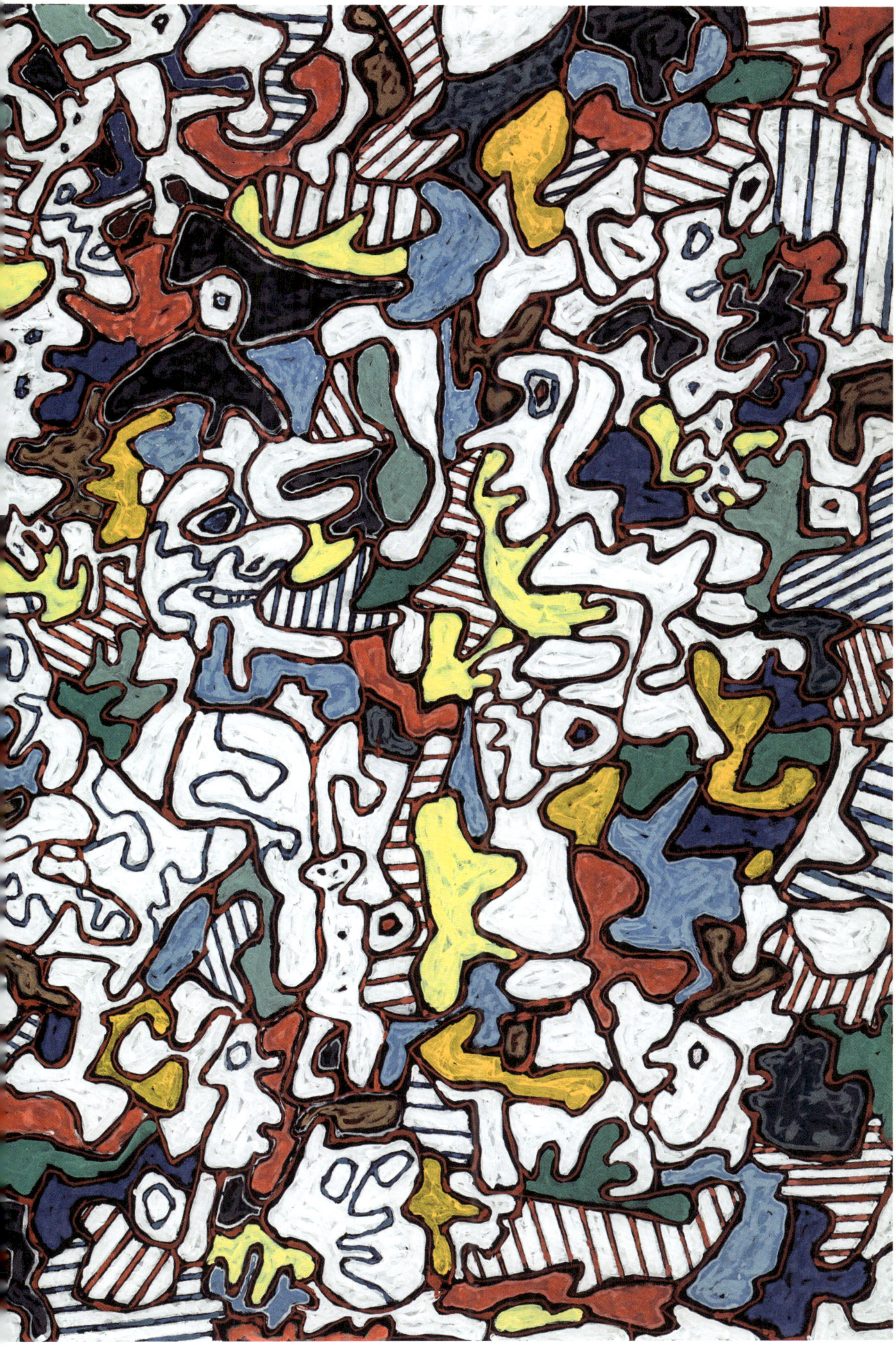

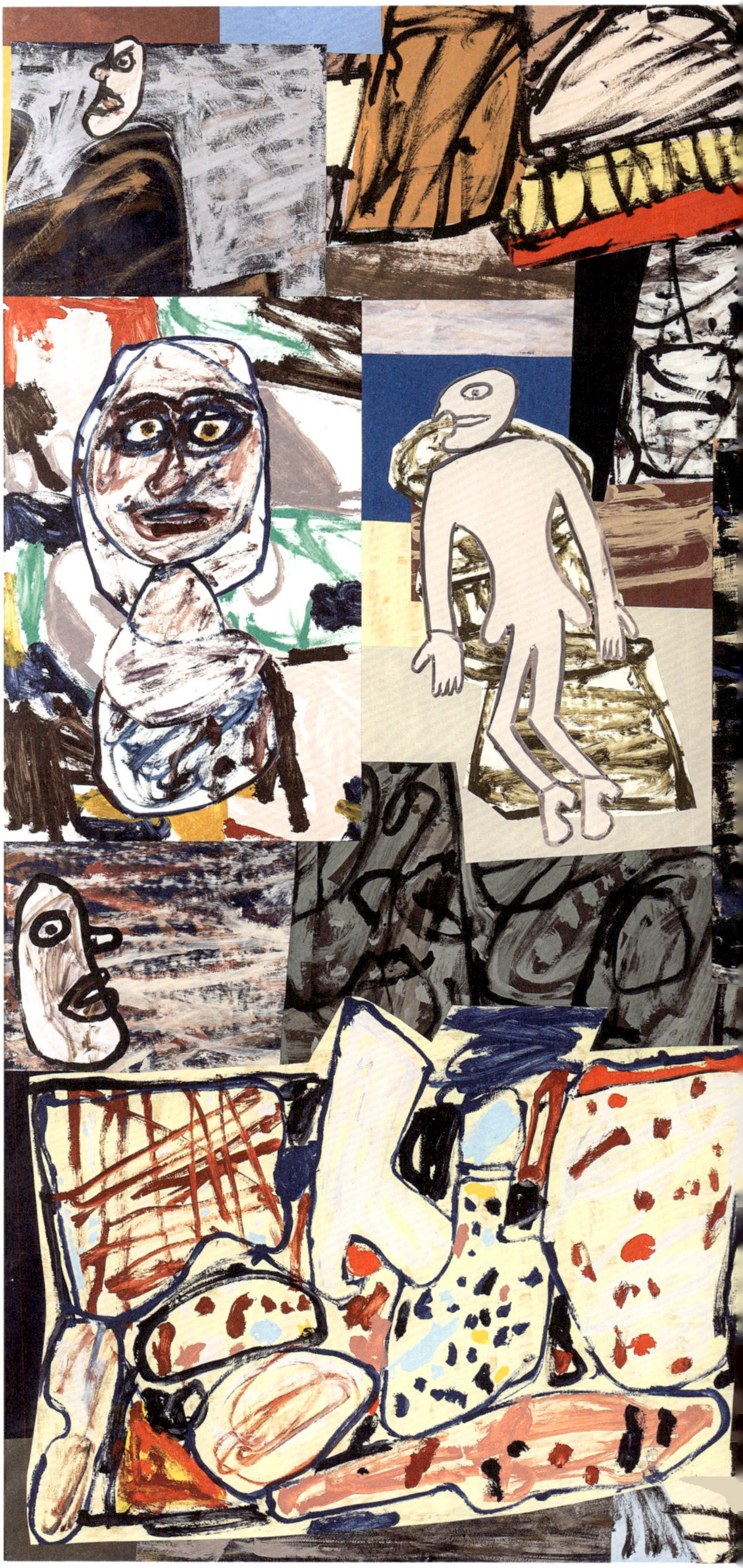

56. Jean Dubuffet. Argument et contexte, March 6, 1977

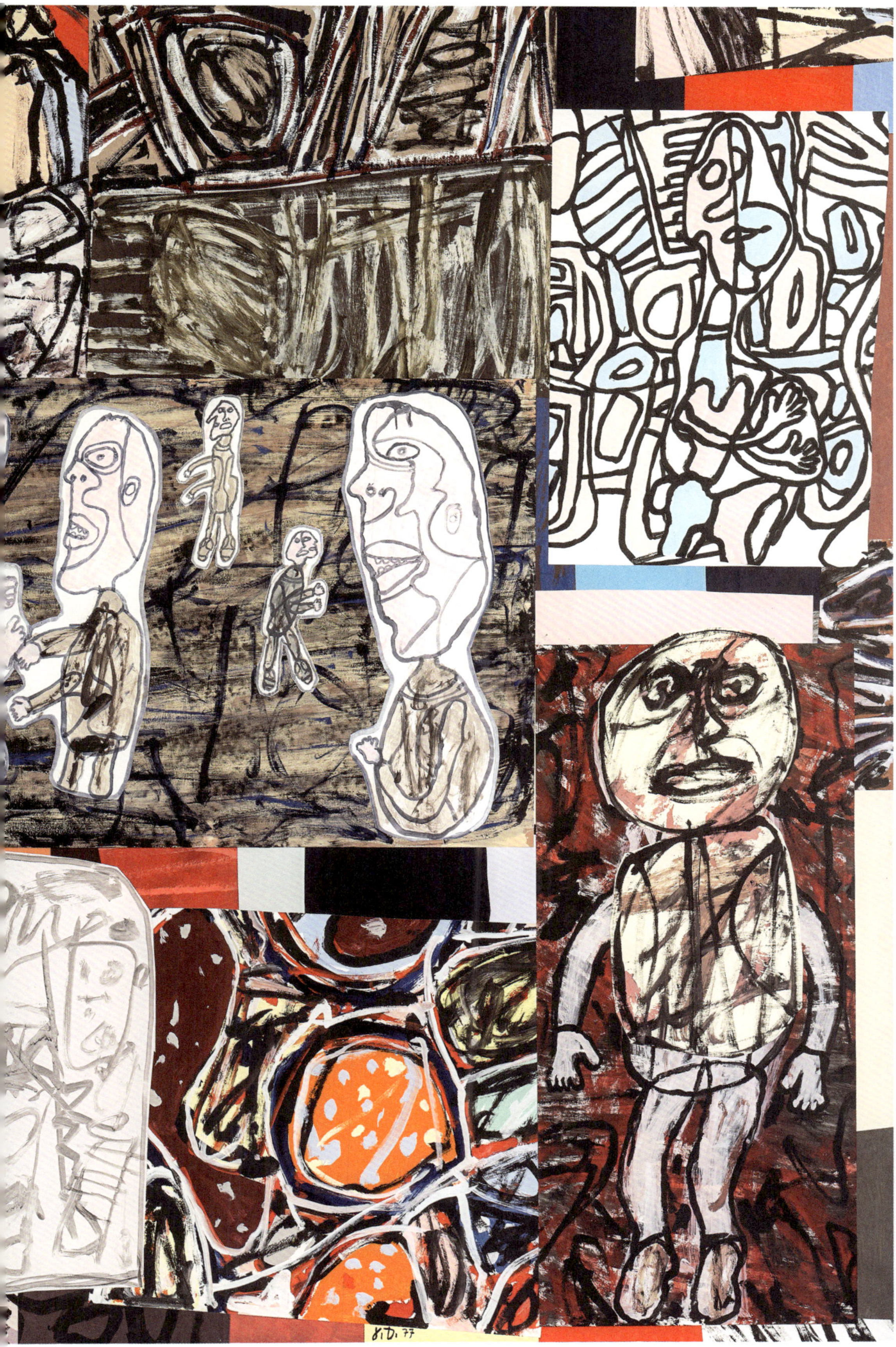
J.D. 77

Du Paris des projets au Paris des chantiers attempted to woo Parisians into accepting some of the most controversial projects under the well-rehearsed arguments of sanitization and modernization.

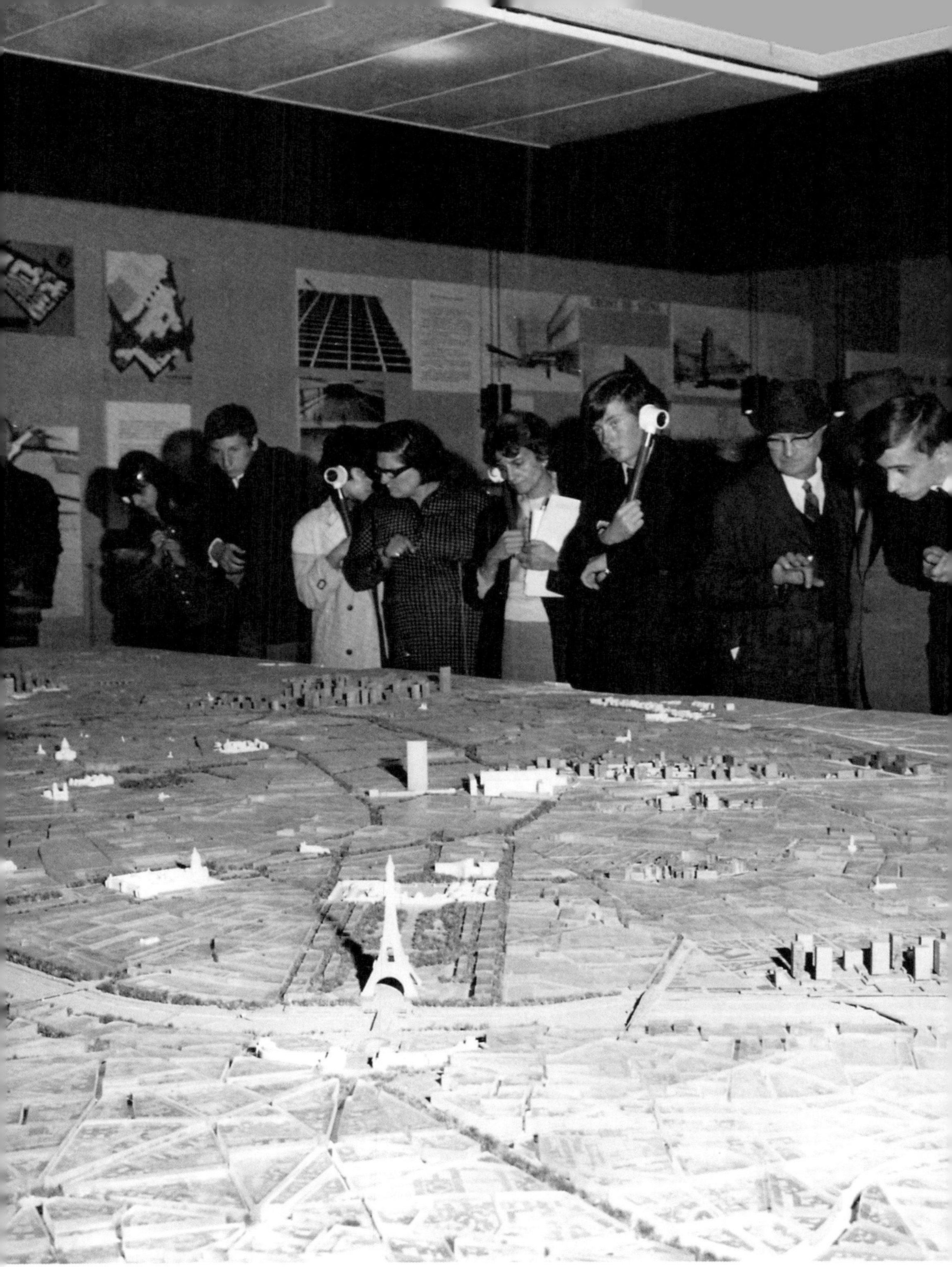

57. Du Paris des projets au Paris des chantiers exhibition, Grand Palais, Paris, March–April 1967

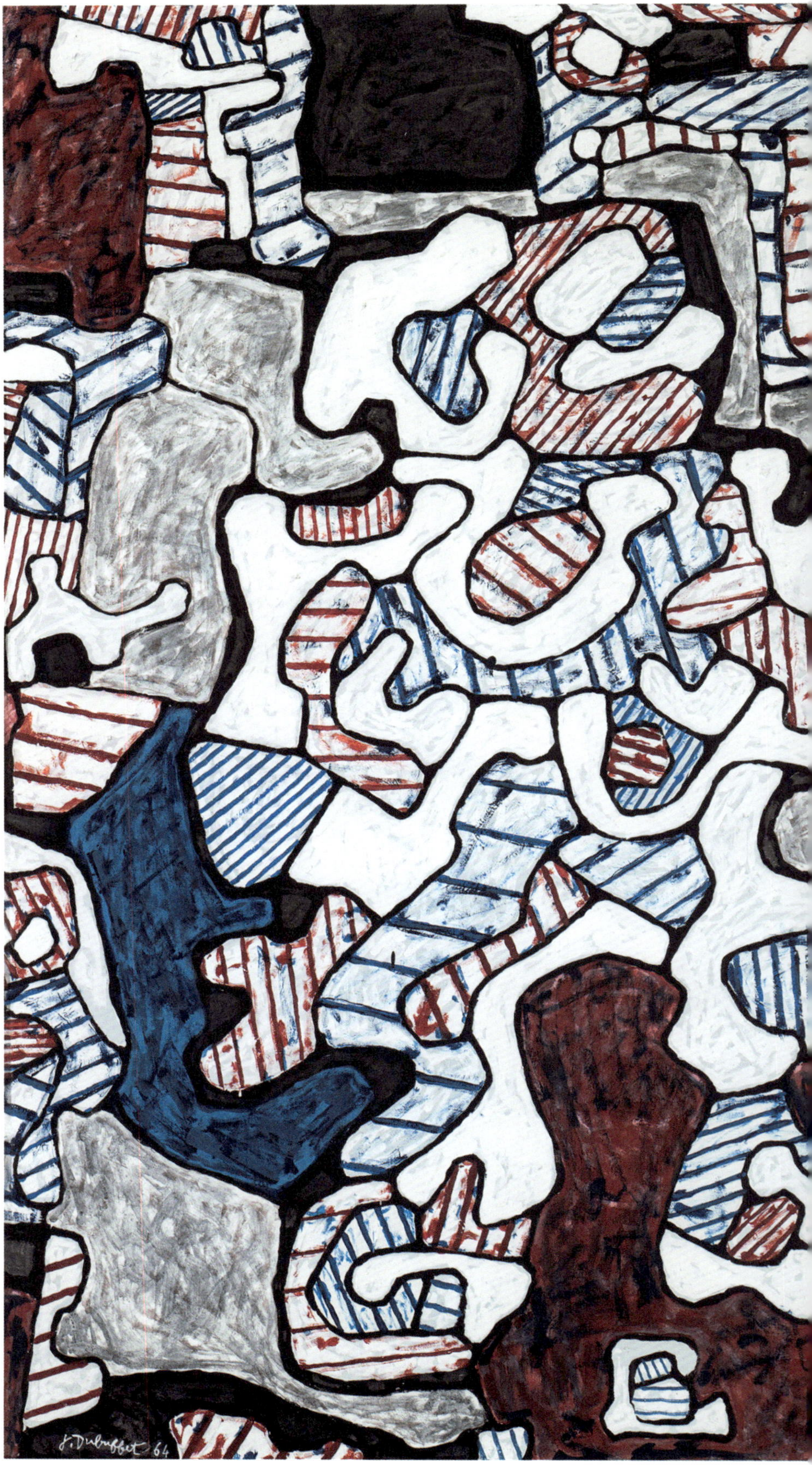

58. Jean Dubuffet. Main leste et rescousse, December 6, 1964

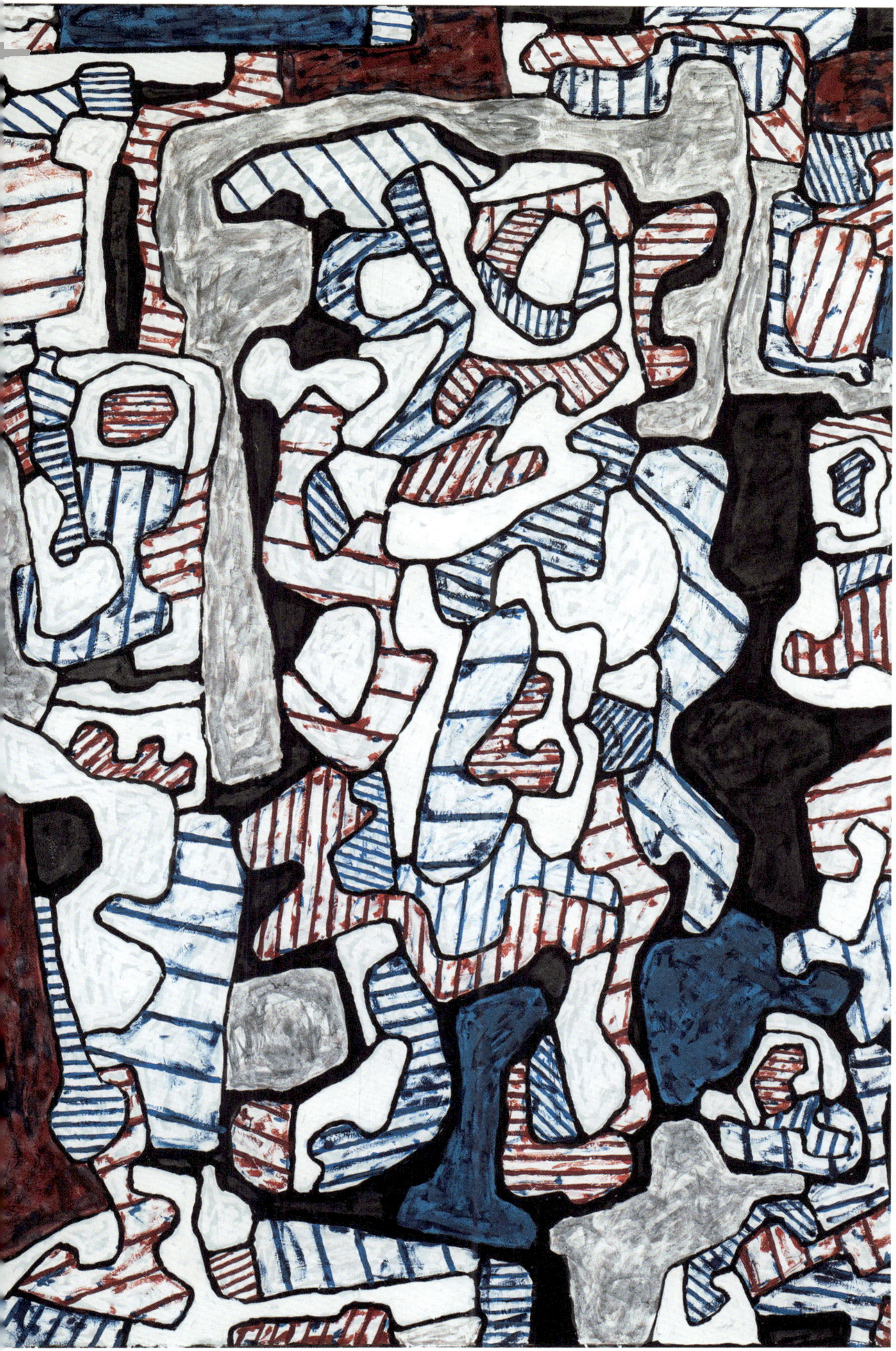

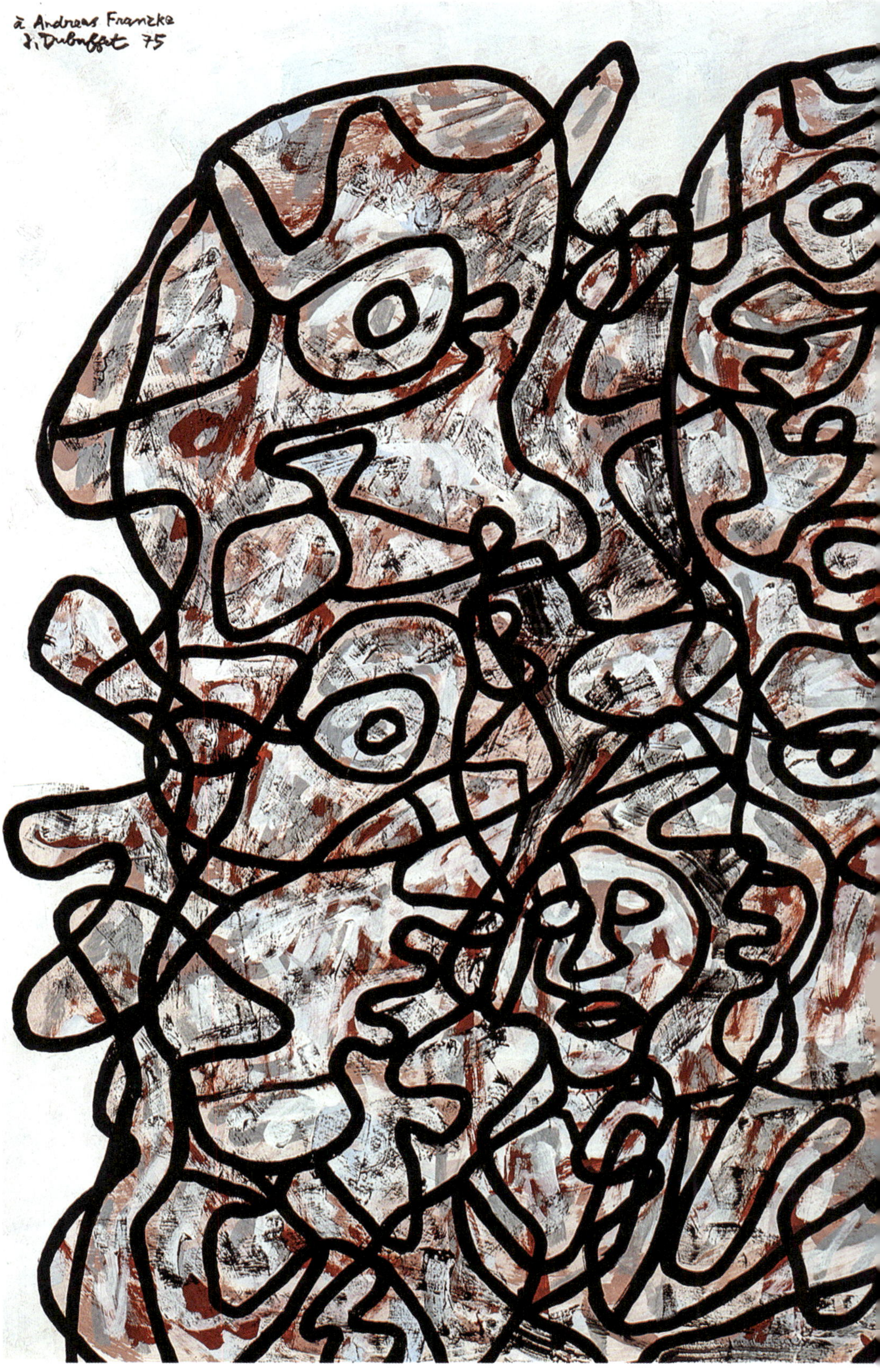

59. Jean Dubuffet. Mondanité IV, March 1, 1975

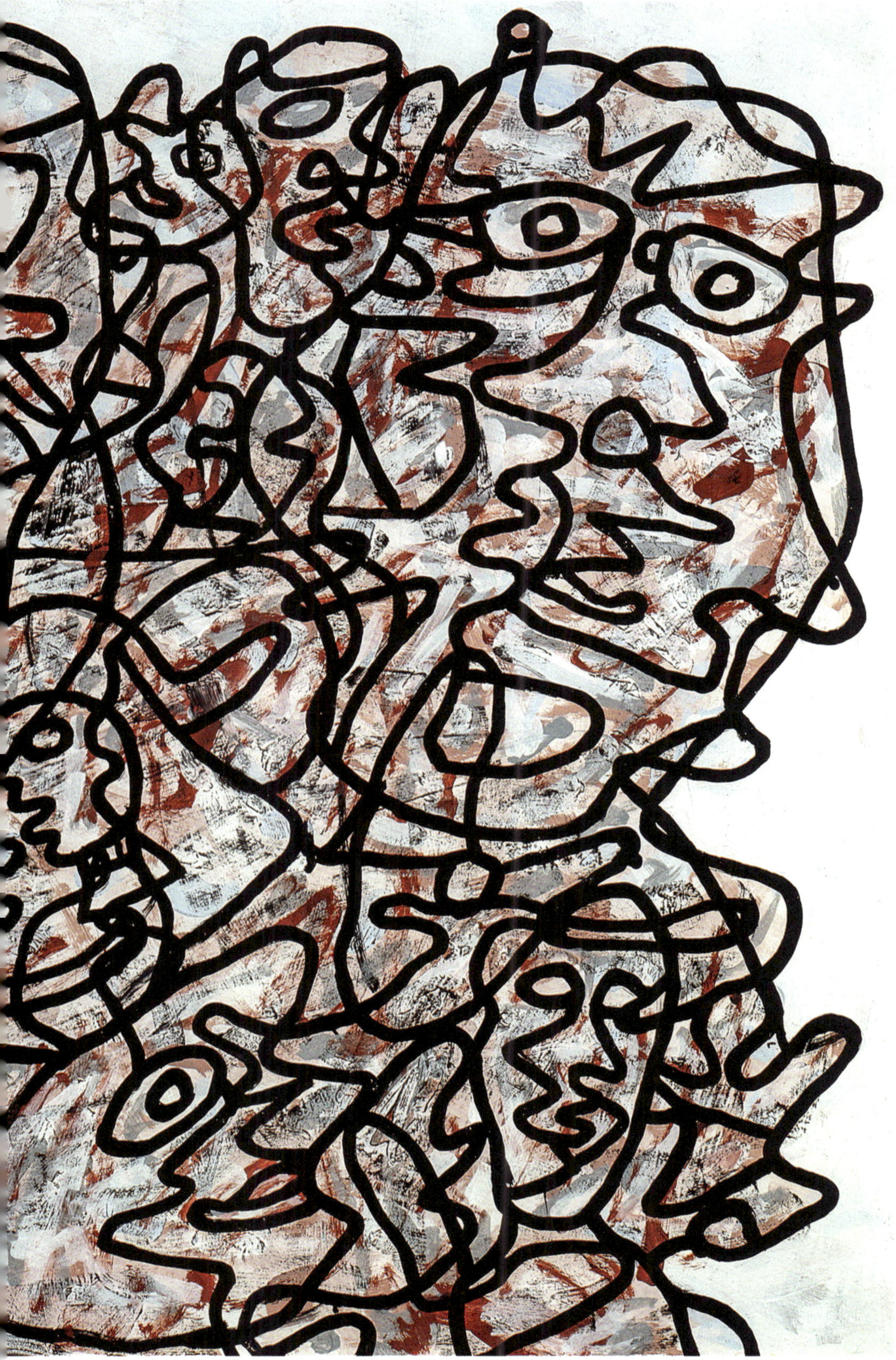

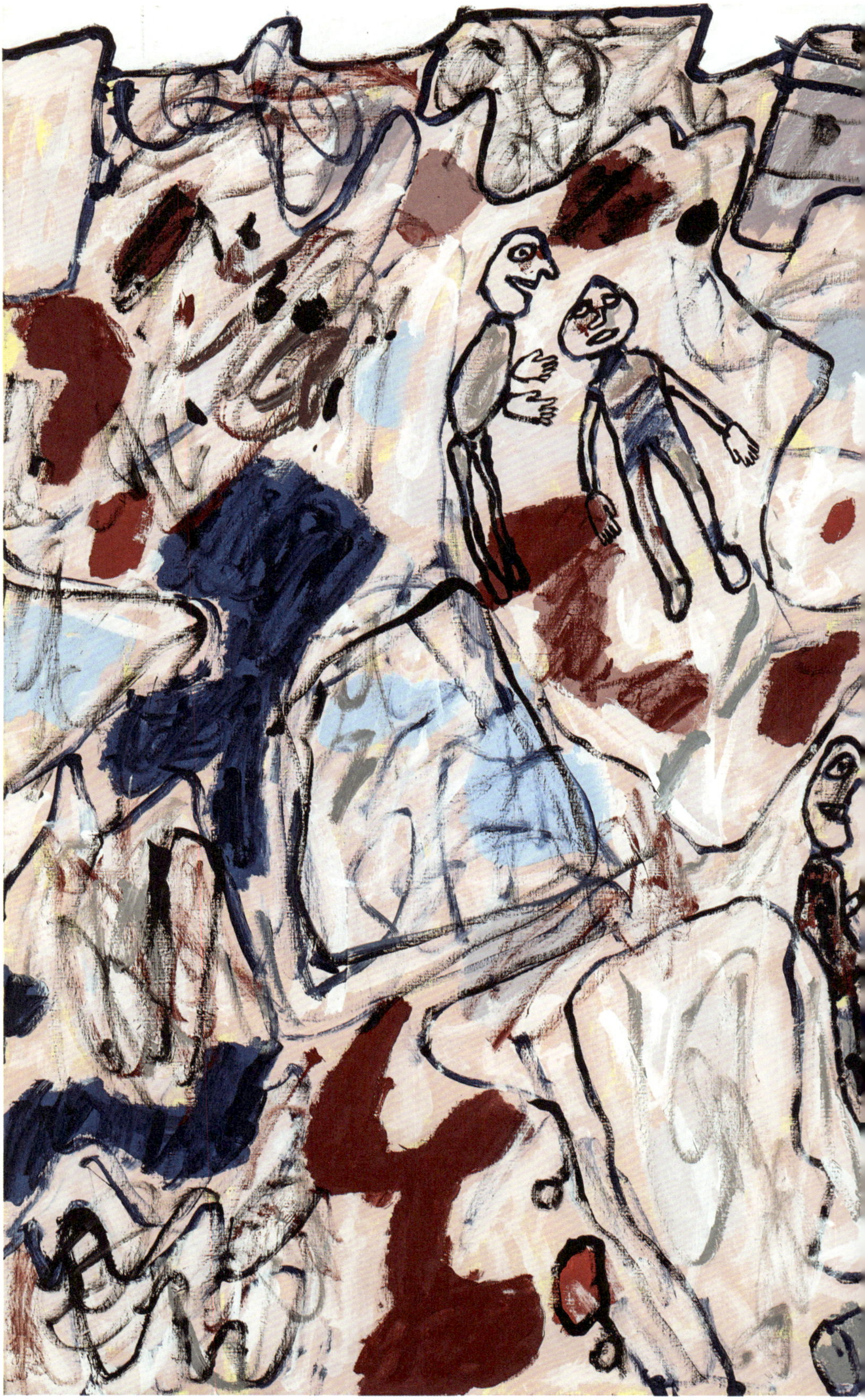

60. Jean Dubuffet. Esplanade aux passants, July 19, 1975

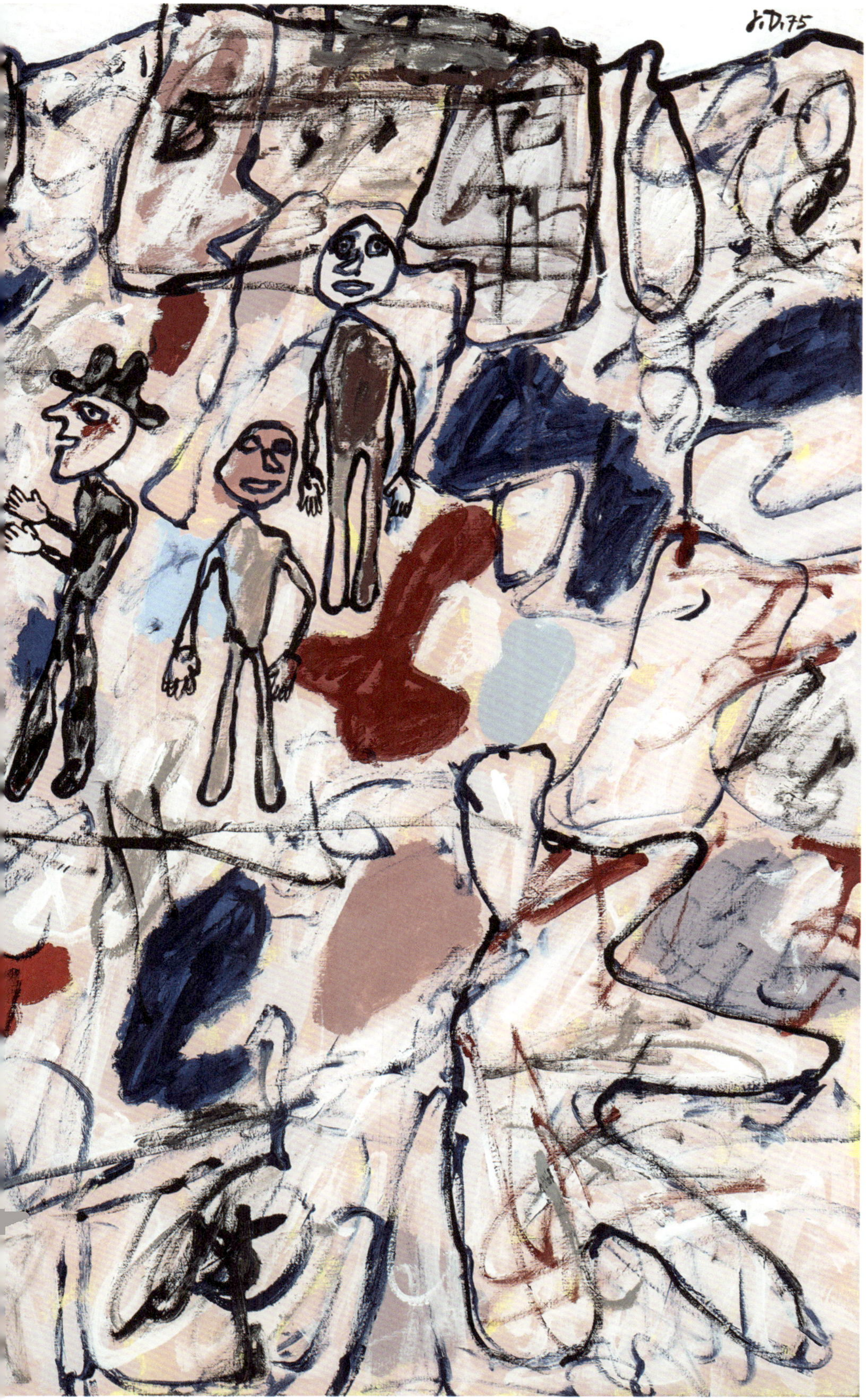
J.D.75

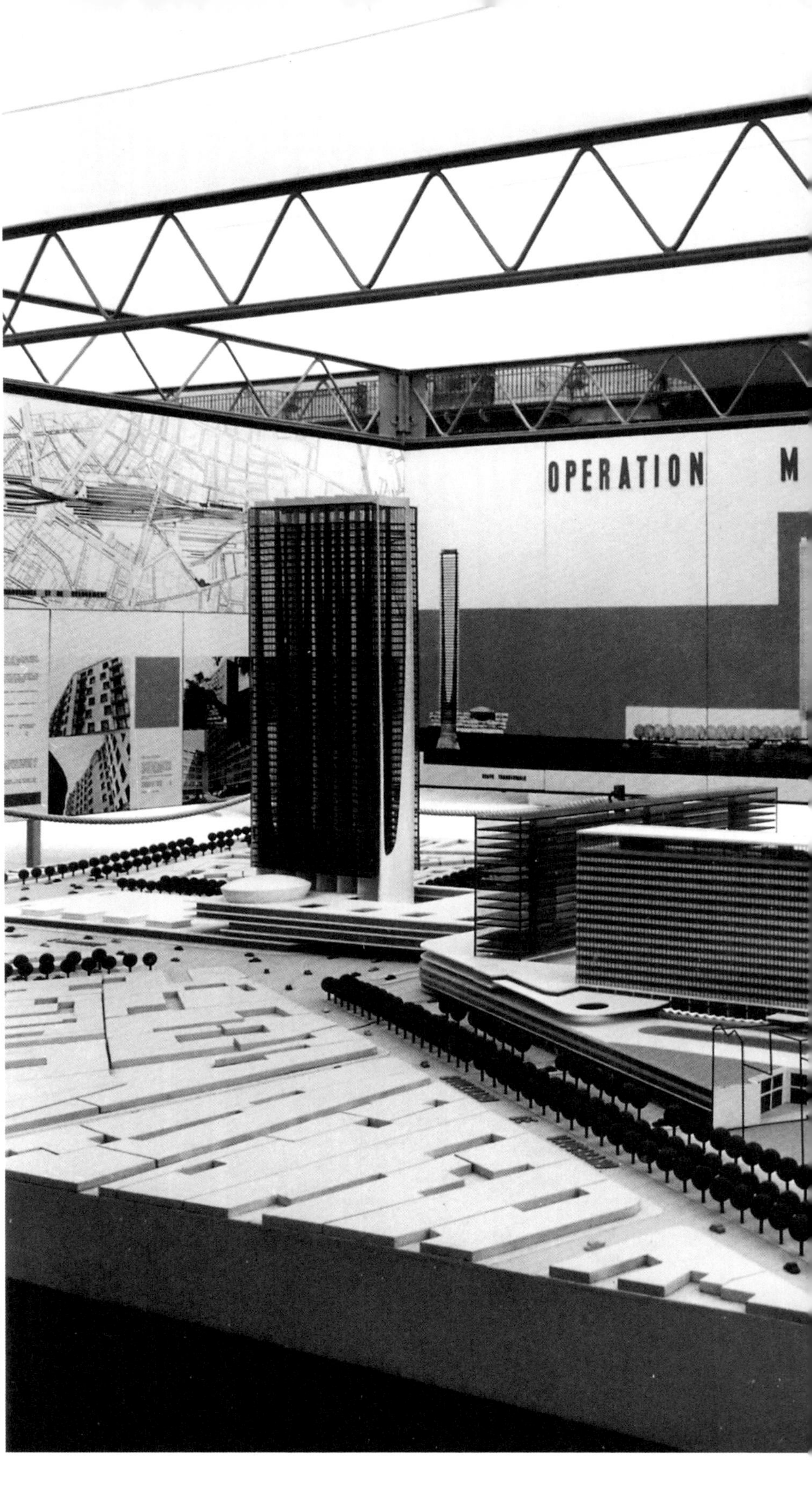

61. Demain Paris exhibition, Grand Palais, Paris, March–April 1961

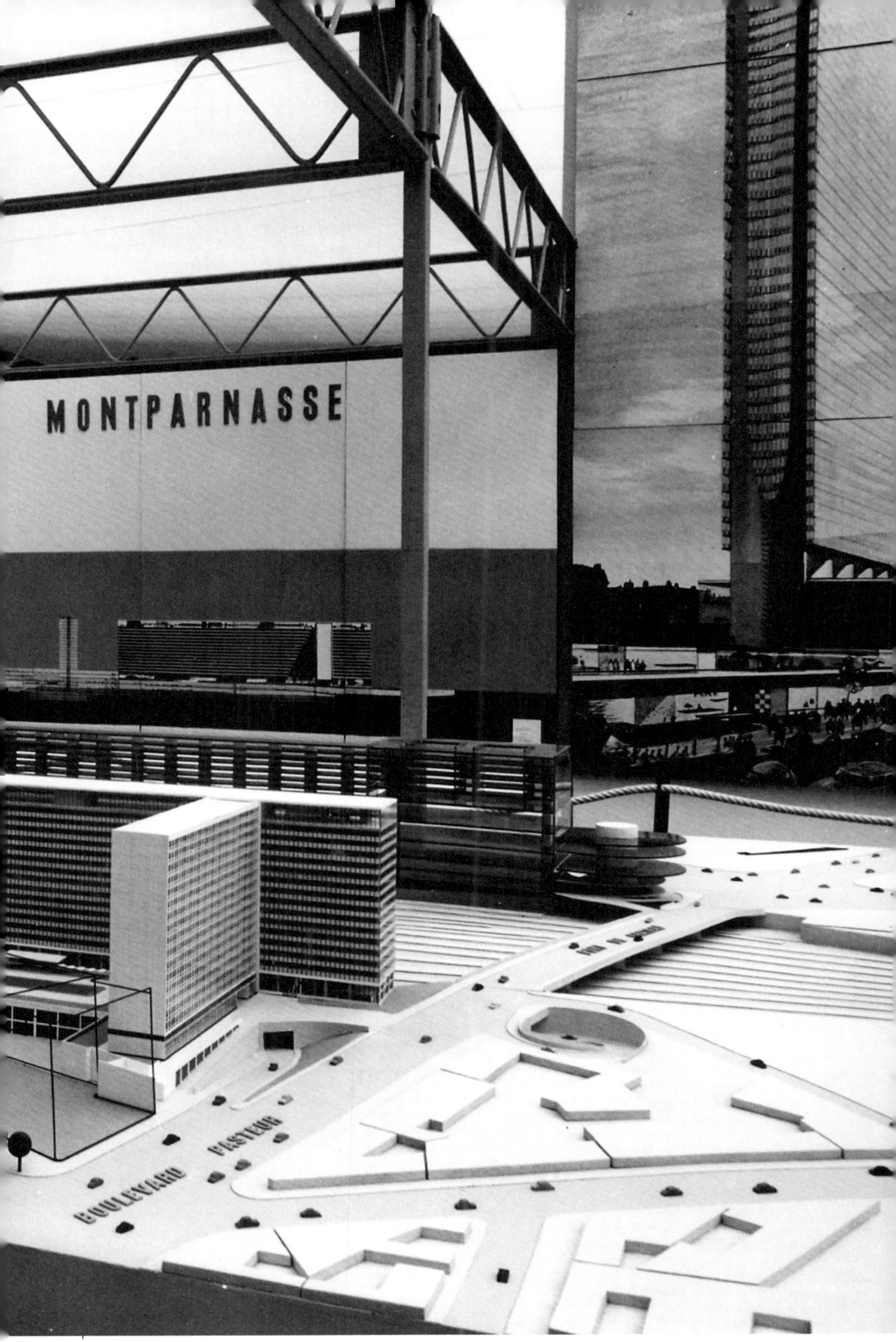
MONTPARNASSE
BOULEVARD PASTEUR

In the tangible materiality of his paintings, these people (whoever they may be) march down city streets, scramble across landscapes, stand in bubble-shaped spaces, and gaze out toward the viewer with outstretched arms.

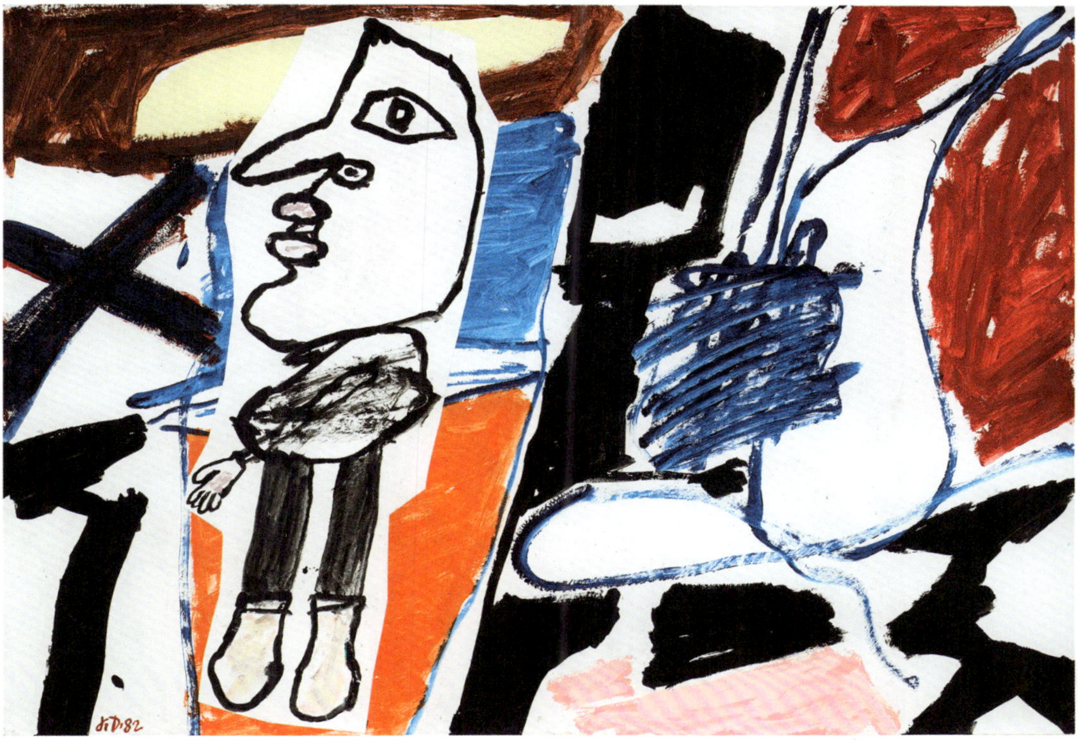

62. Jean Dubuffet. Le passant distrait, July 25, 1982

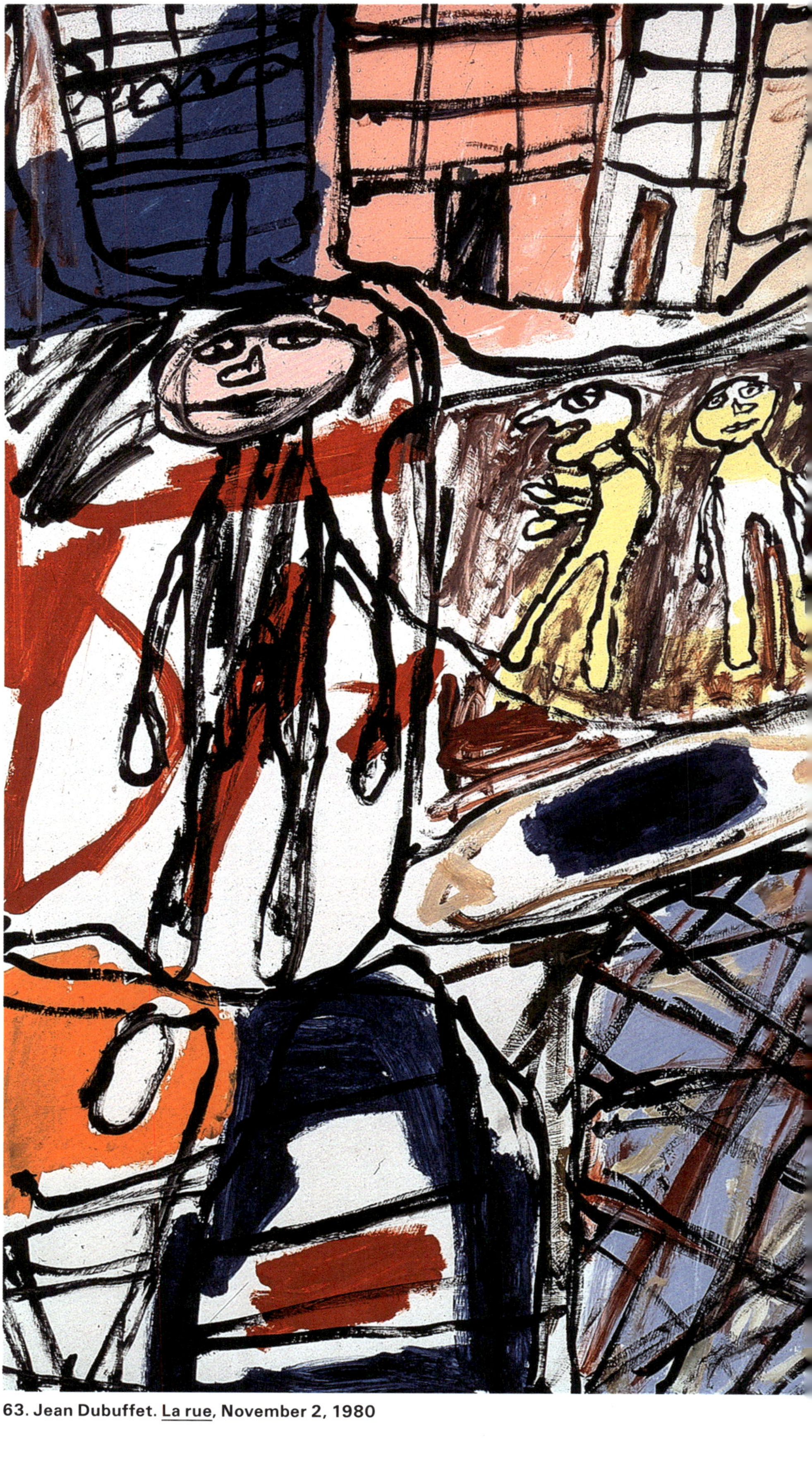

63. Jean Dubuffet. La rue, November 2, 1980

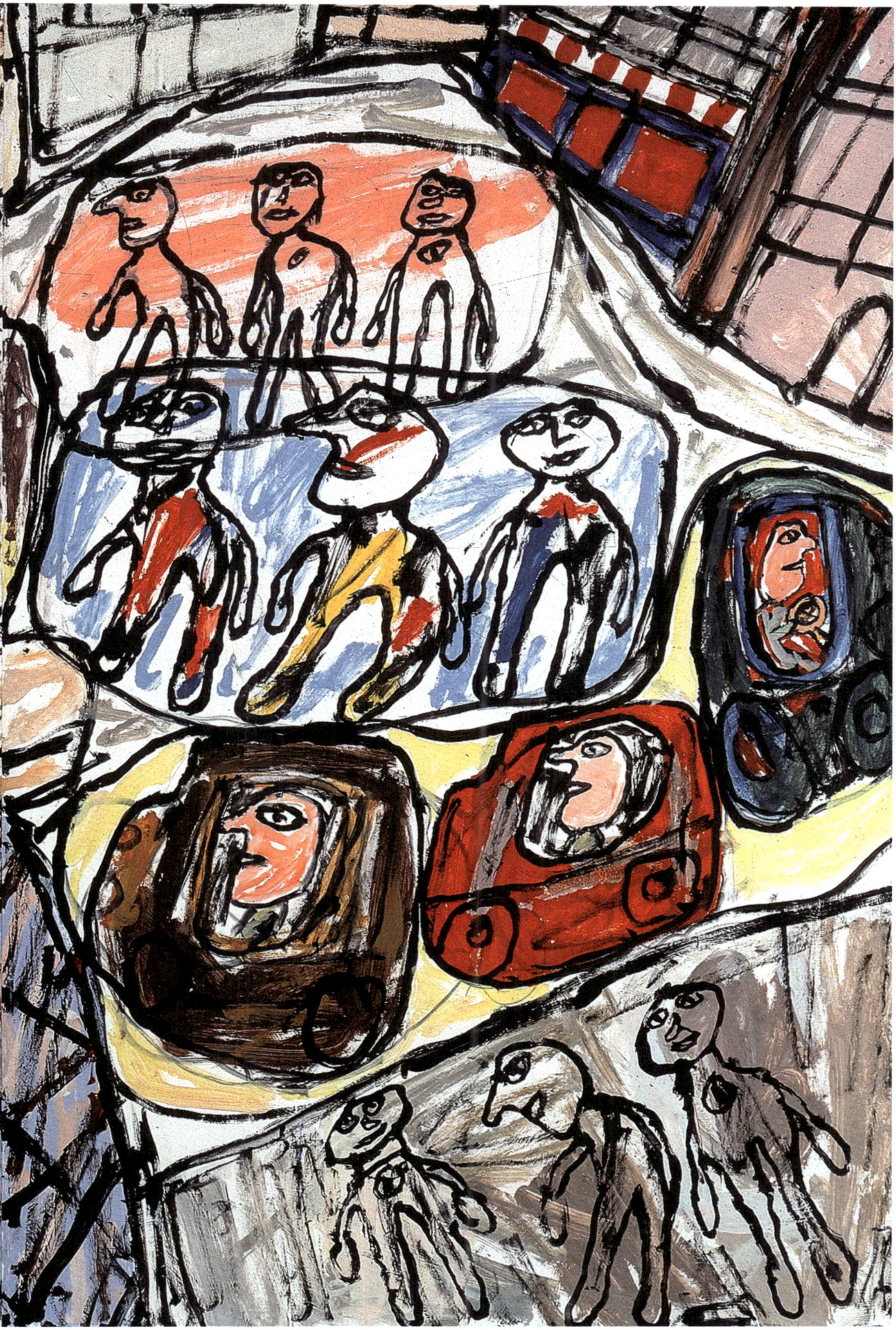

Dubuffet gives us Paris as a complex accumulation of layers, a city that cannot be beheld or grasped as a totality but only as different intersecting views, subtexts, and riddles.

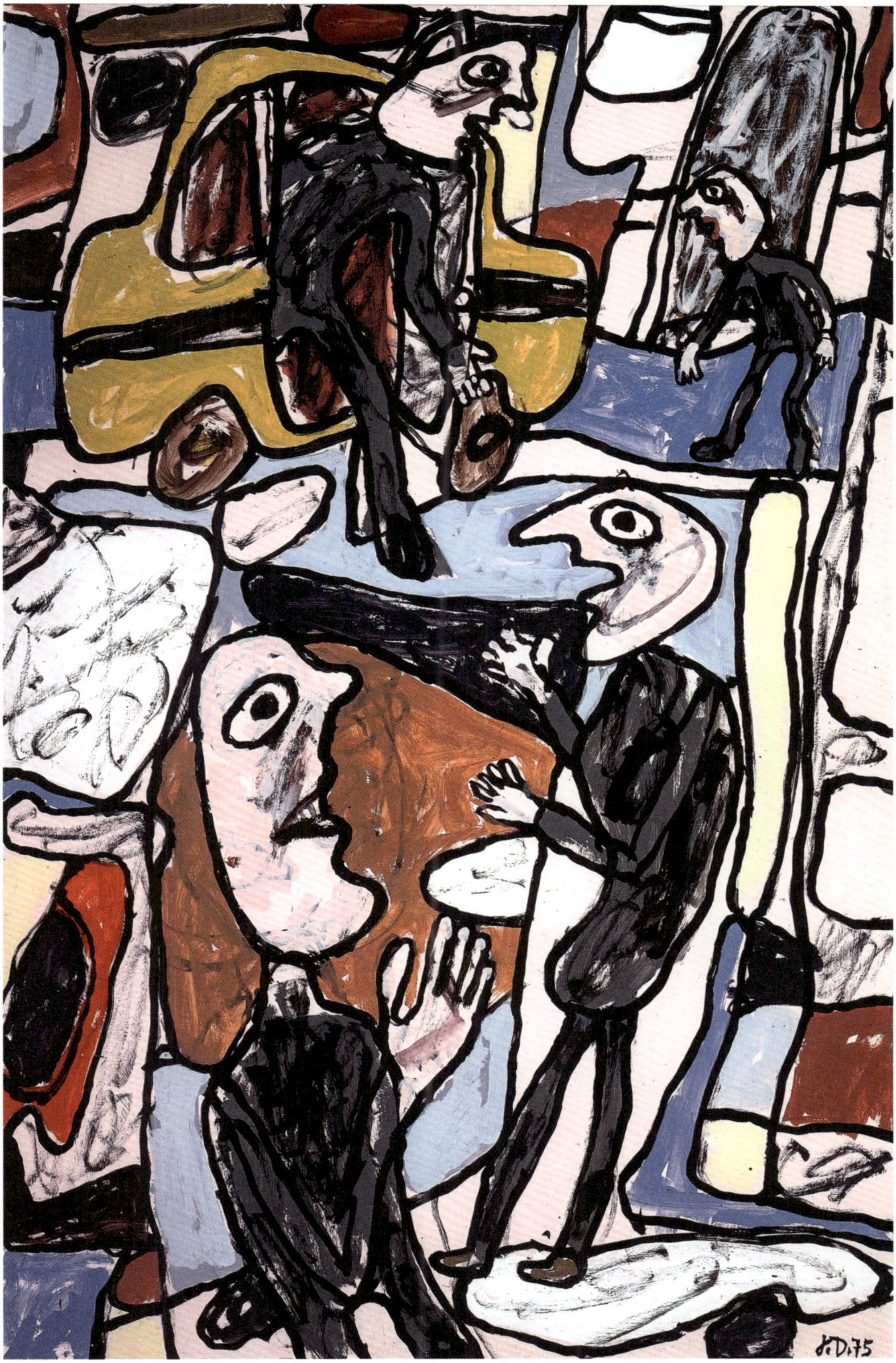

64. Jean Dubuffet. Scène de rue**, June 23, 1975**

Saint-Ouen—The Market (1944)

Jean Dubuffet

There we find—dense dew—man. In the passageways of the Metropolitan Railway (one uses them to reach the Porte de Clignancourt) one finds, in no less profuse quantity, man again, but busy, impatient, man whose thought is in the future position (the term of its route). Closed mussel. In Saint-Ouen, instead, one finds man settled in his present time; available: a radiantly open mussel. Why? That is unclear. Are these exhibits of padlocks, suspenders, can openers, leggings, garters in themselves such an attractive spectacle? Yes, because they are repeated. Because there are alignments and methodical displays of the same object, evenly repeated. A soldier with a gun on his shoulder is without qualities, but four soldiers carrying their guns synchronously on their shoulder—twelve horses beating their forty-eight irons together on the pavement—eighty coffins of the victims of a mining disaster—a hundred padlocks side by side, lying on the same side: that bamboozles the mind, that sings and intoxicates and carries us away! Numbers: oh, my lucky day! Starting from what number? From two. Two padlocks already repeating their lock. . . . But better: two eyes their eyeing—two legs their steps. . . . Man, oh, my lucky day! Man in multitude heaped up there, or flowing, in front of these pourer caps, these gas lighters, all these nice machines—in front, but also behind, because here there is no difference between the merchant and the customer: same face—and this is the unvarying face of the *middle-aged* man, as man most generally is, and that is, if it is necessary to describe him, and it does not take long (finally silence! to the bland Greek marble!), a face with the complexion of mutton stew, or of an old car tire, starred with furrows perfectly shapeless and as if the drawing of the features of each one was the result of a brick thrown in the face—that's what the face of the *middle-aged* man looks like, that of the merchants and that of the customers, they can scarcely be distinguished from one another. Only by where they stand. And as for me, well, that face pleases me. And the clothes, they please me, too; in a uniformly gray-black dusty tone like asphalt—from one to the next a little more jaundiced or faded—and bird-dropping-colored caps and mufflers and pullovers in shades of rubbish, that's how I like them, the clothes. And I'm not the only one. Because here indeed they also sell clothes, which are the same as those worn by the clients, the same colors of bitumen and dirty brown that man likes because they are the colors of man and of his hair, of his streets, of his walls and fences, and of his dirt. Here it i not a party of pheasants or parrots, it's the party of man. So what better for him to hang up, what better for him to lay out to feast upon, than his spangles and trinkets and his little familiar objects and everything that resembles him or makes him up? His combs, his boxers, his little rings? If sheep threw parties, what would they hang up, if not chops and legs and brains and sheep's heads? And his clothes, his lighters, his wristwatches, are indeed pieces of man himself—as wool is part of the sheep. Don't tell me that man is made of skin. Naturally, underneath, he is made of skin, but when do we see that? In rare cases. Man can be peeled like an onion. Man is very much afraid of seeing himself naked; he feels like a peeled onion, like a plucked chicken. Once this skin has been removed, one finds the repulsive meat and deeper in there all these viscera and filthy guts and disgusting pipes that man likes to see even less than his skin and after all the peeling one would find a liquid like that at the core of a coconut, this hot mass of five liters of blood, a full carboy, with that terrible pumping movement of which one cannot think without fainting, but at what moment do you see all these ignominies? Let us rather take man as he is: garnished with his vents—zippers and various holes on the inside—kept neatly closed—and his little watch chains and various pendants gently tinkling around him and his breath of wine, onion, sludge, and polish and let's join his celebration cheerfully on Sunday morning.

Chapter Two

Man in the Street

Je voudrais bien plutôt que mes tableaux amusent et intéressent l'homme de la rue quand il sort de son travail, pas du tout le maniaque, l'initié, mais l'homme qui n'a aucune instruction ni disposition particulières. C'est à l'homme de la rue que j'en veux, moi, c'est pareil à lui que je me sens, c'est avec lui que je veux faire amitié et entrer en confidence et connivence, et c'est à lui que je voudrais, par le moyen de mes ouvrages, donner de l'agrément et de l'enchantement.

—Jean Dubuffet, 1945

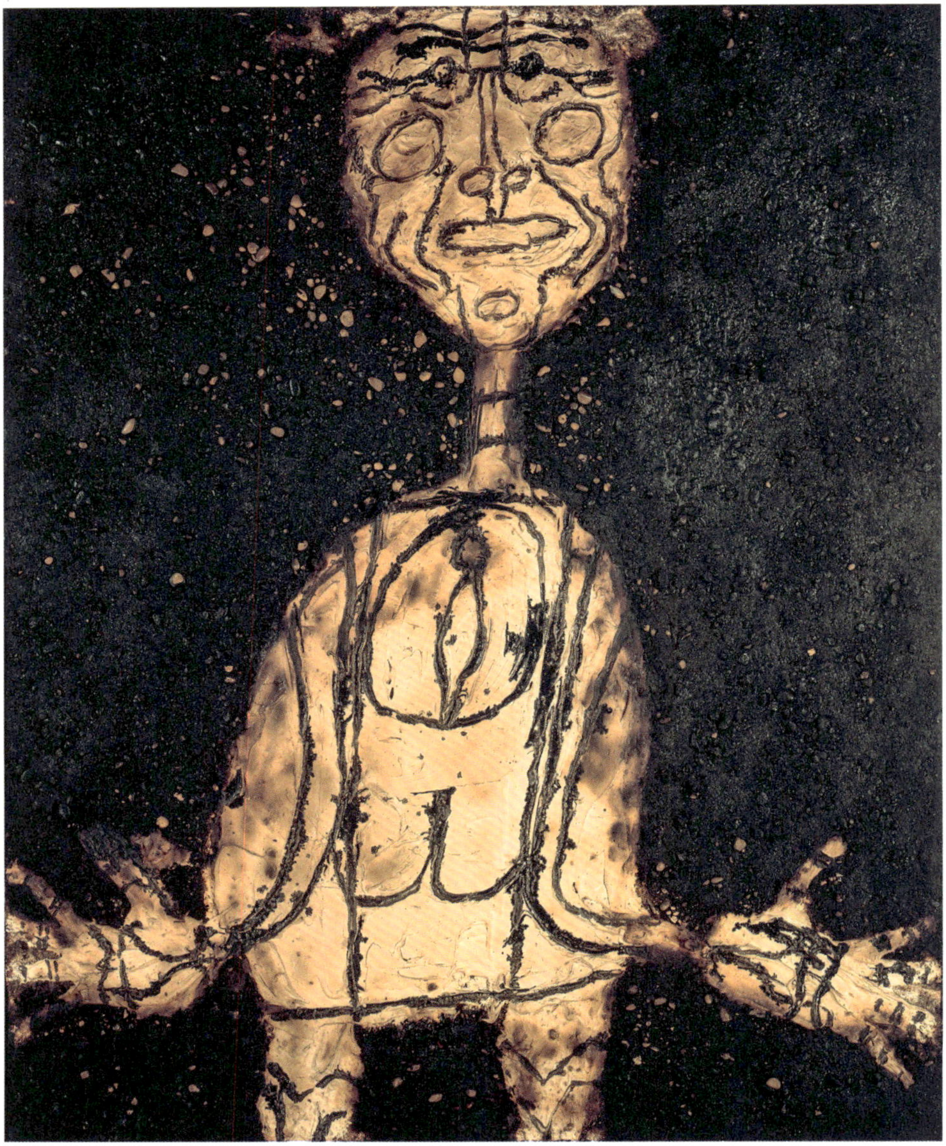

65. Jean Dubuffet. Monsieur Macadam, July 1945

Homme de la rue (man in the street), *homme du commun* (common man), *piéton* (pedestrian), or simply *personnage*, occasionally *citadin* (city dweller) or *passant* (passerby): these terms appear consistently in the titles of Dubuffet's works and in his writings. In the tangible materiality of his paintings, these people (whoever they may be) march down city streets, scramble across landscapes, stand in bubble-shaped spaces, and gaze out toward the viewer with outstretched arms. At first sight, the depictions appear to be mostly generic and timeless: there are very few portraits, apart from those of the artist's wife, Lili, in the mid-1930s and of writers and critics, along with his dealers, in the series Plus beaux qu'ils croient, painted in 1946–47, as well as a couple of self-portraits.[1]

And yet, if we look more attentively at paintings and drawings spanning his career, Dubuffet did allude to social status and identity in various periods of his oeuvre, mainly through details of clothing and titles of works. In his paintings of the 1940s, titles such as Élégante aux escarpins (Elegant Woman with Court Shoes; fig. 12) and Monsieur Macadam (fig. 65), whose protagonist wears a suit and tie, recall the swift, snapshot-like identifications we all make of people we pass on the street, noting a detail of clothing or demeanor that catches our eye and that distinguishes the person *pars pro toto*, while the face is immediately forgotten. In the lithographic album Matière et mémoire (Matter and Memory) of 1945, Dubuffet created several depictions of types identified by their professions, such as Dactylographe (Typist; fig. 66), an approach he followed up in the booklet L'Hourloupe (1963), which introduced the long cycle bearing the same name. There, small figures drawn in ballpoint pen (fig. 67) are captioned with purposefully inventive spellings such as "Nautère" (*notaire*, or notary) and "Jeandarm" (*gendarme*, or constable). Elsewhere in his oeuvre, facial features change from the highly individualized depictions, sometimes nearing caricature, of the early years, when male and female figures abounded in almost equal numbers, to the increasingly anonymous and predominantly masculine faces of the later years (in a rather remarkable comment, Dubuffet once explained that a female figure would be too "particularized, would not have the general, elementary and impersonal character that I aim to give to the figure").[2] Some viewers see in the figures of the artist's later years endlessly repeated self-portraits, gazing at the world with wonder and irony. But for most of us, the figures remain unidentified, their faces sometimes barely sketched in, and yet—perhaps because we are now so used to the simplified visual language of emojis—we immediately read each one of them as joyful, anxious, poker-faced, or angry.

The city, I like to think, is more than a setting for these figures large and small, these urban characters and anonymous silhouettes: not only is it the physical space in which they walk and loiter, but their existence is somehow bound to their surroundings. After all, there can be no pedestrian without a street (fig. 23), no city dweller without a city (see p. 4), and to achieve the suggestion of anonymity that comes with the word "passerby," it is best to picture her or him in an urban setting (fig. 62). Amid these city-related denominations, *homme de la rue* is a *faux ami*, a deceptive cognate that designates an average, typical, or ordinary person. Dubuffet used the expression in his writings, along with *homme du commun*. The meaning of neither is fixed: in his private correspondence and published writings, these expressions refer alternately to Dubuffet himself and to what he perceived or construed as his ideal audience as well as to—and this is reprised by many critics writing about his work—the anonymous figures that populate his paintings.

What reading of those paintings can be revealed if I strip the phrase *homme de la rue* of its metaphorical meaning and understand it instead in a literal manner? This is, in a sense, the starting point and purpose of the present chapter: to rub the representations of figures in urban settings made during different periods of Dubuffet's oeuvre up

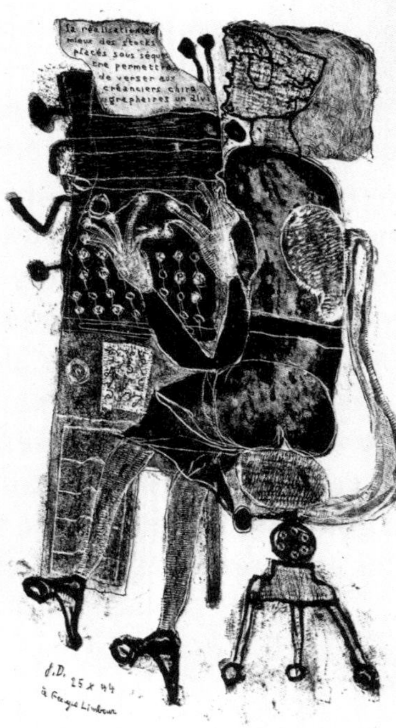

66. Jean Dubuffet. *Dactylographe*, October 25, 1944

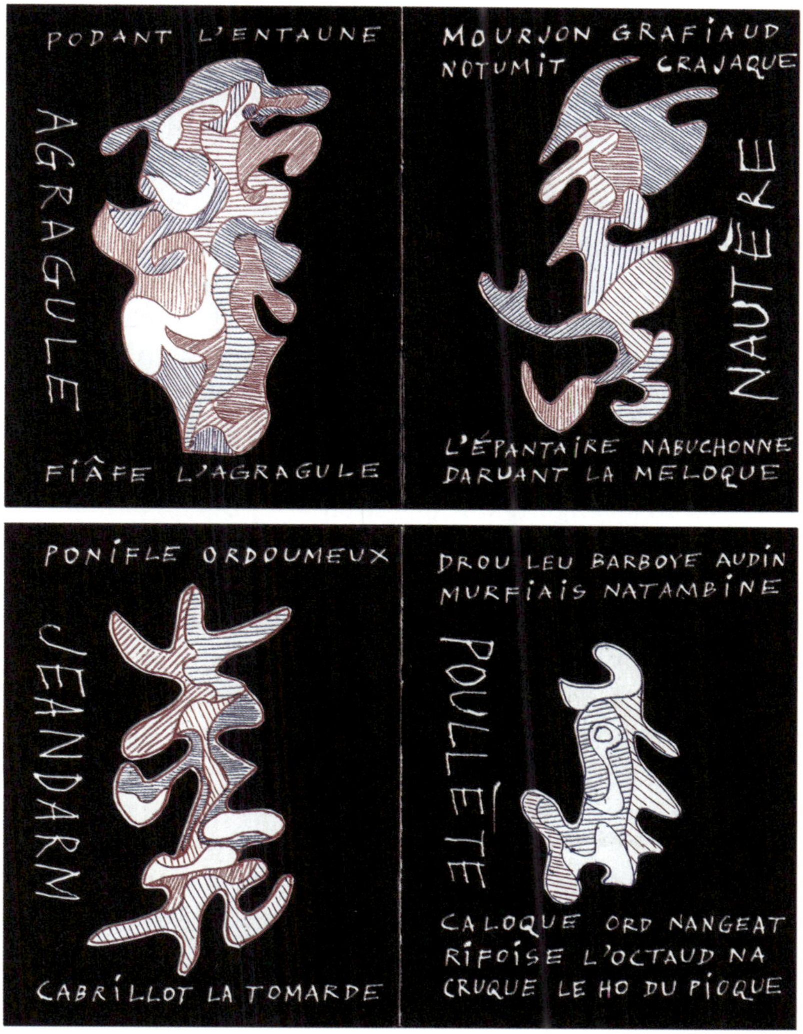

67. Jean Dubuffet. Four pages from L'Hourloupe booklet, published in Le petit Jésus, summer 1963 (original drawings made July 15–25, 1962)

against his changing discourse around the "man in the street" (and the contiguous "common man") in order to understand how the one might infiltrate the other. In considering Dubuffet's writings and works of art in concert and exploring their visual and verbal ambivalences, several affiliations emerge: a rhetoric and practice of the unexceptional or "de-skilled" in art; an idea of the city as an environment that changes over time, adopting, here and there, elements of the outside world as it mutates; and last, an image of anonymity generalized through the idea of the archetype. Ultimately, these three ways in which discourse and painting find common ground make it possible to claim an intractable connection between Dubuffet's images and the urban context in which they were born and in which they live.

"De-skilling": To Paint like the Common Man

"I want to remain a very common man, a simple soldier without a medal or distinction of any kind," Dubuffet wrote to Jean Paulhan in the spring of 1944, explaining his decision to put a temporary stop to the stream of guests visiting his studio, stirred by Paulhan's enthusiasm.[3] At the time he wrote this letter, Dubuffet had known Paulhan for less than a year—enough time to form an intense friendship and enough time as well for Dubuffet to become acquainted with some of the writers and poets who gravitated toward Paulhan's Nouvelle Revue française, one of the most respected literary journals in France, published by Gallimard.[4] In this context, "common man" suggests that Dubuffet may have wanted to preserve a distance from, or maintain his status as an outsider to, that milieu. Did he already fear the corrupting effect of the cultural cognoscenti on his work? Or did he sense the beginnings of an underground succès d'estime that might turn him swiftly into a professional artist, despite his persistent reluctance? It is possible, as the art historian Baptiste Brun has contended, that the idea of the common man, first recorded in this letter to Paulhan, was a tactic for working out a definition of himself in the very short time span during which his status changed from a supposed amateur, working alone, to a darling of the literary world. By calling himself, modestly, a "common man," Dubuffet marked a difference between himself and the literary and artistic set that suddenly surrounded and lauded him. It was also,

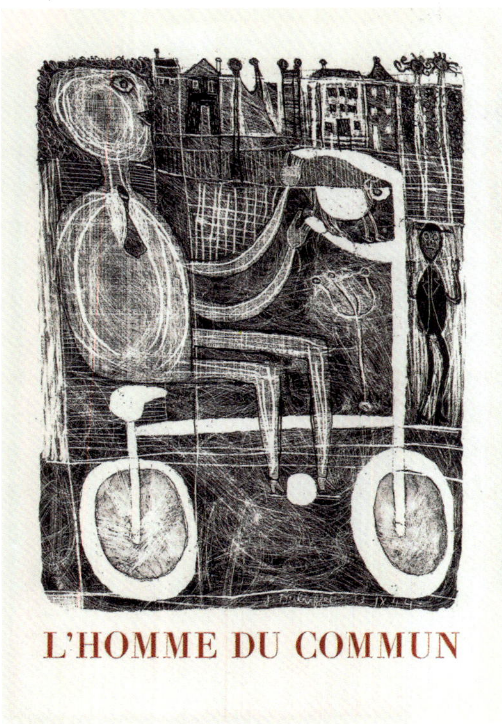

68. Jean Dubuffet, Cyclotourisme, September 13, 1944, published on cover of Pierre Seghers's L'homme du commun (1944)

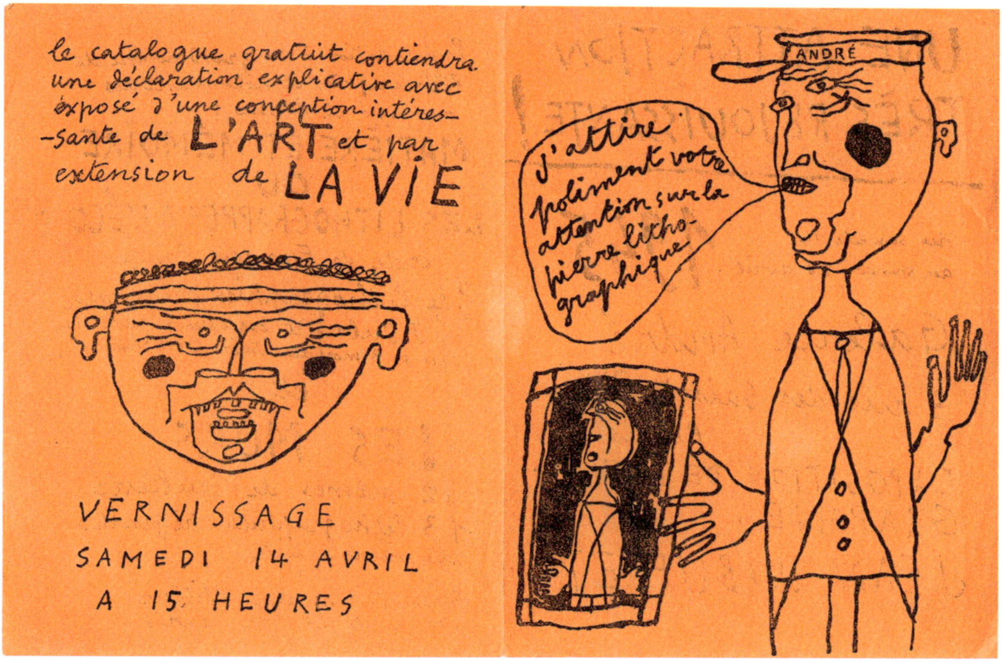

69. Invitation to Exposition de lithographies de Jean Dubuffet exhibition, 1945

possibly, a phrase through which he could take his embarrassment to be seen as a wine dealer dabbling in art—a position that had prompted some early dismissals by critics—and turn it inside out.[5] A year or so after the letter, Dubuffet, for all intents and purposes, transformed the shame of being an outsider into an aesthetic claim: his text "Plus modeste," published under the heading "Notice commune" in the Petit guide du visiteur (Small Guide for Visitors) that accompanied his April 1945 exhibition of lithographs at Galerie André, in the rue des Saint-Pères (reprinted in translation on pp. 53–56 of this volume), recounts fragments of his past life in a colorful and humorous mode, explaining that he had eventually found a way to make art by looking not at other works of art but at the man in the street—for example, a butcher, a woman on a tram, and a shop assistant selling neckties at La Samaritaine.[6] It is in this text, which concludes with his wondering whether art should not be "more modest," that Dubuffet began to publicly build the personal mythology that would accompany his work for many years to come: that of a merchant who, after several unsuccessful attempts at being an artist, finally found a way to become one by "strip[ping] himself of acquired culture."[7]

Between his private utterances of "common man" and the public disclosure of his early life in "Plus modeste," the phrase

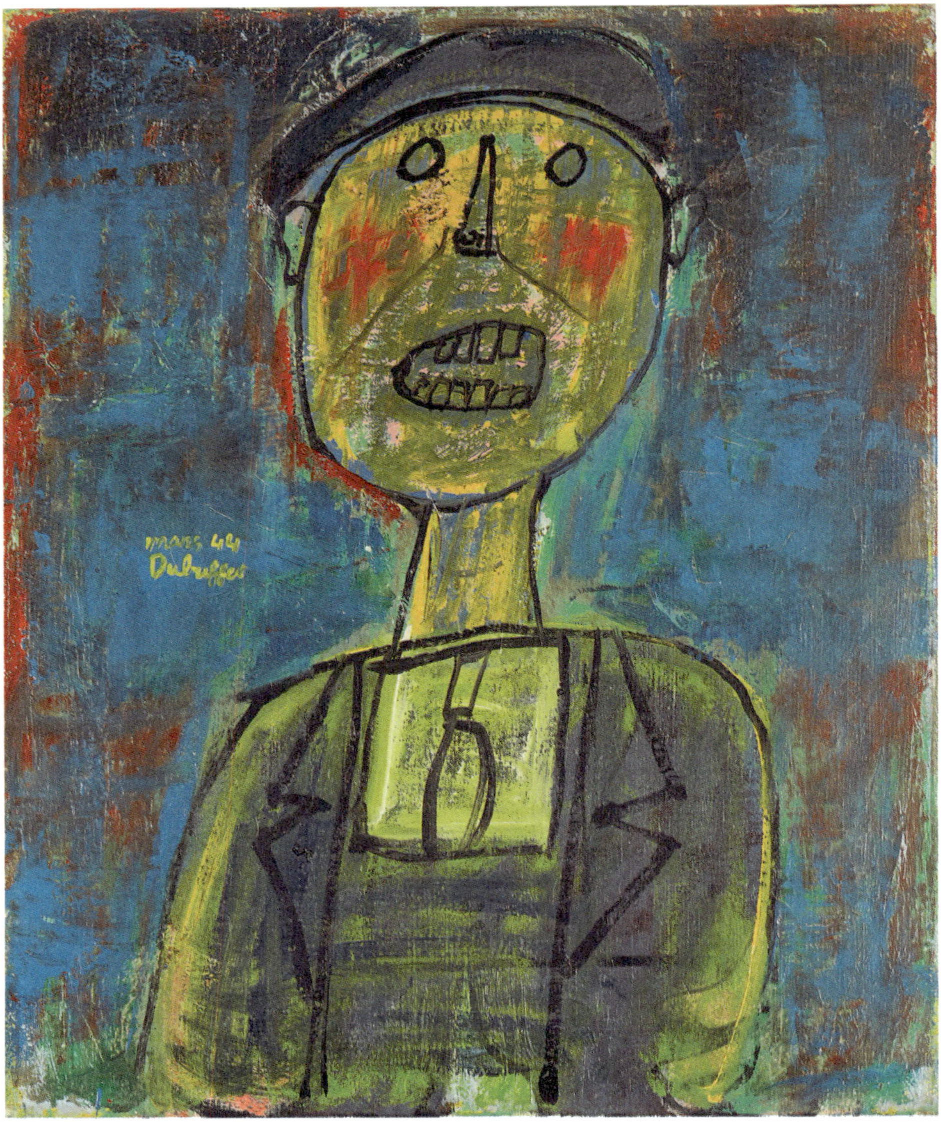

70. Jean Dubuffet. Petit hurleur, March 1944

homme du commun appeared in the title of one of the earliest critical texts dedicated to his work: L'homme du commun ou Jean Dubuffet, by the poet and editor Pierre Seghers (fig. 68). The book appeared in October 1944, a few months after the Liberation of Paris, and coincided with Dubuffet's first solo exhibition at Galerie René Drouin.[8] In his haunting and celebratory text, full of aphorisms and ellipses, Seghers described Dubuffet's painting as "illegal, in a state of permanent insurgency."[9] A few pages on, discussing the artist's preference for representing everyday life, he stated, "Oh, if we let those who write on the walls develop their stories we would see the film of true life unfold."[10] For Seghers, the heroic quality of Dubuffet's work stemmed from his dissonant, individual voice rejoicing in the banality of the average man, a celebration of the ordinary that constituted a resistance to the erasure of the individual enacted by Nazism, which then dominated a large part of Europe: "A project to degrade man can employ one hundred million machine individuals. It can try to stupefy the man for a thousand years, by sterilizing it, by perpetually affixing to it epaulets and visors. Always, at the same moment, another man arrives who proclaims alone that man is free. It is in this sense that Dubuffet's painting is heroic."[11] Seghers, himself a member of the Resistance—whereas Dubuffet steered clear of political engagement in both his life and his work—did not give in to the myth of the artist as genius but instead, reversing the usual rhetoric, perceived him as heroic insofar as he boldly portrayed ordinary humanity.

This ordinary humanity of the common man appeared plentifully in the exhibition at Galerie René Drouin, Tableaux et dessins de Jean Dubuffet. There, amid urban and rural landscapes, Dubuffet's city characters made up a brightly painted crowd.[12] As in "Plus modeste," he identified them through profession or activity. They included, among others, bodyguards, in Gardes du corps (January 1943); a newsboy (literally, "little howler"), in Petit hurleur (fig. 70); a lady trying on a hat, in Essayeuse de chapeau (fig. 73); a violin player, in Le violoniste (March 1944); and a couple of thieves, in Deux brigands (February 1944). While evoking everyday activities, these paintings had little to do with the picturesque photographic genre depicting Parisian street vendors and tradespeople practicing what are commonly referred to as *petits métiers*, examples of which had circulated abundantly since the late nineteenth century. Dubuffet's pictures moved away from anecdote and toward the general—that is where the particular strength of a painting such as Petit hurleur resides. Although the figure strongly suggests, through its clothing and juvenile features, a hackneyed staple of urban life, the *crieur de journaux* (newsboy), Dubuffet played down the picturesque by depicting the eyes as empty circles and simplifying the shape of the body so that it fit within a coarsely sketched oval. That same shape also appears in other works, such as Petit ricaneur (Little Sneerer) of March 1944, suggesting that a kind of generic, modular form could be used to depict different individuals. In addition to these works, almost all the figures were clumsy-looking assemblages of ovals propped on rectangles and larger ovals or sprawled shapelessly across furniture like fried eggs, as in the hilarious Essayeuse de chapeau.

Complementing the intentionally ungainly shapes of his figures, Dubuffet also used a boisterous range of colors to paint their bodies. In a careful study of the artist's use of color in the 1940s, the art historian Daniel Abadie has convincingly shown how Dubuffet's palette in Marionnettes de la ville et de la campagne, with its strident reds, greens, pinks, and yellows, clashed with the traditional scheme of blues and reds associated with the medieval stained glass of Chartres Cathedral and the tin-glazed earthenware of Rouen—a palette that was being reprised, in Vichy France, by the so-called *jeunes peintres de tradition française*.[13] Rejecting the good taste and adherence to the traditions of a "timeless France" promoted by the Vichy government (although the artists in the group were by no means all supporters of that regime), Dubuffet instead promoted the commonplace in two complementary ways: by making portraits of the man (and woman) in the street but also by painting *as* a common man. In other words, Dubuffet initiated a multifold process of "de-skilling" that took the form of a "deconstruction of ideas, habits and practices," to borrow the words of Hubert Damisch.[14]

The forms of Dubuffet's Marionnettes were simplified rather than distorted, and as such, they appeared to directly challenge the unrivaled master of figurative distortion and towering figure of modernism, Pablo Picasso, who also stayed in Paris during the war years, based in his studio on the rue des Grands-Augustins. A clear sign of the authority held by Picasso at this time is that American critics reviewing Dubuffet's first solo exhibition in New York, in January 1947, felt compelled to repeat hearsay: "Transatlantic rumour has it that Picasso doesn't like Dubuffet's work," wrote the critic and art historian Robert Goldwater.[15] There was, according to several testimonies, no love lost between Dubuffet and Picasso, and some works in the Marionnettes series can certainly be read as pitting the man in the street against the master of modernism. Take, for instance, two works that adopt themes often painted by

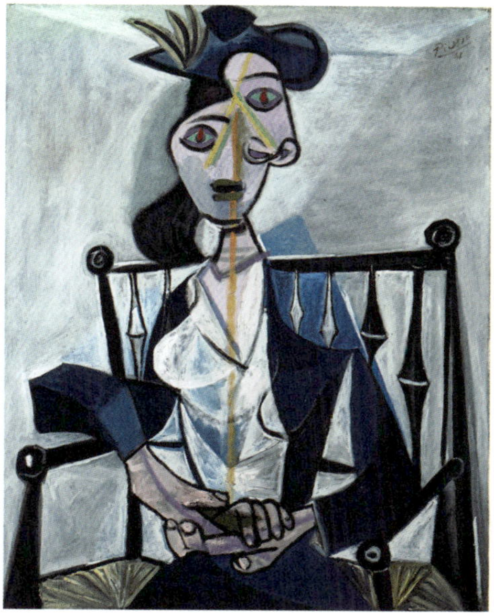

71. Pablo Picasso. Femme assise (Dora Maar), 1941

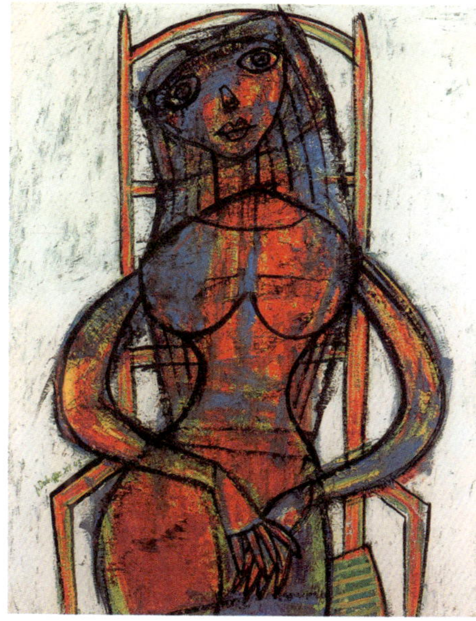

72. Jean Dubuffet. La veuve, November 1943

Picasso in the 1930s and 1940s. La veuve of November 1943 (fig. 72) echoes Picasso's numerous portraits of 1939–41 showing Dora Maar seated in a wood armchair (fig. 71) but substitutes for Picasso's complex Cubist folds, cuts, transparent effects, and harmoniously subdued tones a gawky but provocative arrangement of simple shapes: triangle, heart, rectangles, and hourglass, in sloppily painted reds, yellows, and greens. And how not to read a work of December 1942, with its blithe title Gambade au sofa (fig. 75), as a parody of eroticism in which Dubuffet was poking fun at another of Picasso's canonical themes, that of the reclining nude (fig. 74)? More than just playing with form and color, Dubuffet's pastiches of Picasso invited viewers to dehabituate their eyes from what the artist perceived as a now-contrived tradition of modernist painting, confronting them instead with an urban imagery of the everyday. A search for new ideas and sources of inspiration is what Dubuffet called for in "Avant-projet pour une conférence populaire sur la peinture" (Draft for a Popular Lecture on Painting), a series of lecture notes written in 1945 and published in 1946 in a volume of Dubuffet's writings edited by Jean Paulhan at Gallimard, in which the artist asserted his desire to paint for the "man in the street."[16] Toward the end of that text, he listed a number of (unspecified) paintings by Picasso, Matisse, Rouault, and Modigliani that would be projected as slides, accompanied by the following comment about what he called *la peinture moderniste ou d'avant-garde* (modernist or avant-garde painting):

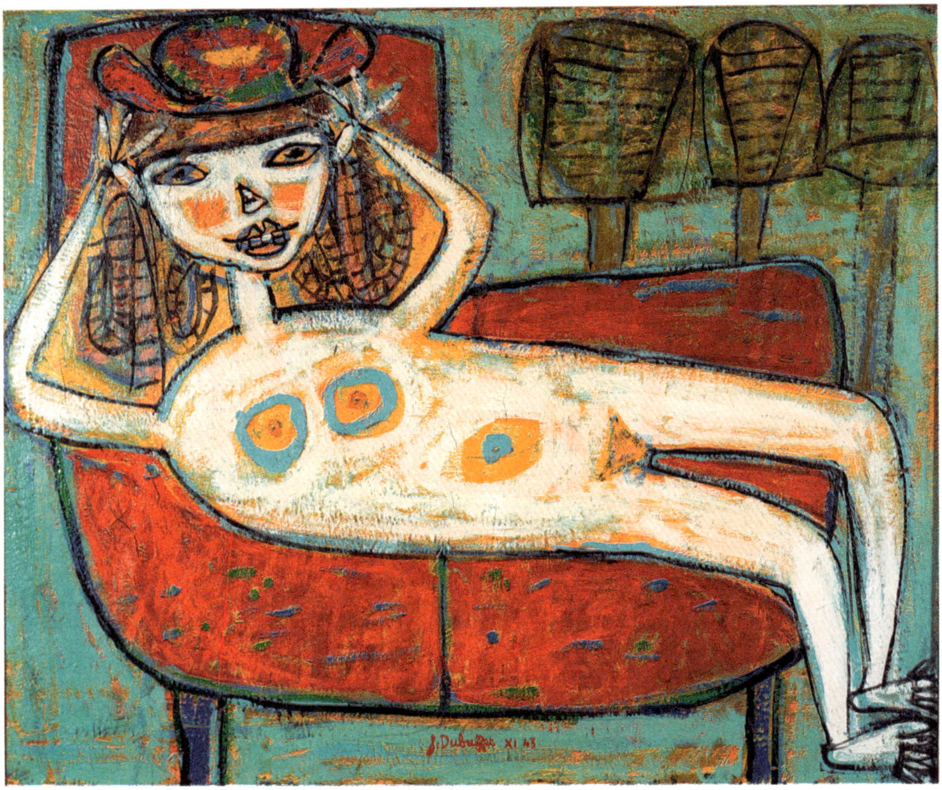

73. Jean Dubuffet. Essayeuse de chapeau, November 1943

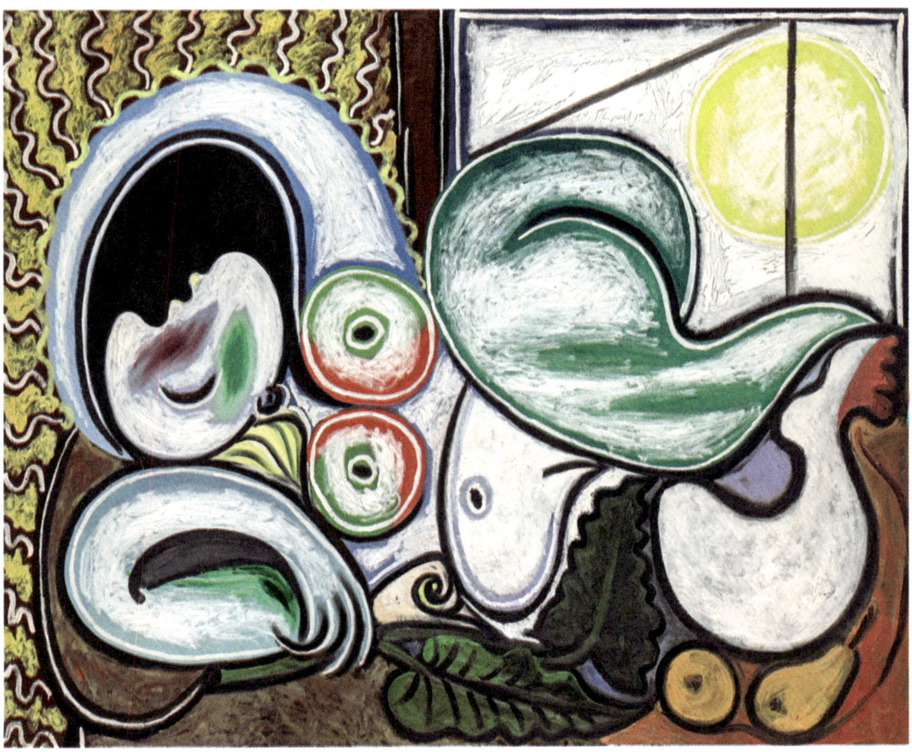

74. Pablo Picasso. Nu couché, April 4, 1932

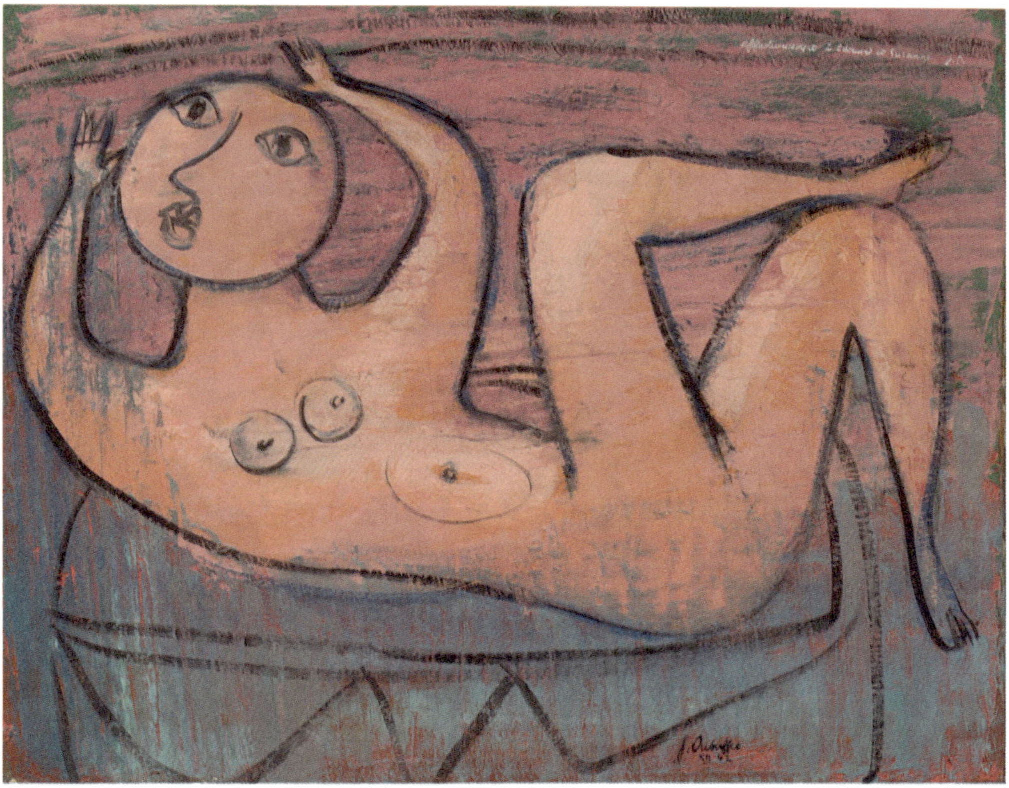

75. Jean Dubuffet. **<u>Gambade au sofa</u>, December 1942**

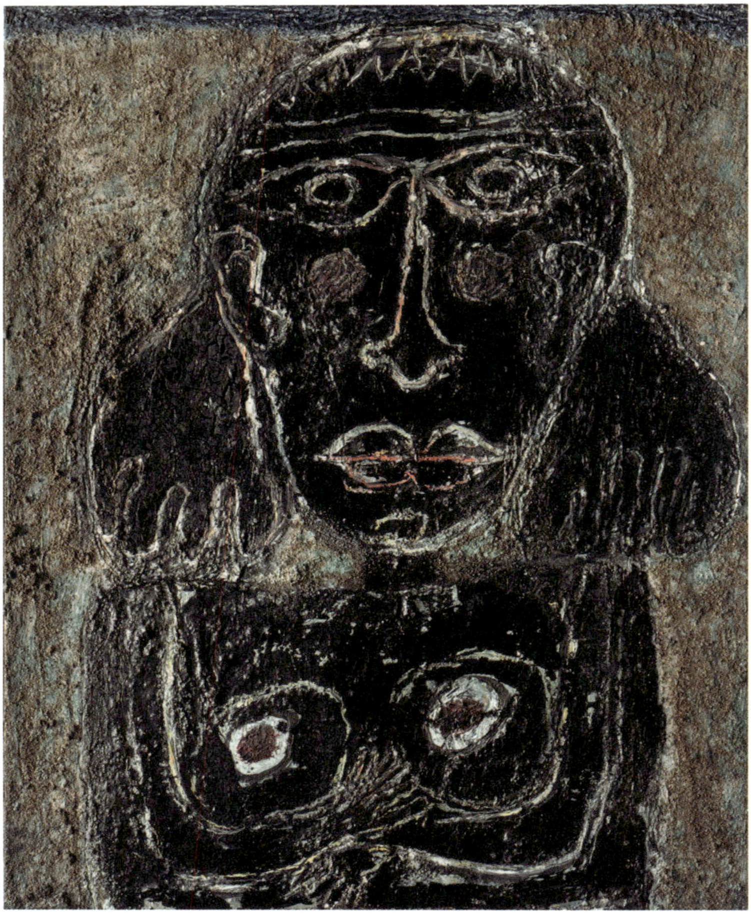

76. Jean Dubuffet. Black Beauty, November 1945

"It appears a little out of breath, anemic. It is in need of a good blood transfusion, a common, and healthy and robust, blood."[17]

But how far could Dubuffet take playing the role of the common man as a tool to deconstruct the "ideas, habits and practices" of high modern art? Already a few months later (although the dating of this letter is uncertain), Dubuffet suggested that the common man posture was but an illusion. Writing to Paulhan, he used it as the two-word summary of what had been his ideal aesthetic standard: "the position I once delighted in dreaming of (that of common man)."[18] The artist seems by then to have discovered that the position of the common man was no longer tenable for him. In the months following his first exhibition in Paris, as if putting into practice this move away from the *homme du commun* in all that character's cheerful diversity, Dubuffet abruptly changed the course of his artistic practice. The bright colors and busy passersby, bodyguards and newsboys, were suddenly out, along with the pastiches of Picasso. Dubuffet embraced the grit of the street.

Figure on Ground: Man "in" the Street

If the Marionnettes were from the city *and* the country, everything in Dubuffet's second series of works, by contrast, spoke of the city. From the title, which included the word "macadam," to the visual references to street graffiti and the colors and materials used in the paintings, to the typography of the title printed inside the catalogue, which replicated that of the ubiquitous *Défense d'afficher* signs stenciled on the walls of Paris (see figs. 77, 78), the city was everywhere. Just as Dubuffet's first exhibition had been a year and a half earlier, his second solo show at René Drouin, Mirobolus, Macadam et Cie, in which forty-eight paintings from the new series were presented, was greeted as a succès de scandale.[19] The gallery's visitor book was again scribbled with insults, and once again, the exhibition had to be guarded to protect the paintings. "What a commotion," wrote Dubuffet to the poet Joë Bousquet. "A policeman had to be put in charge of looking after the paintings . . . and still five of them were damaged."[20] In "L'auteur répond à quelques objections" (The Author Answers a Few Objections), the text he penned for the catalogue of that exhibition, Dubuffet did not write directly about having taken the city as a theme but discussed instead the strange materials (including asphalt, sand, gravel, and mud) he had used to make the thickly encrusted paintings he called *hautes pâtes*.[21] Inviting his readers to find beauty in dirt and junk, he implied that what was most daring

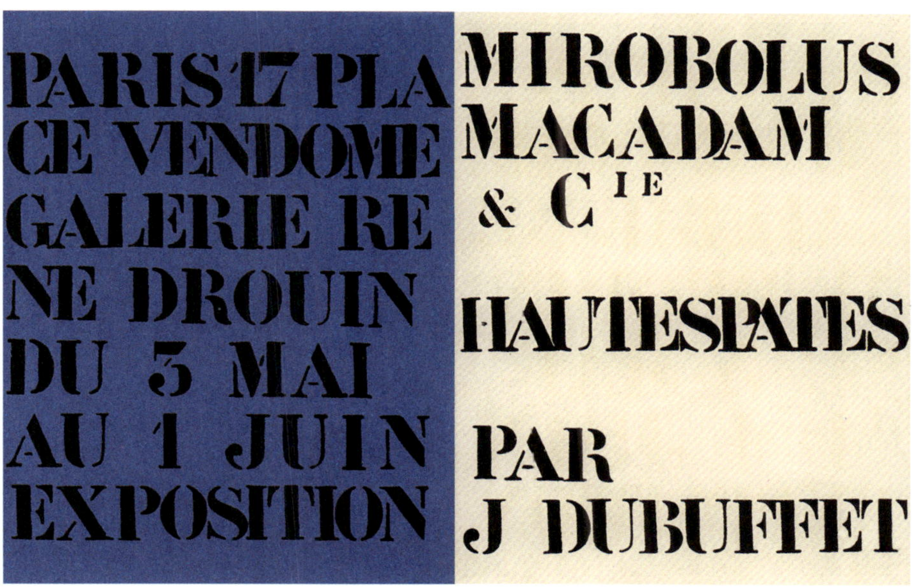

77. Interior spread of catalogue for Mirobolus, Macadam et Cie: Hautes pâtes par Jean Dubuffet exhibition, 1946

in these works was the literal fusion between the materials of the city and its inhabitants, who were crudely sketched, or, rather, scored, into the heavy textures of the paintings.

In Dubuffet's work, *Mirobolus, Macadam et Cie* immediately followed a series of ink drawings of May and June 1944 in which the artist scratched and manhandled the paper—drawings that were themselves fueled by his interest in graffiti, an interest that formed the core of the pivotal lithographic series *Les murs*. In the fifteen images of the series, he depicted figures standing before high walls inscribed with stick figures, anonymous messages, and scratches in a way that suggested an analogy between the depicted walls and the lithographic stones on which the prints had themselves been made (fig. 79). When the lithographs were first exhibited at Galerie André in April 1945, where they illustrated poems by Eugène Guillevic, they echoed a growing interest in graffiti in postwar cultural circles at large.[22] The photographer Brassaï had drawn attention to graffiti in the 1930s with his article "Du mur des cavernes au mur d'usine" (From the Walls of Caves to the Walls of the Factory) in the Surrealist journal *Minotaure*, illustrated with nine photographs taken during his walks around Paris.[23] One of those photographs later appeared on the cover of the poet

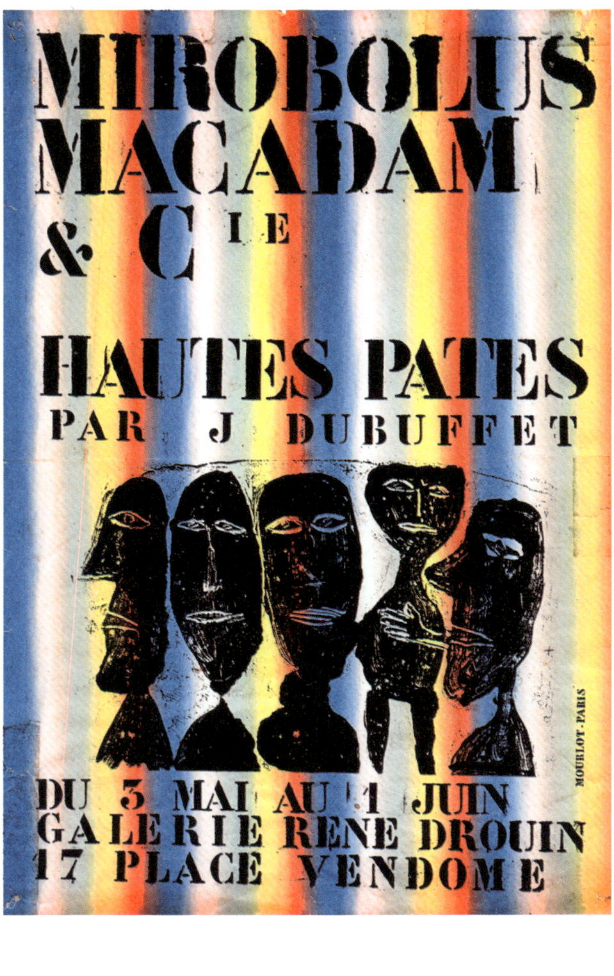

78. Poster for *Mirobolus, Macadam et Cie: Hautes pâtes par Jean Dubuffet* exhibition, 1946

Jacques Prévert's book Paroles, in January 1946, while Brassaï's own book Graffiti, collecting images he had produced over a period of almost thirty years (fig. 80), appeared only in 1961.[24] Dubuffet had acquired several of Brassaï's photographs in the immediate postwar period in the context of the research he was conducting on Art Brut.[25] Also in contact with Dubuffet during this period was the poet and art critic René de Solier, who published an essay entitled "Court traité des graffiti" (Brief Treatise on Graffiti) in April 1946 in the journal Les Cahiers de la Pléiade, published by Gallimard.[26] Almost thirty years later, remembering the walks Dubuffet and Paulhan had taken in the neighborhood of the rue Lhomond as they "hunted" for graffiti, Solier explained that "the common man was a sovereign pedestrian" and suggested that the two men's pursuit of graffiti was a search for basic, anonymous human expression *of* the street as much as *on* the street.[27]

While drawing visually and culturally on graffiti, on the one hand, and using materials in his paintings that can be found on the street or are employed in the building of streets, on the other, were two of the ways Dubuffet indicated his desire to anchor his work in the everyday and the public space of the city, the connection between these works and the city can also be read along different lines. One interpretation was suggested to me by a striking passage I found in Rosemary Wakeman's beautiful 2009 study of public space in postwar Paris, The Heroic City: Paris, 1946–1958. The author explains that in the days following the Liberation in August 1944, the Communist Party section of the 9th arrondissement of Paris had asked local residents to come forward with information on "anyone arrested, deported, or killed during the occupation or sacrificed in the Liberation of Paris so that they could be honored. . . . [Then,] the walls of buildings, sidewalks and trees in the neighborhoods where fighting had taken place were decorated with the names of the dead, inscribed on small pieces of wood along with written testimonials, photographs and flowers in a spontaneous display of public sorrow and witnessing."[28] Wakeman's description is strongly suggestive of a public space marked by figures of absence, people who have disappeared from the pavements of the city and are preserved in its memory, remembered through a picture or a name—a forerunner of the bouquets of flowers and spontaneous mementos that are often seen across Paris (and other cities) after a tragic event.

Whether Dubuffet came across such mementos himself is not known, but Wakeman's description is powerful enough that, for a moment, I can imagine that the artist's figures frozen in midaction, as

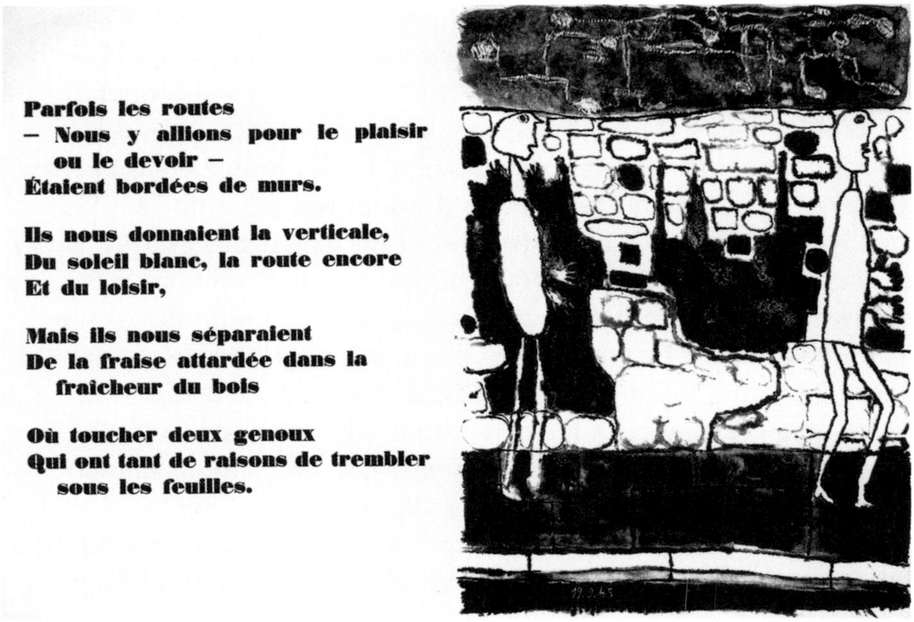

79. Interior spread of *Les murs* (1950), with poems by Eugène Guillevic and lithographs (1945) by Dubuffet

in *Discoureur fossile* (Fossil Babbler) of May 1945, or incised within the tar and rubble of the city, as in *Portrait cambouis* (Sludge Portrait) of December 1945, are endowed with a spectral quality. Something of this appears in a description Dubuffet gave of the latter work, in which he likened it to the image-bearing "cast-iron plates in fireplaces."[29] Although the artist was rarely one for pathos, the idea that the dead could be inscribed within a painting was not completely alien to him. In the spring of 1944, his correspondence with Jean Paulhan betrayed a rare moment of despondency following the news of the tragic death of his friend and mentor Max Jacob. "During these days, which were all filled with sadness, this death of Max and then this wall of ghosts that I saw emerge at the ceremony, old moving memories, and also penetrated by the surrounding sadness, in the first place your own, I worked melancholically on a small painting—no, not small, it is big—it is a view of Paris, a building with a balcony, and a street populated by a wan humanity (very haunted)."[30] The painting in question, *Vue de Paris, tout le monde aux fenêtres* (View of Paris, Everyone at the Windows) of April 1944, was later accidentally destroyed, but the black-and-white photograph of it that remains, showing stick figures painted in ghostly, translucent, light-colored paint, peering out from balconies, gives some idea of the work Dubuffet described as a "votive monument."[31]

Honoring the dead in the streets of Paris was one of the means by which Parisians reclaimed a public space that had been under the control of Occupation forces and the collaborationist Vichy regime for the greater part of the war. In *The Heroic City*, Wakeman describes the moments following the Liberation, with "people walking, marching, dancing, processing in an intense political theatre outside the

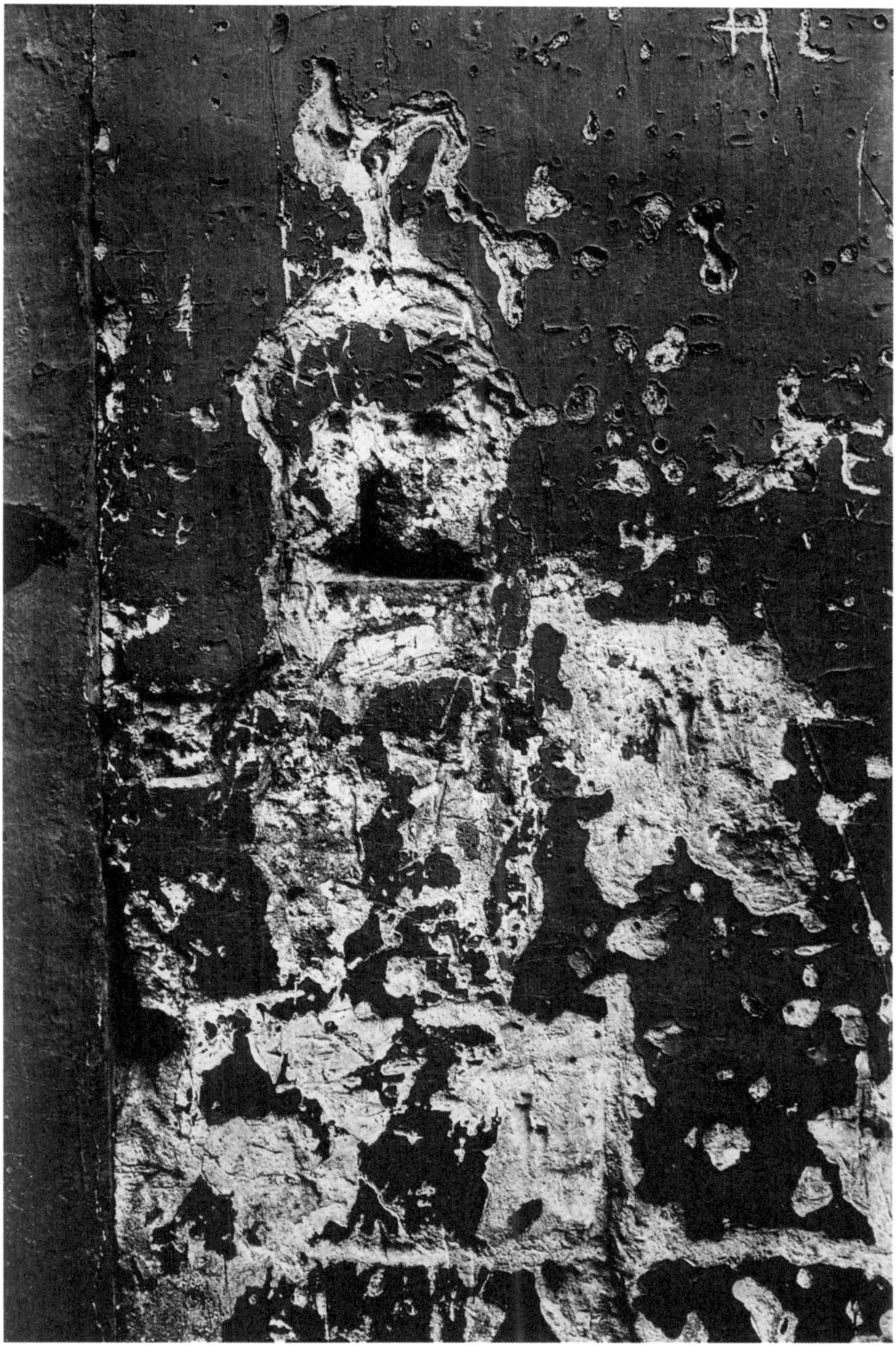

80. Brassaï. Untitled, from the series Graffiti, 1945–55

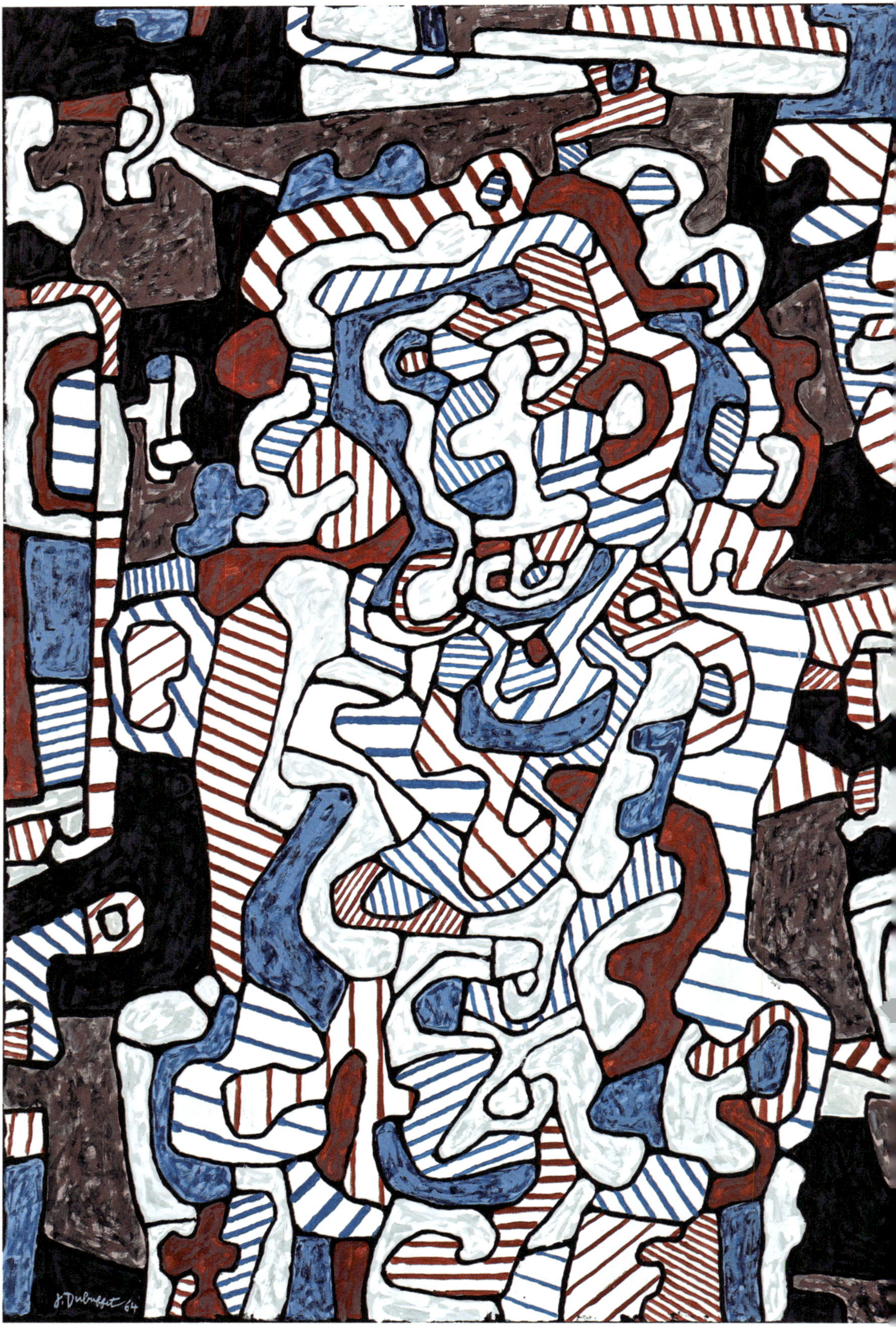

81. Jean Dubuffet. Époux en visite, December 12, 1964

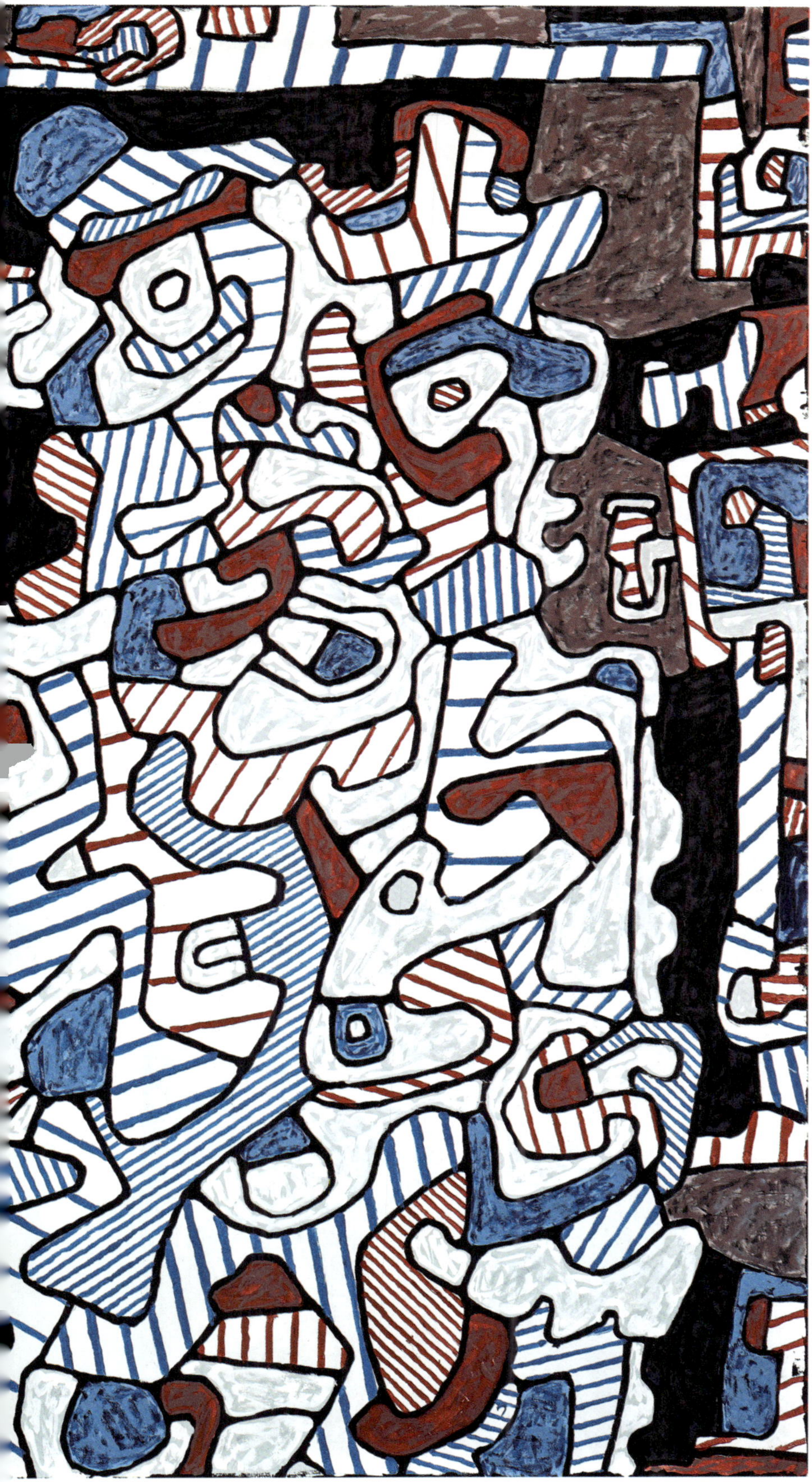

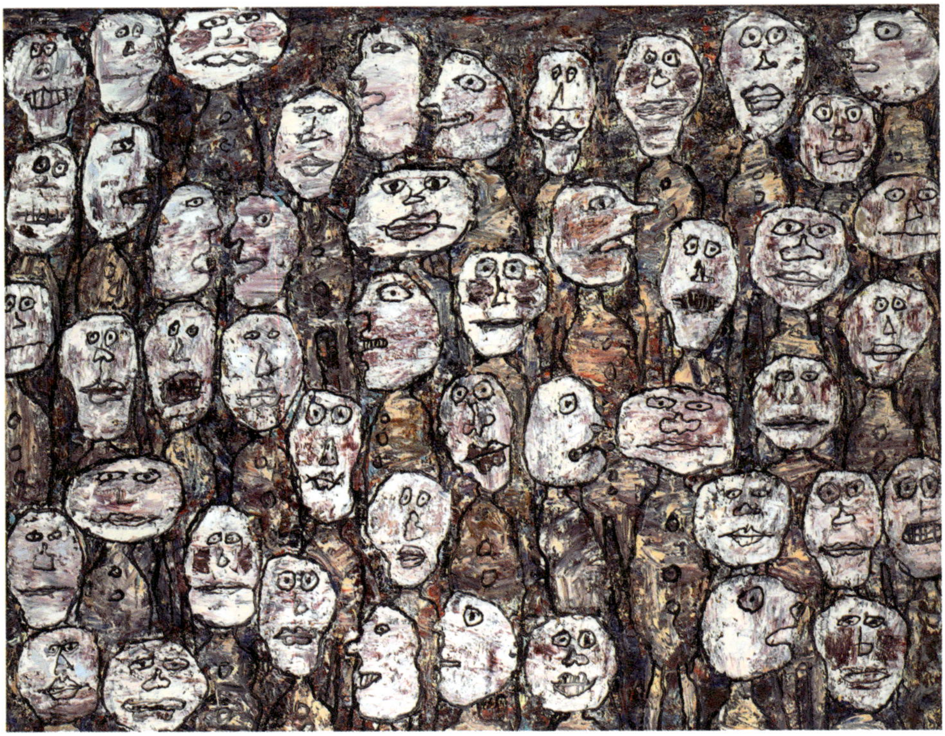

82. Jean Dubuffet. Affluence, March 22–23, 1961

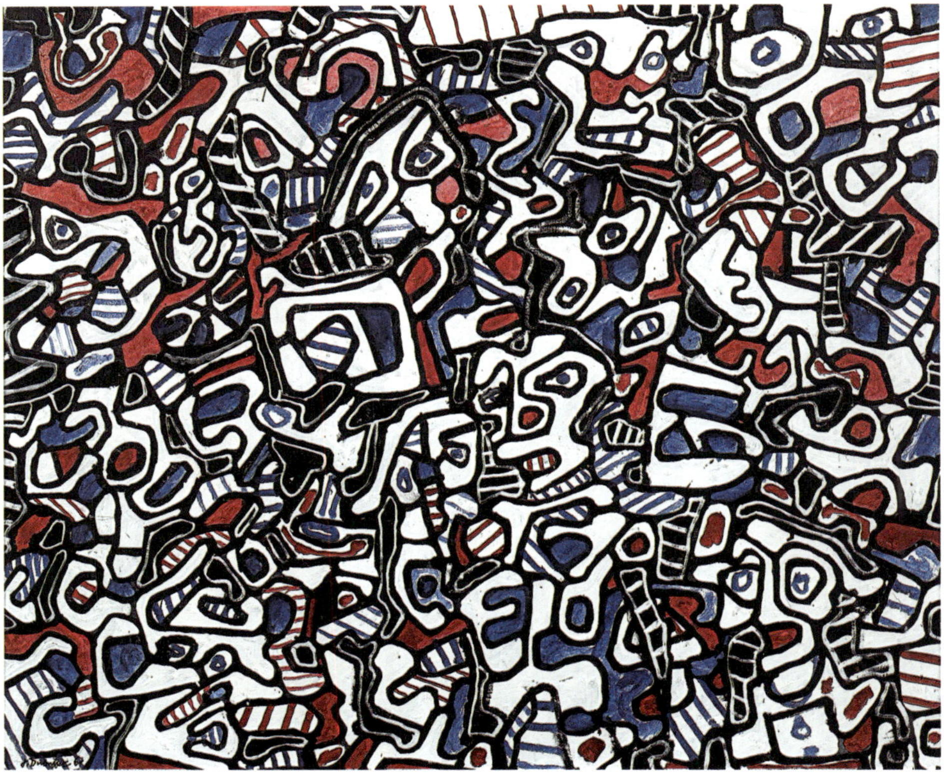

83. Jean Dubuffet. Affluence, January 16, 1967

official halls of power. Hundreds of thousands descended into the streets on a regular basis, evoking a multitude of traditional practices and topographies and creating new ones. Public ceremony and spectacle were ways of claiming civic life and citizenship—they were a political instrument."[32] A number of paintings in Dubuffet's Mirobolus series foreground bodily gestures, albeit frozen in thick paint: Danseurs (Dancers) and Le nœud au chapeau (The Bow on the Hat) of February 1946, Gambadeuse d'asphalte (Asphalt Saunterer; fig. 18), and Élégante aux escarpins (fig. 12) all suggest snapshots of people in a crowd in movement, dressed up and celebrating the city's liberation. Here, the nondescript browns and blacks and faded colors of the clothing serve as a reminder of the wearers' intimate connection with the street. Dubuffet made this connection explicit in "Saint-Ouen—le marché," a short text of 1944 about the famous flea market at the Porte de Clignancourt (translated in full on pp. 125–26): "Here they also sell clothes, which are the same as those worn by clients, the same colors of asphalt and dirty brown that man likes because they are the colors of man and of his hair, of his streets, of his walls and fences, and of his dirt."[33]

After Célébrations du sol, Assemblages, Texturologies, and other series throughout the 1950s in which the figure receded to a lesser role, the "man in the street" made a full-fledged reappearance in Dubuffet's work in the context of Paris Circus in 1961. But whereas Mirobolus had consisted mostly of large-scale, individual figures identified by a detail of clothing or a physical feature, in Paris Circus the individual was usually left aside in favor of the crowd. To some extent, this change reflected a reality discovered by Dubuffet when, after spending a little over five years living in Vence, in the South of France, he returned to Paris at the beginning of 1961. One difference must have been striking: only a third of the prewar population of the city had remained in Paris during World War II, but the population had bounced back after the Liberation and increased throughout the 1950s, thanks to the development of industry and services and the rural exodus they entailed. More than a million people arrived in Paris between 1945 and 1960.[34] Fittingly, street scenes in Paris Circus, such as Vire-volte (fig. 20), depict swarms of similar-looking pedestrians scurrying around the streets. The 1961 painting Affluence (fig. 82) exemplifies this shift: it looks as if the artist has taken a fragment of one of his street scenes and placed it under a magnifying glass. In the resulting composition, which seems to extend beyond the limits of the canvas, a subdued, dove-gray background is lightened up by a multitude of roundish, ashen faces displaying a disparate array of expressions, ranging from surprise to withdrawal, while the corresponding bodies disappear into the molten grays of the asphalt. Six years later, within the context of the Hourloupe cycle begun in 1962, Dubuffet painted a second picture with the same title. This Affluence (fig. 83) has, at first glance, little to do with its homonym. Its surface is covered with intricate shapes like puzzle pieces in blue, red, and white, with darker blue and black highlights. Only a prolonged and attentive look reveals countless distraught faces, squashed and squeezing through the crowd. Their expressions are less subdued than in the 1961 painting, more powerful and anguished, despite the narrowing of palette and the simplification of forms.

Would it be possible to read the Hourloupe cycle as foregrounding some kind of turn toward a more social and less formal

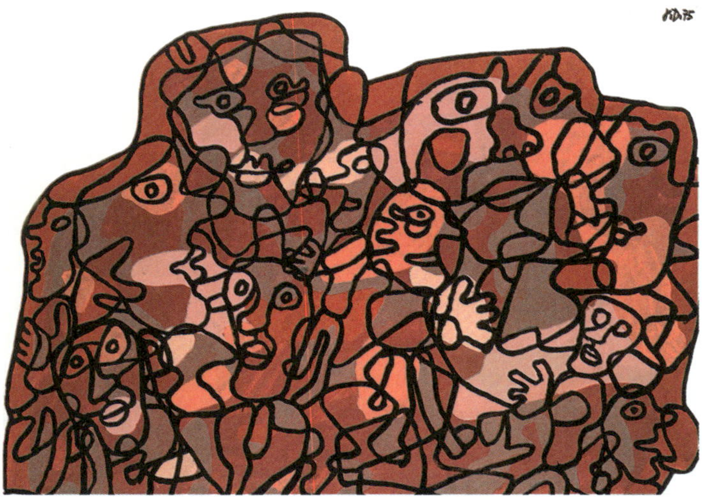

84. Jean Dubuffet. Mondanité XVIII, March 13, 1975

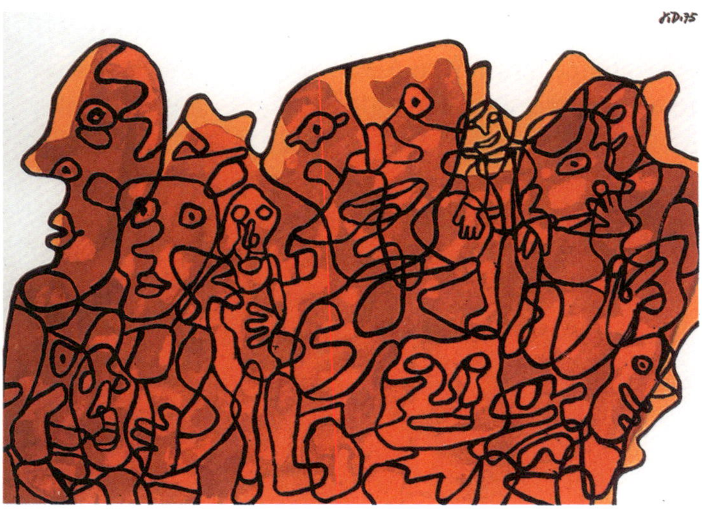

85. Jean Dubuffet. Mondanité XXII, March 19, 1975

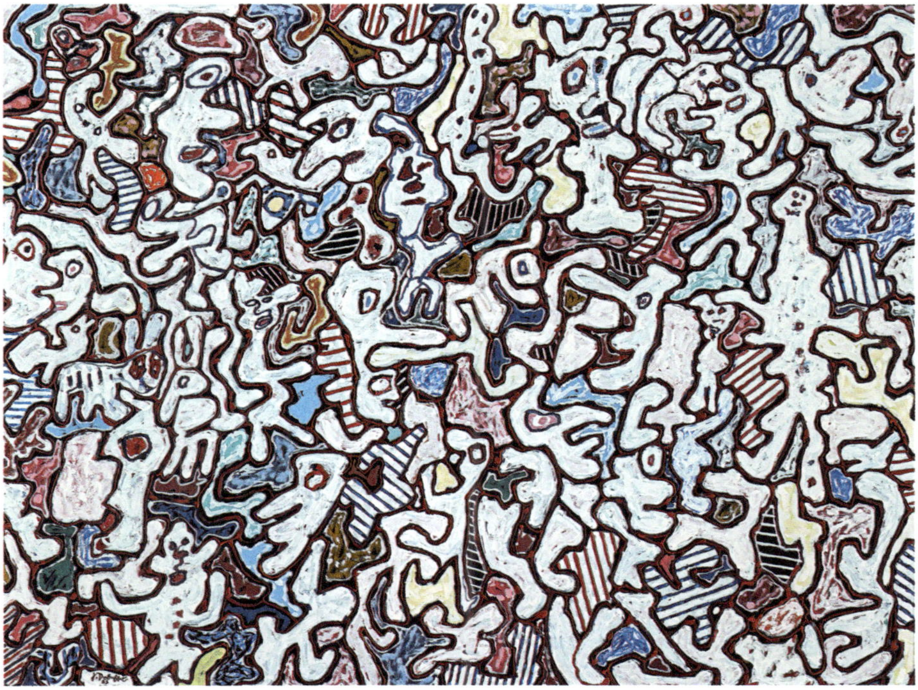

86. Jean Dubuffet. *Vertu virtuelle*, June 25, 1963

understanding of the figure in the city? The drawings in the 1963 booklet *L'Hourloupe*, mentioned earlier, would support this claim. But I am also thinking of another depiction of a crowd painted in the same year, *Être et paraître* (To Be and to Seem; fig. 55), in which outlines of figures can barely be made out as they disappear and reappear within the confines of the canvas. The title can be read in multiple ways: in relation to the deliberate ambiguity between tangibility and illusion that characterizes *L'Hourloupe* as a whole, with its optical games and elusively recognizable figures, and in reference to the way people act in society, concealing their true selves behind composed attitudes. Two paintings from the beginning of the *Hourloupe* series, each depicting two figures side by side—*Main leste et rescousse* (Nimble Free Hand to the Rescue) and *Époux en visite* (Spouses on a Visit), both of 1964 (figs. 58, 81)—similarly evoke an ambivalence of posture and action and a social game of appearances in which background and figure merge almost completely. No longer working with tar and asphalt but with a restricted palette of primary colors, Dubuffet inscribed his figures in the social texture of the city at the same time as he wrote them into the visual composition of his paintings.

Archetypes and Men in Suits

Next to the phrases *homme du commun* and *homme de la rue*, another recurring linguistic penchant that points to a generic idea of human beings in Dubuffet's texts and paintings is the word "archetype." I have avoided it until now because, contrary to the other two, which leave greater room for interpretation, "archetype" is less ambiguous, or, rather, it is ambiguous in a different way, to consider which it is necessary once again to walk several paths through Dubuffet's oeuvre. The dictionary defines archetype as a "prototype" or "typical specimen," and this is the meaning Dubuffet seemed to be acknowledging when he painted, in 1945, the work entitled Archétypes (fig. 87). In the explanatory notes published in the catalogue of the exhibition Mirobolus, Macadam et Cie, he described the painting as "a couple of people, bodies in frontal view, heads in profile, traced in the manner of graffiti by a cursive incision."[35] Unusually for one of his *haute pâtes*, Archétypes depicts not one but two figures, a naked, rather wrinkled man and woman who cannot fail to evoke the discovery of mortality that befell those original prototypes, Adam and Eve, whom Lucas Cranach depicted in their beautiful fragility in the mid-sixteenth century (fig. 88). Indeed, it is possible to read Archétypes as an expression of universal humanism: writing to Paulhan several months before painting it, Dubuffet had explained, "My system rests indeed on the identical character of all men." He repeated the argument in another letter: "There is in man—all man (cf. my system)."[36] Such a postulate inevitably recalls the words of the architect Le Corbusier, who, in 1925, in L'art décoratif d'aujourd'hui (The Decorative Art of Today), argued that human needs "are few; they are identical among men, men being all made in the same mold since the most distant times that we know."[37] Of course, World War II separated Le Corbusier's claim, usually understood from the perspective of a universalism born out of the Enlightenment, from Dubuffet's postwar statements. When it was presented at the Museum of Modern Art, New York, in the exhibition New Images of Man (1959), Archétypes seemed a reminder of the frailty of human existence, a return to a degree zero of humanity.[38] And yet, Le Corbusier must have recognized something familiar in Dubuffet's archetypal figures when he acquired, in 1943, the year of its creation, Dubuffet's painting Danseuse de corde (the story is that Le Corbusier thereby became the artist's first collector, having been given the painting by a Dubuffet who was then reluctant to sell his work—another proof, if needed, of the latter's desire to cling to an idea of himself as an *homme du commun* and amateur artist). Danseuse de corde (Rope Dancer) belongs stylistically to the same group of works as Gardes du corps (1943)—a couple of mustachioed male nudes that somewhat anticipate Archétypes—and all these works were contemporary with the elaboration of Le Corbusier's Modulor, an anthropometric measuring system designed to place a standardized human proportion at the center of architecture (fig. 89).[39] But Dubuffet's unsightly couple seems more concerned with waving goodbye to the Garden of Eden than with incarnating an ideal human measure. Baptiste Brun, drawing on Dubuffet's known acquaintance with the philosopher Gaston Bachelard, who introduced the Jungian notion of the "archetype" to French readers in the 1940s, sees Archétypes, the first painting of Mirobolus, Macadam et Cie, as a programmatic picture, something of a manifesto, in which Dubuffet jointly affirmed his desire to let the material of the work "speak for itself" and his intention to offer a provocative reinvention of the representation of the human figure.[40]

"The word archetype evokes for me something like a schematic generic prototype from which all individual particularity is omitted. It should be observed that the very first painting in my series 'Mirobolus, Macadam et Cie,' made in 1945, is titled 'Archétypes.' Depersonalization is certainly a constant feature of all my characters. Not only of my characters but also of all the objects I depict."[41] This is Dubuffet writing in 1963, a few months after initiating L'Hourloupe. There is an undoubted consistency in the artist's idea of the archetype. The formulation echoes words he had written in 1944: "I like to paint general facts. if I paint a sunken path, I want it to be an archetype of a sunken path . . . and if I paint the effigy of a man it seems to me sufficient that my painting evoke indeed a human face but without accidental particularities, which are so vain."[42] And yet, a decade or so later, at the end of L'Hourloupe, new details began to appear in Dubuffet's figures that contradicted this generic nature praised by the artist: business suits, waistcoats, and ties are clearly identifiable in the small drawings of Crayonnages, in Lieux abrégés, in many figures of Théâtres de mémoire—as exemplifed, for instance, in Avantage aux cravates (fig. 90)—and in the various Sites that followed in the late 1970s and early 1980s (figs. 140, 141, 154, 155). What could account for this sudden, widely generalized presence of the man in a suit in Dubuffet's work? I write "widely generalized" because, in the 1940s, the suit clearly demarcated the *monsieur* from both the military man and the newsboy, and Dubuffet, citing in the 1947 text "Causette" (Chat) a tunic gifted to him by his artist friend Gaston Chaissac, expressed with a certain glee an interest in blue-

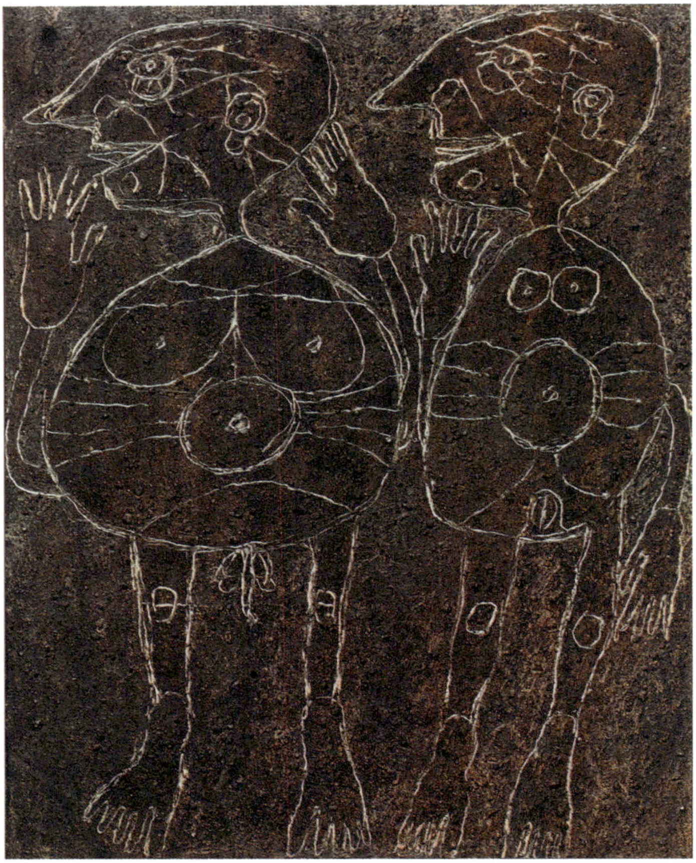

87. Jean Dubuffet. Archétypes, May 1945

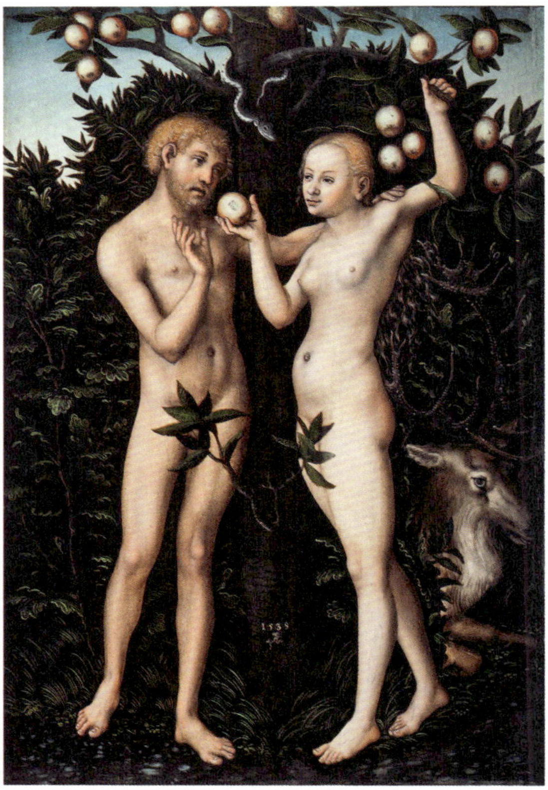

88. Lucas Cranach the Elder. Adam and Eve, 1538

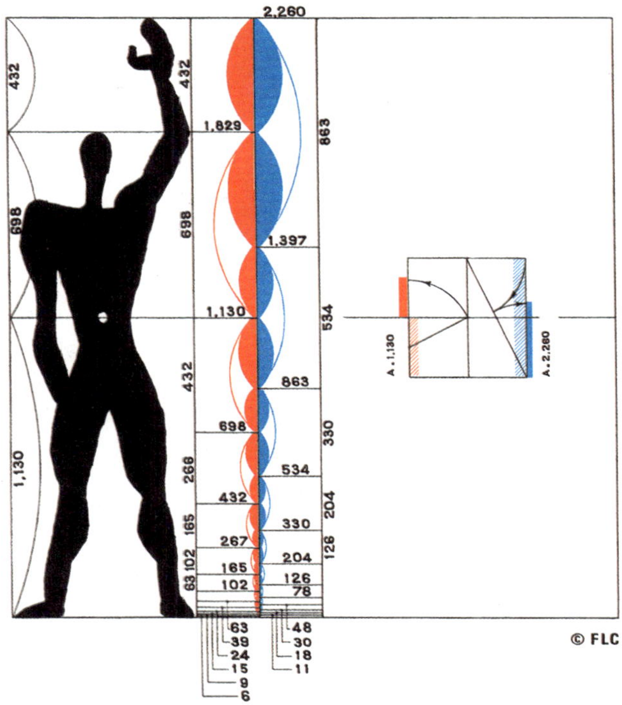

© FLC

89. Le Corbusier. Le Modulor, 1946

collar clothing that led him to haunt the working-class neighborhoods in Aubervilliers and Billancourt, looking for clothes to purchase.[43]

From the 1950s to the 1970s, as France's population moved from country to city and the tertiary sector and new industries expanded, modernization affected society in many ways. One of the "archetypal" figures of this revolution in the workforce was the *cadre*, a category born in the mid-1930s in the context of the ideological strengthening of the idea of the middle class, in opposition to the proletariat. *Cadre*, an untranslatable French term, was used to "describe men whose place in a company couldn't be precisely defined," as Kristin Ross succinctly puts it in her book on the modernization of French culture in the 1950s and 1960s.[44] While the number of *cadres* grew throughout the postwar era, the term came to stand for much more than a position in a company or a salary bracket. It embodied a particular social group and even a way of life and pattern of consumption, which were targeted as such by advertising (for example, the well-known French chain of stores FNAC, an acronym for Fédération nationale d'achat des cadres, was created especially for this category).[45] The *cadre* also epitomized a new kind of rootless capitalism. In his 1982 study of *cadres*, the

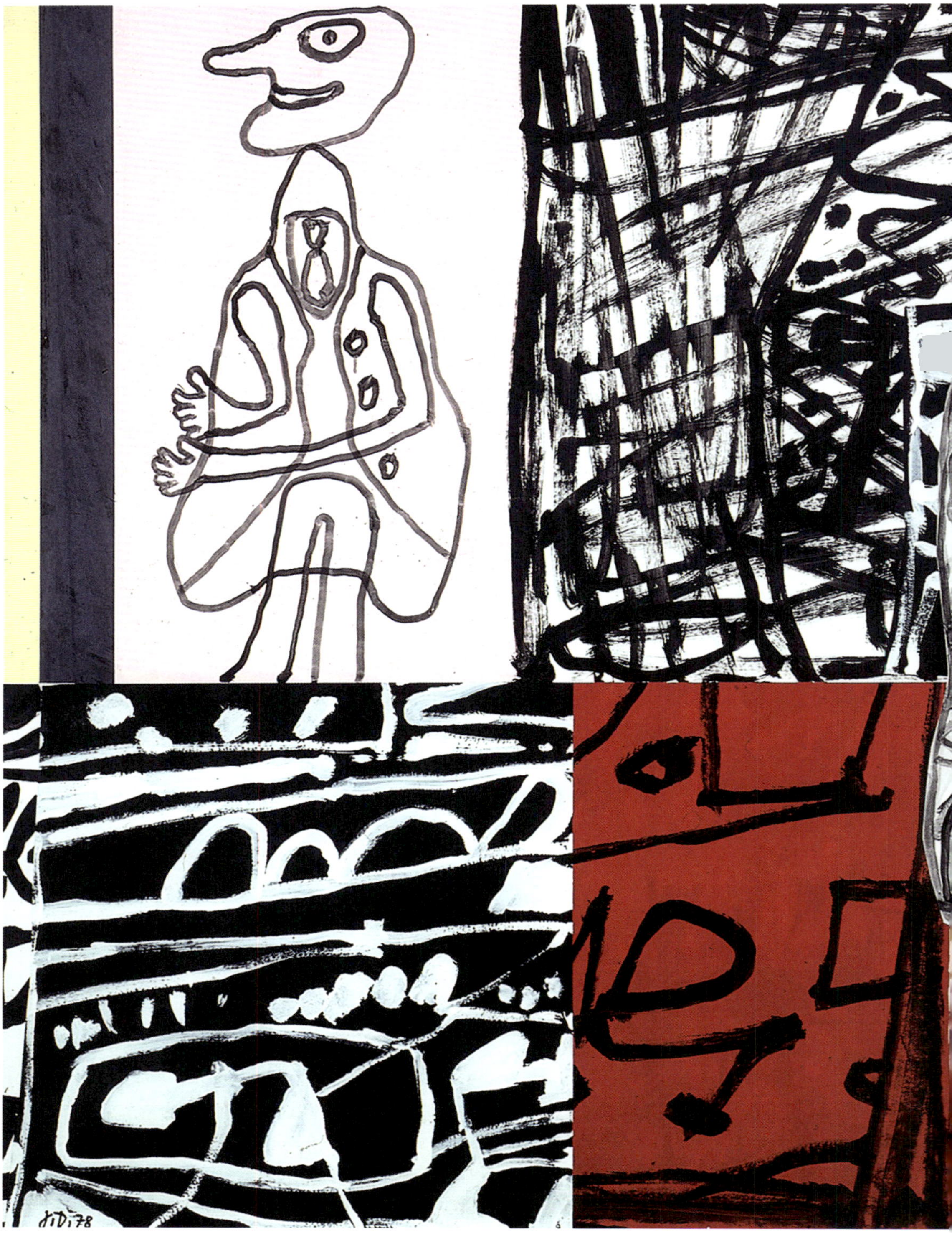

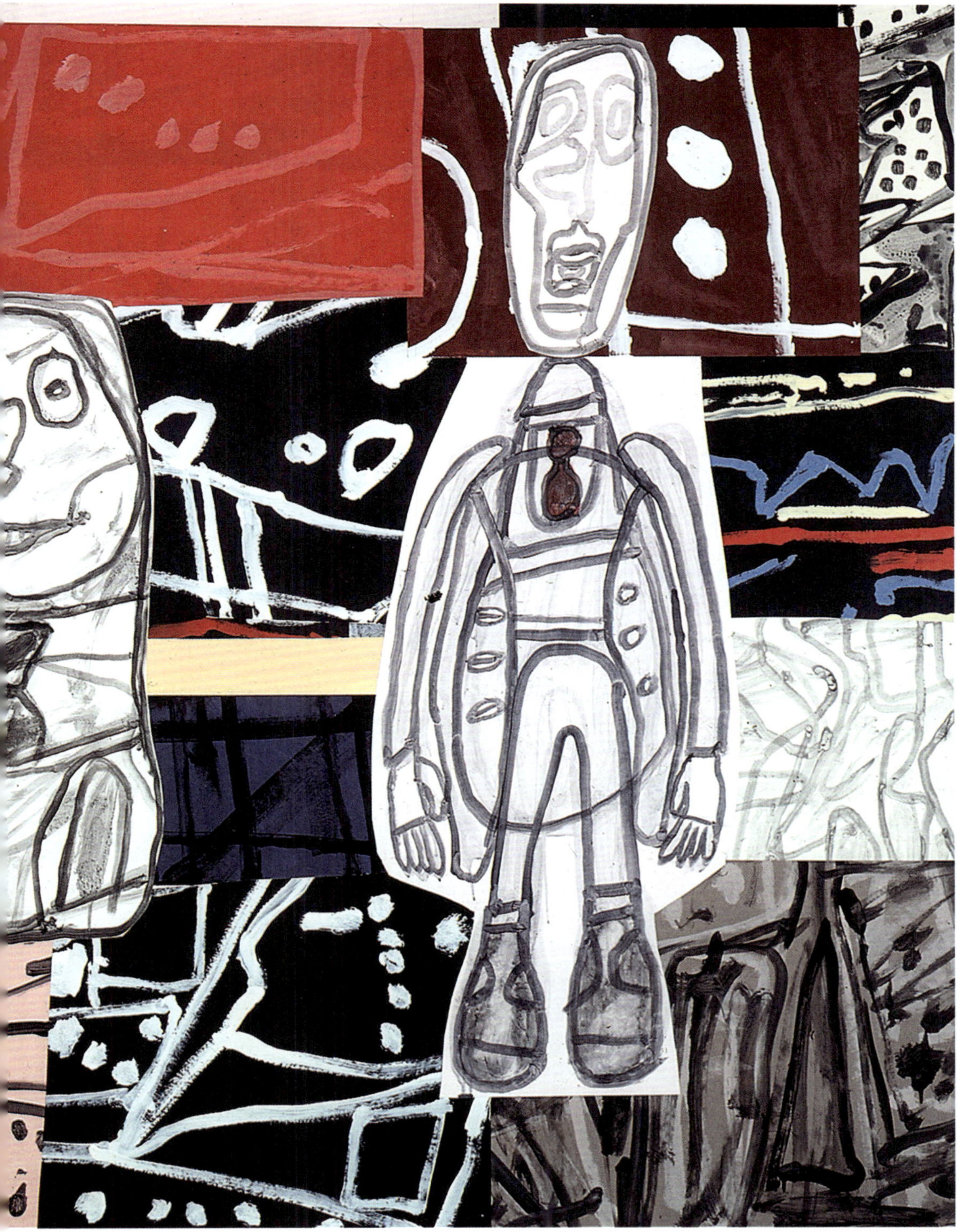

90. Jean Dubuffet. Avantage aux cravates, March 8, 1978

sociologist Luc Boltanski explained that these employees, a key category in large, multinational companies that were importing new management ideas from the United States, reflected the globalization of the economy.[46] *Cadres* were different from civil servants and from workers in small or family companies. Although the name suggests a certain power and certain responsibilities (*cadre* can be translated literally as "frame"), as Boltanski pointed out in his analysis of the testimony that introduces the book, the *cadre* does not correspond to a clear cultural or social group with an established identity (beyond the shallow stereotype circulated by advertising). Through the analyses of Boltanski and Ross and their use of key ideas of modernization, rootlessness, and Americanization, the *cadre* suggests similarities with certain features of modern architecture and urbanism that sprouted in the new business neighborhoods that were developed in France from the 1960s onward: the tower, the slab, and the concrete deck. One emblem of this convergence is the ubiquitous image of businessmen walking across empty esplanades dotted by skyscrapers, such as the one reproduced on the cover of Boltanski's book (fig. 92). Could it be that Dubuffet's archetype became, in the 1970s, the man in a suit, the *cadre* walking around a public garden on a lunch break or across one of those concrete esplanades, as in Promenade au jardin (Walk in the Garden; fig. 99) or Esplanade aux passants (fig. 60), both of 1975?

But Dubuffet did not always need to depict businessmen in three-piece suits to evoke the idea of a cold and impersonal modernity. In Le citadin (see p. 4), a monumental effigy of a city dweller with an inscrutable expression, lost in a topography that seems to make little sense, he achieved it by means of technique. The work resulted from the projection of a small drawing by Dubuffet onto a canvas, where, having been enlarged in the process, it was painted by assistants. One of a small series called Peintures projetées, which the artist designed in the context of the series Paysages castillans et sites tricolores (Castilian Landscapes and Three-Color Sites), it suggests the idea of a technocrat who projects the small plans he has produced in the confines of his office onto the world at a large scale. Dubuffet may have been inspired to work in such a way, distinguishing design from production, by his collaboration with the automobile manufacturer Renault, for which, in the early 1970s, he produced a series of wall pieces and began a monumental outdoor commission that was eventually canceled, leading to a bitter legal conflict.[47]

And yet, this greater distance from the work, this abstraction of the artist's touch, also points to the conceptual nature of the notion of the archetype. A couple of years earlier, Dubuffet had written to the poet Jacques Berne: "The common man does not exist if not as ideational archetype. And ideational is not saying enough,

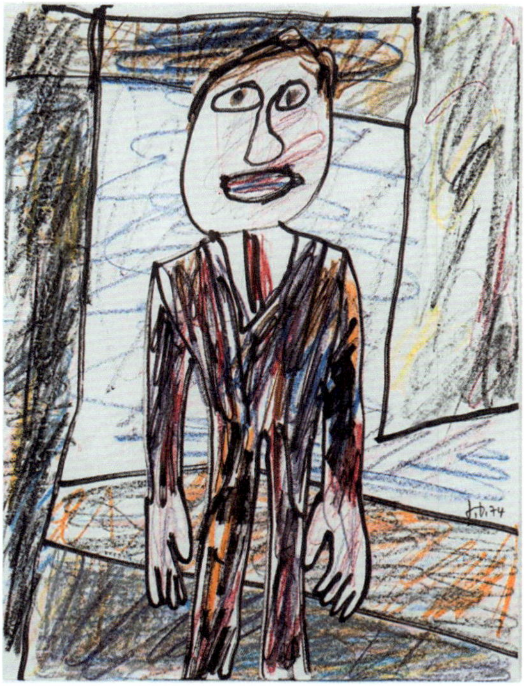

91. Jean Dubuffet. Promeneur en ville, 1974

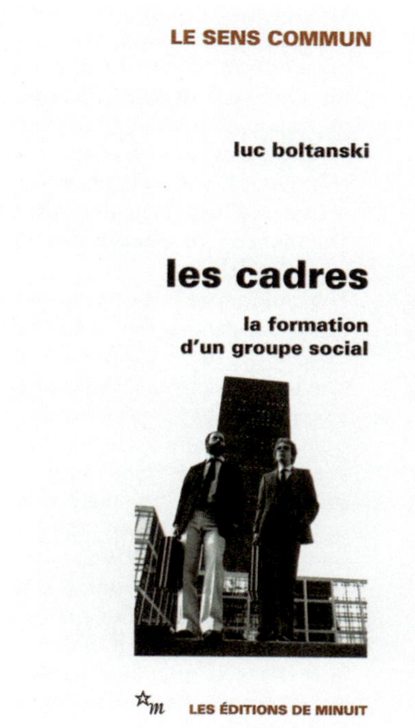

92. Cover of Luc Boltanski's Les cadres (1982)

better to say utopian. It is probably impossible. . . . For the idea implied by the common man is that of a man who would not be, at any level, conditioned."[48] Looking back at his early dream of a common man who would not be conditioned by culture, Dubuffet now acknowledged its impossibility in the real world but granted it an existence within the realm of ideas, in which the *homme du commun* existed as a stand-in for the artist and a facilitator for the viewer to gain access to the conceptual world of the painting, perhaps even more than it existed as a character in the picture itself.

Epigraph: Jean Dubuffet, "Avant-projet pour une conférence populaire sur la peinture" (January 1945), PES, vol. 1 (1967), 50. "I would much rather that my paintings be found amusing and interesting by the man in the street when he comes out of work, not the obsessed, the initiated, but the man who has no particular education or disposition. It is the man in the street I am after, whom I feel closest to, with whom I want to make friends and enter into confidence and connivance, and he is the one I want to please and enchant by means of my work." Translated into English in Peter Selz, The Work of Jean Dubuffet (New York: The Museum of Modern Art, 1962), 10.

1 The majority of Dubuffet's portraits of Lili are dated 1935–36, and they are all reproduced in the revised edition of CTJD, vol. 1, Marionnettes de la ville et de la campagne, 1917–1945 (Paris: Minuit, 1993). His portraits of literary figures were first shown in the exhibition Portraits à ressemblance extraite, à ressemblance cuite et confite dans la mémoire, à ressemblance éclatée dans la mémoire de M. Jean Dubuffet, Galerie René Drouin, Paris, October 7–31, 1947.

2 Jean Dubuffet, Bâtons rompus, PES, vol. 3 (1995), 142.

3 Dubuffet to Jean Paulhan, April 13 [1944], in Jean Dubuffet and Jean Paulhan, Correspondance 1944–1968, ed. Julien Dieudonné and Marianne Jakobi (Paris: Gallimard, 2003), 77. Baptiste Brun, in his doctoral dissertation, extensively researched the archeology of the phrase "common man" in relation to Dubuffet, and I am indebted to that research in my discussion of its occurrences in and around the artist's writings of the 1940s. Baptiste Brun, "De l'homme du commun à l'art brut: 'Mise au pire' du primitivisme dans l'œuvre de Jean Dubuffet; Jean Dubuffet et le paradigme primitiviste dans l'immédiat après-guerre, 1944–1951," PhD diss., Université Paris Ouest Nanterre, 2013, 134. My translation.

4 Paulhan was the editor of La Nouvelle Revue française from 1924 to 1940 and from 1953 to 1968.

5 Brun, "De l'homme du commun à l'art brut," 13.

6 La Samaritaine was a large department store located near the Pont Neuf in Paris from 1869 to 2005.

7 Selz, Work of Jean Dubuffet, 11.

8 Pierre Seghers, L'homme du commun ou Jean Dubuffet (Paris: Poésie 44, 1944).

9 Ibid., 13.

10 Ibid., 24

11 Ibid., 28–29.

12 The denomination "Marionnettes de la ville et de la campagne" first appeared as the title of the first volume of the artist's catalogue raisonné (CTJD), published by Jean-Jacques Pauvert in 1966.

13 Daniel Abadie, "Réflexion aux couleurs de Jean Dubuffet," in Hubert Damisch, ed., Jean Dubuffet (Paris: Jeu de Paume, Conférences et Colloques, 1992), 50. The *jeunes peintres* moniker comes from the exhibition Vingt jeunes peintres de tradition française, which took place at Galerie Braun, Paris, in May 1941. The participating artists included Jean René Bazaine, Alfred Manessier, Charles Lapicque, and Édouard Pignon. For an analysis of the exhibition, see Laurence Bertrand Dorléac, L'art de la défaite, 1940–1944 (Paris: Seuil, 1993).

14 Hubert Damisch, "Dubuffet, Jean, 1901–1985," in Encyclopedia Universalis (Paris: Encyclopedia Universalis, 1971), vol. 5, 828–30. Translated into English by Nicholas Huckle in Hubert Damisch and Jean Dubuffet, "Writings and Correspondence, 1961–1985," October, no. 154 (Fall 2015), 51.

15 Robert Goldwater, "Dubuffet's Diablerie," View 7, no. 3 (1947), 47–49. See also other examples of reactions by American critics in Sophie Berrebi, The Insider as Outsider: Dubuffet and the United States, 1945–1962, PhD diss., Courtauld Institute of Art, 2003, 14–15.

16 Jean Dubuffet, Prospectus aux amateurs de tous genres (Paris: Gallimard, 1946).

17 Dubuffet, "Avant-projet pour une conférence populaire sur la peinture," 52.

18 Dubuffet to Jean Paulhan, [July 1944], in Dubuffet and Paulhan, Correspondance 1944–1968, 118.

19 Mirobolus, Macadam et Cie: Hautes pâtes par J Dubuffet, Galerie René Drouin, Paris, May 3–June 1, 1945. Part of the name of many French businesses, "et Cie" is an abbreviation for *et Compagnie* (and Company).

20 Dubuffet to Joë Bousquet, "Monday evening Pentecost" [June 1946], reprinted in Daniel Abadie, ed., Dubuffet, exh. cat. (Paris: Éditions du Centre Pompidou, 2001), 363.

21 This text was originally published under the title "Réhabilitation de la boue" in the catalogue of the Galerie René Drouin exhibition. Reprinted in PES, vol. 2 (1967), 63–66.

22 Exposition de lithographies de Jean Dubuffet, Galerie André, Paris, April 14–30, 1945. The exhibition presented the series of lithographs entitled Matière et mémoire, which were accompanied by a text by Francis Ponge and published concurrently as an album, and the lithographs of Les murs, made at the invitation of Guillevic, who had written several poems on the theme. Guillevic's poems and Dubuffet's fourteen lithographs were also published as an album, in 1950, by Éditions du Livre, printed by Mourlot. Baptiste Brun gives a good overview of this interest in graffiti in postwar Paris; see Brun, "De l'homme du commun à l'art brut," 166–78. See also Karolina Ziebinska-Lewandowska, Brassaï: Graffiti, le langage des murs, exh. cat. (Paris: Éditions du Centre Pompidou/Xavier Barral, 2016).

23 Brassaï, "Du mur des cavernes aux mur d'usine," Minotaure, no. 3–4 (1933), 6–7. Both the text and the photographs are by Brassaï.

24 Brassaï, Graffiti (Paris: Éditions du Temps, 1961).

25 Fourteen photographs of graffiti by Brassaï have been identified in the archives of the Musée de l'art brut, Lausanne, probably purchased directly from Brassaï by Dubuffet around 1945–47. See Brun, "De l'homme du commun à l'art brut," 172–74.

26 I am particularly grateful to Baptiste Brun for pointing out this astonishing publication in his dissertation: René de Solier, "Court traité des graffiti" [extracts], Les Cahiers de la Pléiade, no. 1 (April 1946), 52–65. The essay was a fragment of a book that was never published in its entirety. Dubuffet discussed his relationship with Solier in "Biographie au pas de course," PES, vol. 4 (1995), 487–88.

27 René de Solier, "Au temps des graffiti, et ensuite," in Jacques Berne, ed., Dubuffet (Paris: L'Herne, 1973), 274.

28 Rosemary Wakeman, The Heroic City: Paris, 1946–1958 (Chicago: University of Chicago Press, 2009), 100.

29 Jean Dubuffet, "Indications descriptives," PES, vol. 2 (1967), 424.

30 Dubuffet to Jean Paulhan, [March 25, 1944], in Dubuffet and Paulhan, Correspondance 1944–1968, 60. The word *mélancoliquement* (melancholically) was added in handwriting to the otherwise typed letter.

31 Ibid., 61.

32 Wakeman, Heroic City, 14.

33 Jean Dubuffet, "Saint Ouen—le marché" (1944), PES, vol. 1 (1967), 109.

34 Wakeman, Heroic City, 22.

35 Jean Dubuffet, "Indications descriptives," PES, vol. 2 (1967), 423.

36 Dubuffet to Jean Paulhan, 1944, PES, vol. 2 (1967), 227, and Dubuffet to Paulhan, [April 7, 1944], in Dubuffet and Paulhan, Correspondance 1944–1968, 71.

37 Le Corbusier (Charles-Édouard Jeanneret), The Decorative Art of Today, trans. James Dunnett (Cambridge, MA: MIT Press, 1987).

38 See Peter Selz, New Images of Man (New York: The Museum of Modern Art, 1959).

39 Kent Minturn shows Dubuffet's Danseuse de corde side by side with a plan of Le Corbusier's Modulor of 1946, arguing, somewhat sketchily, that Dubuffet's Archétypes "nullif[ies] Le Corbusier's 'gold standard' of proportion and undermine[s] the notion of the human figure as an ideal for universally recognized sign." Kent Mitchell Minturn, "Physiognomic Illegibility: Jean Dubuffet's Postwar Portraits," in Jean Dubuffet: Anticultural Positions, exh. cat. (New York: Acquavella, 2016), 8.

40 Baptiste Brun mentions the contemporaneity of Dubuffet's interest in archetype with that of some of the New York School artists, such as Barnett Newman, Jackson Pollock, and Adolph Gottlieb, all avid readers of the psychoanalyst Carl Jung. See Brun, "De l'homme du commun à l'art brut," 110–11. For Dubuffet's encounters with Gaston Bachelard and his reading of Bachelard's publications, see pp. 102–21.

41 Dubuffet to Max Loreau, June 1963, PES, vol. 2 (1967), 374.

42 Jean Dubuffet, "Notes pour les fins lettrés" (1945), PES, vol. 1 (1967), 74.

43 "Causette" was originally published in the catalogue for the exhibition Portraits à ressemblance extraite, à ressemblance cuite et confite dans la mémoire, à ressemblance éclatée dans la mémoire de M. Jean Dubuffet, peintre, Galerie René Drouin, Paris, October 7–31, 1947. Reprinted in PES, vol. 2 (1967), 67–73. On Dubuffet's interest in clothing and costume, see Sophie Berrebi, "L'épingle à nourrice: Dubuffet, image, habit," in Anne Lacoste, Sam Stourzé, and Sophie Webel, eds., Jean Dubuffet: L'outil photographique (Arles: Photosynthèse, 2017), 243–51.

44 Kristin Ross, Fast Cars, Clean Bodies: Decolonization and the Reordering of French Culture (Cambridge, MA: MIT Press, 1995), 167.

45 See Jean Dubois, Les cadres dans la société de consommation (Paris: Cerf, 1969).

46 Luc Boltanski, Les cadres (Paris: Minuit, 1982), 63–65.

47 On the technique of the Peintures projetées, see, in particular, Anne Lacoste and Sophie Webel, "Jean Dubuffet: L'outil photographique," in Lacoste, Stourzé, and Webel, Jean Dubuffet: L'outil photographique, 35. On Dubuffet's work with Renault, see Daniel Abadie, Dubuffet as Architect, trans. Elaine Briggs, exh. cat. (Paris: Hazan, 2011), 150–77, and Didier Semin, "From Hourloupe to Castille: Dubuffet at Renault," in Ann Hindry, ed., Renault and Art: A Modern Adventure (Paris: Hazan, 1999), 71–105.

48 Dubuffet to Jacques Berne, February 3, 1972, in Jean Dubuffet, Lettres à JB (Paris: Hermann, 1991), 249.

That year, Dubuffet also began to sculpt with blocks of expanded polystyrene. Using tools made expressly for the purpose from hot wires, he shaped objects, "utensils," mile markers, tables, and, finally, in 1967–69, a series of monuments and architectural projects.

While some critics decried Dubuffet's use of plastic-looking polyester resin and epoxy, those materials nonetheless corresponded to the increased artificiality of the modern city acknowledged by historians of urbanism.

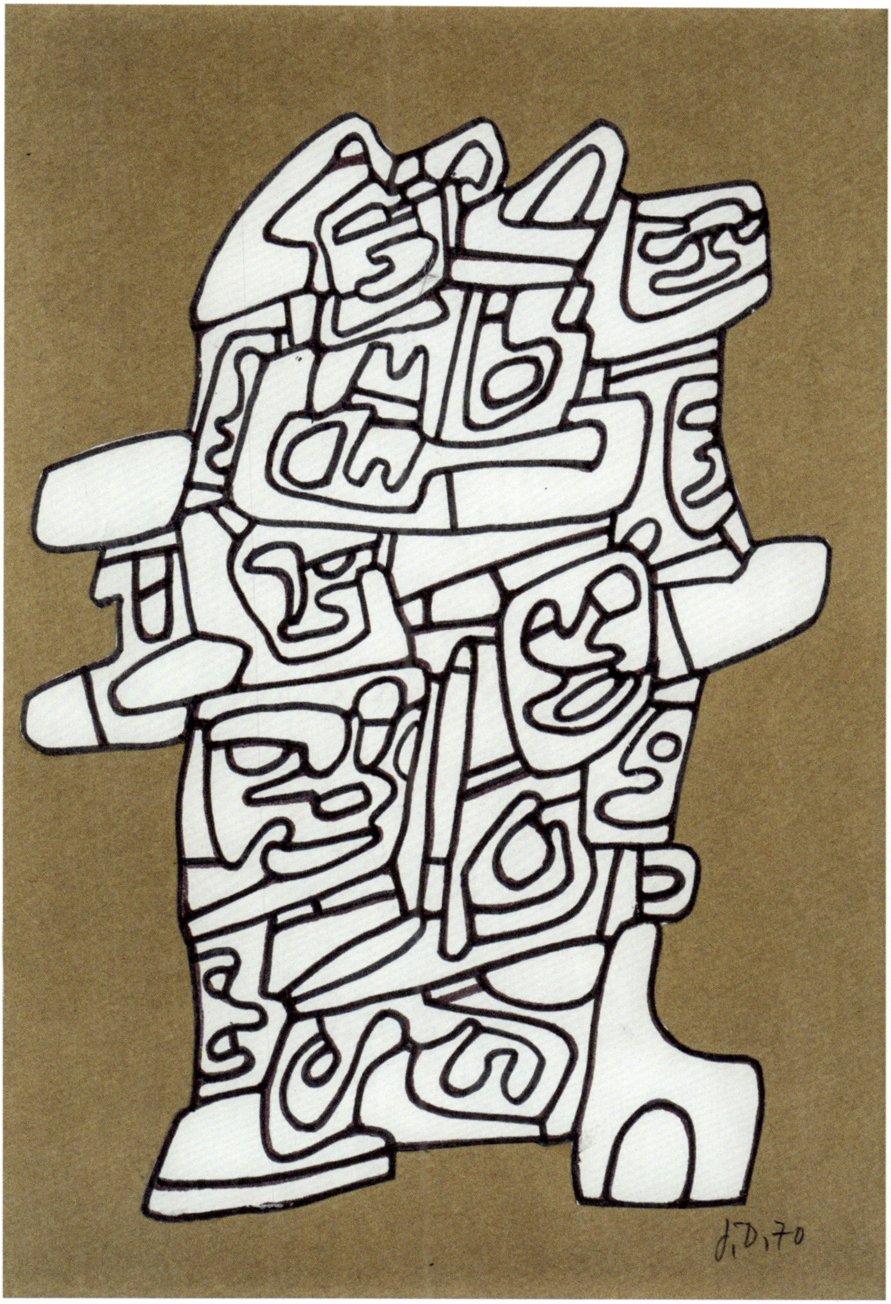

93. Jean Dubuffet. Dessin pour un monument, July 28, 1970

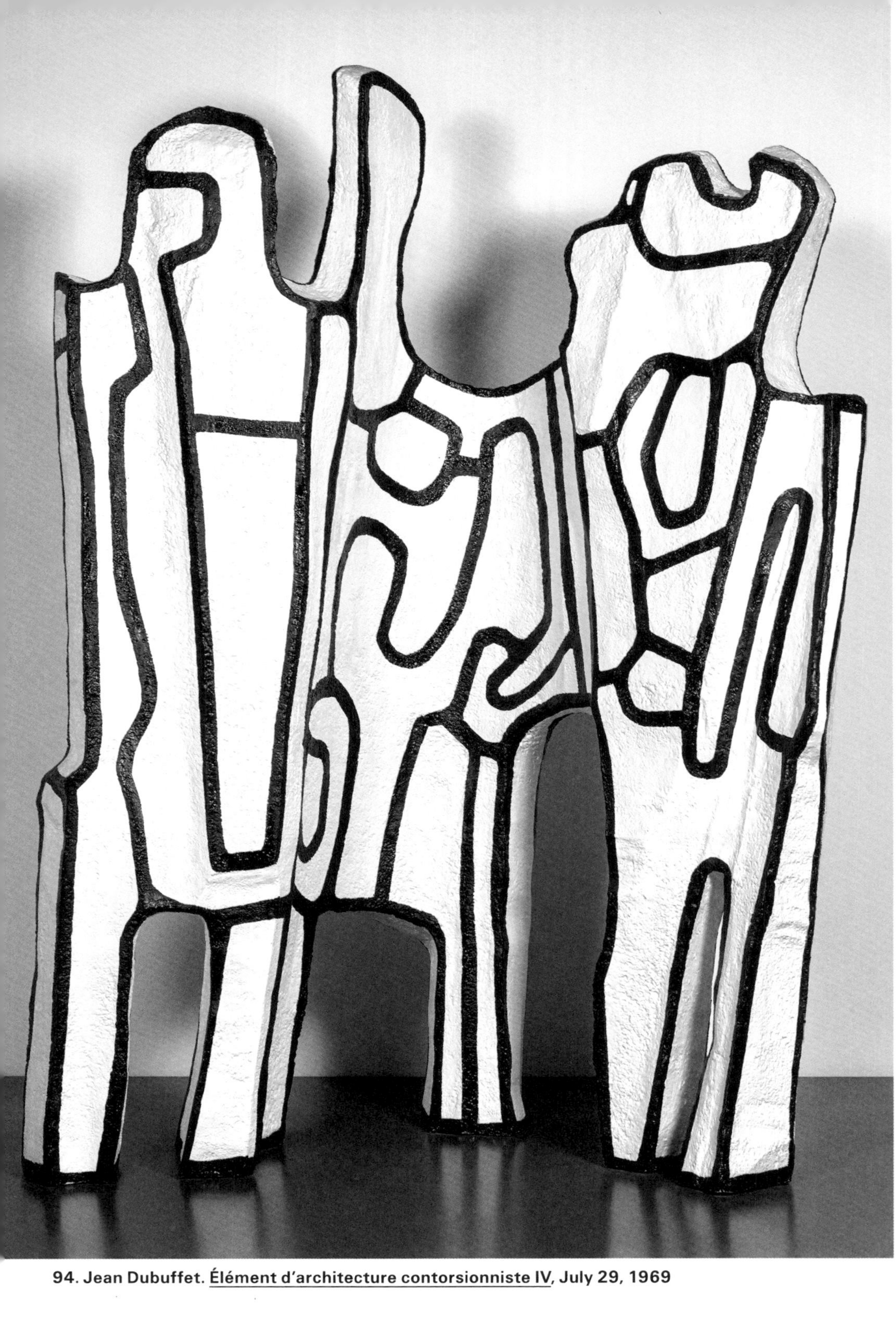

94. Jean Dubuffet. Élément d'architecture contorsionniste IV, July 29, 1969

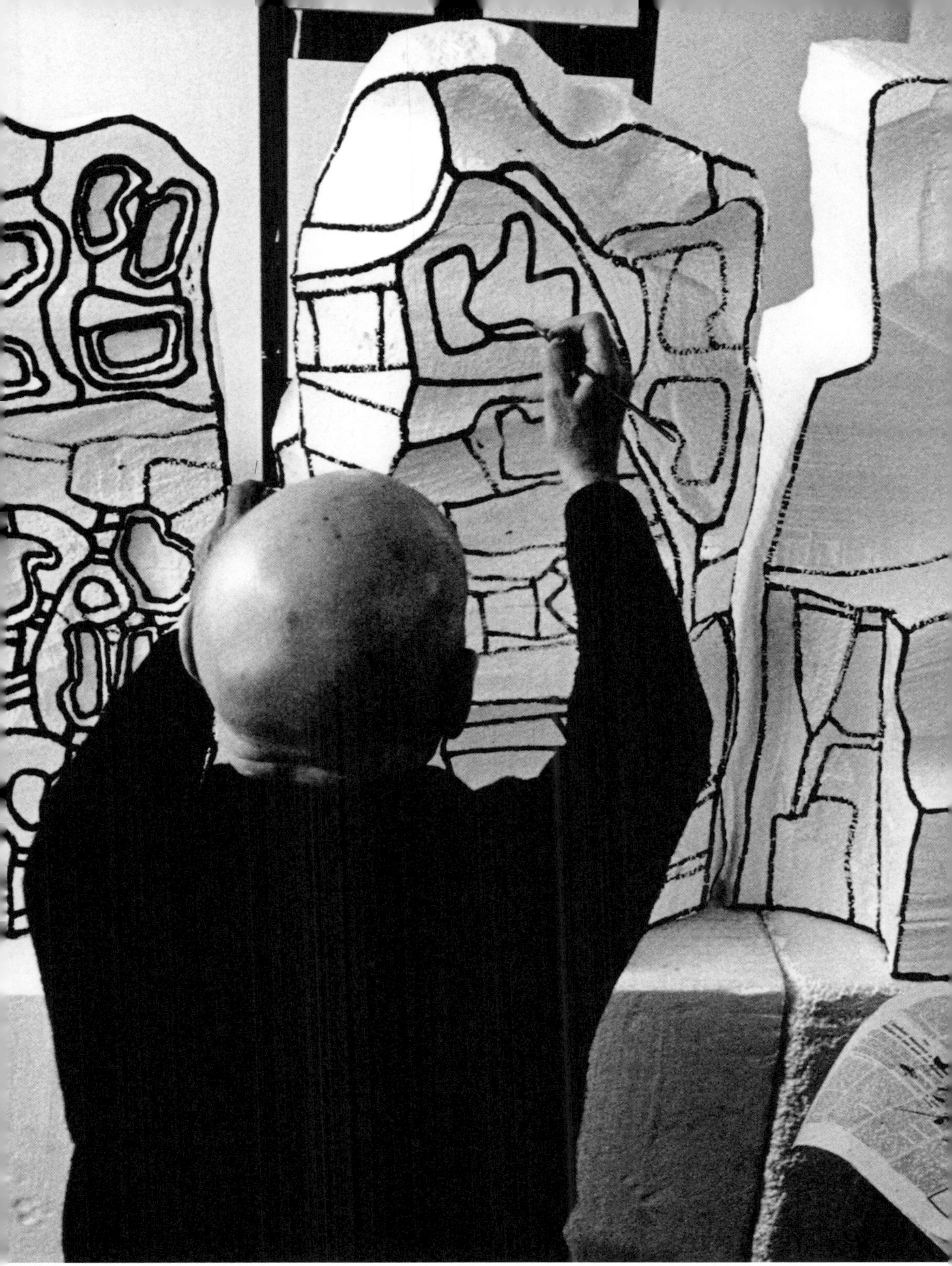

95. Kurt Wyss (photographer). Jean Dubuffet working on expanded polystyrene elements of La rue, Paris, 1970

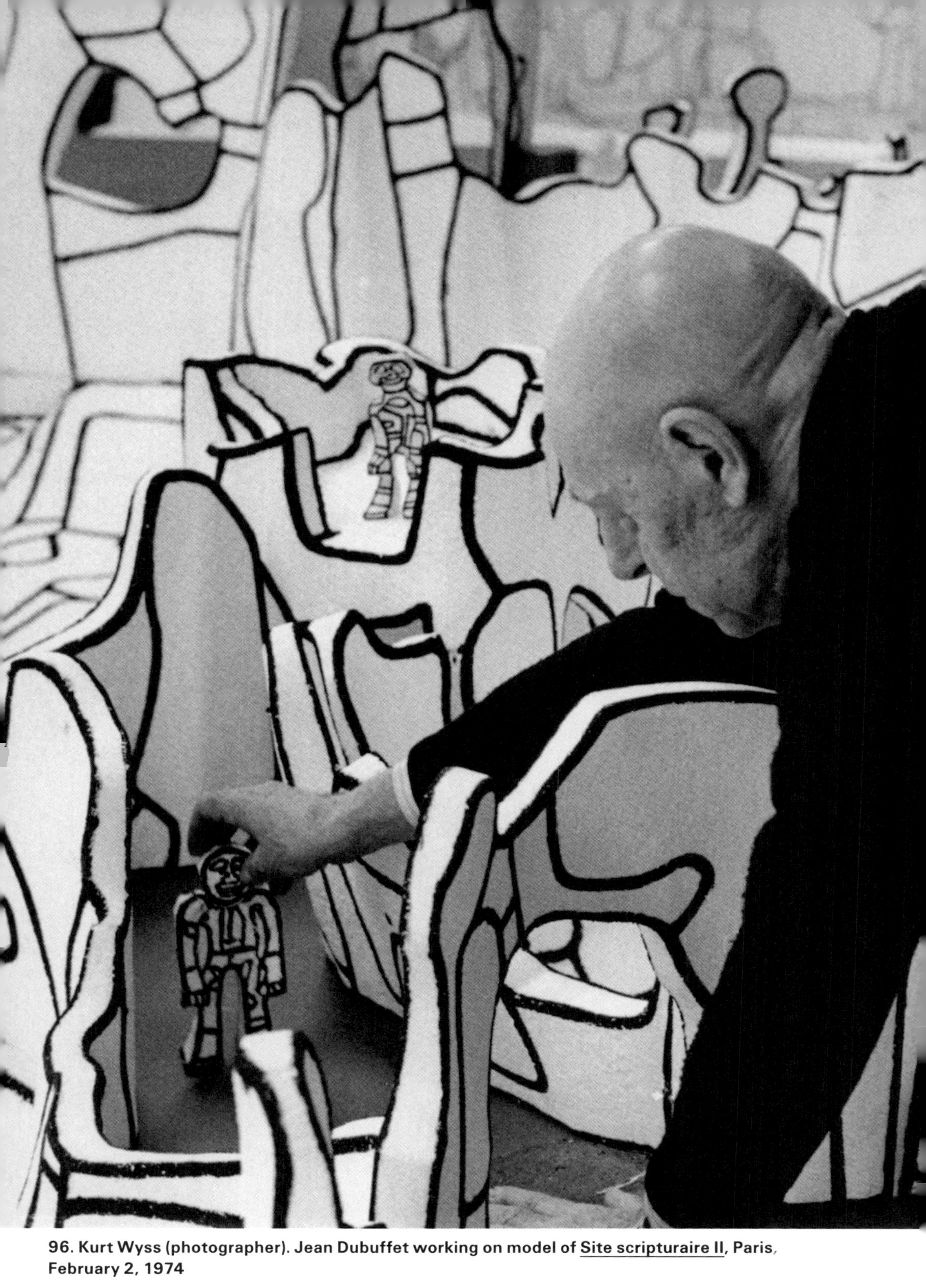

96. Kurt Wyss (photographer). Jean Dubuffet working on model of Site scripturaire II, Paris, February 2, 1974

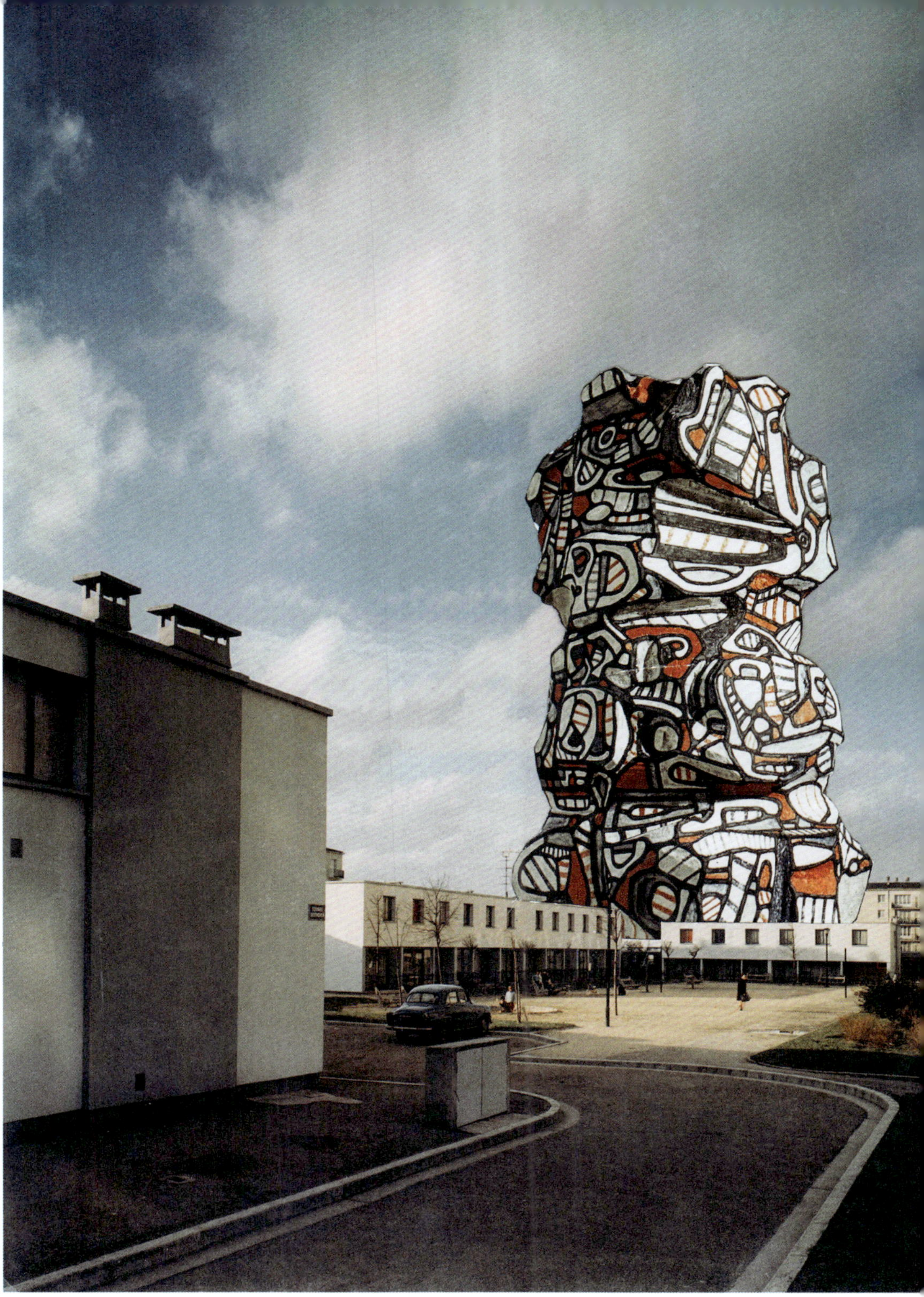

97. Jean Dubuffet (Wolf Slawny, photographer). Photomontage with Tour aux figures, November 1967

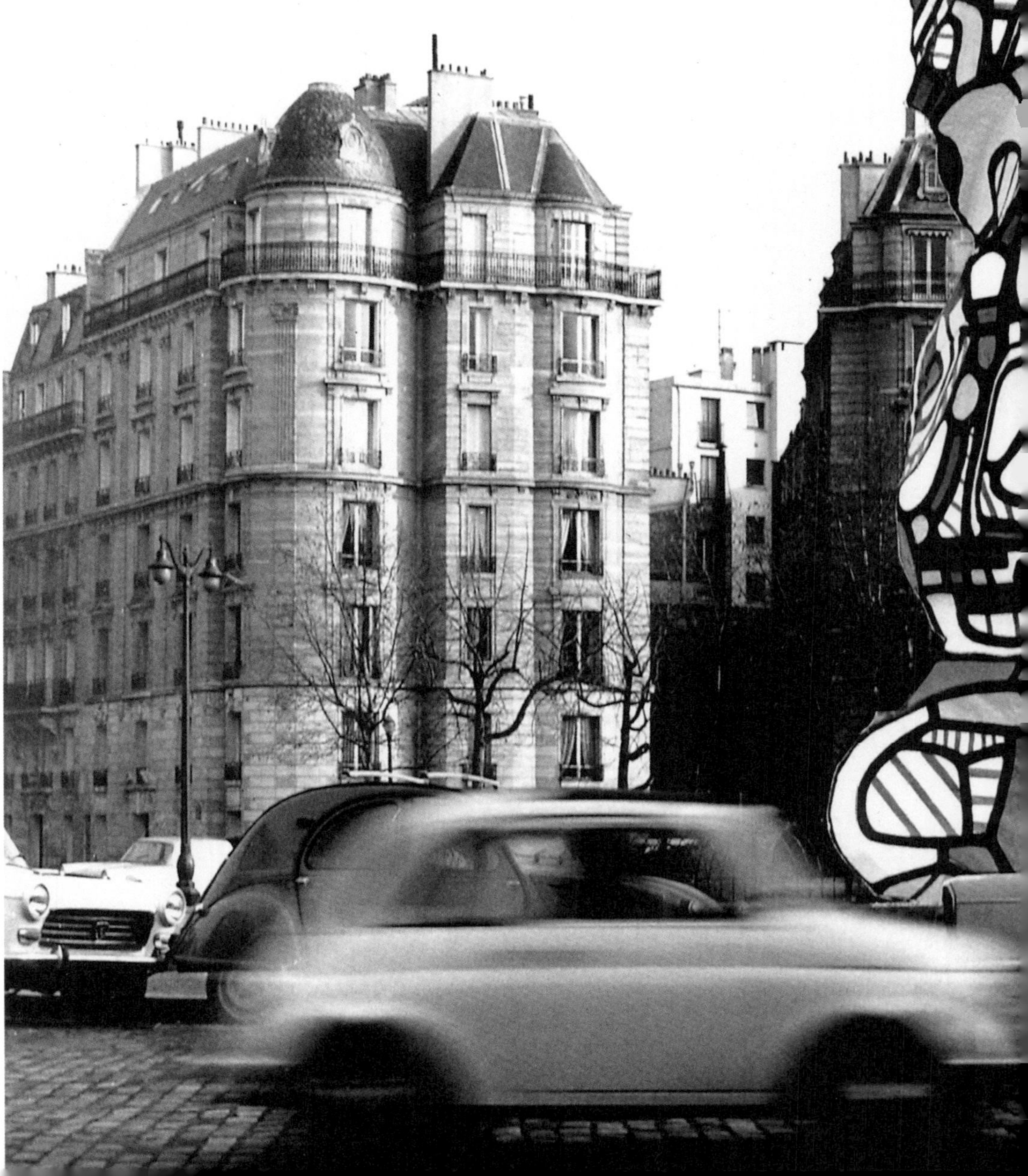

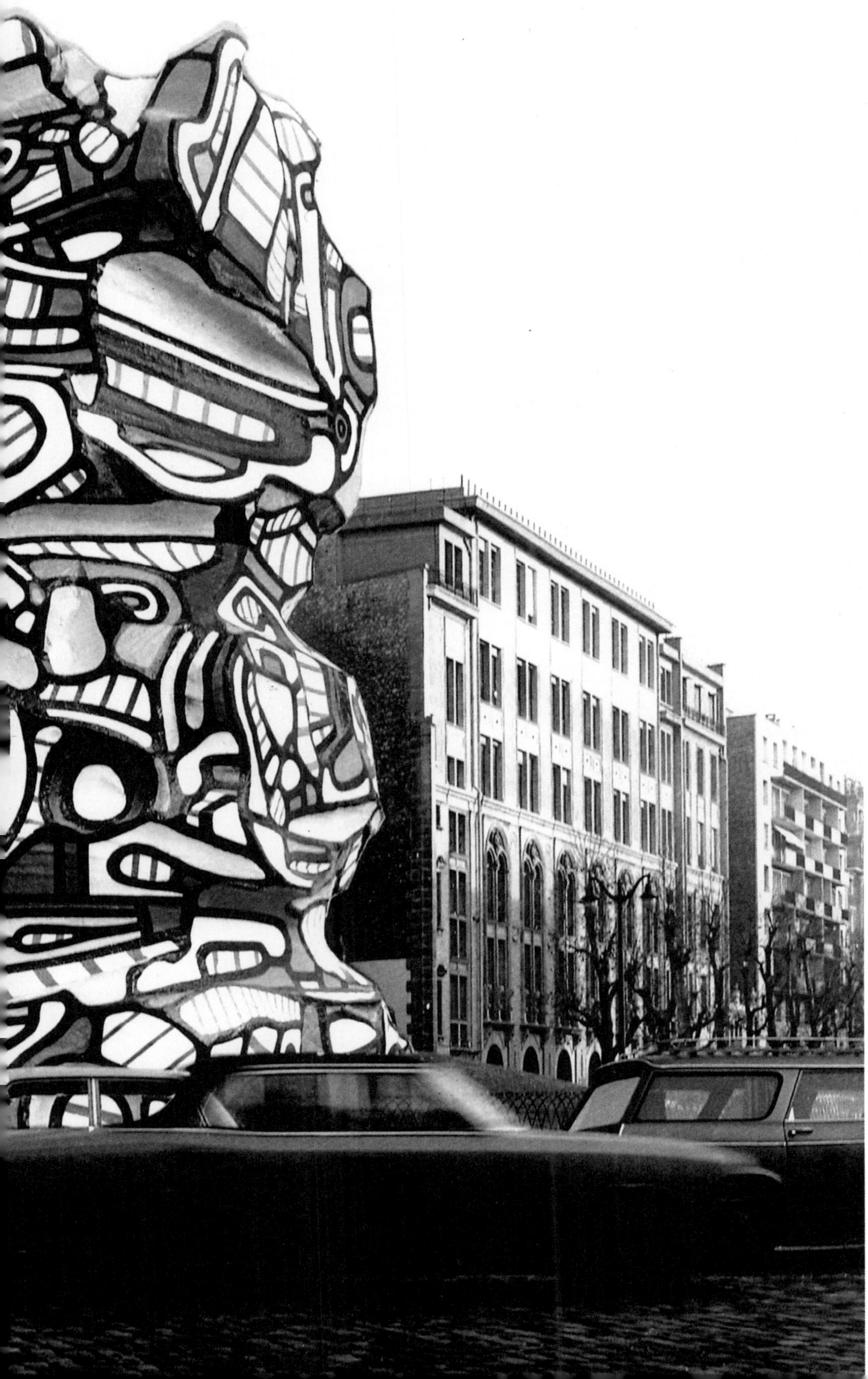

98. Jean Dubuffet (Augustin Dumage, photographer). Photomontage with *Tour aux figures*, 1967

The paintings in the series Lieux abrégés represent figures in largely indefinable areas. While some are explicitly about rural spaces, most, including Promenade au jardin, depict moonlike environments in which male figures dressed in simplified business suits wander aimlessly.

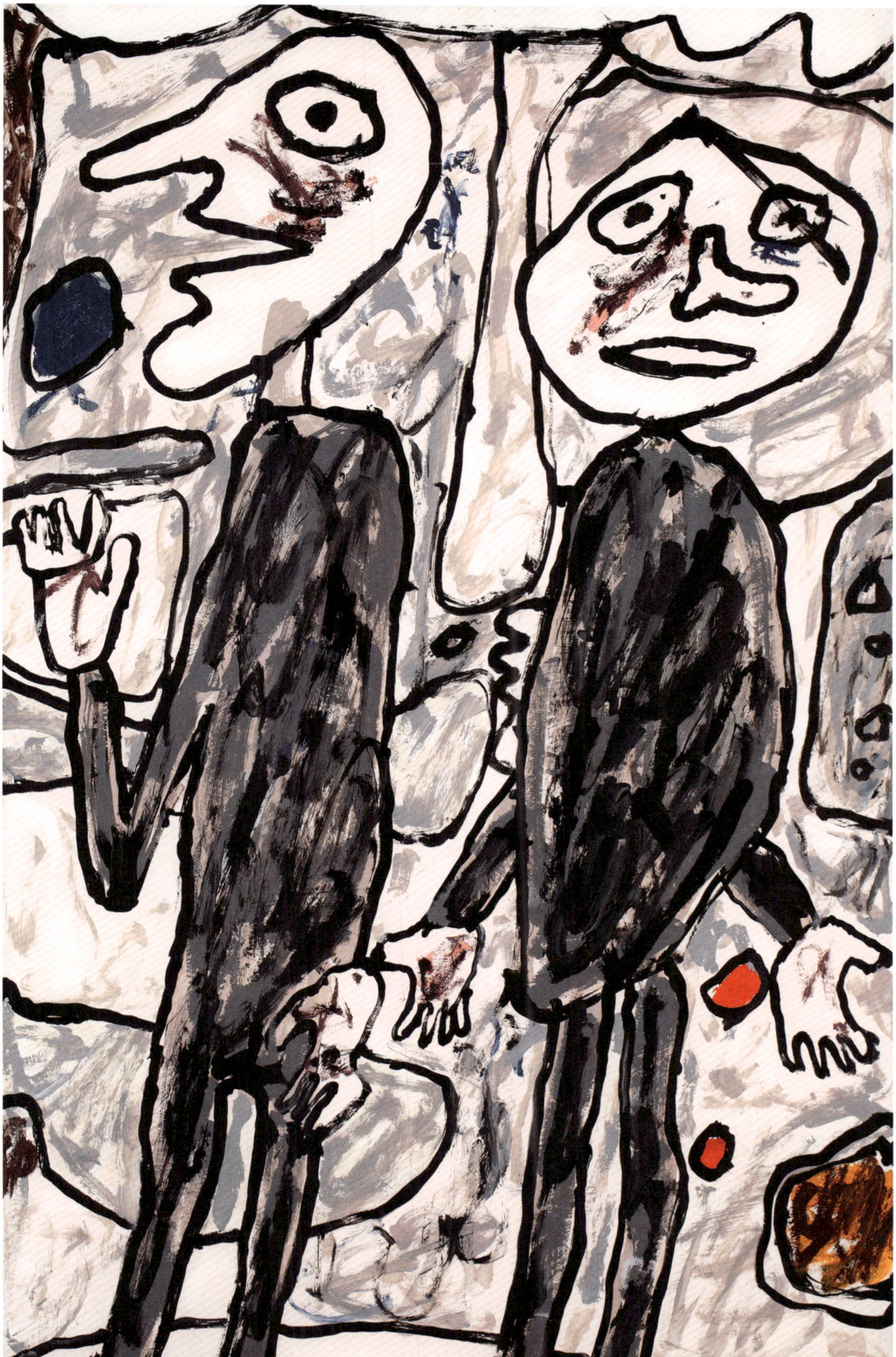

99. Jean Dubuffet. Promenade au jardin, June 21, 1975

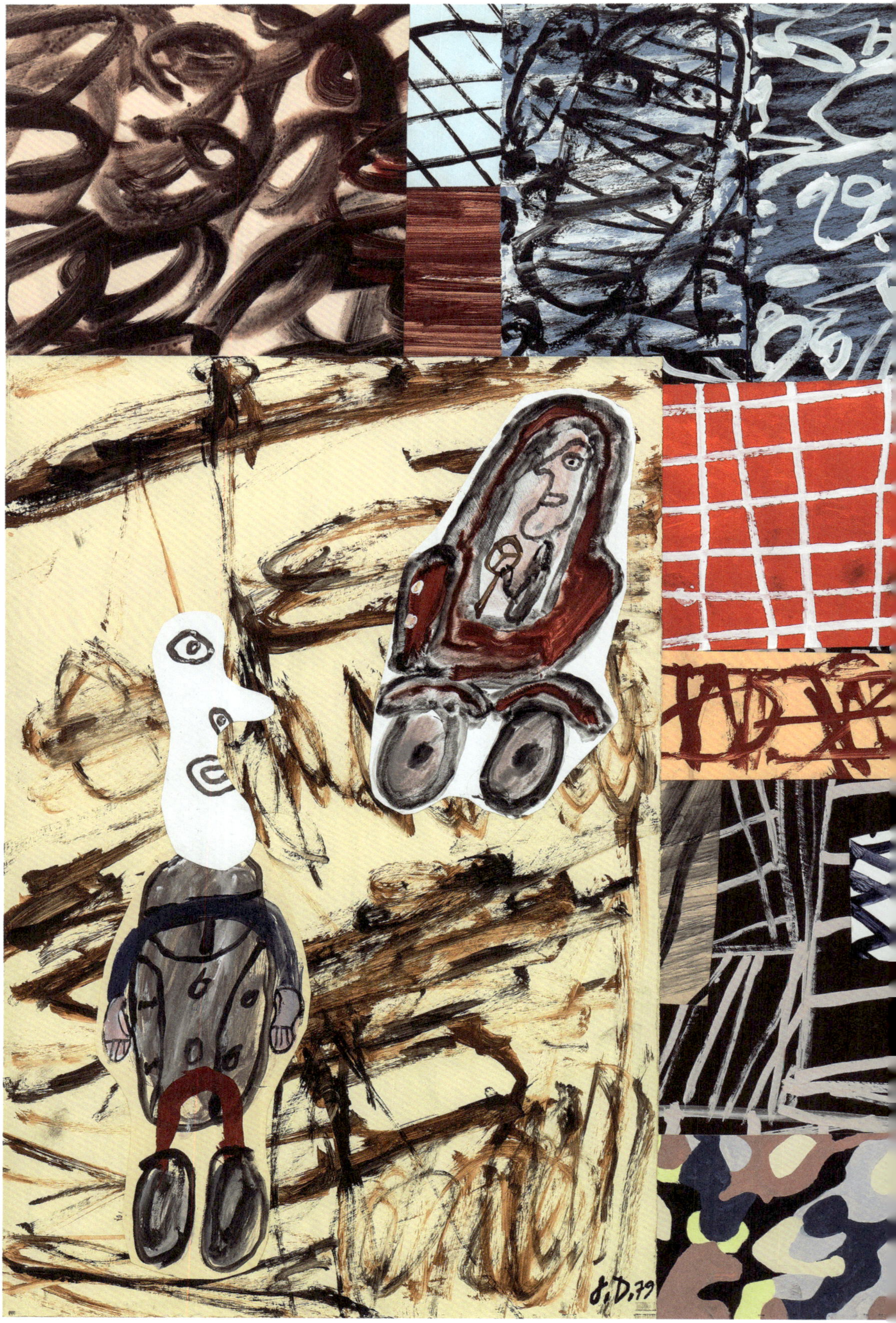

100. Jean Dubuffet. Parages fréquentés, October 17, 1979

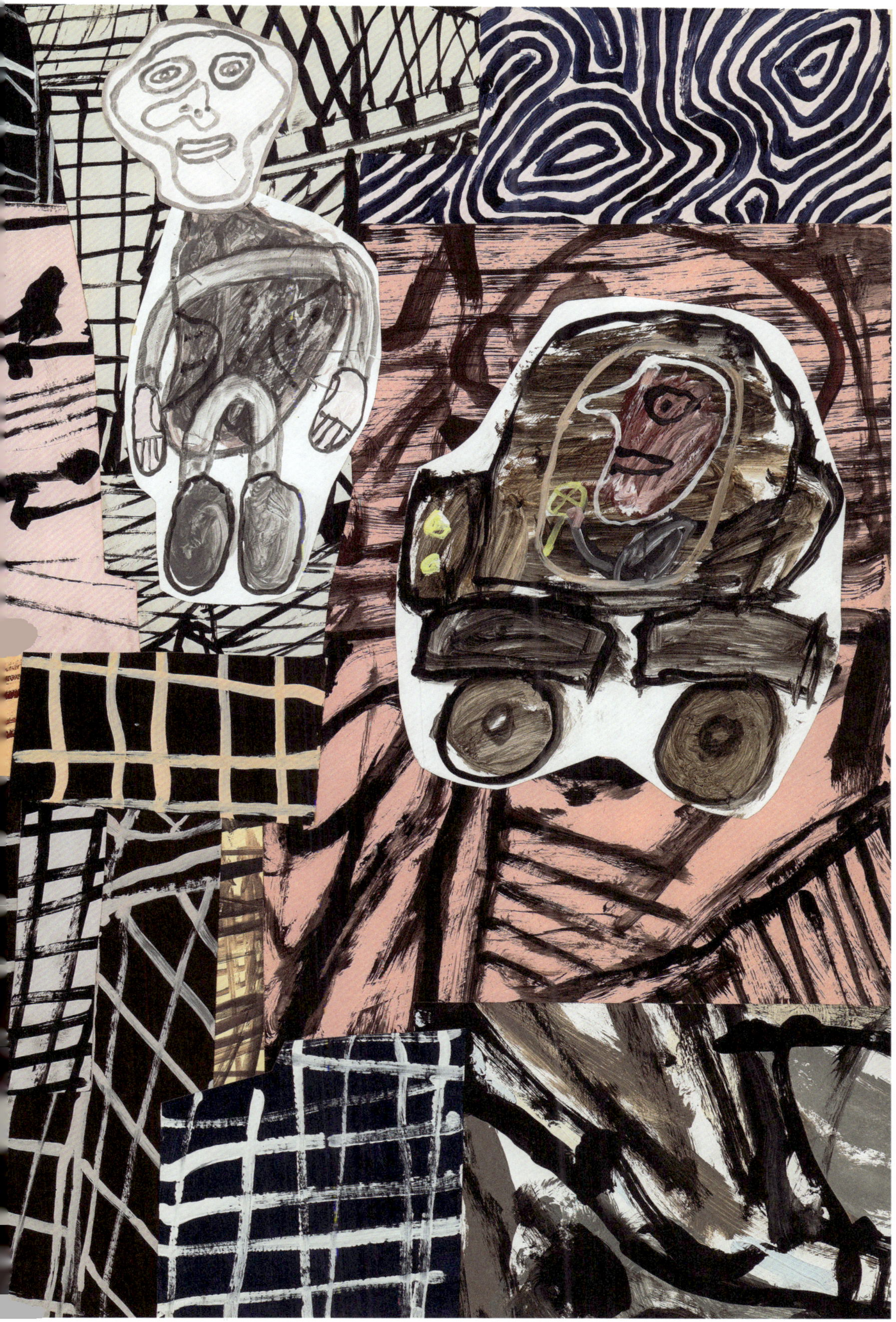

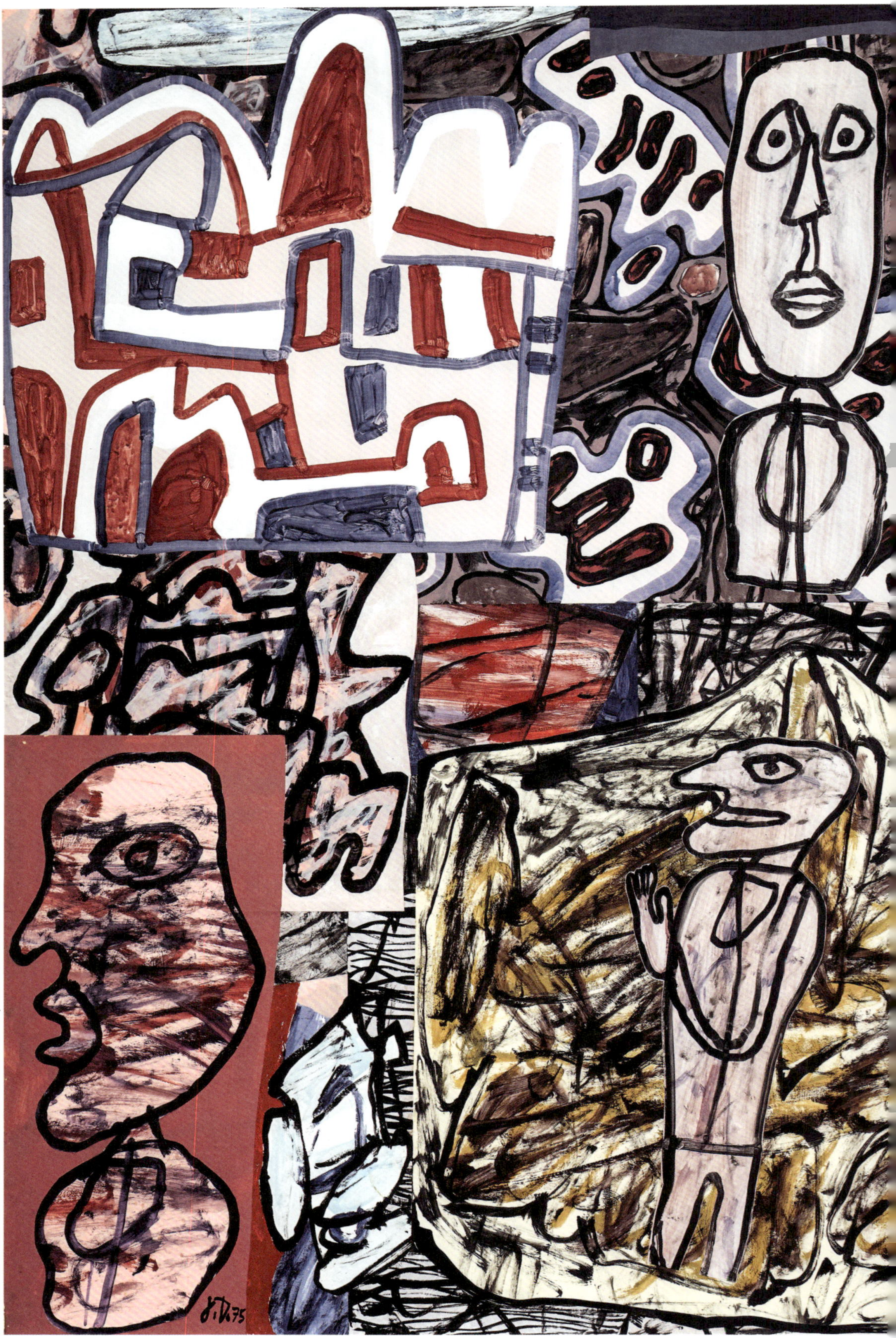

101. Jean Dubuffet. Carnet de voyage, December 10, 1975

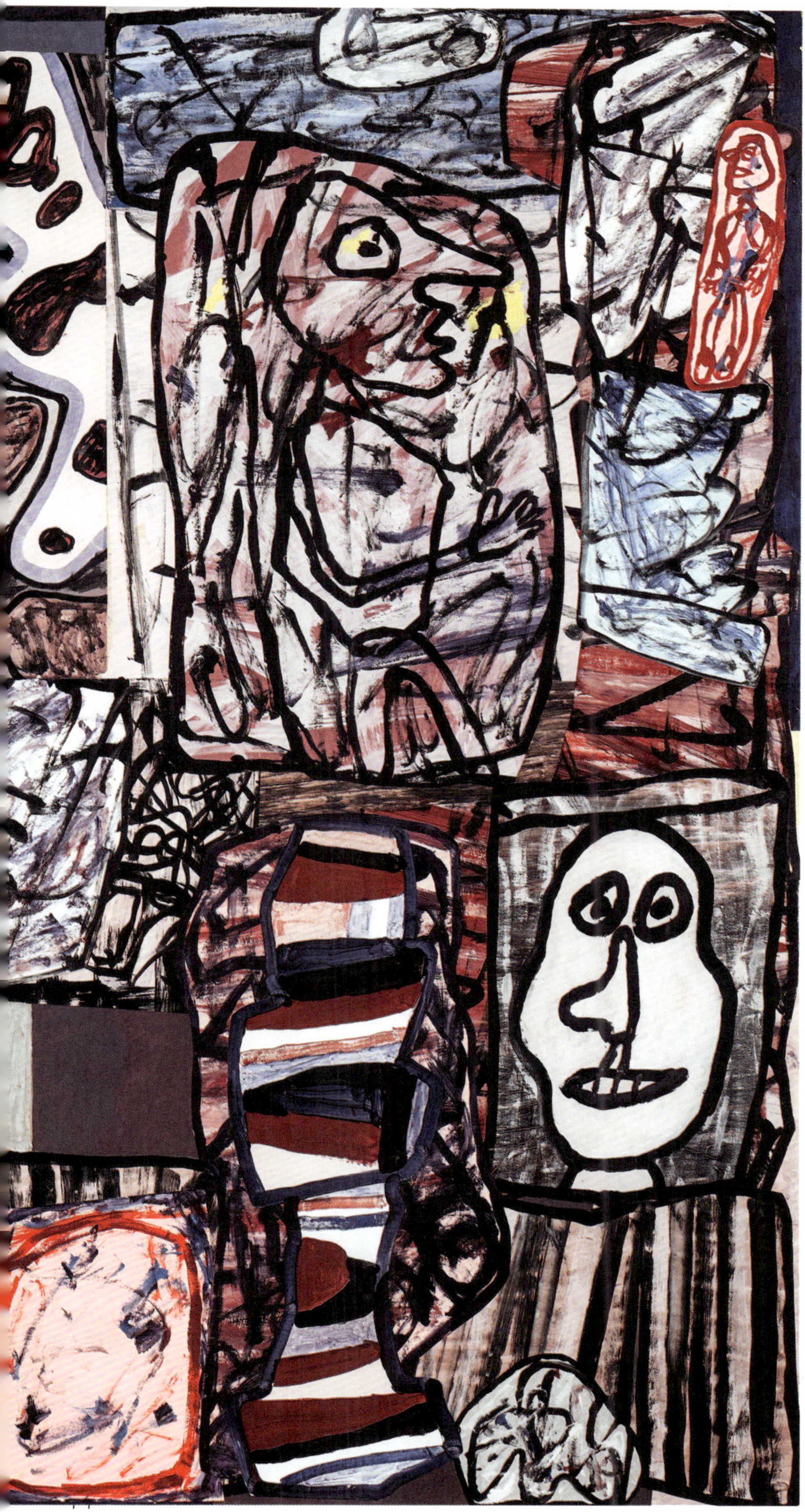

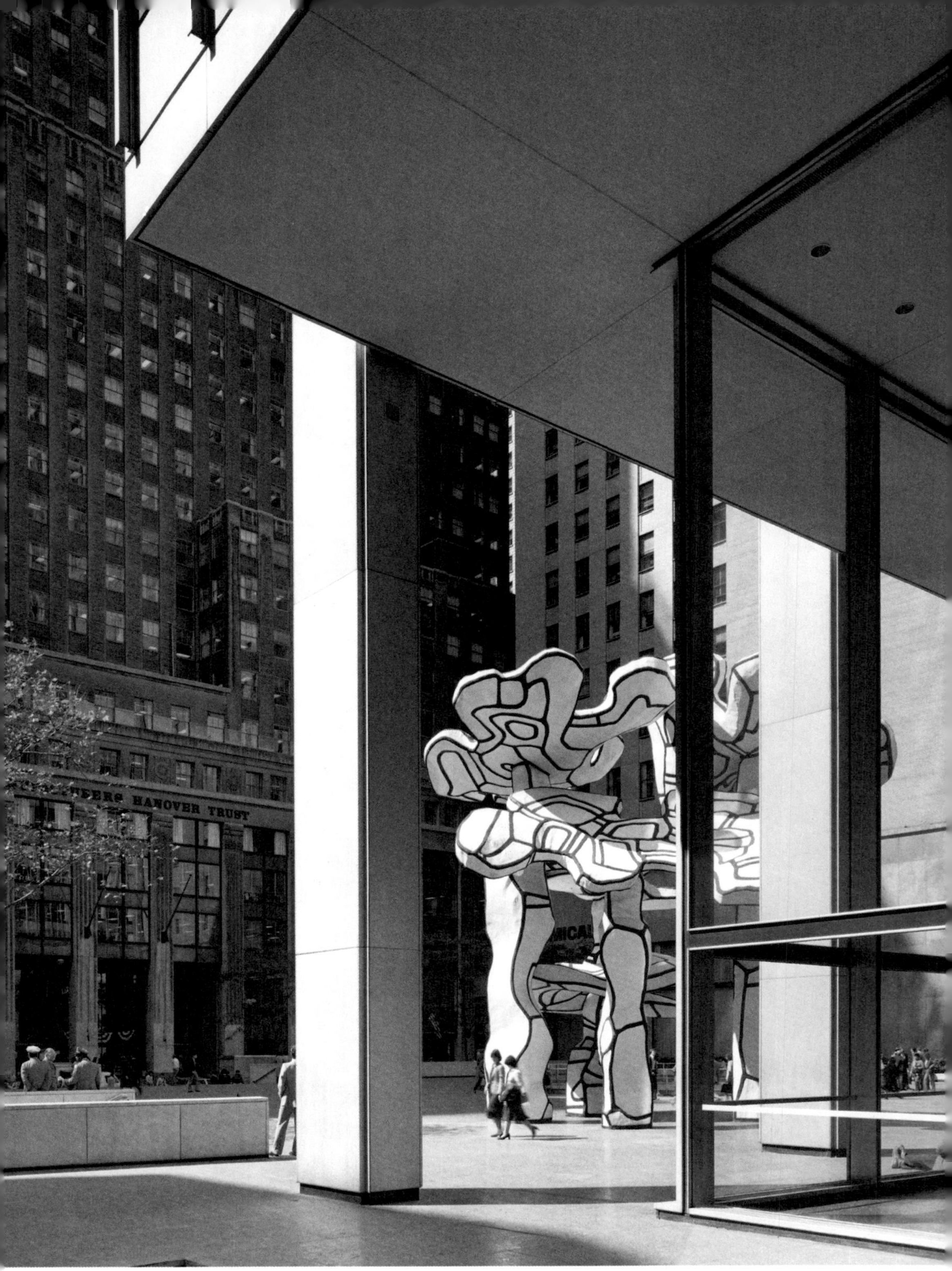

102. Jean Dubuffet. Groupe de quatre arbres, April 1971–July 1972, installed at 1 Chase Manhattan Plaza (28 Liberty Street), New York

The matte and opaque surfaces contrasted with the shiny aluminum and black glass of the building's façade, while the tangled, coiling black lines of the sculpture emphasized the neat verticals behind it.

Habitat urbain and other works in the series Brefs exercices d'école journalière can be seen as satirical takes on such a rectilinear architecture, depicting figures enclosed in cage-like environments.

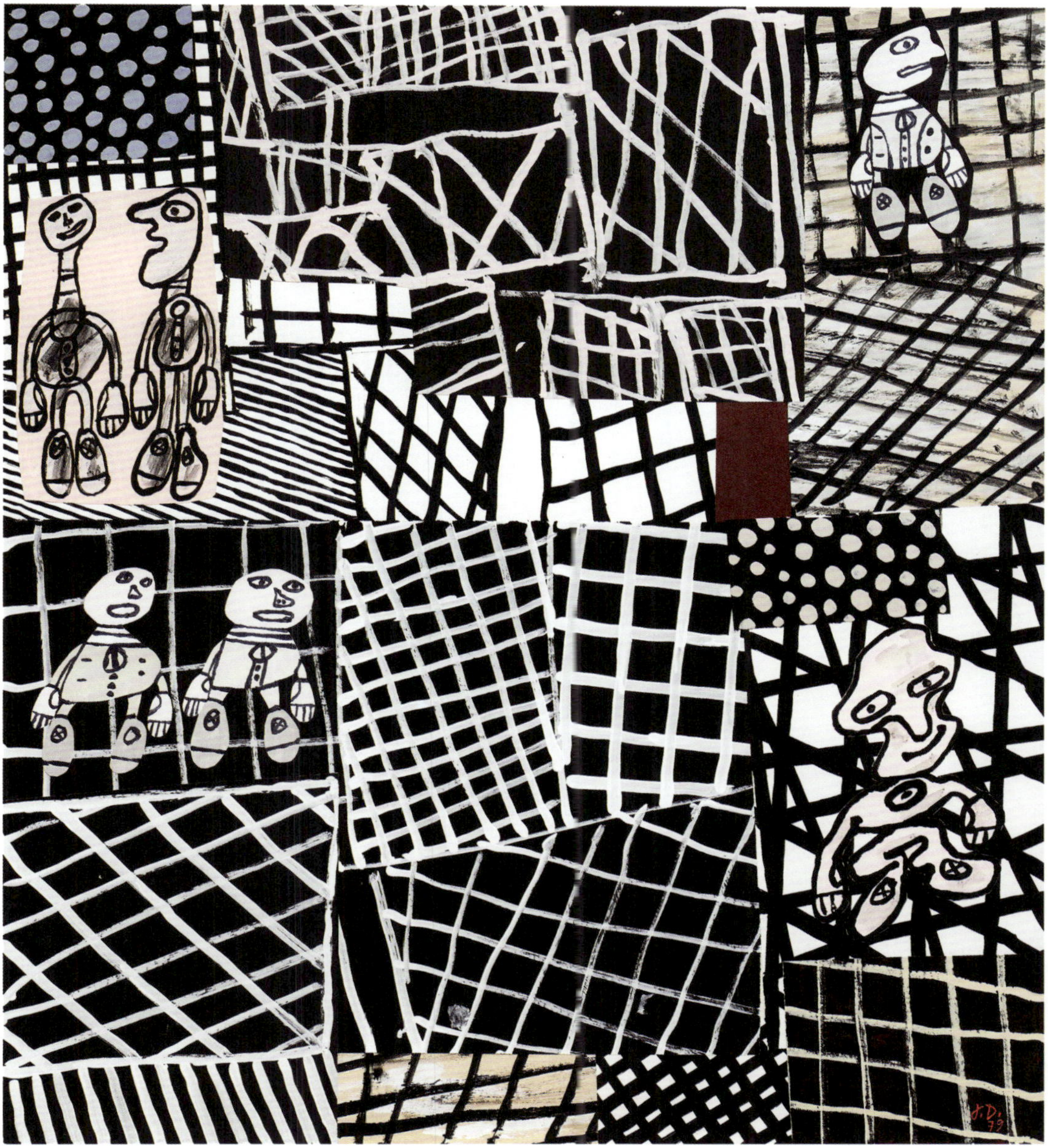

103. Jean Dubuffet. Habitat urbain, May 28, 1979

Radical Realism (1983)

Jean Dubuffet

Here I am at the end, weary of all instituted images: human effigies, to start with, then trees, houses, and all identifiable objects. I no longer believe in the old inventory of figures in whose form some want to confine the world. It appears to me as false and sterile, I reject it. I want to put things back to the point of their beginning, to their zero point, before the institution of any vocabulary. I do not want anything that can bear a name, I want to free myself from the old nomenclature that I was led to believe listed reality. I want to transport my vision of what is around us to a different level, I want to live from now on in a change of reality. I no longer want it to be given to me, I want to make it at my own leisure. Of course, I feel an urgent need, like everyone else, that the edifice of my vision and of all my thought be seated on solid foundations of reality. But having ceased to believe in that embarrassing prosthesis of reality that had been inculcated in me, I must make myself another that suits my use better. There are as many realities as we want there to be, let each find his own. Instead of adapting my thought to a reality that is imposed on me, I consider it healthier to see myself well anchored in the realism I aspire to, to conform, on the contrary, my own prosthesis of reality to the image of my thought. And no longer the other way around. It is legitimate, at my age, to use prostheses and adapt them to my needs. Now armed with my new perspective, I will set about taking stock of all the facts of the world. Work to be done.

Chapter Three

The Slab, the Tower, and L'Hourloupe

Le désir de constituer des sites habitables—ou plus précisément des interprétations mentales de sites édifiés en trois dimensions et à l'échelle même des sites réels évoqués, de manière à rendre habitables ces interprétations—prit origine en 1962 à partir des vues de Paris du cycle Paris Circus. L'idée de construire un element architectural bariolé (une boutique ou préférablement un groupe de boutiques, un fragment de rue) dans la même forme fantasque que les peintures et les gouaches de ce cycle évoquait les rues de Paris occupa des ce moment la pensée de l'auteur, frappé par l'idée de l'équivoque resultant d'habiter physiquement (au lieu de seulement les imaginer au vu d'un tableau) des interprétations mentales de sites et d'architectures.

—Jean Dubuffet, 1980

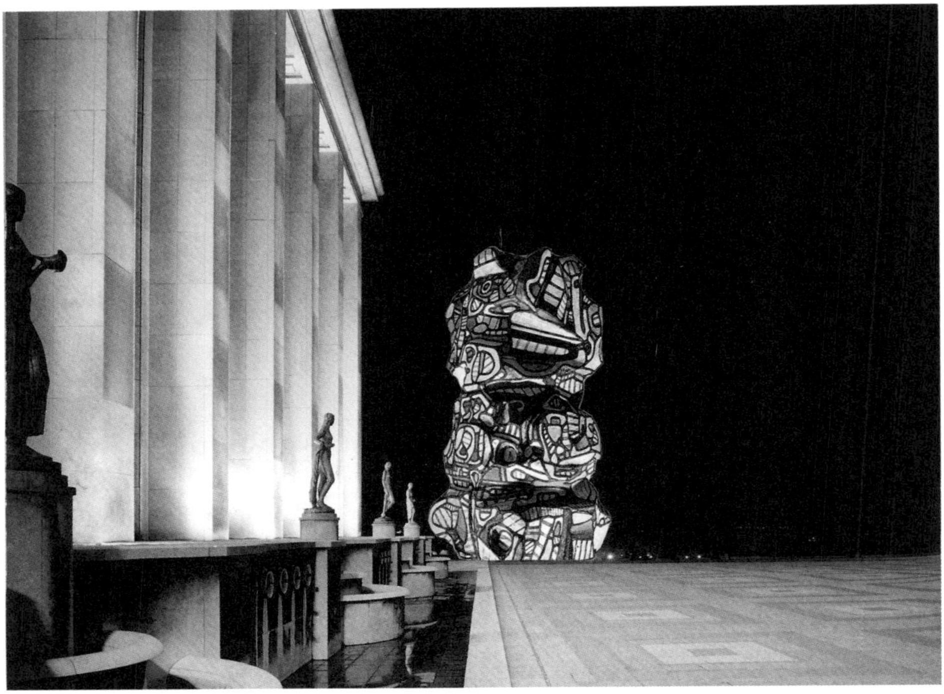

104. Jean Dubuffet (Augustin Dumage, photographer). Photomontage with Tour aux figures (with Eiffel Tower concealed), 1967

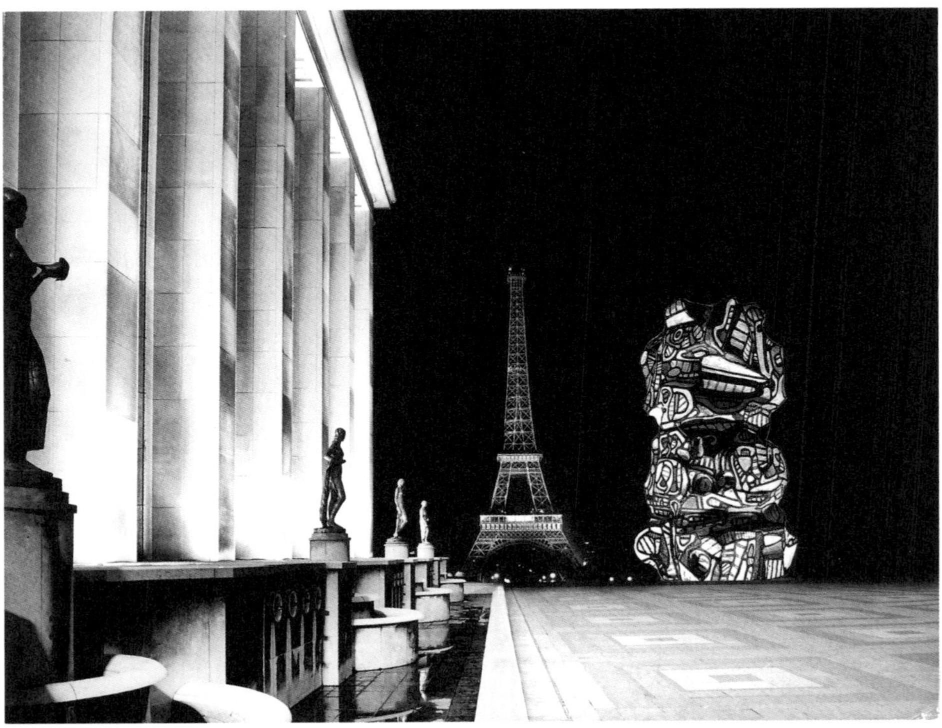

105. Jean Dubuffet (Augustin Dumage, photographer). Photomontage with Tour aux figures (with Eiffel Tower visible), 1967

Now you see it, now you don't! Like playing peekaboo, Dubuffet obliterates the Eiffel Tower under his own tower, the *Tour aux figures* (Tower with Figures), in one of two photomontages showing the view from the esplanade of the Palais de Chaillot by night (fig. 104). In the other (fig. 105), the Eiffel Tower is back, eerily flanked by the *Tour aux figures* in a picture that breaks the symmetry of the iconic vista. In a third, distinct photomontage, a monumental, bulbous white outgrowth covered in sinuous lines and hatch marks is inserted into the regular alignment of buildings on a generic Haussmannian street; in yet another (fig. 110, far right), a bumpy and similarly embellished façade encroaches on the elegant curve of the place des Victoires.

These *photographies truquées* (trick photographs), as the artist called them in a letter to Françoise Choay, show an entirely different approach to the city on his part.[1] No longer content with observing it or depicting its inhabitants and their peculiar demeanors, Dubuffet now imagined his work to be present in the middle of the urban environment, ostensibly reinventing himself, at the age of sixty-seven, as an architect. At least, this is what the small book entitled *Dubuffet: Édifices*, and the accompanying exhibition of his architectural models that opened at the Musée des arts décoratifs in December 1968, suggest. 1968: quite a year to be making such a bold move, when architects and urban planners were being decried for their generic towers and slabs haphazardly slapped onto an increasingly dehumanized urban fabric. *Non aux bidonvilles, non aux villes bidon: l'urbanisme est un acte politique* (No to shantytowns, no to fake towns: urbanism is a political act) and *Sous les pavés, la plage* (Under the pavement, the beach) were two of the better-known slogans stenciled on posters and painted on walls around Paris in May and June 1968 (fig. 106). In March of that year, in *Le droit à la ville*, Henri Lefebvre had critiqued the ideology of urban planning and its submission to capitalism, claiming a "right to urban life" that he characterized as a "right to freedom, to individualization in socialization, to habitat and to inhabit. A right to the *oeuvre*, to participation and *appropriation* (clearly distinct from the right to property)."[2] Lefebvre's writings on urbanism found a wide echo in the late 1960s and early 1970s, resounding, for example, in the controversy that arose around the destruction and replacement of the old glass-and-steel architecture of Les Halles, an iconic architectural landmark designed in the 1850s by Victor Baltard, which was left empty after the transfer of the central food market out of the city to Rungis in February 1969.

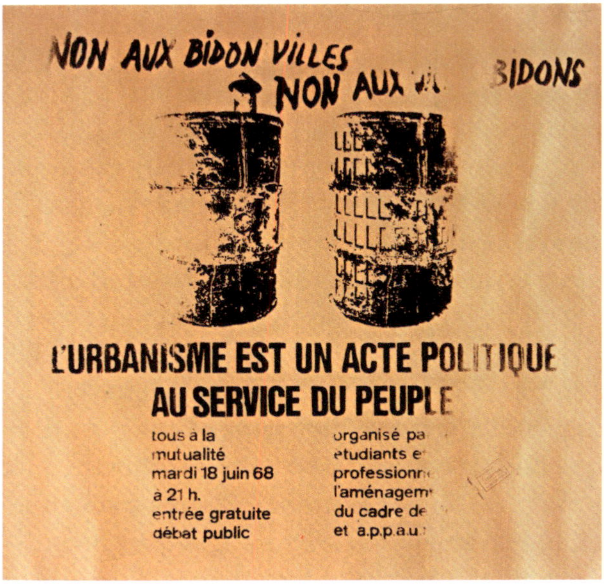

106. Poster by the Association pour la participation du public à l'architecture et à l'urbanisme (A.P.P.A.U.R.), May 1968

It would be misleading to argue that Dubuffet's move had much to do with the demonstrations and strikes of May 1968—even in view of his diatribe against the fossilized character of established culture, published that same year as the stand-alone book *Asphyxiante culture*.[3] And yet, by the same token, it is impossible to ignore, as scholars sometimes do, the convergence between the public rejection of the worst aspects of the authoritarian and profit-driven urban planning of Paris and Dubuffet's simultaneous attempt to rethink architectural forms in the city.[4] The architecture critic Marcel Cornu, whose savage and well-informed study of the gentrification of Paris and its "conquest" by high capitalism came out in 1972, praised, during the same period, Dubuffet's "wise ideas" about architecture.[5]

Dubuffet's foray into architecture in 1968 inaugurated an especially prolific phase of his work.[6] Within a decade, he completed the *Hourloupe* cycle begun in 1962 and embarked upon the large-scale *Théâtres de mémoire* series. He also produced a stage performance, *Coucou Bazar* (1973); made dozens of architectural models; and completed three large-scale outdoor constructions, in New York (1972), the southeastern Paris suburb Périgny-sur-Yerres (1973), and Otterlo, The Netherlands (1974). Other projects would be realized later, and the artist ensured that this process could continue beyond his death, notably by setting up a foundation.[7] Large retrospective exhibitions of his work took place in 1973 in Paris and New York, and prior to that, his sculptures and models were exhibited internationally and reviewed widely. He also conversed and corresponded with architecture critics, scholars of urbanism, and architects.[8] Yet, to call him an "architect," or even a "paper architect," would be too simple, ignoring the slippages between several words Dubuffet used frequently and sometimes interchangeably—"architecture," "edifice," "monument," "project," and "model"—as well as the elusiveness of his thinking about architecture in general. A second exhibition of his three-dimensional projects at the Musée des arts décoratifs, *Jean Dubuffet: Le Salon d'été et autres*, organized in 1978, went some way toward clarifying these slippages, so that bookending this chapter, chronologically and conceptually, between the two exhibitions of 1968 and 1978 may render visible the various forms of Dubuffet's engagement with the idea of the city and its reality as well as his thinking with and against architecture.[9]

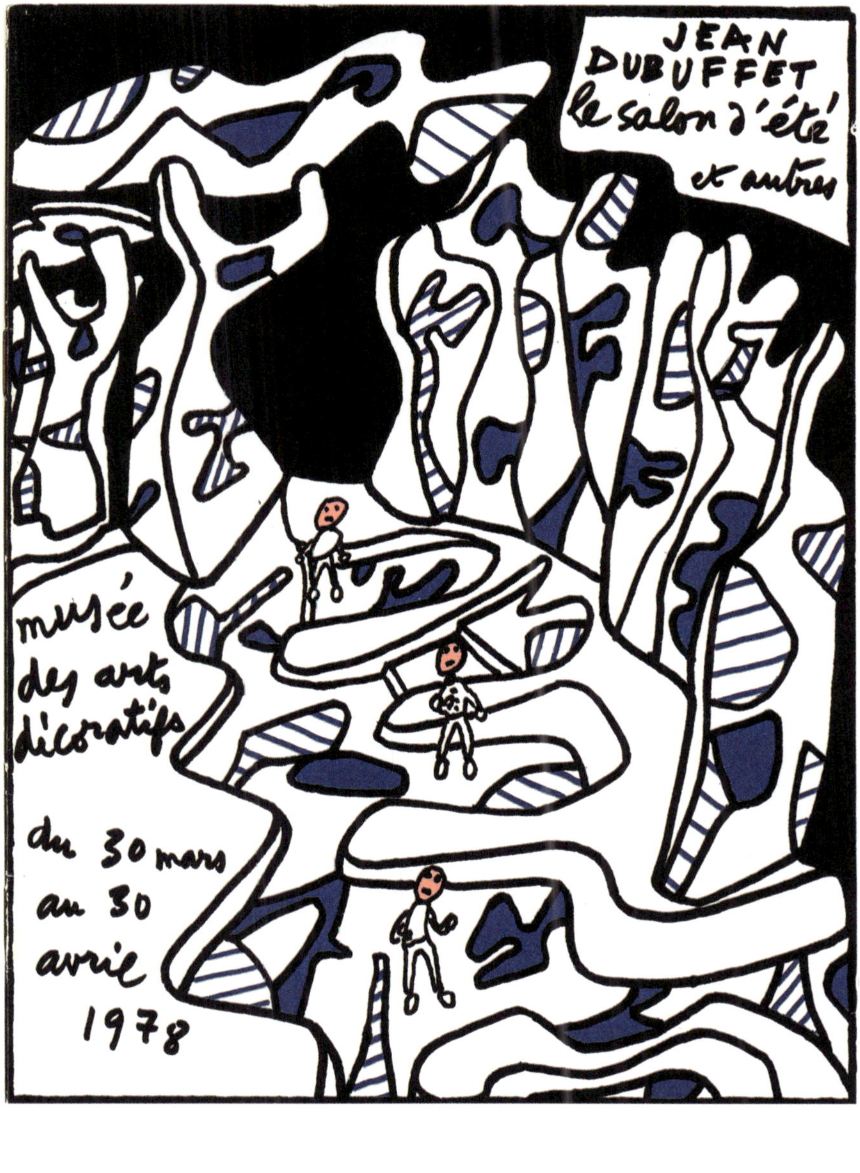

107. Jean Dubuffet. Cover of catalogue for *Jean Dubuffet: Le Salon d'été et autres* exhibition, 1978

Around *Édifices*: The Expanded *Hourloupe* in Context

The first of the two exhibitions held at the Musée des arts décoratifs, *Jean Dubuffet: Édifices, projets et maquettes d'architecture*, opened on December 11, 1968.[10] The photographs kept in the archives at the Fondation Dubuffet show a relatively sparse and bright space dotted with architectural maquettes varying in height from approximately half a meter to the three-meter-tall model for the *Tour aux figures* (from about twenty inches to ten feet). They were all presented on plinths and complemented by nearby wall panels reproducing several photomontages enlarged to two by three meters (about six and a half by ten feet), in which the models were inserted into views of Paris (figs. 108, 109).[11] The small book (or "brochure," as Dubuffet called it) *Édifices*, published jointly by the artist's two main galleries, Jeanne Bucher in Paris and Beyeler in Basel, introduced seven of these "architectural projects," including *Tour aux figures*, *Château bleu*, *Petit hôtel particulier* (Small Mansion), and *Pavillon à deux étages* (Two-Story Pavilion). Each is described and illustrated with diagrams, maps, photomontages, and/or photographs (fig. 110). The text, authored by the artist, is sharp, at times to the point of bluntness. His use of the conditional tense is sparse, while the present and future simple tenses abound, giving the impression that the conversion from model and plan to final, full-scale form had already been flawlessly worked out. "The tower is 24 meters high," he wrote of the *Tour aux figures*. "This is a small town house two stories high, set down between other buildings lining an avenue," reads the first sentence describing *Petit hôtel particulier*.[12] Also included were details concerning the innovative materials to be used to build the edifices (epoxy and concrete), notes concerning their upkeep, and, in one case, a fully worked-out internal structure.

Dubuffet's correspondence with the historian of urbanism Françoise Choay suggests that the two had discussed the possibility that she write the text for a publication about these architectural models, which he had been busy designing since July 1967. In a letter dated November 29, however, he delayed the writing project, explaining that his *travaux d'architecture* had become more advanced and that he was now working on the "interior of these buildings—shape and placement of the rooms, stairwells, elevator, etc."[13] Eight months later, Dubuffet had decided to write the text himself. He explained to Choay: "I would like this brochure to be exempt from aesthetic considerations, but rather purely descriptive and documentary, and abundantly illustrated with reproductions of models, plans, and technical sketches."[14] Between the two letters, Dubuffet had pushed the publishing project away from the classic format of an exhibition catalogue, with a text penned by a specialist, to

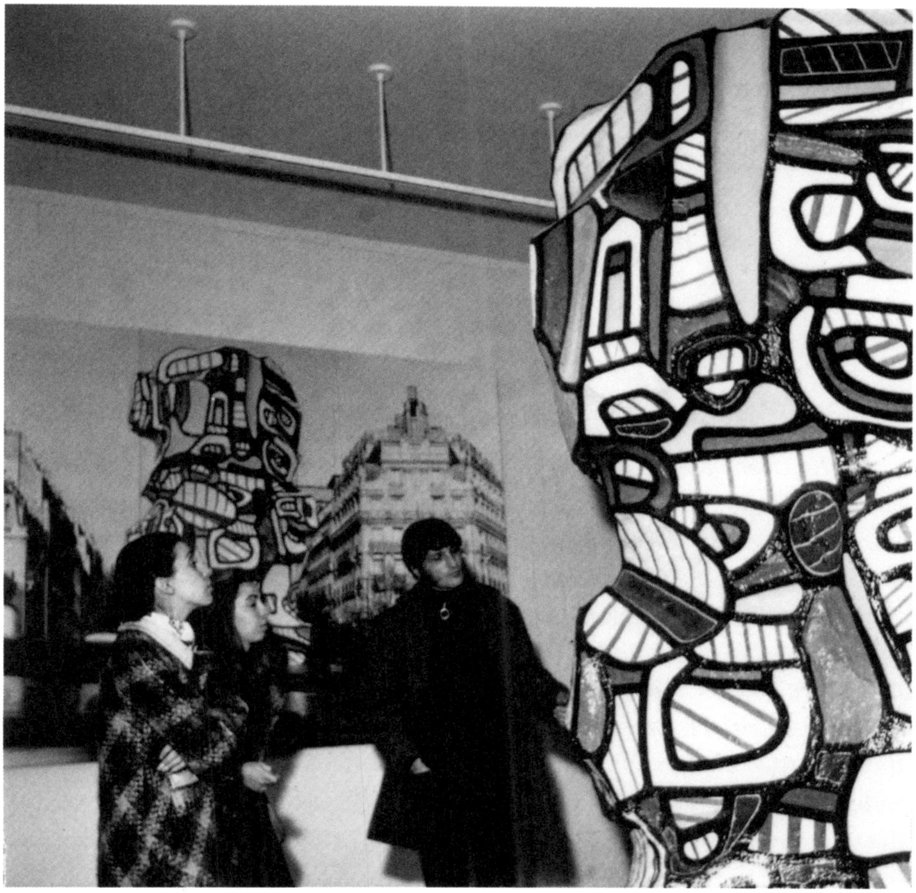

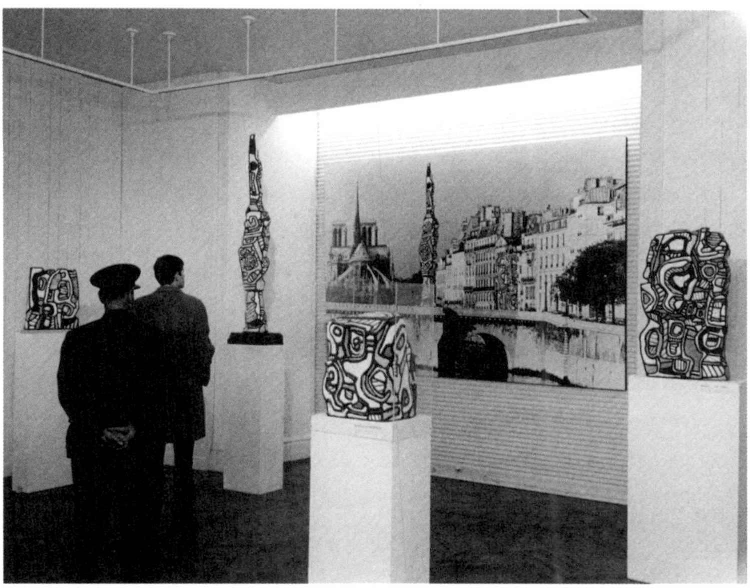

108, 109. Jean Dubuffet: *Édifices, projets et maquettes d'architecture* exhibition, Musée des arts décoratifs, Paris, December 11, 1968–February 10, 1969

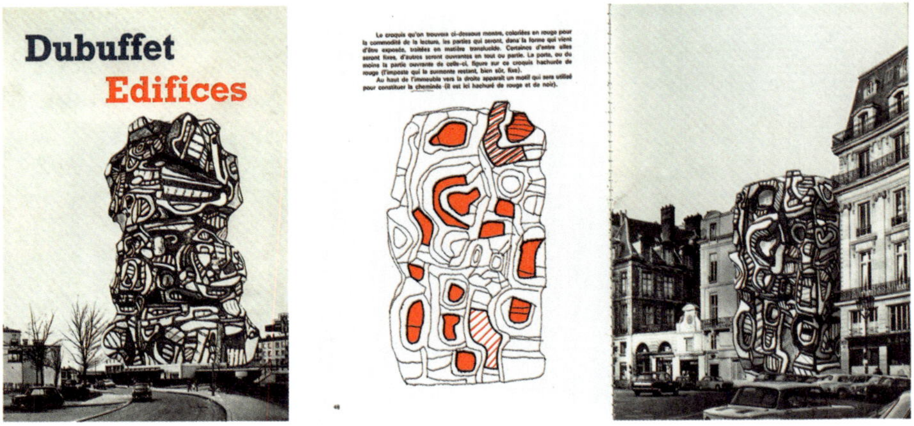

110. Jean Dubuffet. Cover and interior spread of *Dubuffet: Édifices* (1968)

something more anonymous. While practical reasons may have accounted, in part, for this change of plan—a presentation of Dubuffet's projects at the Museum of Modern Art in New York had been scheduled for October 1968—there was certainly a deliberate choice on the artist's part to produce a publication that had all the appearances of an architecture firm's brochure, with professional diagrams and descriptive text.[15] The publication tallied with the design of the exhibition at the Musée des arts décoratifs, enhancing the contrast with the outlandishness of Dubuffet's proposals, which, with their uneven floors, amorphous windows, and irregular structures made up of curves and diagonals, countered almost all rules of conventional building.

The architectural models were, in 1968, the latest development within *L'Hourloupe*, the cycle of work that followed *Paris Circus* and its brief offshoot, *Légendes*. Max Loreau, the scholar who began to compile the information for Dubuffet's thirty-eight-volume catalogue raisonné in 1961, recounted the well-rehearsed story of the beginnings of *L'Hourloupe*, which eventually became Dubuffet's longest-running series, in the introduction to the twentieth volume.[16] According to that account, the series emerged out of a series of doodles Dubuffet made in red ballpoint ben while on the telephone in July 1962. He then added accents in blue ballpoint, cut out the figures, and placed them on black backgrounds, discovering that the doodles became visually striking when submitted to these manipulations. The booklet *L'Hourloupe* (1963) was the first result of this series of drawings, providing a kind of matrix for the future work. Over the following few months, Dubuffet continued to separate figures from ground, making gouaches and paintings in which the hectic city atmosphere that had characterized *Paris Circus* gradually subsided and the palette significantly darkened, so that black now dominated. In some cases, he pasted painted figures displaying the same jagged lines as the blue-and-red drawings into loosely outlined urban settings, and during the winter of 1962–63, *Rue Poisse* and *Rue*

Tournique Bourlique (figs. 23, 111) still depict silhouettes of buildings and imprecise indications of streets; the striking use of black, however, imparts a ghostly quality to the translucent white figures that clamber across an environment that seems to be in the process of liquefying. Throughout 1963 and 1964, Dubuffet alternated between works with the appearance of a tightly fitting puzzle—such as the striking Être et paraître of July 1963 (fig. 55), in which areas with blue and white hatch marks on a white ground alternate with pieces painted in full color—and paintings and gouaches with a central motif or figure and a plainer background. Many works of 1962 and 1963 bear titles that continue to refer directly to the city. One series of gouaches, for example, is called Paris plaisir (Paris Pleasure), and invented street names abound. In the summers of 1963 and 1964, Dubuffet painted several works on the theme of the Pas-de-Calais region, including a number of views of the town of Étaples (such as Maison d'Étaples of August 1964). By the end of that year, however, the artist was keen to mark a difference between his current and his earlier work. "The paintings of the 'Hourloupe' are not at all based on the relations

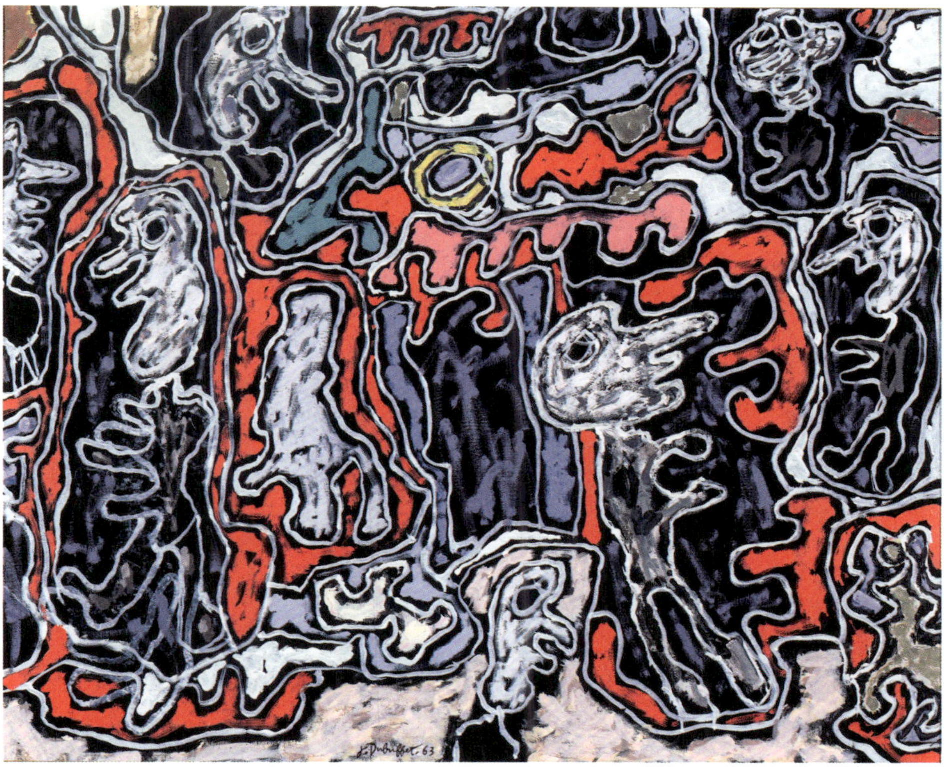

111. Jean Dubuffet. Rue Tournique Bourlique, February 26, 1963

between Man and the city. Those of 'Paris Circus' are, indeed, but not 'L'Hourloupe,'" he wrote to the art critic Otto Hahn.[17]

Alongside these paintings, which became increasingly large (for instance, *Les inconsistances* [The Inconsistencies], of February–March 1964, measures 130 by 780 centimeters, or about 4 by 25 1/2 feet), Dubuffet continued to produce small drawings in ballpoint pen showing figures and, later, objects of everyday life. The latter, in turn, led him, from 1965 on, to paint everyday objects he called "utensils," including clocks, bottles, coffeepots, and teacups (figs. 112, 113). These were the first works in which Dubuffet used vinyl paint, which came to replace oil paint (before it was itself, in time, replaced by acrylic). He continued to paint landscapes with figures throughout 1965, although such a description became superfluous, in some cases, when landscape and figures were no longer clearly distinguishable from one another. That year, Dubuffet received a commission from the town of Nanterre for two monumental ceramic panels to be placed in the hallway of the faculty of letters for a new university. Dubuffet eventually pulled out of the project, and one of the two large paintings he had made as models for the panels, *Nunc stans* (May–June 1965), was acquired by the Solomon R. Guggenheim Museum in New York.

In the months that followed, the themes of the everyday and the interior extended to paintings with titles evocative of staircases and houses, such as *Demeure II (avec seuil et cheminées)* of March 1966 (fig. 114). That year, Dubuffet also began to sculpt with blocks of expanded polystyrene. Using tools made expressly for the purpose from hot wires, he shaped objects, "utensils," mile markers, tables, and, finally, in 1967–69, a series of monuments and architectural projects. These creations were given a new lease on life after a

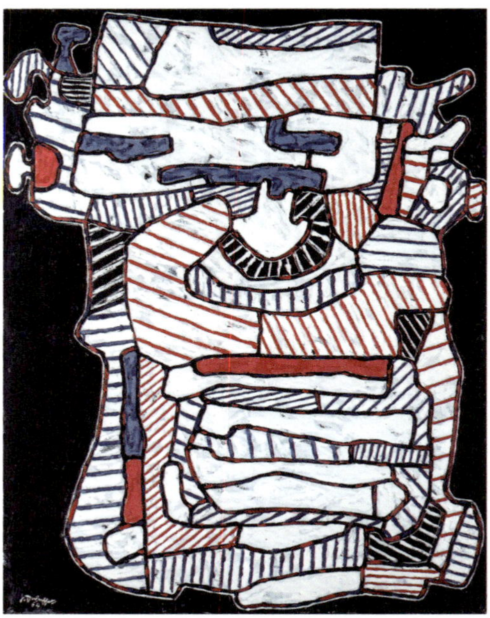

112. Jean Dubuffet. *Machine à écrire I*, June 29, 1964

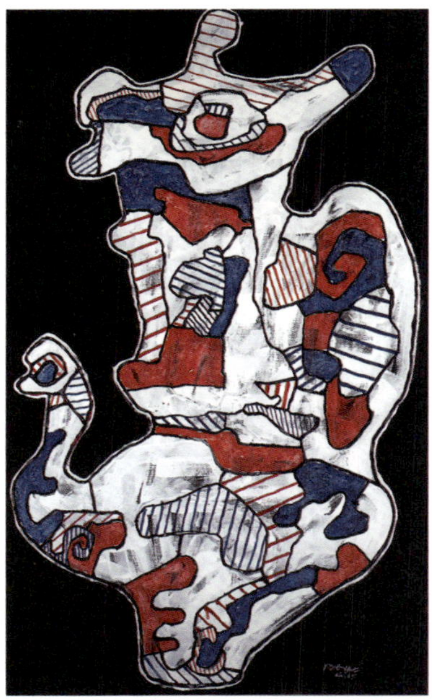

113. Jean Dubuffet. *Cafetière V*, December 17, 1965

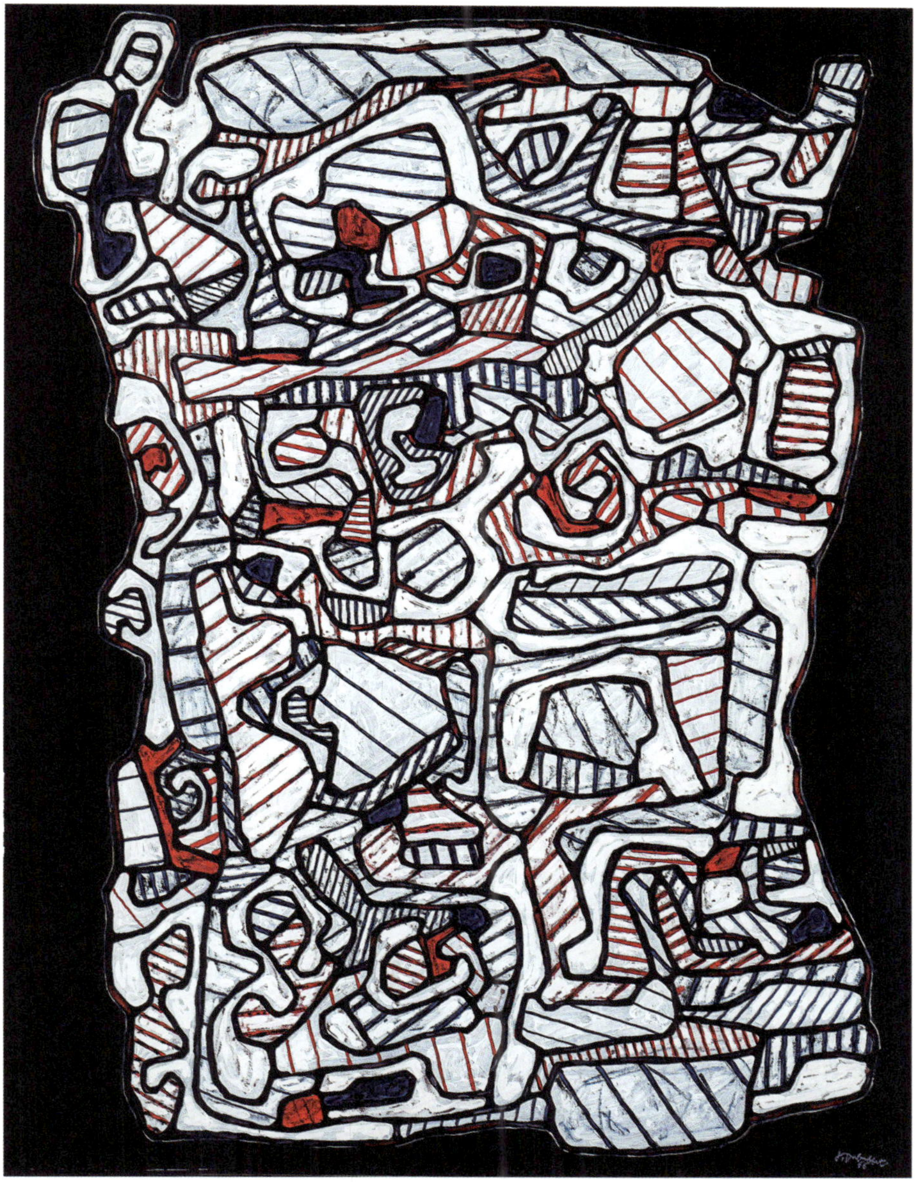

114. Jean Dubuffet. Demeure II (avec seuil et cheminées), March 25, 1966

technical assistant worked out a means of replicating them in a more hard-wearing polyester resin through a process that preserved the textural qualities and original lines and areas of color painted on the Styrofoam by the artist. In 1967, Dubuffet began to make his first models intended for enlargement and conceived his first environment-type work, Cabinet logologique (1967–69). In a text written ten years later, the artist described the latter as a “figuration of the universe.

I mean of a subjective universe, the universe such as it appears digested by my thoughts."[18] By the end of the 1960s, Dubuffet's visual universe was dominated by reds, blues, and sinuous black lines on dead-white grounds, which he described in a 1969 letter to his American dealer Arne Glimcher as an

> uninterrupted meandering and resolutely uniform hand-writing. . . . Perhaps some will object that the term *logos* is here used in the opposite of its meaning, as it generally defines the operation of the mind that names and classifies whereas my own process is rather, on the contrary, to erase categories and regress toward an undifferentiated continuum.[19]

Such a formulation, which, in the context of 1960s France, would have resonated as a departure from the then-dominant theories of semi-otics and structuralism, contributed to the idea that Dubuffet was precipitating himself into an austere, highly individualistic formal vocabulary, emphatically "other" from a contemporary art scene that had absorbed the visual language of popular culture. This reading—of Dubuffet's self-imposed distance, both personal and aesthetic, from the art world—was underscored by critics such as Barbara Rose, who, in a 1979 article, referred to L'Hourloupe as nothing less than a "grave."[20] In France, the critic Geneviève Bonnefoi, writing about Dubuffet's first architectural models, similarly contended—echoing, to a large extent, Dubuffet's own words—that "a particular obsession manifests itself here . . . that of the *closed place*, enclosed on the outside, and self-sufficient."[21] This idea of L'Hourloupe as a hermetic, self-sufficient world became a truism in much of the writing on the artist both then and now, and yet, looking at it from the perspective of the theme of the city, it demands to be questioned and addressed.

The notion of a "hermetic" Hourloupe is closely connected to the idea of a multiplication and spread of its visual language that carried the artist from the first small drawings to the monumental constructions of the Villa and Closerie Falbala, built in Périgny-sur-Yerres to shelter the Cabinet logologique in 1971–73. It also draws very much on the similarity between the material favored by Dubuffet and the idea of growth in multiple dimensions: indeed, the grainy texture of "expanded" polystyrene, commercialized as a packing material by the petrochemical industry in 1960–61, embodies the idea of irrepressible growth, akin to the gradually expanding size and variety of the Hourloupe objects and architectural projects.[22] This sense of a proliferating and hermetic world is also conveyed in the design of several exhibitions of the artist's monuments and sculptures held in 1968–71. A case in point is Jean Dubuffet: Peintures monumentées, which took place from December 1968 to February 1969 at Galerie Jeanne Bucher in Paris. Photographs kept in the

Dubuffet archives show the sculptures presented on the walls, floor, and ceiling, closely surrounding the viewer (one or two pictures even show visitors touching the work) and creating an allover, environment-like space. Almost two years later, the *Edifices and Monuments* exhibition in Chicago repeated, as far as the archival photographs show, this aesthetic of an enclosed, idiosyncratic world.

By contrast, the exhibition *Édifices, projets et maquettes d'architecture*, taking place at the Musée des arts décoratifs at the same time as the show at Jeanne Bucher, threw a very different light on the work. It manifested a continuity with Dubuffet's interest in building that, from the street views of the early *Hourloupe* to the *Demeures* (Homes), disappeared only rarely from the cycle. Moreover, while it is true that Dubuffet's architectural spaces were sometimes made for a single inhabitant, the artist nonetheless envisaged them, as the large photomontages on the museum walls made clear, within the direct context of the city. Finally, the exhibition's inclusion in a program of architecture shows and events at the Musée des arts décoratifs inserted Dubuffet into a particular history and theory of architecture and urbanism that the institution was keen to present. Other exhibitions mounted there between 1965 and 1971 included *Oscar Niermeyer*, in 1965; *Ricardo Porro*, in 1968; Bernard Rudofsky's *Architectures méconnues—architectes inconnus* (Little-Known Architectures, Unknown Architects), in 1969, which reprised, under a new title, the Museum of Modern Art's 1964 exhibition *Architecture without Architects*; and the two-part *Pionniers du XXe siècle* devoted to Hector Guimard, Victor Horta, Henry van de Velde, and Antoni Gaudí. Latin American architects, Art Nouveau pioneers, an idiosyncratic Catalonian modernist, and vernacular architecture: these subjects taken together outline alternatives to the Le Corbusier- and Bauhaus-driven modernist traditions that, in the late 1960s, had become assimilated into the ubiquitous generic forms of the International Style, or, as the architecture critic Ada Louise Huxtable called it, "high modern corporate style."[23] Alongside these exhibitions, François Mathey, the museum's director and a longtime Dubuffet supporter, opened his doors in 1965–67 to a series of lectures by the Groupe d'intervention d'architecture prospectiviste (GIAP), which brought together architectural thinkers and practitioners around the ubiquitous Michel Ragon (who, in another life, in the 1950s, had written about Dubuffet's work).[24] Dubuffet's first architectural exhibition thus took place in a setting within which strong, individualistic voices representing

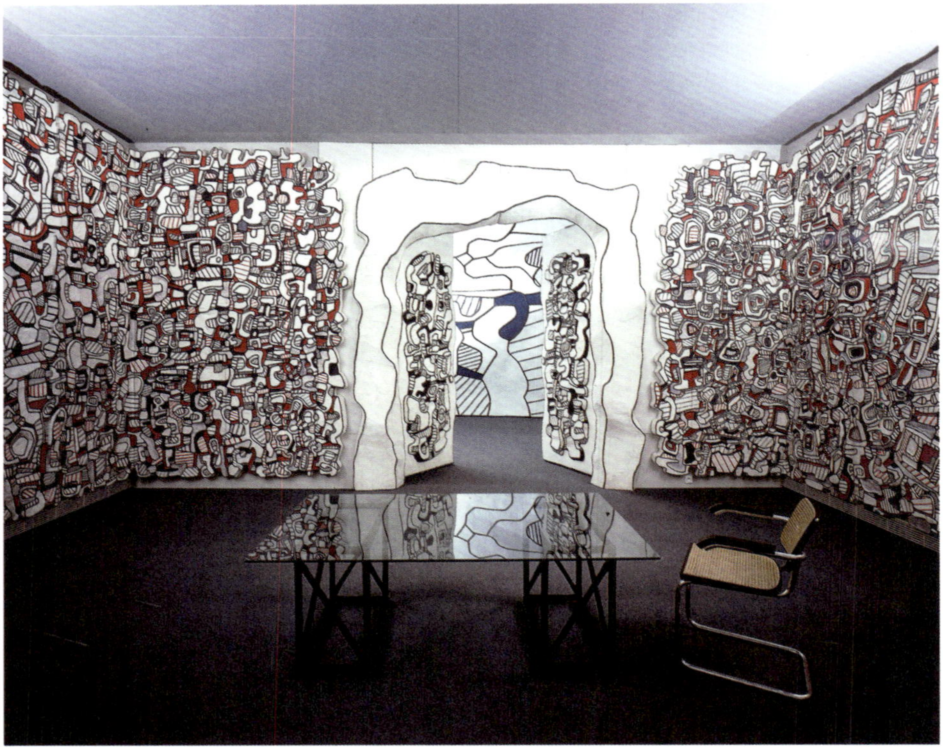

115. Jean Dubuffet. Cabinet logologique, August 1967–February 1969

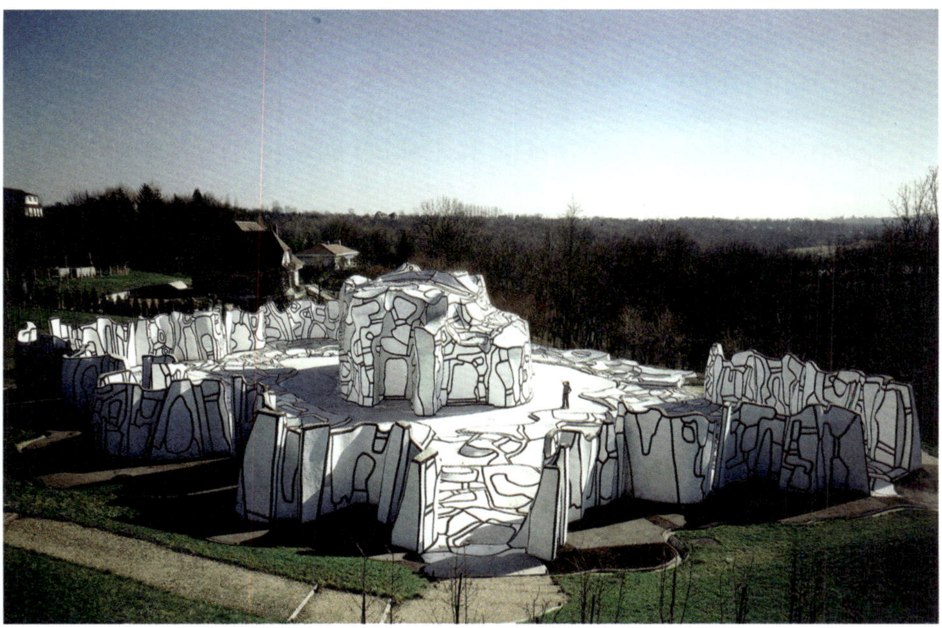

116. Jean Dubuffet. Closerie Falbala, Périgny-sur-Yerres, built 1971–73

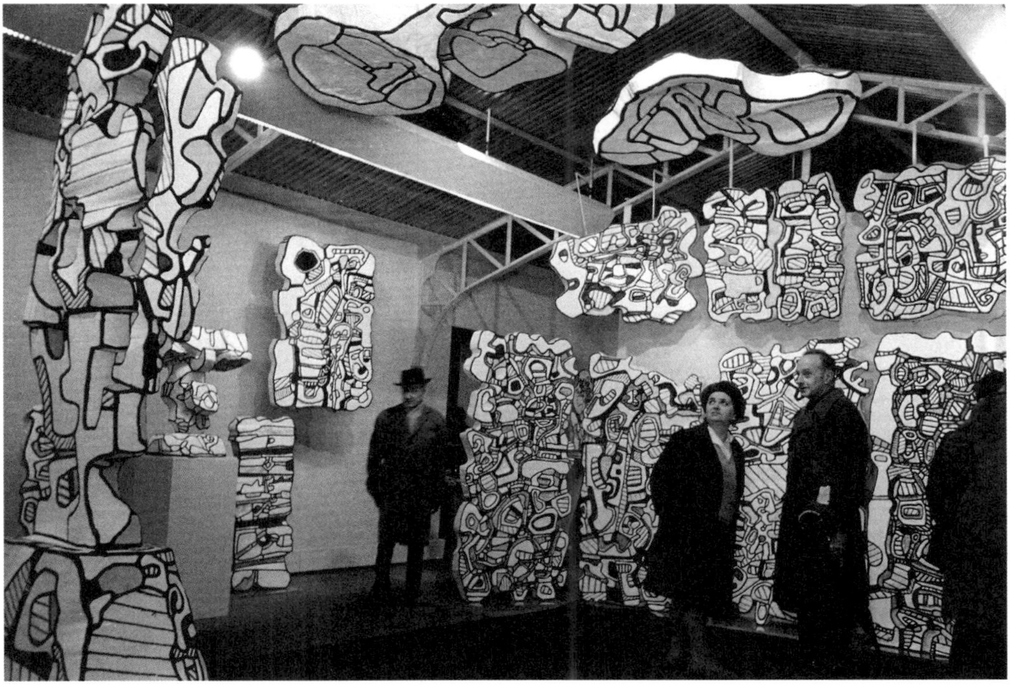

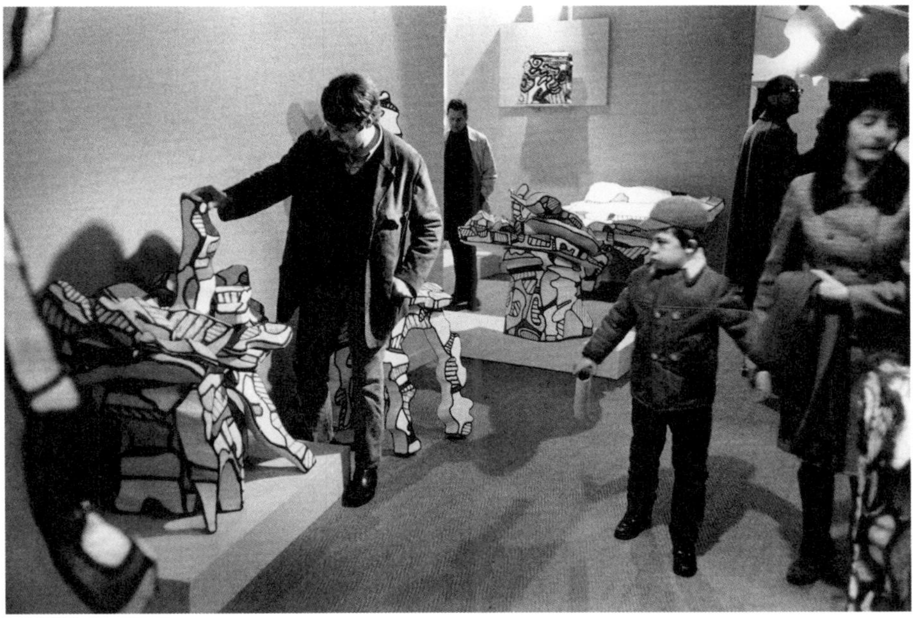

117, 118. Jean Dubuffet: Peintures monumentées exhibition, Galerie Jeanne Bucher, Paris, December 12, 1968–February 8, 1969

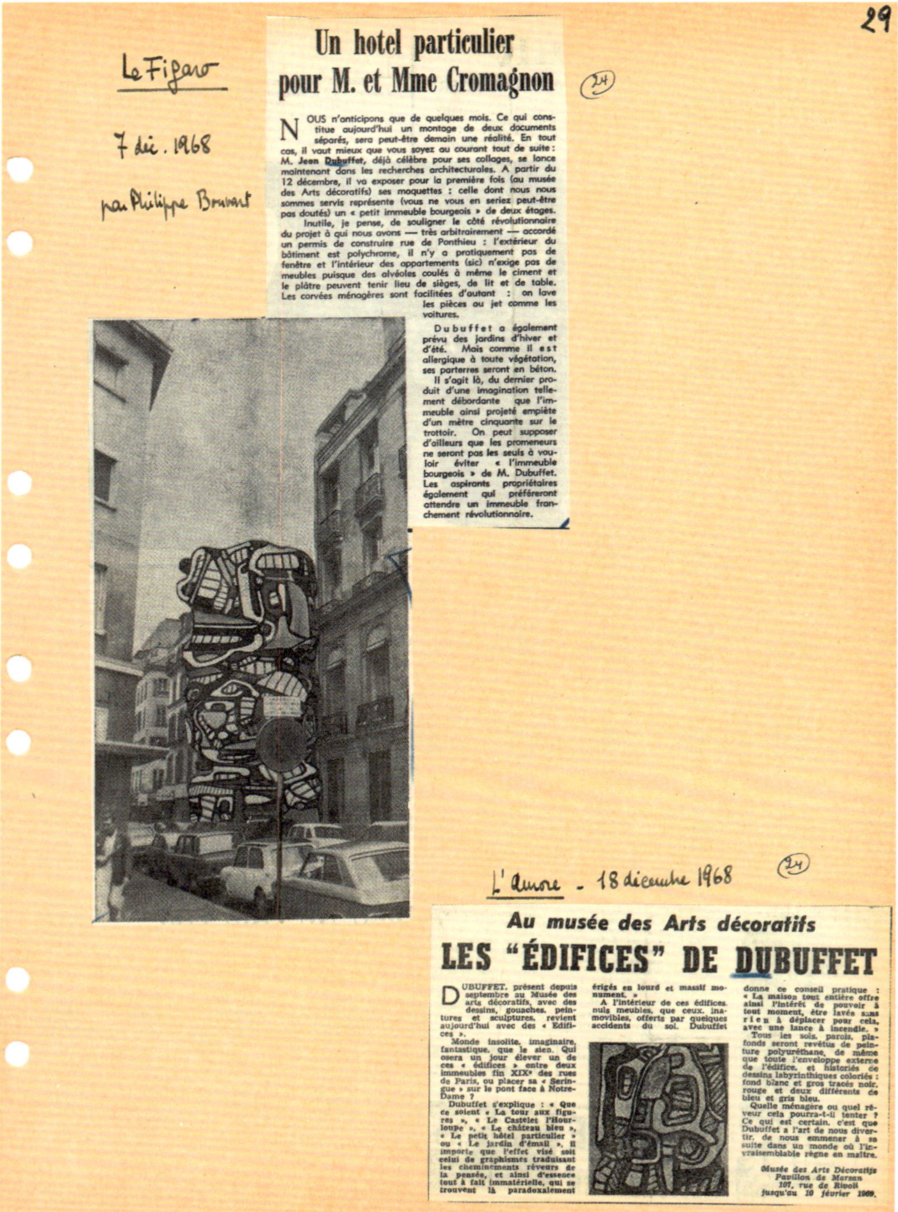

29

Le Figaro

7 déc. 1968

par Philippe Bouvard

Un hotel particulier pour M. et Mme Cromagnon

NOUS n'anticipons que de quelques mois. Ce qui constitue aujourd'hui un montage de deux documents séparés, sera peut-être demain une réalité. En tout cas, il vaut mieux que vous soyez au courant tout de suite : M. **Jean Dubuffet**, déjà célèbre pour ses collages, se lance maintenant dans les recherches architecturales. A partir du 12 décembre, il va exposer pour la première fois (au musée des Arts décoratifs) ses maquettes : celle dont nous nous sommes servis représente (vous ne vous en seriez peut-être pas doutés) un « petit immeuble bourgeois » de deux étages.

Inutile, je pense, de souligner le côté révolutionnaire du projet à qui nous avons — très arbitrairement — accordé un permis de construire rue de Ponthieu : l'extérieur du bâtiment est polychrome, il n'y a pratiquement pas de fenêtre et l'intérieur des appartements (sic) n'exige pas de meubles puisque des alvéoles coulés à même le ciment et le plâtre peuvent tenir lieu de sièges, de lit et de table. Les corvées ménagères sont facilitées d'autant : on lave les pièces au jet comme les voitures.

Dubuffet a également prévu des jardins d'hiver et d'été. Mais comme il est allergique à toute végétation, ses parterres seront en béton.

Il s'agit là, du dernier produit d'une imagination tellement débordante que l'immeuble ainsi projeté empiète d'un mètre cinquante sur le trottoir. On peut supposer d'ailleurs que les promeneurs ne seront pas les seuls à vouloir éviter « l'immeuble bourgeois » de M. Dubuffet. Les aspirants propriétaires également qui préféreront attendre un immeuble franchement révolutionnaire.

L'Aurore - 18 décembre 1968

Au musée des Arts décoratifs

LES "ÉDIFICES" DE DUBUFFET

DUBUFFET, présent depuis septembre au Musée des arts décoratifs, avec des dessins, gouaches, peintures et sculptures, revient aujourd'hui avec des « Edifices ».

Monde insolite, imaginaire, fantastique, que le sien. Qui osera un jour élever un de ces « édifices » entre deux immeubles fin XIXe des rues de Paris, ou placer sa « Seringue » sur le pont face à Notre-Dame ?

Dubuffet s'explique : « Que ce soient « La tour aux figures », « Le Castelet l'Hourloupe », « Le château bleu », « Le petit hôtel particulier » ou « Le jardin d'émail », il importe que l'effet visé soit celui de graphismes traduisant les cheminements rêveurs de la pensée, et ainsi d'essence tout à fait immatérielle, qui se trouvent là paradoxalement érigés en lourd et massif monument. »

A l'intérieur de ces édifices, nuls meubles, que ceux, inamovibles, offerts par quelques accidents du sol. Dubuffet donne ce conseil pratique : « La maison tout entière offre ainsi l'intérêt de pouvoir à tout moment, être lavée sans rien à déplacer pour cela, avec une lance à incendie. »

Tous les sols, parois, plafonds seront revêtus de peinture polyuréthane, de même que toute l'enveloppe externe de l'édifice, et historiés de dessins labyrinthiques coloriés : fond blanc et gros tracés noir, rouge et deux différents de bleu et gris bleu.

Quelle ménagère ou quel rêveur cela pourra-t-il tenter ? Ce qui est certain, c'est que Dubuffet a l'art de nous divertir, de nous emmener à sa suite dans un monde où l'invraisemblable règne en maître.

Musée des Arts Décoratifs
Pavillon de Marsan
107, rue de Rivoli
jusqu'au 10 février 1969.

119. Page from scrapbook of press coverage for Dubuffet's exhibitions in the archives of the Fondation Dubuffet, Paris

different forms of theory, vision, and practice of architecture coexisted. There is nothing in the Dubuffet archives that clarifies whether it was Dubuffet himself or Mathey who initiated the exhibition of December 1968.[25] But Dubuffet did fully control, as his correspondence shows, the conception of Édifices, penning the text of the book, commissioning the architect Antoine Butor to make technical drawings, and instructing the photographers Augustin Dumage and Wolf Slawny to produce, in collaboration with himself, the photomontages.

The critical reception of the exhibition in the French and international press included some examples of philistinism and caricature but also serious appraisals and consideration of Dubuffet's projects within the realm of utopian architectural thinking. Numerous critics and journalists attempted to connect Dubuffet's models to past styles. One saw in the Hourloupean patterns of the models "swarming shapes like a Maya sculpture,"[26] while another described them as archaizing dwellings and at least one mentioned the Catalonian magus Gaudí: "The Edifices of Jean Dubuffet reveal a Gaudí of the twentieth century," wrote the critic François Pluchart.[27] Some reporters made connections between Dubuffet's projects and other artists' ventures into architecture or architectural utopias, such as Niki de Saint Phalle's Hon, the woman-shaped walk-in sculpture realized in Stockholm in collaboration with Jean Tinguely in 1966, and Yves Klein's designs for "air architecture," developed with Claude Parent.[28] Dubuffet's projects were thus perceived to be connected both with a history of art and with the time in which they were produced. One critic even described his architectural projects as "a kind of 'mental prosthesis' made to help Man live in a civilization in which he feels unwell."[29]

Extending the reach of these reviews, the photomontages extensively circulated as illustrations to press articles. These striking visual documents, along with the informed tone of many critics, suggest that Dubuffet's work was indeed perceived within the context of debates around urbanism that were very much present in everyday life: "The population at large was bombarded with the frequent coverage of construction work in the press, on the radio and on the television," explains the architectural historian Jacob Paskins in his 2016 book Paris under Construction; newspapers abundantly reported "proposals for new urbanism schemes, the construction of new infrastructure, or the opening of new buildings."[30] For instance, in 1967, the popular weekly magazine Paris Match published an issue on the "Paris of tomorrow" that reprised some of the main large-scale urban projects being developed at that time (fig. 120), while the large exhibition Du Paris des projets au Paris des chantiers (From the Paris of Projects to the Paris of Construction Sites) attempted to woo Parisians into accepting some of the most controversial projects under the well-rehearsed arguments of sanitization and modernization (figs. 121, 122). Presented in March and April 1967 under the glass canopy of the Grand Palais, this sequel to 1961's Demain Paris again included the monumental architectural model of Paris (fig. 57). Observing the plans for the Port of Gennevilliers, place d'Italie, boulevard Périphérique, Porte Maillot, and, of course, the concrete slabs making up the *grands ensembles* that Godard critiqued the same year

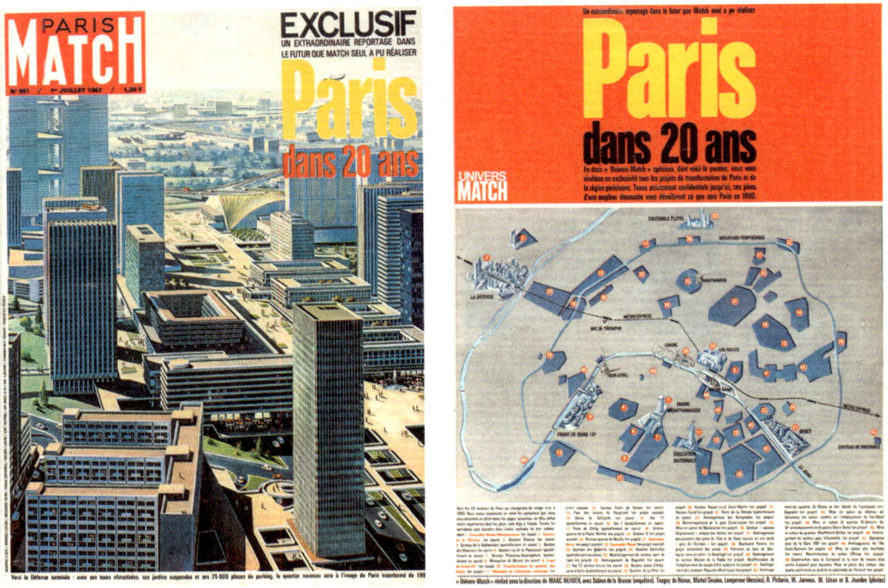

120. Cover and interior page of Paris Match, July 1, 1967

in his film Deux ou trois choses que je sais d'elle (Two or Three Things I Know about Her), the critic André Fermigier mused, "Will this be the Paris of the year 2000? I do not think so, it looks to me very 1960. . . . The shape nearly universally adopted is that of a gathering of high-rises lined up, back to back, shifted from one another but always at right angles: like a game of dominos propped up vertically, a weakened Mies van der Rohe."[31] Fermigier's articles penned between 1967 and 1983 first for the center-left fortnightly Le nouvel Observateur and then for the center-left daily Le Monde show something of the context in which Dubuffet's models were received. Fermigier notably reviewed the large exhibitions emanating from public authorities as well as a myriad of smaller exhibitions by local associations, rejecting official projects, proposing alternative ones, and reminiscing about endangered historical neighborhoods. He also pointed up a certain sense of collective weariness with the International Style and the more degraded, generic forms of the tower and the slab it generated under the guise of modernization.[32] In a December 1968 article discussing the plans for an entirely rebuilt neighborhood around place d'Italie, which were on view in the *mairie* (town hall) of the 13th arrondissement, he succinctly noted: "Triumph of the domino and of the parallel bars."[33]

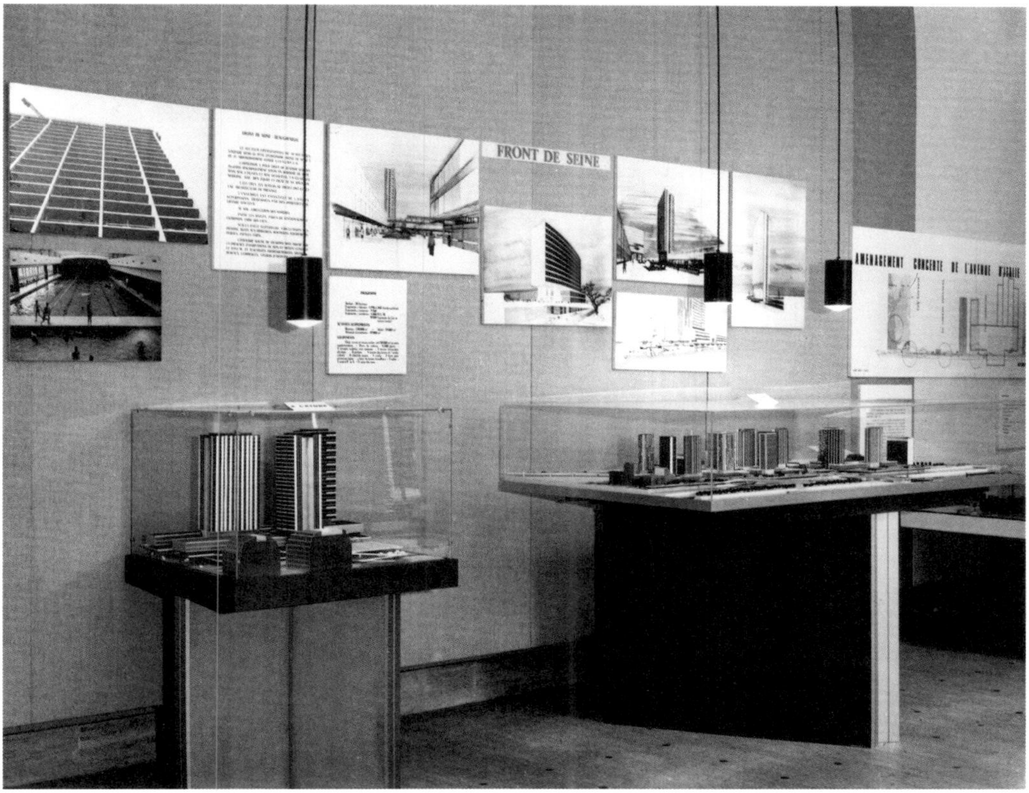

121. *Du Paris des projets au Paris des chantiers* exhibition, Grand Palais, Paris, March–April 1967

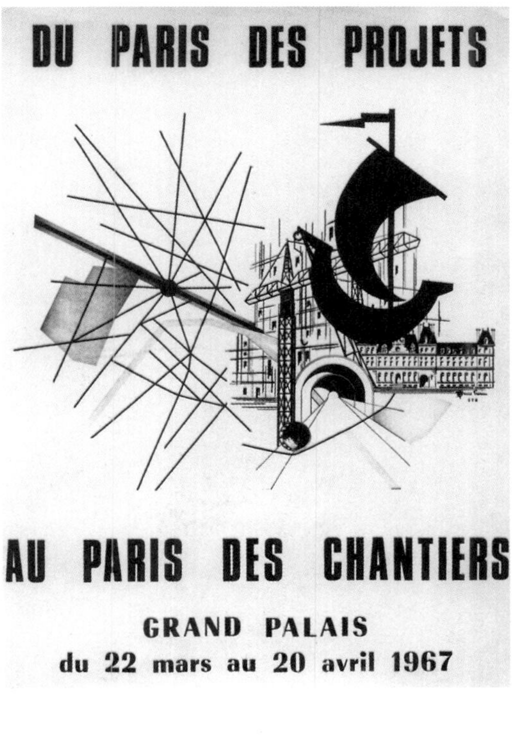

122. Poster for *Du Paris des projets au Paris des chantiers* exhibition, 1967

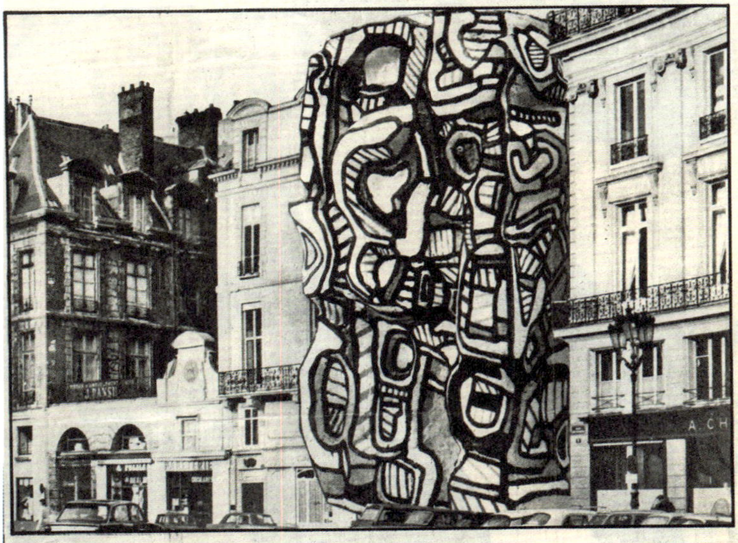

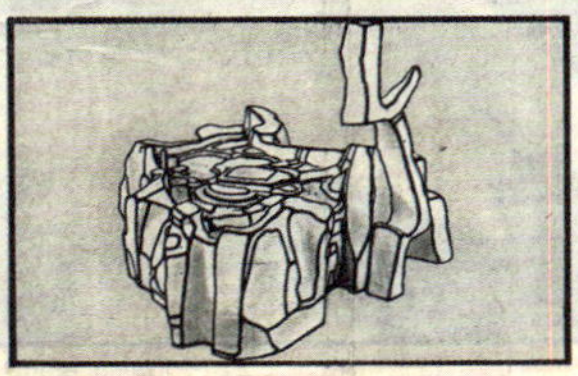

Novità architettoniche in Francia

TREDICI PROGETTI PER TRASFORMARE PARIGI

di BRUNO ZEVI

PARIGI. I primi risultati del concorso internazionale indetto dall'ente "Construction et Humanisme"; i lavori della Défence, già valutabili, per quanto attiene all'indirizzo architettonico, osservando il grattacielo della Tour Nobel a Puteaux; la crisi dell'Ecole des Beaux-Arts; infine, due mostre al Musée des Arts Décoratifs e quella di Mondrian all'Orangerie. Ecco gli eventi più discussi nella capitale francese in questa stagione particolarmente depressa. Ne diamo un rapido resoconto.

Al concorso di "Construction et Humanisme" hanno partecipato, con 87 progetti, gruppi di professionisti di 28 nazioni. Straordinario successo dell' iniziativa cui non corrisponde tuttavia un risultato culturale parimenti positivo. I due temi, "Création d'une ville nouvelle" e "Création d'une structure associant habitat, bureaux, équipements publics et services, dans le cadre d'un programme de rénovation d'un centre de ville à population très dense" avrebbero dovuto stimolare proposte coraggiose, immagini urbane capaci di captare l'attenzione di un vasto pubblico. Invece, c'è ben poco di nuovo. Le ipotesi presentate sono classificabili entro tre categorie: A. Visioni utopistiche, farragine di mastodontiche strutture conoidali o romboidali accatastate secondo congegni privi perfino di fascino pop; B. Riedizioni di città-giardino e di città-satelliti solo tecnologicamente aggiornate rispetto ai prototipi di cinquant'anni fa; C. Tentativi di riconcentrazione urbana ricchi di contenitori integranti le varie funzioni della città. Quest'ultima tendenza è certamente la più attuale ma, nelle specifiche applicazioni, si rivela o troppo professionale o troppo astratta. Da un lato, tecniche di industrializzazione edilizia che imprigionano l'architettura in reticolati rigidi e monotoni; dall'altro, ideologie inadatte a materializzarsi in un'organica morfologia. Quanto al "centre de ville", è una nozione anacronistica, ottocentesca, cui occorre sostituire una diversa gamma di relazioni funzionali tuttora imprecisate.

La giuria ha scelto tredici progetti i cui modelli saranno esposti nella prima quindicina di marzo a Cannes, durante la settimana del "Grand Prix International d'Urbanisme et d'Architecture". La selezione finale avverrà allora e probabilmente darà luogo a contrasti e polemiche.

"Construction et Humanisme" ha sede nella Tour Nobel, il primo edificio realizzato del complesso della Défence. L'orrore di questo colossale sventramento di Parigi appare già in tutta la sua evidenza. Nel caso migliore, avremo una brutta replica di Park Avenue, con l'esibizionistico corteo di insignificanti involucri vitrei; ma qui mancherà l'alimento di un tessuto metropolitano ad altissima densità. Su altra scala, i blocchi della Défence costituiscono una facciata alla Haussmann sprovvista di un organismo vitale alle spalle. Speculazione neocapitalistica e scenografia neoclassica in forme pseudo-moderne si sposano con la benedizione del generale.

Di fronte a tale spettacolo, la rabbia degli studenti è più che giustificata. Ma la scuola d'architettura versa in gravissima crisi, e la contestazione non trova modo di esprimersi. Si è verificata una spaccatura pericolosa. I professori e gli studenti moderati hanno ripreso l'attività didattica, mentre la sinistra resiste e condiziona la riapertura dei corsi e dei seminari all'inserimento della facoltà nell'ambito universitario. Ma fino a quando potrà insistere su questa posizione di rifiuto? Il malumore si estende, i giovani non intendono perdere un anno e cominciano a criticare l'intransigenza massimalista.

Veniamo alle tre mostre. Paradossalmente, quella di Piet Mondrian costituisce quasi una novità per la cultura media francese. Il celebre pittore si trasferì a Parigi dalla nativa Olanda nel 1911 e vi risiedette fino al 1938, lavorando nell'atelier della rue du Départ; ma nessun museo ha mai acquistato una sua opera, e questa esposizione, peraltro incompleta, è la prima che si effettui nella capitale. Sedotta dalla prestigiosa figura di Le Corbusier, l'avanguardia francese ha ignorato la ricerca di "De Stijl" e solo adesso scopre questa componente fondamentale del movimento moderno. Gli architetti affollano l'Orangerie ma non sempre riescono ad individuare le implicazioni del messaggio di Mondrian nel loro campo.

Al Museo delle Arti Decorative, la mostra dell'architettura preistorica e primitiva allestita da Bernard Rudofsky, proveniente da New York, ha dato luogo ad un episodio incredibilmente ridicolo. Il titolo originale della rassegna è "Architecture without architects", ma gli ordini professionali l'hanno ritenuto offensivo. Non possono ammettere, nella loro grettezza corporativa, che esista un'architettura spontanea, costruita senza l'intervento del demiurgo laureato. Perciò la mostra è stata ribattezzata "Architectures méconnues - Architectes inconnus", senza il permesso dell'autore. Ionel Schein, uno degli animatori più vivaci della cultura architettonica parigina, è furibondo: « La gente scherza su questo episodio, ma non è affatto trascurabile. Dimostra che le giornate di maggio hanno cambiato poco o nulla. I vecchi notabili, con la loro prosopopea, hanno rialzato la cresta. Quando si riesce a svisare il titolo di un'esposizione giunta dagli Stati Uniti, tutto è possibile, anche la Défence, anche la ripresa dell'insegnamento senza alcuna garanzia di ottenere i mutamenti istituzionali promessi. Siamo in piena involuzione. La burocrazia, il conformismo, i soliti tromboni tornano a prevalere e sono così stupidi da illudersi che quanto è accaduto a maggio non possa ripetersi ».

Nelle sale adiacenti, gli "Edifices" di Jean Dubuffet. Si respira un'aria nuova, a metà tra l'espressionismo e l'informale. Totem mostruosi, che sembrano lanciare anatemi e invettive contro un panorama urbano sterilizzato dai processi dell'industrializzazione edilizia. Enormi sculture cave, deformi e gesticolanti, cromaticamente stridenti, denunciano una volontà di ribellione che mutua la disperazione col grottesco.

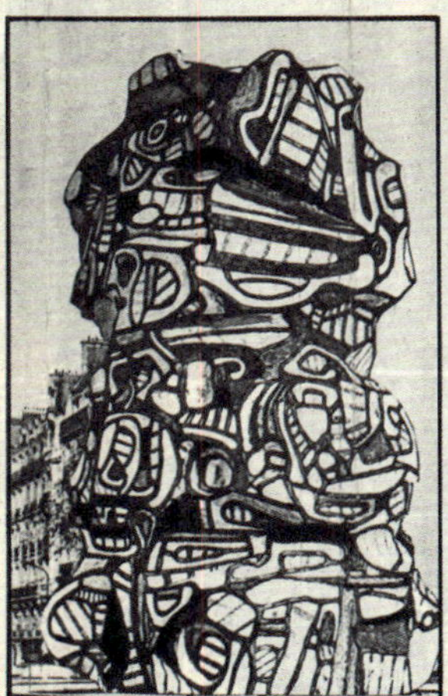

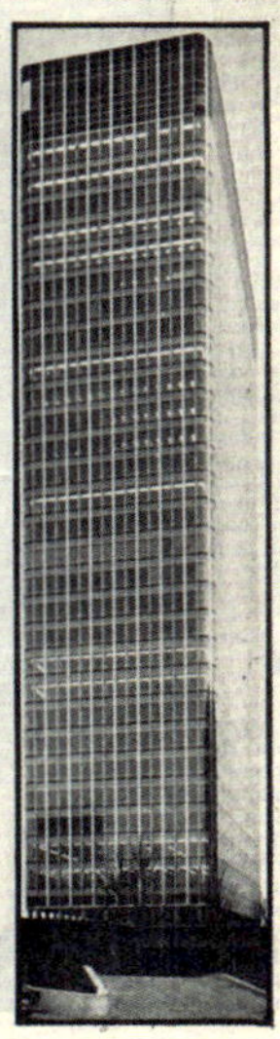

"Tour aux Figures" progettata da Jean Dubuffet. A destra: la Tour Nobel a Puteax, il primo grattacielo del complesso della Défence. Accanto al titolo: "Castelet l'Hourloupe", disegno esposto nella mostra "Edifices". In alto, "Pavillon à deux étages". Questa mostra è una protesta contro l'industrializzazione edilizia.

123. Bruno Zevi's article in L'Espresso, February 2, 1969, featuring Dubuffet's Tour aux figures, from a scrapbook in the archives of the Fondation Dubuffet, Paris

Against Functionalism

André Fermigier, who, in another instance, lauded one of Dubuffet's monument projects, was part of a category of critics who considered Dubuffet's proposals a salutary response in the context in which they appeared.[34] For the architect and author Bruno Zevi, Dubuffet's Tour aux figures was the complete antithesis of the high-rises gradually appearing in Paris and at La Défense. In an article for the Italian weekly L'Espresso, he published a photograph of it side by side with one of the Tour Nobel, the first high-rise to be completed at La Défense, in 1966, with a caption referring to Dubuffet's show at the Musée des art décoratifs and reading, "This exhibition is a protest against industrialized building" (fig. 123).[35]

This juxtaposition demonstrates the need for Dubuffet's proposals, and notably the Tour aux figures, to be read against the background of the functionalism that was then dominant in Parisian architecture. At the time Dubuffet was developing this project, another tower was capturing the imagination—and the ire—of commentators and Parisians at large. This was the Tour Montparnasse. Again, Fermigier's lapidary tone succinctly conveys a sense of the building's reception even as it was still in progress: "I admire the total lack of shame on the part of the architects who presented the projects for the high-rises to be built at the roundabout of La Défense and the location of the former Montparnasse station. Personally, I would have lost sleep over it."[36] The form reprised and transformed by Dubuffet in the Tour aux figures was thus not only one of the staples of the modern architectural vocabulary; it was also a form perceived as "inhuman," resolutely foreign to the architectural vocabulary of Paris and seen, in that Gaullist era, as an unwelcome American import. The project for the Tour Montparnasse was highly publicized and fiercely debated throughout the 1960s, before the building was finally erected, between 1969 and 1973. Part of these debates concerned the height of the tower, which constantly fluctuated over the years: in 1957, it was planned to be 50 meters (164 feet) tall; in 1959, 183 meters (600 feet); and finally, in 1967, it reached 200 meters (656 feet, or 67 floors). These changes testify to the competing voices of politicians, planners, architects, and the public in the years the project was under way.[37] Photographs taken from the beginning of the rue de Rennes showing the progress of the tower are among the most spectacular views of Paris during this era (fig. 124).

By the time the Tour Montparnasse was completed, high-rises were undergoing a general backlash, being widely denounced as an "attack against the city" and a symbol of a brand of urban planning that was in need of reform.[38] To wit, in 1974, the newly elected president Valéry Giscard d'Estaing declared a ban on the building of towers in central Paris that is still in effect today.

Within this context, Dubuffet's own towers, with their combination of modularity and idiosyncrasy, read both in stark opposition and as ironic comments on the phenomenon and very idea of the tower. The motif itself reappeared in a number of his projects, including the Tour de chantourne of 1967, Tour aux récits (Tower with Stories) of 1973, and Tour ballerine (Ballerina Tower) of 1974. Each exhibits irregular bumps and curves, and each façade is painted in blues, reds, and black and white, with planes of hatched and solid color. Depending on the angle at which they are viewed, vaguely human silhouettes or grinning faces peer through interlacing lines. This anthropomorphic and illusionistic character is a far cry from the rectilinear structures and geometric façade patterns of typical high-rises, injecting an element of fantasy into the modernist idea of the tower. Hence, one critic noted, "Dubuffet has made a transfer from utilitarian to obsessional functionalism."[39] Dubuffet's towers stand as far as possible from any kind of industrialized building, and yet, they display a similar lack of sensitivity to context that was criticized by authors in reference to the high-rises then being built across the country. Fermigier, for example, repeatedly deplored the ubiquity of the "domino" in urban planning. Dubuffet envisaged several possible heights for his towers and, in the case of the Tour aux figures, pasted it into a half-dozen photomontages in urban and suburban contexts, making it appear in different surroundings as if, like a modern high-rise, it could be erected just about anywhere. Moreover, while some critics decried Dubuffet's use of plastic-looking polyester resin and epoxy, those materials nonetheless corresponded to the increased artificiality of the modern city acknowledged by historians of urbanism.[40]

The interior layout of the Tour aux figures shows more clearly how Dubuffet gradually distanced himself from the traditional tower-block idea. In his first idea for the inside, he evoked something close to an ordinary residential building: "a building with apartments each divided into rooms conceived in the usual way."[41] The second plan was given a title, L'Aérogire, as was the third and final one, Le Gastrovolve, and each of these took on an individualized, sculptural quality.[42] In Édifices, Dubuffet described the intended use of the latter: "Instead of being divided by rooms at the different levels, the tower is conceived of as an ascending path, interrupted by landings, ramps, and staircases which lead sinuously from the bottom to a

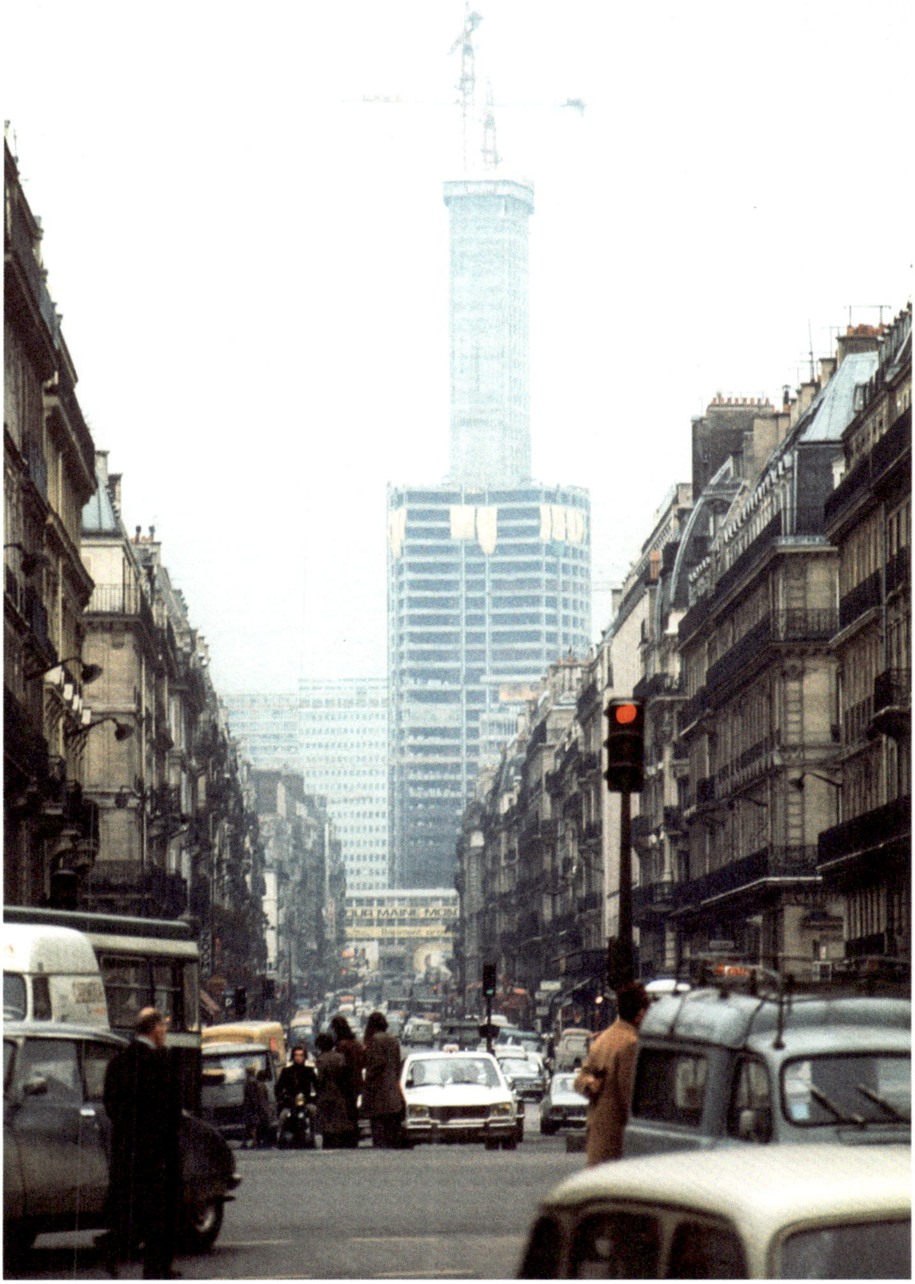

124. Tour Montparnasse under construction, Paris, February 16, 1972

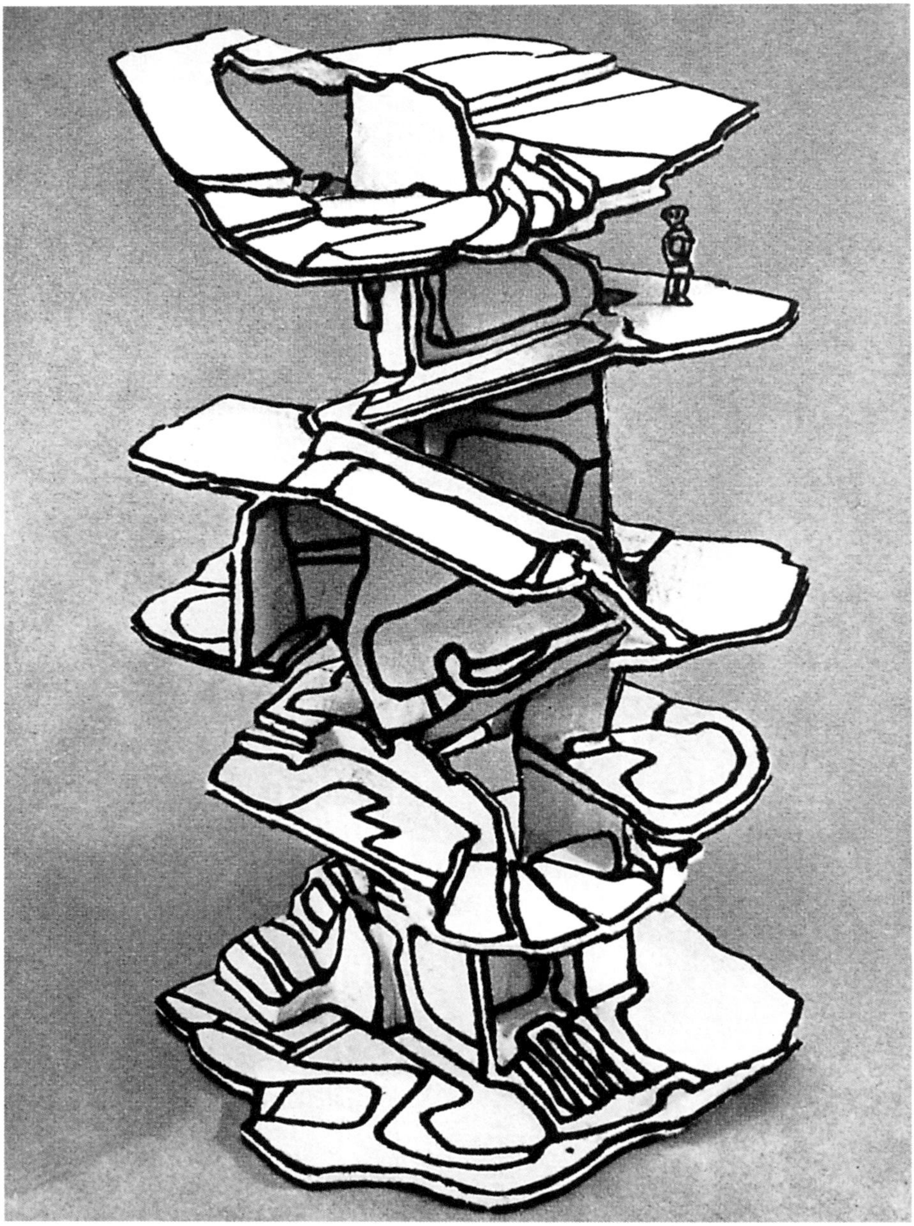

125. Jean Dubuffet. Le Gastrovolve (1968), reproduced in Dubuffet: Édifices (1968)

great hall in the summit. Its course would much resemble a walk in the mountains."[43] Reviewing the Tour aux figures and Le Gastrovolve in the context of the Musée des arts décoratifs exhibition, Marcel Cornu praised both the architectural quality of Dubuffet's interior volumes and his ability to construct a continuous volume from one space to another. For Cornu, in an argument that seems to pit anonymous industrial architecture against the humanist idea of the architect as artist, Dubuffet could be an inspiration for the architecture of the day, down to his innovative construction techniques: engineers, Cornu claimed, were fascinated by Dubuffet.[44] Françoise Choay similarly argued for the importance of Dubuffet's architecture projects within contemporary culture: "The work of a Dubuffet today cannot be dissociated from investigation into the human sciences," she wrote a few years later in a text on Dubuffet and language.[45]

It is in the letters Dubuffet exchanged during this period with Cornu and Choay that the artist's antagonism to late international modernism becomes unambiguous. In a letter to Cornu of January 1969, written to thank him for the aforementioned article, he reflected: "The architecture of our time is appalling—completely devoid of imagination, based on sordid economic considerations, made without effort, stuck to the rectilinear, the parallelepipedal box of such miserable invention."[46] Habitat urbain of 1979 (fig. 103) and other works in the series Brefs exercices d'école journalière (Brief Daily School Exercises) can be seen as satirical takes on such a rectilinear architecture, depicting figures enclosed in cage-like environments. By the time he was producing two-dimensional works

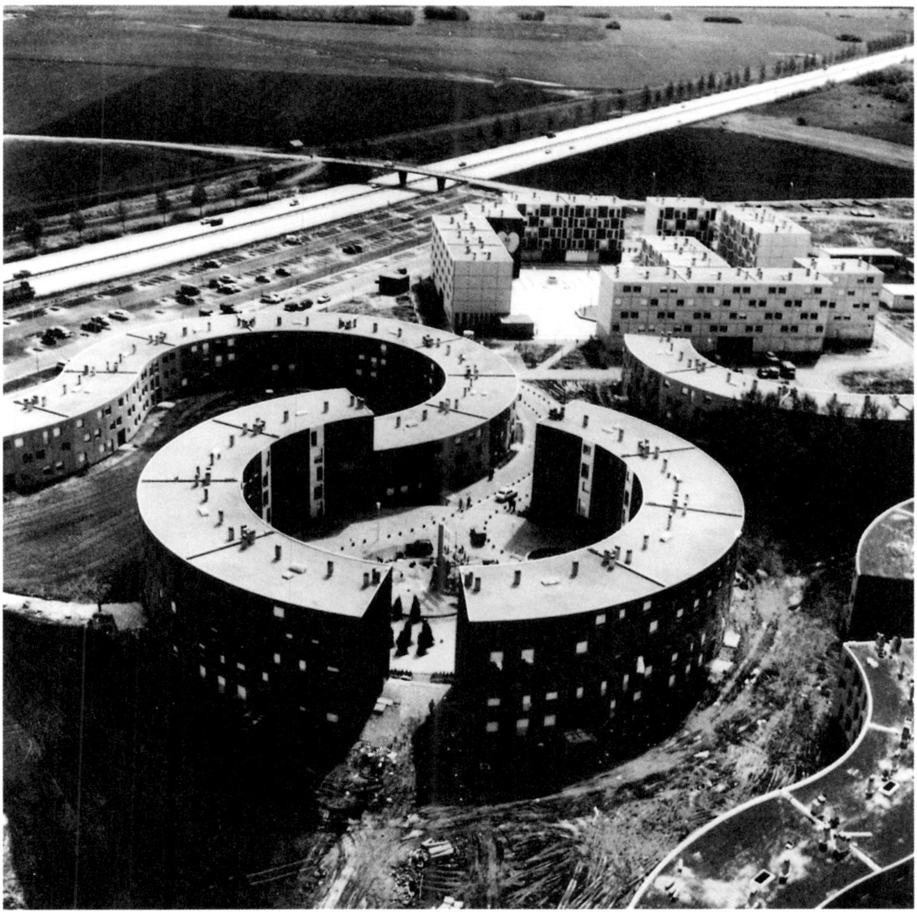

126. Aerial view of La Grande Borne, Grigny, built 1967–69

such as these, Dubuffet was looking back at his architectural projects, and in 1977, in a text that is worth citing at length, he explained what he believed to be the effect of rectilinear architecture on the human imagination:

> We have all lived constantly since birth surrounded by angled planes and rectilinear elements. We sleep in a parallelepipedal room, on a rectangular bed and our furniture is, too. We are deeply conditioned by the constant companionship of the horizontal and the vertical, by the right angle, the strict rectangle. . . . It is certain that this fact has an influence on our thinking and an important role in the way it functions. I have had a great deal of curiosity about our ability to get away from inhabiting these plane, straight geometrical structures and to adapt ourselves without discomfort to living in places where the plane, the straight line, and the square are abolished. The experience I have had of buildings I have built or that are currently under way leads me to think that we can do it, that we even feel it as a regenerating liberation and release. I also feel that a habitation of this new kind is likely to cause a significant and perhaps very rewarding change to the structures and movements of our thinking."[47]

"To live in ideas"? Architecture, Monument, Sculpture

The clarity of Dubuffet's vision as it is expressed in the preceding text begs the question of the extent to which he aimed to build habitable edifices. The American Institute of Architects awarded him its annual medal of honor in June 1982, explaining that his works "provide not only scale, focus, color and texture but clear insights into the nature of the architecture they complement—its space, volume, structure and surface—blending architecture and sculpture into a single entity."[48] It was the only prize that Dubuffet ever accepted, and the precise wording used by the AIA's director, Robert M. Lawrence, suggests that the prize committee perceived Dubuffet's work primarily as a reflection on the nature of architecture. An exchange of letters with Choay shows how she encouraged him to become more involved with actual architectural practice. At the end of 1967, she had sent the artist a brochure concerning an unspecified project by the architect Émile Aillaud, whose work mixed functionalism with literary and poetic references. Upon returning it to her, Dubuffet commented:

> I have not understood if the city in question is actually built or if it is at the stage of a project.
>
> It would not be my thing to live there. I would feel better in some low neighborhood of Paris or London. The idea of a city that, instead of being formed over the course of centuries, little by little, by the game of circumstances, has been created all in one go, in an arbitrary location, weighs heavily on the well-being of its dweller. . . . I think that I would feel more comfortable if, instead of this deliberate [design], the city resulted from putting everything into a hat, throwing it in the air and taking things as they fall back down. I feel a great need to anchor myself in the nondeliberate. And I am sure that everyone senses this very strongly. A great deal of the nondeliberate, chaos, and irrationality should be given to such urbanism plans.[49]

The brochure having been returned, it is impossible to identify which of Aillaud's projects it may have concerned; however, given the dates, it may well have been La Grande Borne, the large housing estate of almost four thousand dwellings built by Aillaud between 1967 and 1969 in the communes of Grigny and Viry-Châtillon, near Paris, which remains, along with the Tours Nuages in Nanterre (1977), his

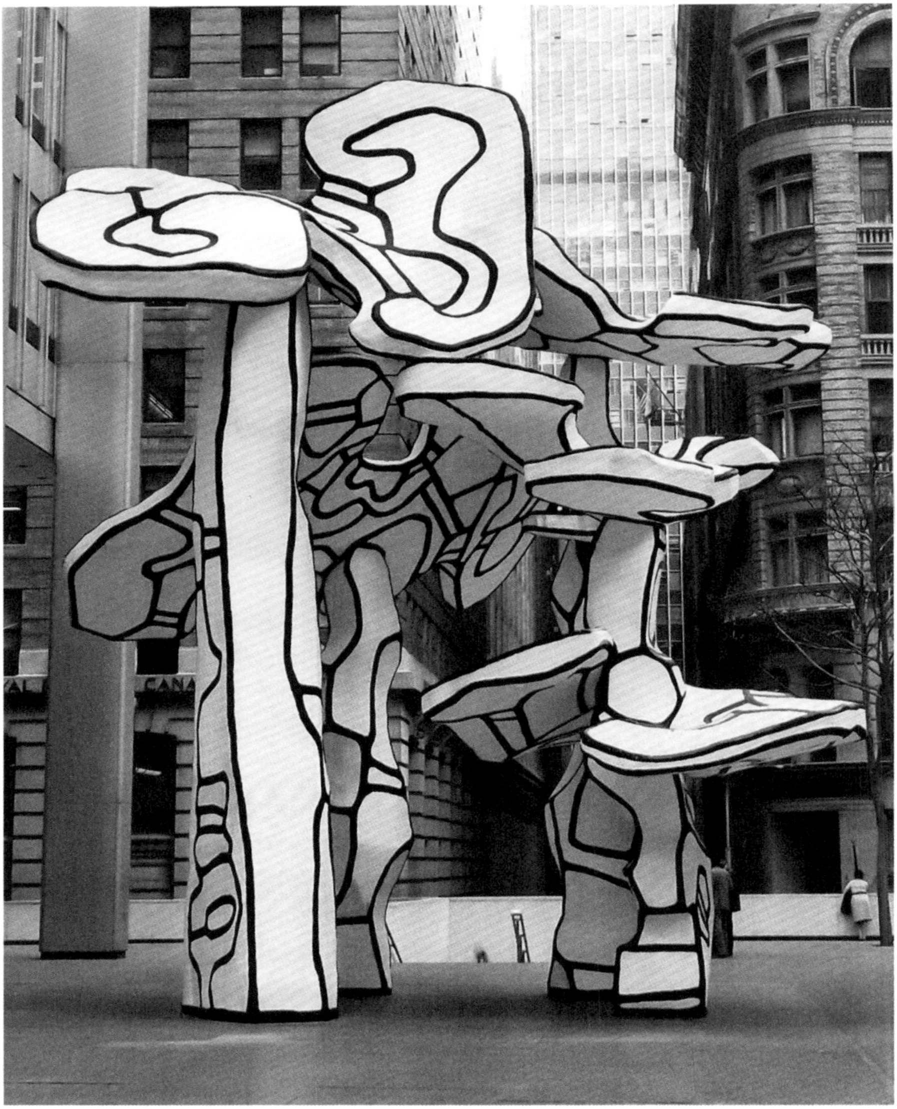

127. Jean Dubuffet (Al Mozelle, photographer). Groupe de quatre arbres, April 1971–July 1972, installed at 1 Chase Manhattan Plaza (28 Liberty Street), New York

best-known achievement (fig. 126). In designing the experimental development, Aillaud surrounded himself with artists to create an alternative to the slabs and towers typical of postwar public housing complexes, proposing instead a labyrinthine project full of small plazas with colorful walls and works of public art.

In her reply dated February 24, 1968, Choay agreed with Dubuffet concerning the "uncomfortable aspect of the new 'pseudo-cities' built in haste from scratch" and pointed out the weaknesses of Aillaud's work: "What you reproach, with reason, to Aillaud, is that he has, by lack of talent, missed the appearance of chaos and the nondeliberate."[50] Despite this failure, Choay's interest in Aillaud—and the reason, I believe, she sent Dubuffet the brochure—is that he was attempting to find an alternative to the postwar *grands ensembles*: "It is today's geometric and simplistic forms that are meaningless or at any rate are of an extreme weakness," she wrote,

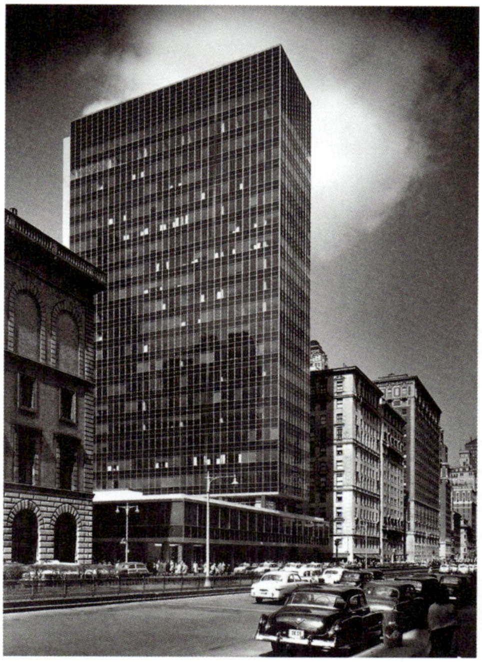

128. Lever House (built 1948–52), New York

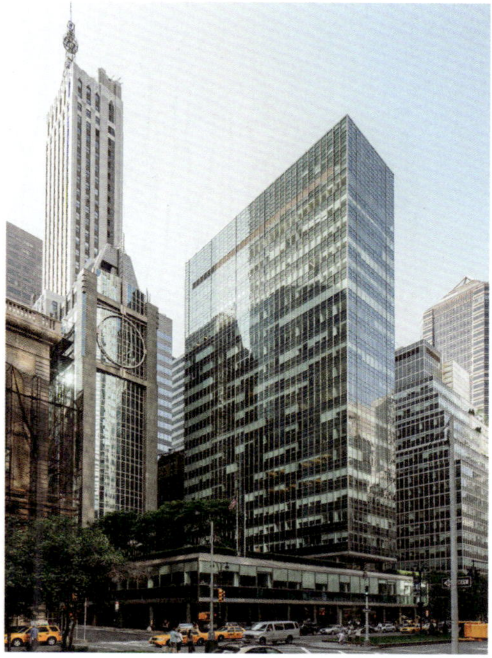

129. Lever House in 2011

before concluding, "According to me, this objective of an 'irrational' urban ensemble, to use your word, can only be reached through the playful mode of art. But our urbanists are not there yet, that is why I would love it if you would, one day, move beyond your current strange constructions toward developing a real project of a neighborhood."[51]

There are no further letters from Dubuffet responding to this invitation from Choay, and his later oeuvre does not suggest that he ever ventured into designing such a project. In the years that followed, Dubuffet built only one "house" for himself: the Villa Falbala, a windowless habitat composed of an entrance, a corridor, and the Cabinet logologique, surrounded by a walled garden, the Closerie Falbala. It is impossible to know whether this was of his own accord or because no commission for a housing project ever came his way.

When commissions did come to Dubuffet, they were for works to be inserted either within a sculpture park, as was the case with the Jardin d'émail (Enameled Garden), destined for the grounds of the Kröller-Müller Museum in Otterlo, or into an urban context dominated by late-modernist-style architecture. Such was the case with Groupe de quatre arbres (Group of Four Trees; 1971–72), commissioned for the base of 1 Chase Manhattan Plaza (also known as 28 Liberty Street), a sixty-floor high-rise designed by Gordon Bunshaft, off Wall Street in downtown New York City. Upon hearing of Bunshaft's

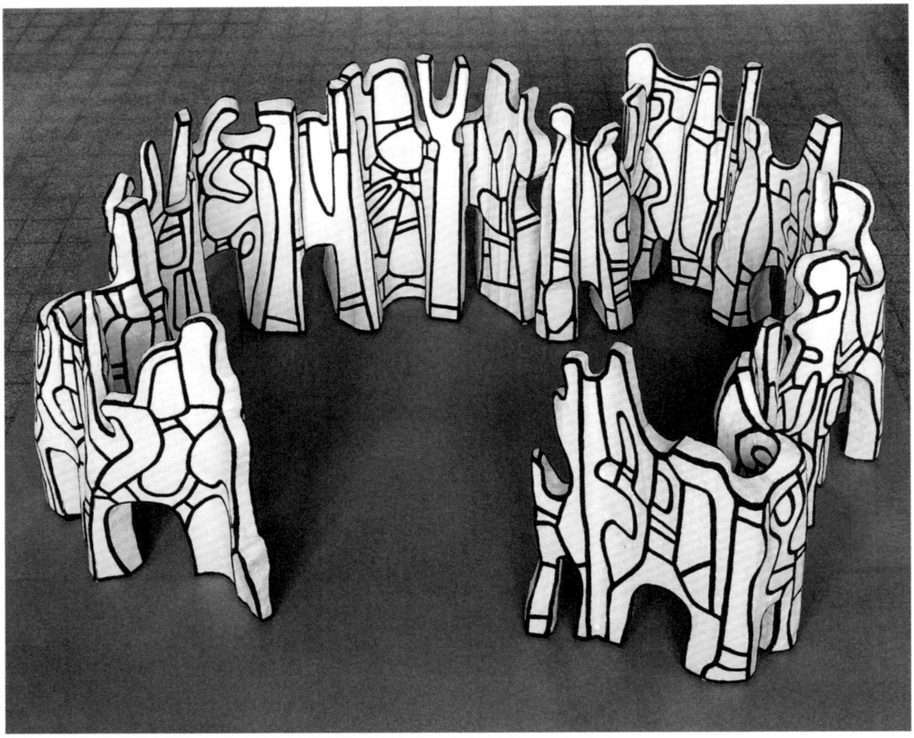

130. Jean Dubuffet. Le cirque, January 2, 1970

interest in his work, Dubuffet wrote to the architect in December 1968: "What would interest me chiefly would be the building of my Tour aux figures at a height of 80 feet with its interior layout, Le Gastrovolve, as it is described in the Édifices brochure."[52] A collector of Dubuffet's work, Bunshaft was the designer of Lever House (figs. 128, 129), a landmark of the International Style, and the head architect of Skidmore, Owings & Merrill (SOM), the firm that came to most emphatically represent the generalization of this "high modern corporate style" around the world. The Tour aux figures was immediately deemed unsuitable for the project, in terms of both form and height, and in the long, drawn-out process of the commission that ensued, Dubuffet produced almost a dozen proposals before the twelve-meter-tall (thirty-nine-foot) cluster of black-and-white trees, tops gently overlapping one another, was unanimously chosen by the selection comittee.[53] Its final dimensions were adjusted to form a canopy for the atrium of Bunshaft's skyscraper and responded point by point to the nearby architecture. The matte and opaque surfaces contrasted with the shiny aluminum and black glass of the building's façade, while the tangled, coiling black lines of the sculpture emphasized the neat verticals behind it. This contrast was important to the architect, as he would express a few years later in relation to another project: reacting in a letter to Dubuffet about a photomontage showing the Tour ballerine in front of Bunshaft's Banque Lambert, on avenue Marnix in Brussels (now ING Bank), he noted, "I think your piece looks perfect in size and in contrast to

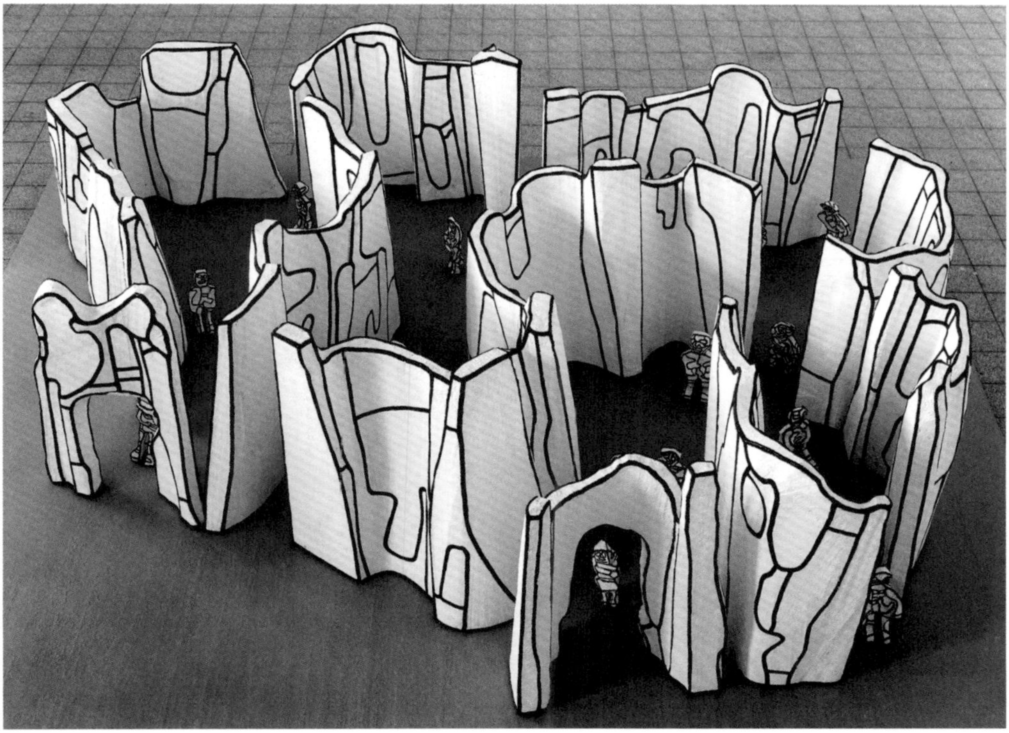

131. Jean Dubuffet. Rues et immeubles de la ville, July 1969

the small pattern of the Banque Lambert."[54] For an architect such as Bunshaft, Dubuffet's edifices appear to have belonged firmly to the realm of sculpture—a kind of sculpture that sometimes earned the derogatory moniker "plop art," whose purpose was merely to enhance or contrast with the features of the modernist architecture nearby.

If this was a far cry from Dubuffet's articulate reflection on architecture, it also signaled the irresoluble conundrum of interventions by artists in the public realm. However much Dubuffet could lament the rectilinear surroundings in which we are brought up, with their parallelepipedal rooms and "rectangular beds," they are nonetheless the context in which his constructions gain meaning—as any visit to the site of Groupe de quatre arbres confirms. Moreover, could it be that Dubuffet's projects, in reality, aimed to remain, to a certain extent, at a stage of—if not nonrealization—then at least nonlivability? Such is the effect produced by some of his most beautiful models: La rue (fig. 139), a stretch of ghostlike buildings lined up to evoke a street, and Rues et immeubles de la ville (Streets and Buildings of the City; fig. 131), a mazelike network of façades and openings for passersby to wander through and become disorientated.

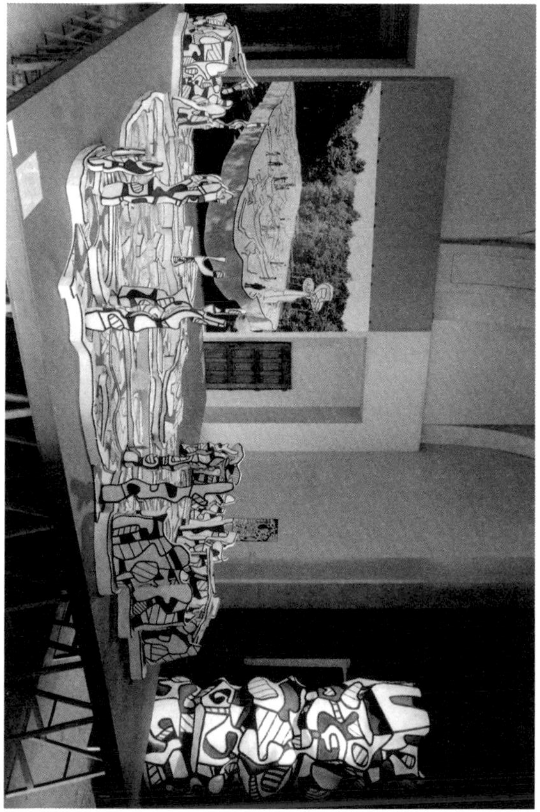

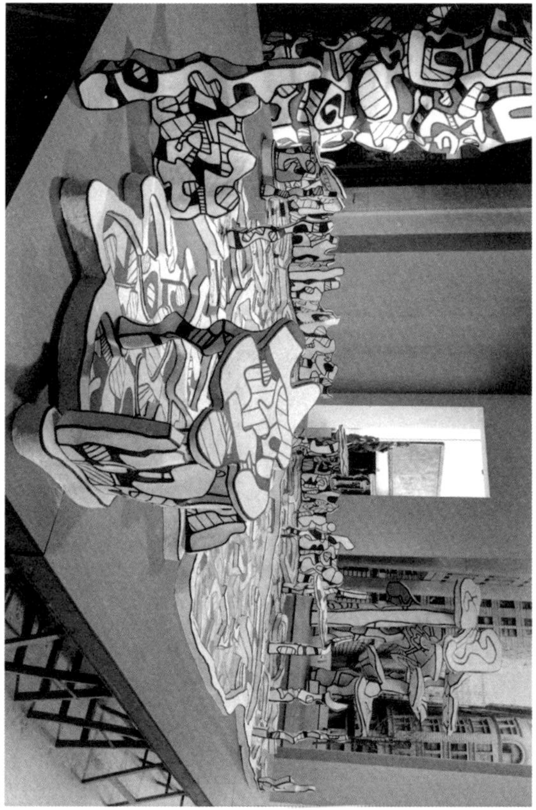

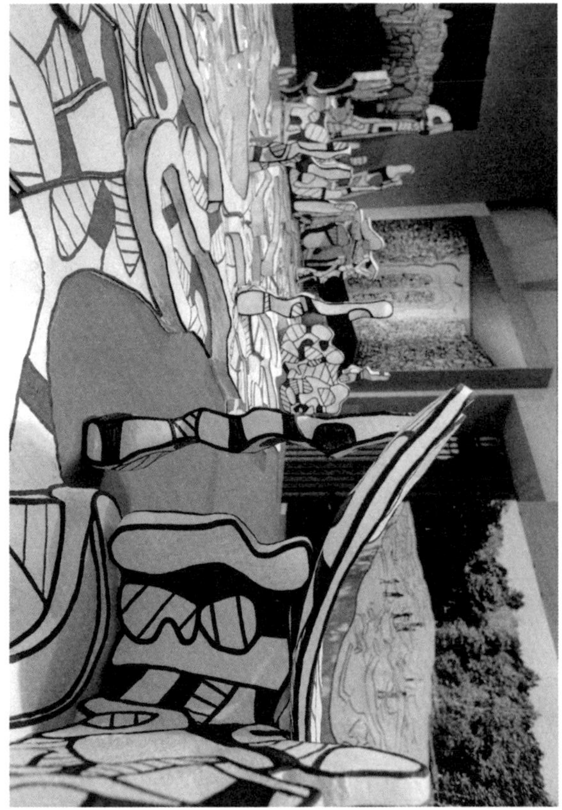

132–34. Jean Dubuffet: Le Salon d'été et autres exhibition, Musée des arts décoratifs, Paris, March 30–April 30, 1978

Even if these constructions were to be realized on a monumental scale, they would remain structures to be looked at and walked across, or through, rather than lived in. They move fluidly between architectural form and monuments of a new type—"monuments," as Choay later wrote, "that commemorate no historical event and mark no collective memory, that negate natural sites and ignore neighbors."[55]

The Musée des arts décoratifs exhibition of 1978 sustained this ambiguity and emphasized the fluidity of Dubuffet's practice even if its declared purpose was to present to the public the model of the *Salon d'été*, a large, concrete, garden-like environment of white and dark blue commissioned in 1974 for the front of Renault's new headquarters in Boulogne-Billancourt. Construction had begun in January 1975 before being halted by the company, and the building-in-progress was buried under a layer of concrete in 1977. A lawsuit followed during which Dubuffet gained wide international support from figures in the cultural world. The 1978 exhibition took place during the appeals process, which Dubuffet won (he decided to leave the salon buried). *Jean Dubuffet: Le Salon d'été et autres* presented the final model for the project alongside models of other structures that had been built in the past decade: *Groupe de quatre arbres*, the Closerie Falbala, *Cabinet logologique*, and *Jardin d'émail*. On the walls, five large photographs, ranging in size from two by three to three by seven meters (six and a half by almost ten feet to nearly ten by twenty-three feet), showed the realizations in their contexts and created a more immersive and visual environment than the drier architectural exhibition of 1968. As such, it was essentially the exhibition of an artist rather than that of an architect, and the visual continuity between photographs and models echoed the fluidity between idea and realization and the power of destabilization generated by that fluidity, to which Dubuffet alluded in a note written in 1977: "I aimed to create habitats of a mental character, belonging to the reign of ideas and movements of the mind, having only a body that is artificial, illusory, fantasy. To live in ideas, that was my aspiration."[56]

Epigraph: Jean Dubuffet, "Habitats, Closerie Falbala, Salon d'été" (1980), introduction to *CTJD*, vol. 31, 7–9, reprinted in *PES*, vol. 3, 366. "The desire to create habitable sites—or more precisely, mental interpretations of sites built in three dimensions and at the very scale of the real sites referred to, in order to make these interpretations livable—finds its origins in 1962 in the views of Paris of the Paris Circus cycle. The idea of building a colorful architectural element (a shop or preferably a group of shops, a fragment of a street) in the same whimsical form as the paintings and gouaches of this cycle evoked the streets of Paris occupied from this moment on the thought of the author, struck by the equivocal idea resulting from living physically (instead of only imagining them in the light of a painting) in mental interpretations of sites and architectures."

1 Dubuffet to Françoise Choay, November 29, 1967, *PES*, vol. 3 (1995), 496. The artist mentions that he has made "trick photographs" and briefly describes two of them.

2 Henri Lefebvre, *The Right to the City*, in Henri Lefebvre, *Writings on Cities*, ed. and trans. Eleanor Kofman and Elizabeth Lebas (London: Blackwell, 1996), 158, 173–74. On the reception of the book in the context of the May 1968 events, see Laurence Costes, *Lire Henri Lefebvre, Le droit à la ville: Vers la sociologie de l'urbain* (Paris: Ellipses, 2009).

3 Jean Dubuffet, *Asphyxiante culture* (Paris: Minuit, 1968), published in English as *Asphyxiating Culture and Other Writings*, trans. Carol Volk (New York: Four Walls Eight Windows, 1988).

4 For a close analysis of several of Dubuffet's architecture projects, see Daniel Abadie, *Dubuffet as Architect*, trans. Elaine Briggs, exh. cat. (Paris: Hazan, 2011).

5 Marcel Cornu, *La conquête de Paris* (Paris: Mercure de France, 1972); Marcel Cornu, "Dubuffet dans le ventre de la mère architecture," *Les Lettres françaises*, January 8, 1969, 24. The latter is reprinted in *CTJD*, vol. 24, *Tour aux figures, Amoncellements, Cabinet logologique* (Paris and Geneva: Weber, 1972), 145–46.

6 Although his first architectural models are dated 1967, I am taking the year 1968 as the first public appearance of his architecture projects.

7 The mission of the Fondation Dubuffet, set up by the artist in 1973 and officially recognized by the State in 1974, is to preserve and administer his archives and collection, including the Villa and Closerie Falbala. The Fondation Dubuffet is the sole owner of the rights to enlarge and build from Dubuffet's architectural models.

8 *Jean Dubuffet: A Retrospective*, Solomon R. Guggenheim Museum, New York, April 16–July 29, and *Jean Dubuffet*, Galeries nationales du Grand Palais, September 27–December 20, 1973, extended until December 31. Notably, Dubuffet exchanged letters with the architecture critic Marcel Cornu, historian of urbanism Françoise Choay, and architects Gordon Bunshaft and I. M. Pei.

9 Abadie, *Dubuffet as Architect*. Kent Minturn calls Dubuffet a "paper architect" in "Architect without Walls," *Architectural Review*, August 29, 2015, https://www.architectural-review.com/view/jean-dubuffet-architect-without-walls/8684655.

10 *Jean Dubuffet: Édifices, projets et maquettes d'architecture*, Musée des arts décoratifs, December 11, 1968–February 10, 1969.

11 Archives Fondation Dubuffet, Paris.

12 Jean Dubuffet, *Edifices*, trans. Teri Wehn (New York: The Museum of Modern Art, 1968), 39.

13 Dubuffet to Françoise Choay, November 29, 1967, *PES*, vol. 3 (1995), 497.

14 Dubuffet to Françoise Choay, July 11, 1968. Archives Fondation Dubuffet, Paris.

15 These exhibitions were *Jean Dubuffet: Peintures monumentées*, Galerie Jeanne Bucher, December 12, 1968–February 8, 1969; *Édifices*, Musée des arts décoratifs, December 11, 1968–February 10, 1969; *Jean Dubuffet at the Museum of Modern Art*, The Museum of Modern Art, New York, October 2–27, 1968, which traveled to San Francisco, Saint Louis, and Chicago; and *Edifices and Monuments by Jean Dubuffet*, Art Institute of Chicago, December 19, 1970–January 31, 1971.

16 Max Loreau, "Présentation" (March 1966), *CTJD*, vol. 20, *L'Hourloupe I, 1962–1964* (Paris: Fondation Dubuffet, 1995), 7, 15.

17 Dubuffet to Otto Hahn, December 29, 1964, *PES*, vol. 2 (1967), 487.

18 Jean Dubuffet, "Le cabinet logologique"(1978), *PES*, vol. 3 (1995), 357. This text was written for the catalogue of the exhibition *La Fiat invita all'incontro con Jean Dubuffet*, Palazzo della Promotrice delle Belle Arti al Valentino, Turin, June 15–July 15, 1978.

19 "Simulacres: Lettre à Arnold Glimcher," September 15, 1969, PES, vol. 3 (1995), 354–55. This letter appeared in French in the catalogue published by Pace Gallery to accompany the New York exhibition Jean Dubuffet: Simulacres (November 8, 1969–January 7, 1970).

20 Barbara Rose, "Jean Dubuffet: The Outsider as Insider," Arts Magazine 53, no. 8 (April 1979), 146–54.

21 Geneviève Bonnefoi, "Édifices et monuments de Jean Dubuffet, La quinzaine littéraire, December 1968, 21.

22 Ibid.

23 Ada Louise Huxtable, The Tall Building Artistically Reconsidered: The Search for a Skyscraper Style (Berkeley: University of California Press, 1982), 50.

24 Larry Busbea, Topologies: The Urban Utopia in France, 1960–1970 (Cambridge, MA: MIT Press, 2007), 89.

25 What is known, however, is that Mathey and Dubuffet enjoyed a productive exchange: the Musée des arts décoratifs hosted Dubuffet's first large institutional retrospective, a prelude, in 1960, to the retrospective organized at the Museum of Modern Art, New York, in 1962, and it was there, rather than to any museum of modern art, that Dubuffet chose to make a substantial donation of his works in 1967.

26 Pierre Mazars, "Pas de quartier pour Dubuffet," Le Figaro littéraire, December 16, 1968.

27 "Édifices," unsigned brief announcement for the exhibition Édifices, Le nouvel Observateur, December 30, 1968; François Pluchart, "Dubuffet tord le cou à la culture," Combat, August 5, 1968.

28 Christiane Duparc, "La folie des grandeurs," Le nouvel Observateur, January 6, 1969.

29 Jacques Michel, "L'escalade de Jean Dubuffet," Le Monde, January 12, 1969.

30 Jacob Paskins, Paris under Construction: Building Sites and Urban Transformation in the 1960s (New York: Routledge, Taylor & Francis, 2016), 9.

31 André Fermigier, "Le troisième siège de Paris: Allez voir au Grand Palais les dominos de l'an 2000, c'est de votre vie qu'il s'agit," Le nouvel Observateur, April 12, 1967, reprinted in André Fermigier, La bataille de Paris: Des Halles à la Pyramide; Chroniques d'urbanisme (Paris: Gallimard, 1991), 34.

32 On this subject, see Virginie Picon-Lefèbvre, Paris—Ville Moderne: Maine-Montparnasse et la Défense, 1950–1975 (Paris: Norma, 2003), 85.

33 André Fermigier, "Paris en 1972: Ce qui se prépare aux Halles et porte d'Italie devrait intéresser tous les français," Le nouvel Observateur, December 9, 1968, reprinted in Fermigier, La bataille de Paris, 94.

34 André Fermigier's opinion is cited in Brigitte Gilardet, Réinventer le musée: François Mathey, un précurseur méconnu (1953–1985) (Dijon: Les Presses du réel, 2014), 313.

35 Bruno Zevi,"Tredici progetti per trasformare Parigi," L'Espresso, February 2, 1969, 20.

36 Fermigier, La bataille de Paris, 35.

37 See Picon-Lefèbvre, Paris—Ville Moderne, 263. André Malraux supported the project of the tower in a discourse that merged the future and the past (see p. 267). Malraux, then minister of cultural affairs under President Charles de Gaulle, was also one of the few figures Dubuffet cited by name in Asphyxiante culture.

38 Picon-Lefèbvre, Paris—Ville Moderne, 160. On the debates concerning high-rises in France, see "Vie et mort des gratte-ciels," the special issue released by the magazine L'Architecture d'aujourd'hui (April–March 1975).

39 Michel, "L'escalade de Jean Dubuffet."

40 See Picon-Lefèbvre, Paris—Ville Moderne, 13, 15.

41 Loreau, "Présentation" (1972), CTJD, vol. 24, Tour aux figures, Amoncellements, Cabinet logologique (Paris and Geneva: Weber, 1972), 7.

42 Numbers 7–12 in the catalogue raisonné show the different proposals for the inside layout; ibid., 20–23.

43 Dubuffet, *Edifices* (New York), 12.

44 See Cornu, "Dubuffet dans le ventre de la mère architecture."

45 Françoise Choay, "Dubuffet aux bornes de l'écriture," *Cahiers de l'Herne*, no. 22 (May 1973), 319.

46 Dubuffet to Marcel Cornu, January 12, 1969, *PES*, vol. 3 (1995), 497.

47 Jean Dubuffet, "Concernant le statut de plusieurs de mes monuments et éléments architecturaux" (January 22, 1977), *PES*, vol. 3 (1995), 516. Hubert Damisch gives no indication regarding the purpose or destination of this text.

48 Robert M. Lawrence, "Memo," *Newsletter of the American Institute of Architects*, no. 622 (March 19, 1982), reprinted in *PES*, vol. 4 (1995), 636. See also Dubuffet's letter to Robert M. Lawrence in response to the award, *PES*, vol. 4 (1995), 421.

49 Dubuffet to Françoise Choay, December 10, 1967. Archives Fondation Dubuffet, Paris.

50 Françoise Choay to Dubuffet, February 24, 1968. Archives Fondation Dubuffet, Paris.

51 Ibid.

52 Dubuffet to Gordon Bunshaft, December 20, 1968. Archives Fondation Dubuffet, Paris.

53 For an overview of the commissioning process, see Harriet F. Senie, *Contemporary Public Sculpture: Tradition, Transformation, and Controversy* (New York: Oxford University Press, 1992), 117.

54 Gordon Bunshaft to Dubuffet, January 31, 1975. Archives Dubuffet Foundation, Paris.

55 Françoise Choay, "Les édifices de Jean Dubuffet," *L'Œil*, no. 221 (1973), 16–17.

56 Dubuffet, "Concernant le statut de plusieurs de mes monuments et éléments architecturaux," 515.

Tremor on the Eye (1962)

Jean Dubuffet

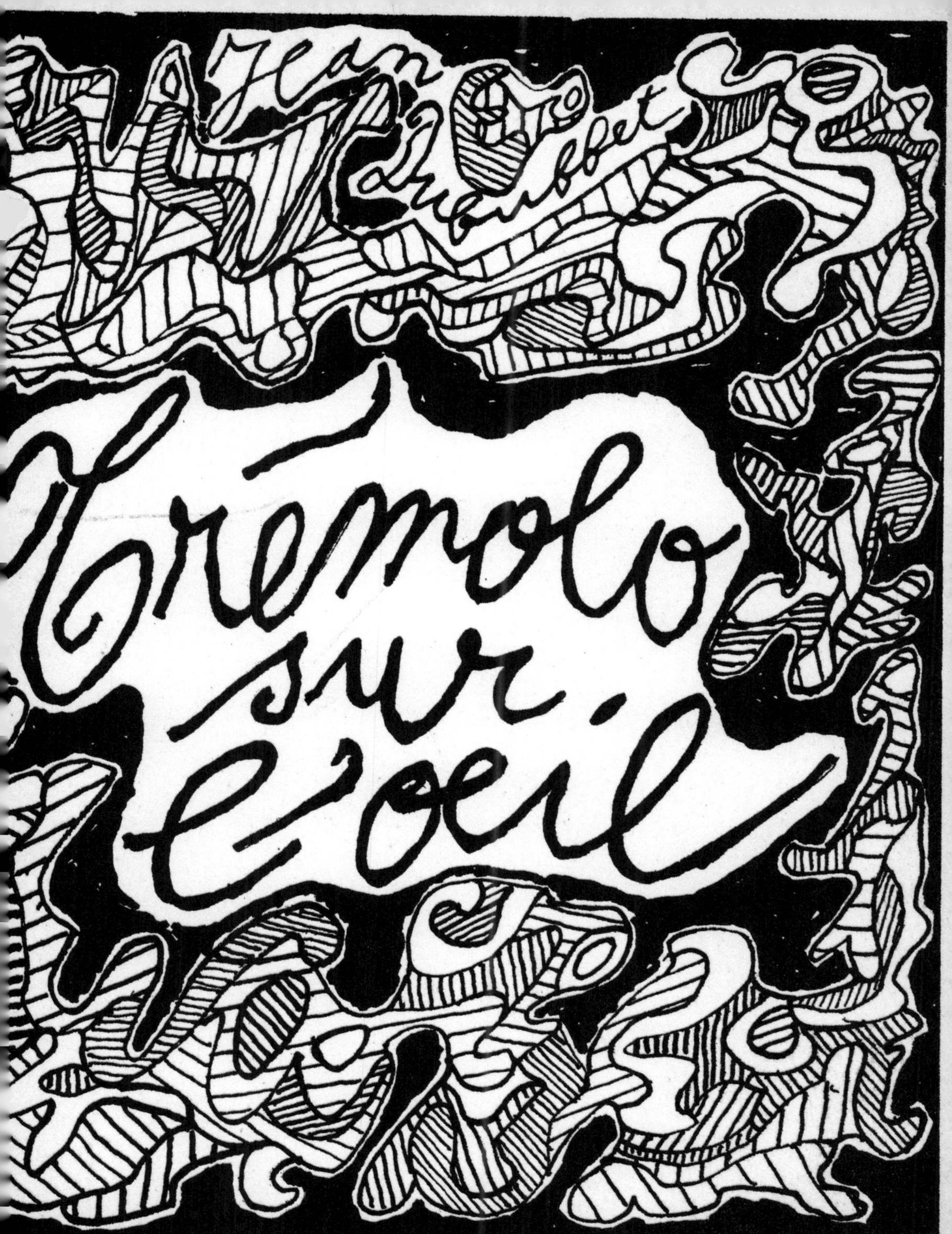

135. Jean Dubuffet. **<u>Trémolo sur l'œil</u>, 1962–63**

Outrepasse contrecarre
avandule La Nocivité
galoche Retourne poches
alive et rit Attention
soutenue gare aux suites
onsultation périodique
arte à la source entrée
ratuite soins prophy-
lactiques fermé le
amedi jusqu'à
midi vadrouille floraison

Oversteps thwarts lavandula *The Noxiousness Clog* Turn pockets **drool and laugh** SUSTAINED ATTENTION beware of the consequences *PERIODIC CONSULTATION* dead loss FREE ENTRANCE *prophylactic care* **CLOSED ON SATURDAYS** UNTIL NOON stroll flowering

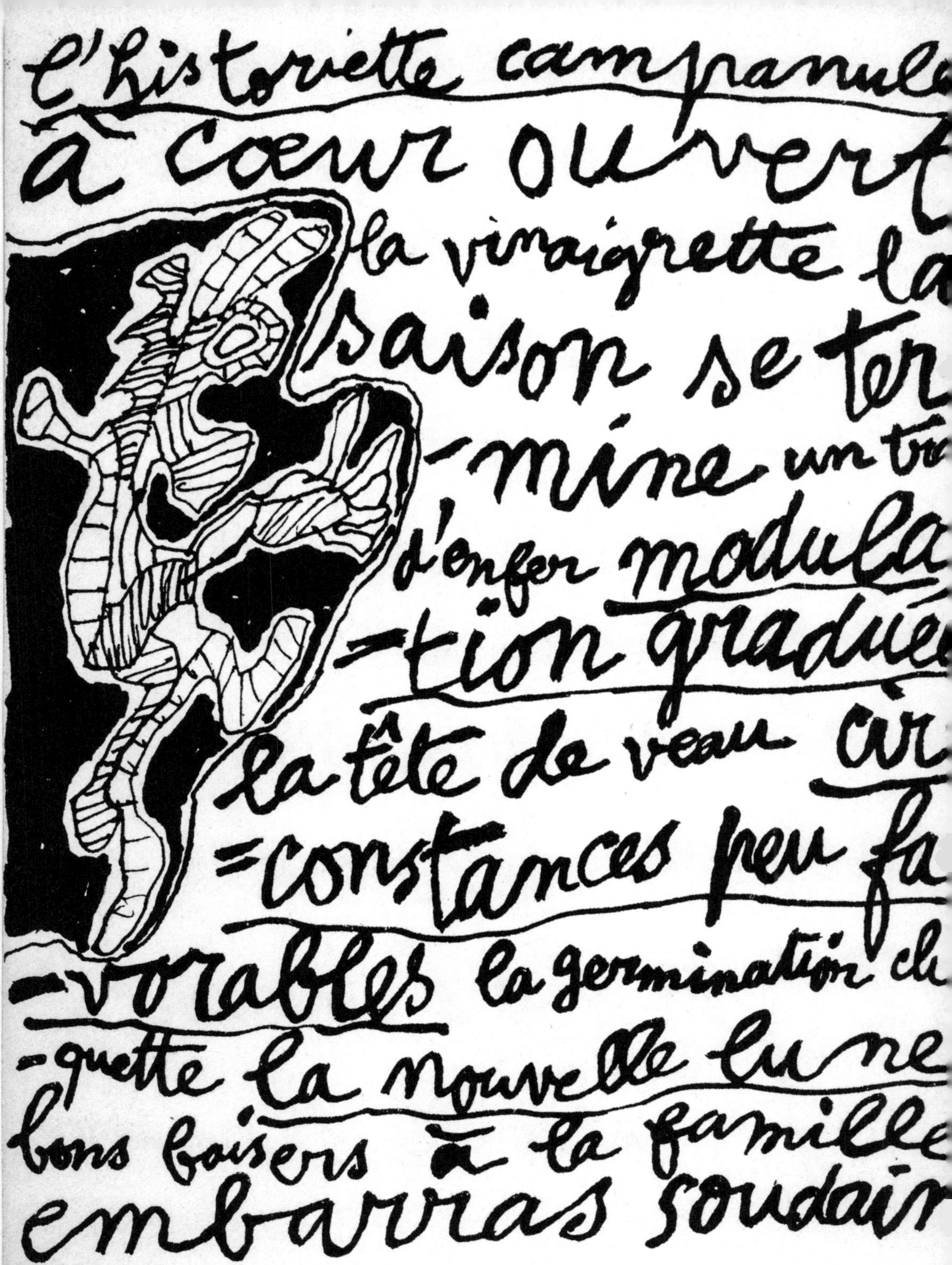

the bellflower tale **OPEN HEART** the vinaigrette *THE SEASON IS ENDING* full steam GRADUATED MODULATION la tête de veau **UNFAVORABLE CIRCUMSTANCES** the germination rattles *the new moon* kisses to the family SUDDEN EMBARRASSMENT

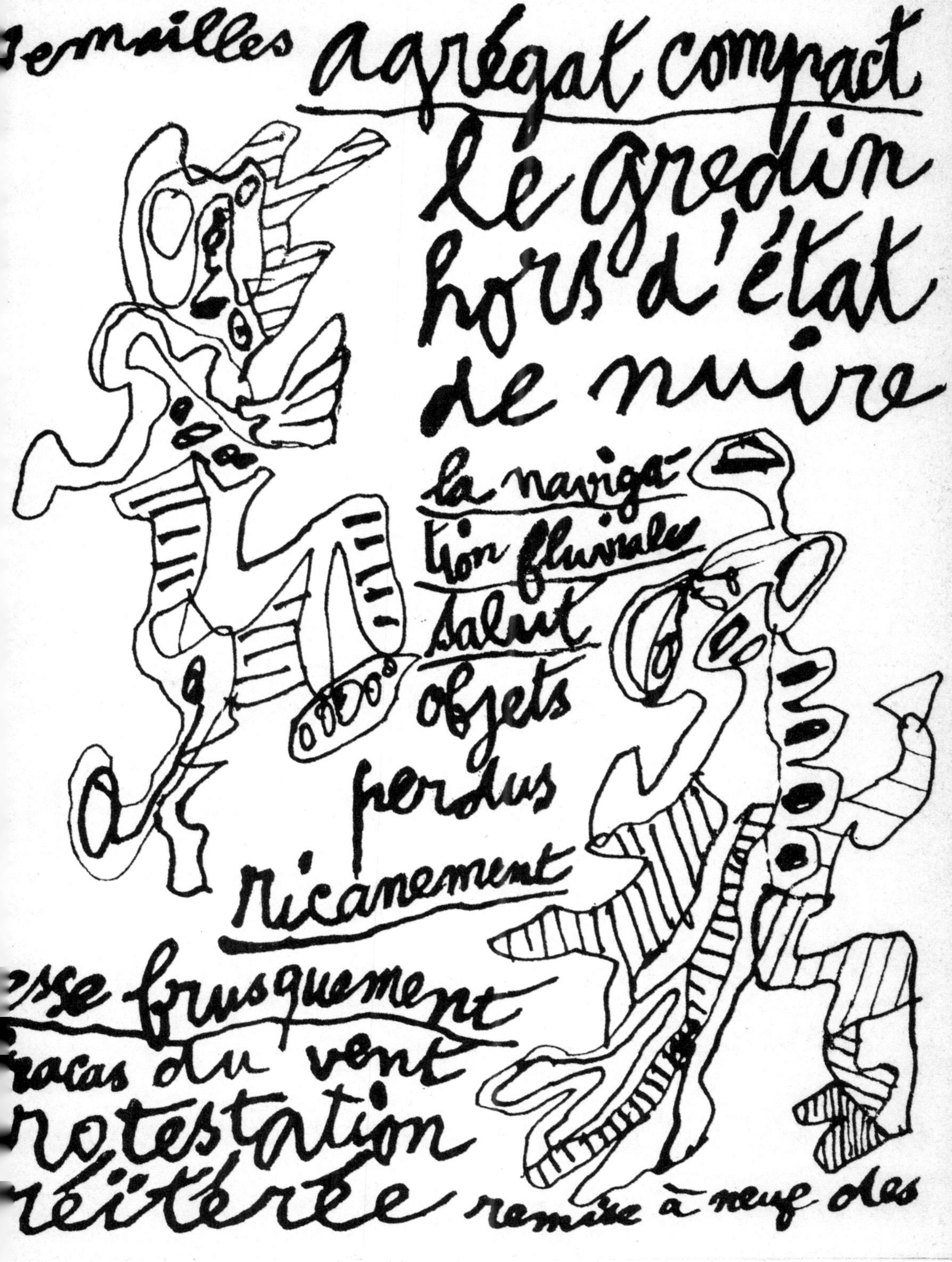

sowing <u>*COMPACT AGGREGATE*</u> **the rascal rendered harmless** <u>the river navigation greeting</u> LOST AND FOUND <u>cease sneer</u> suddenly wind thunder *REPEATED PROTEST* refurbishment of the

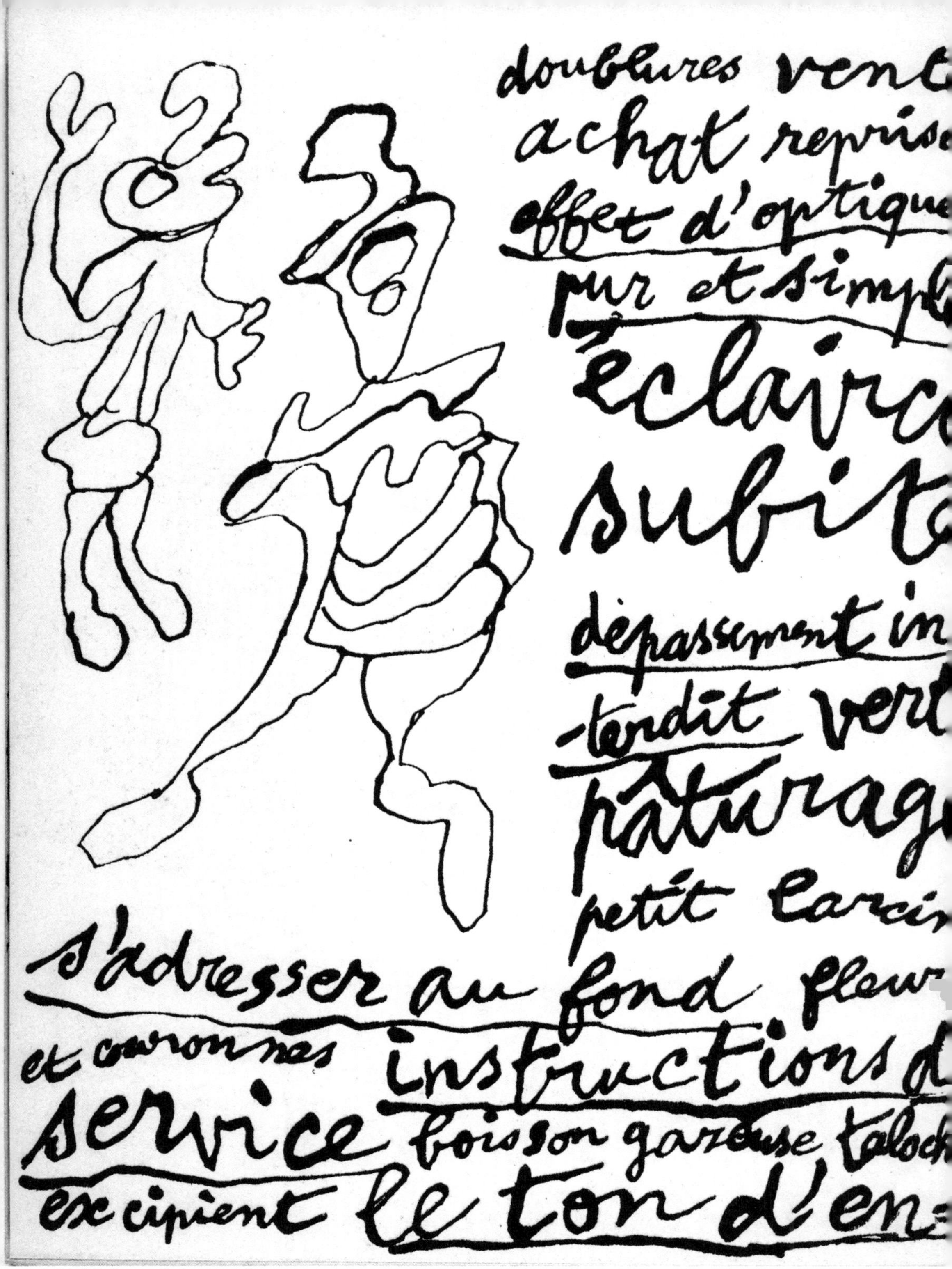

linings **sell buy** return optical effect pure and simple **SUDDEN SUNSHINE** no passing GREEN PASTURES petty larceny *contact at the back* flowers and wreaths **operating instructions** fizzy beverage slap excipient *SOUNDING DOWN IN THE*

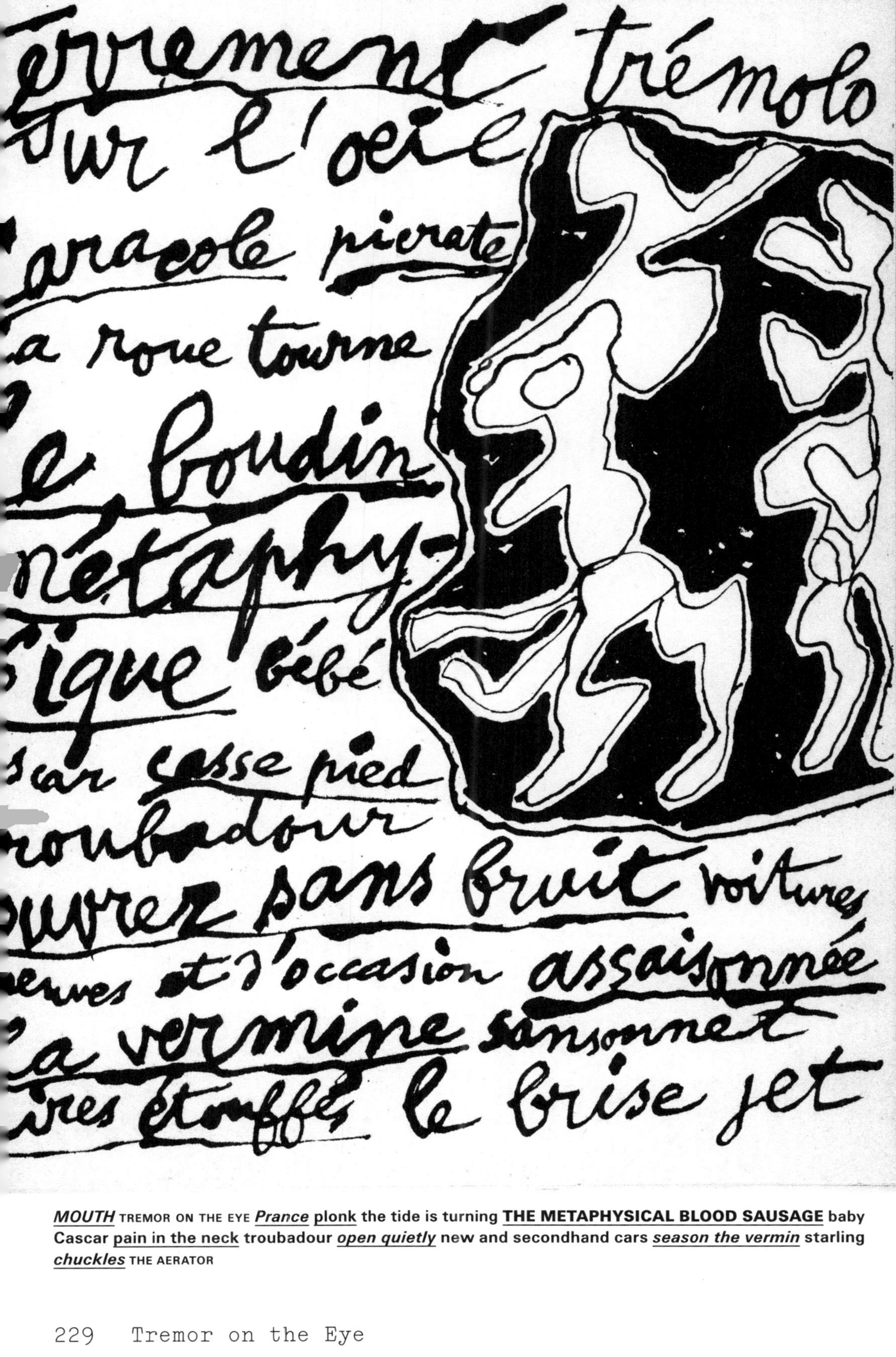

MOUTH TREMOR ON THE EYE ***Prance*** **plonk** the tide is turning **THE METAPHYSICAL BLOOD SAUSAGE** baby Cascar **pain in the neck** troubadour ***open quietly*** new and secondhand cars ***season the vermin*** starling ***chuckles*** THE AERATOR

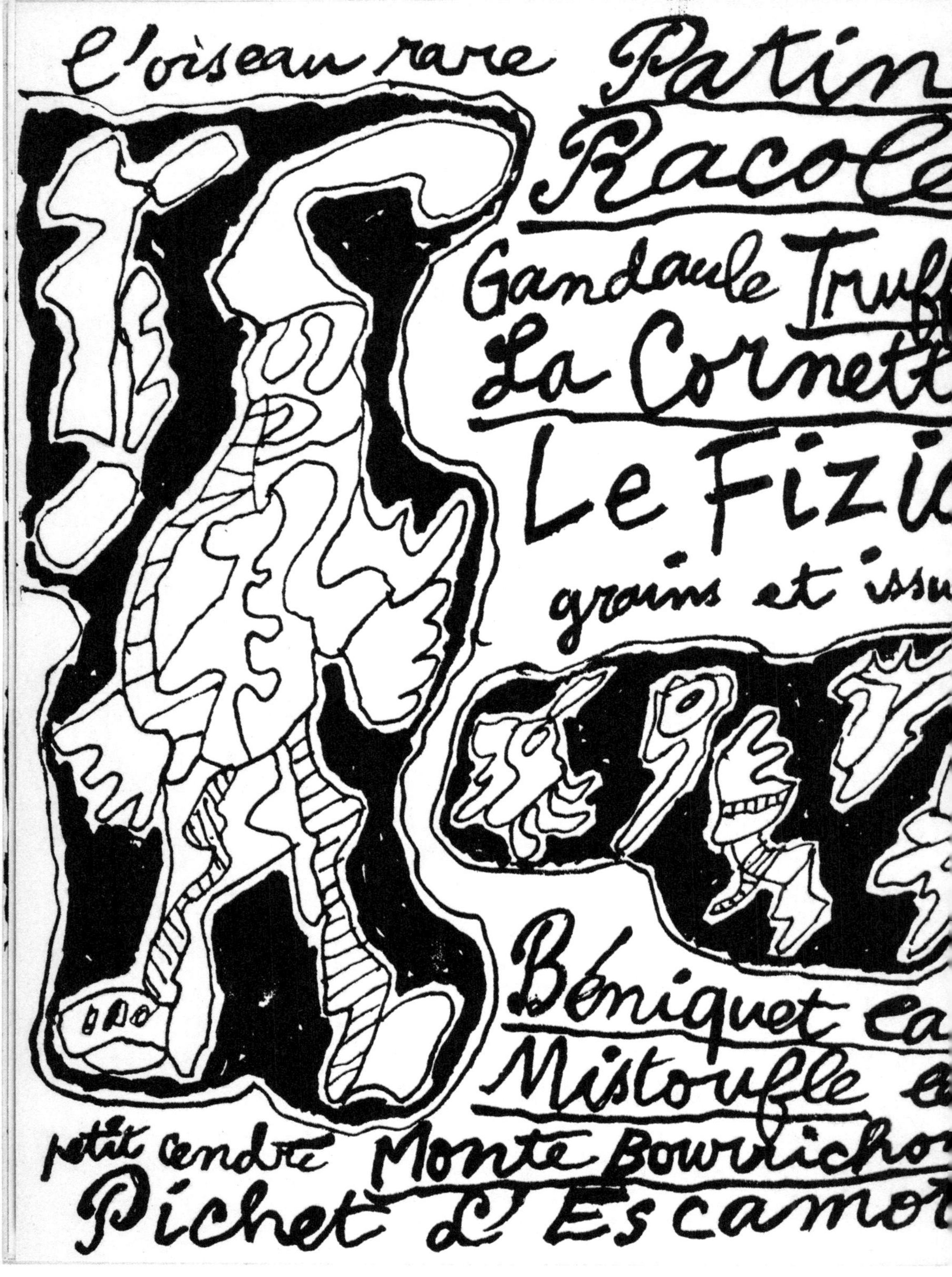

one in a million **SKATE DRUM UP** Gandaule *TRUFFLE THE CORNET* **THE FIZICO** grains et issues **Béniquet the Pauper** le petit cendré IDEAS PUT IN THE HEAD **PITCHER RETRACT**

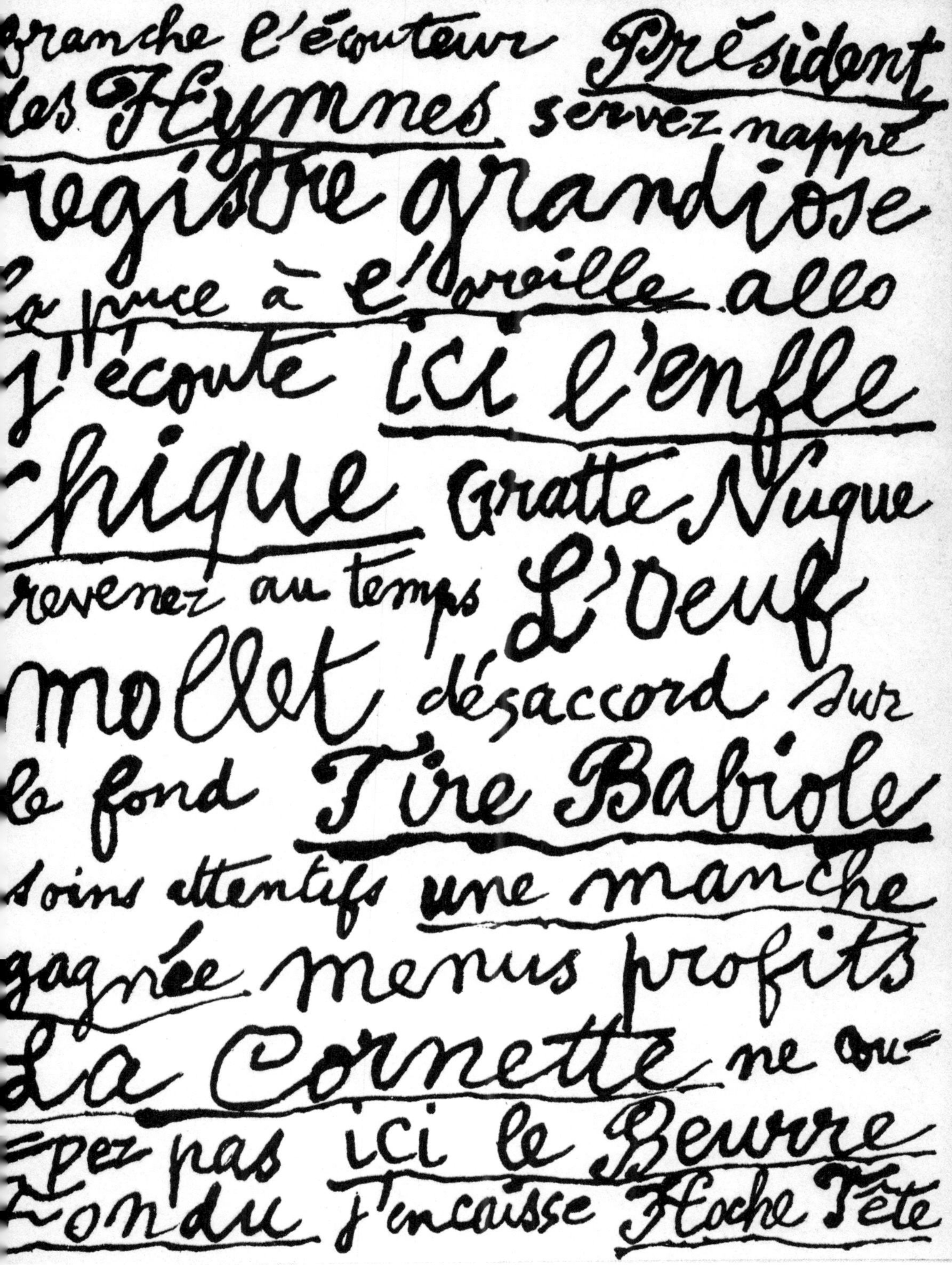
ranche l'écouteur Président
les Hymnes servez nappe
registre grandiose
a puce à l'oreille allo
j'écoute ici l'enfle
chique Gratte Nuque
revenez au temps L'Oeuf
mollet désaccord sur
le fond Tire Babiole
soins attentifs une manche
gagnée menus profits
La Cornette ne cou-
pez pas ici le Beurre
ondu j'encaisse Hoche Tête

plug in the earphone *President of the Hymns* serve tablecloth GRANDIOSE REGISTER a flea in the ear allô j'écoute **HERE BLOWN-UP CHEEK** **Neck Scratcher** come back to the time *THE POACHED EGG* disagreement on the substance STEAL BAUBLES attentive care *a round won* SMALL GAINS THE CORNET ne coupez pas **here the Melted Butter** I collect *Wag Head*

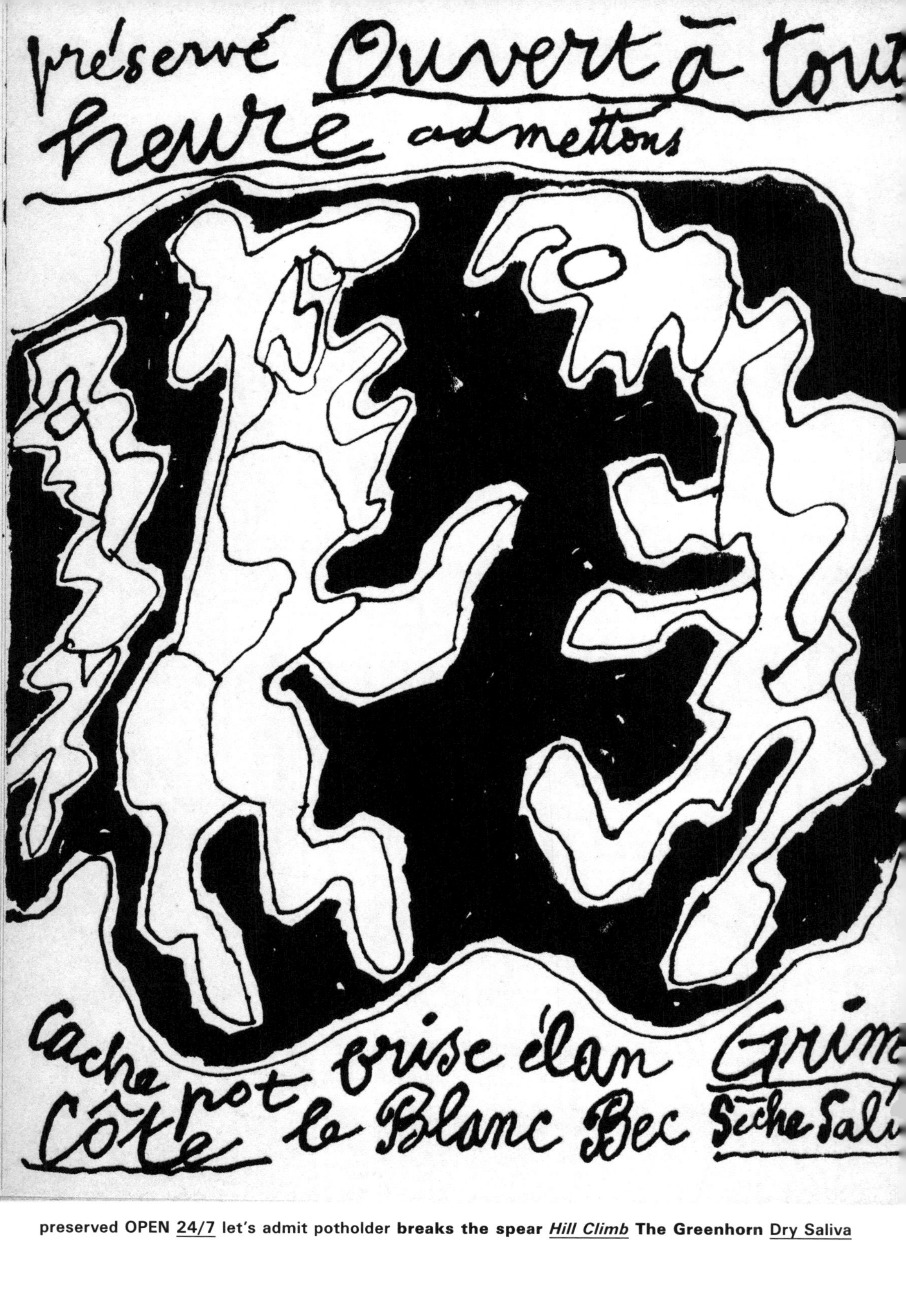

preserved OPEN 24/7 let's admit potholder **breaks the spear** *Hill Climb* **The Greenhorn** Dry Saliva

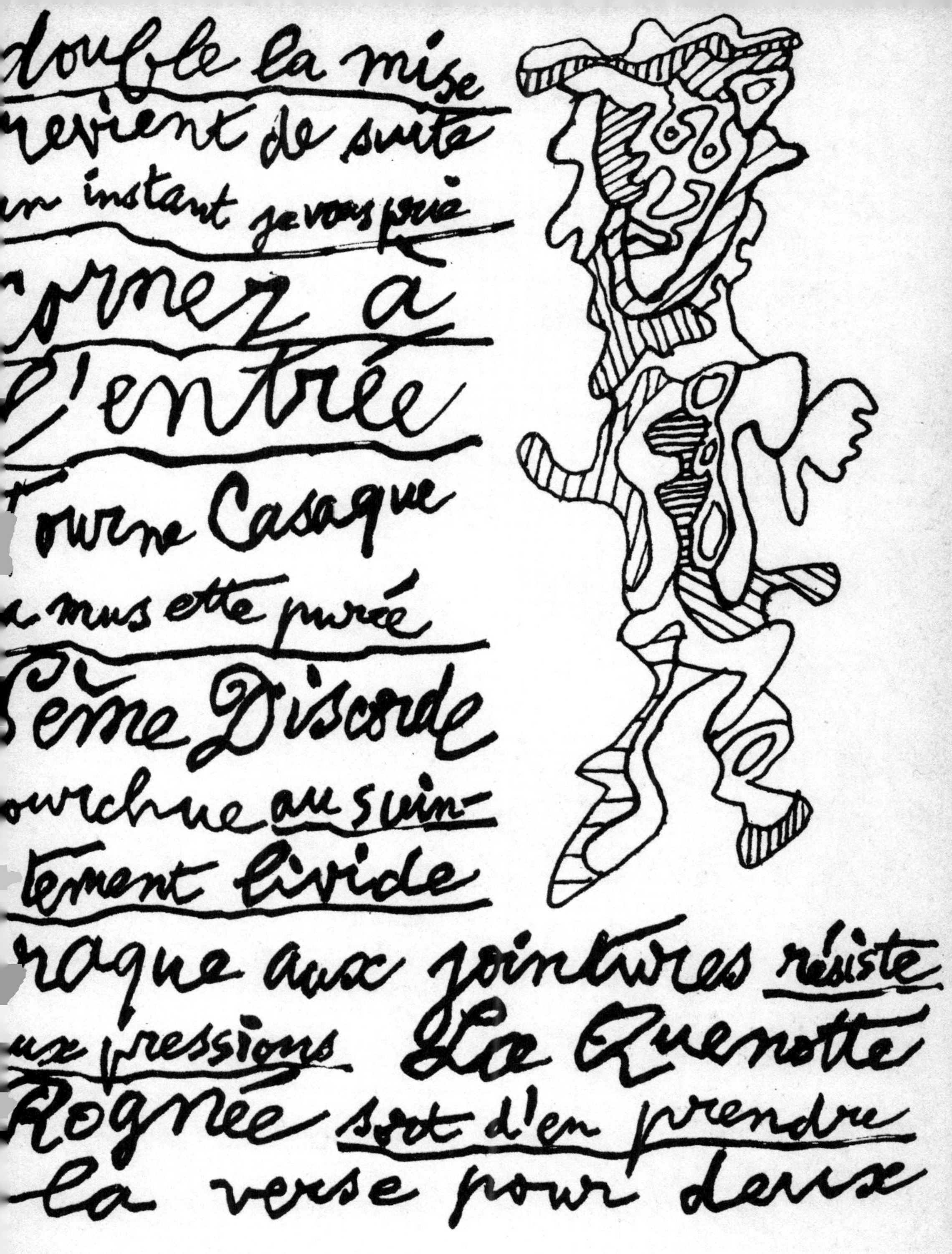

double the bets be right back one moment *please RING DOORBELL AT THE ENTRANCE* Turn Tail lunchbag purée **Sowing discord** forked to the livid oozing *bursting at the joints* resists pressure WORN-AWAY BABY TOOTH steps out a catch pours it for two

Fringue Ribote
romance Perce Pâté
craint la chaleur un peu
de patience tambou
battant sucre à volonté
Courbe échine
ventre à terre chass
gardée résultat semon
gai matin frise poulet
les traits tirés casquette
lavandière Confiance mé=
=ritée tord boyau res=
=cousse à fond perdu

BUTTERMILK GARMENTS romance *Drill Pâté* keep away from heat have some patience with much fanfare sugar as desired **kowtow** run wild *chasse gardée* result warning GAY MORNING chicken frieze *drawn-out features* cap washerwoman *EARNED TRUST* rot gut **rescue** sunk investments

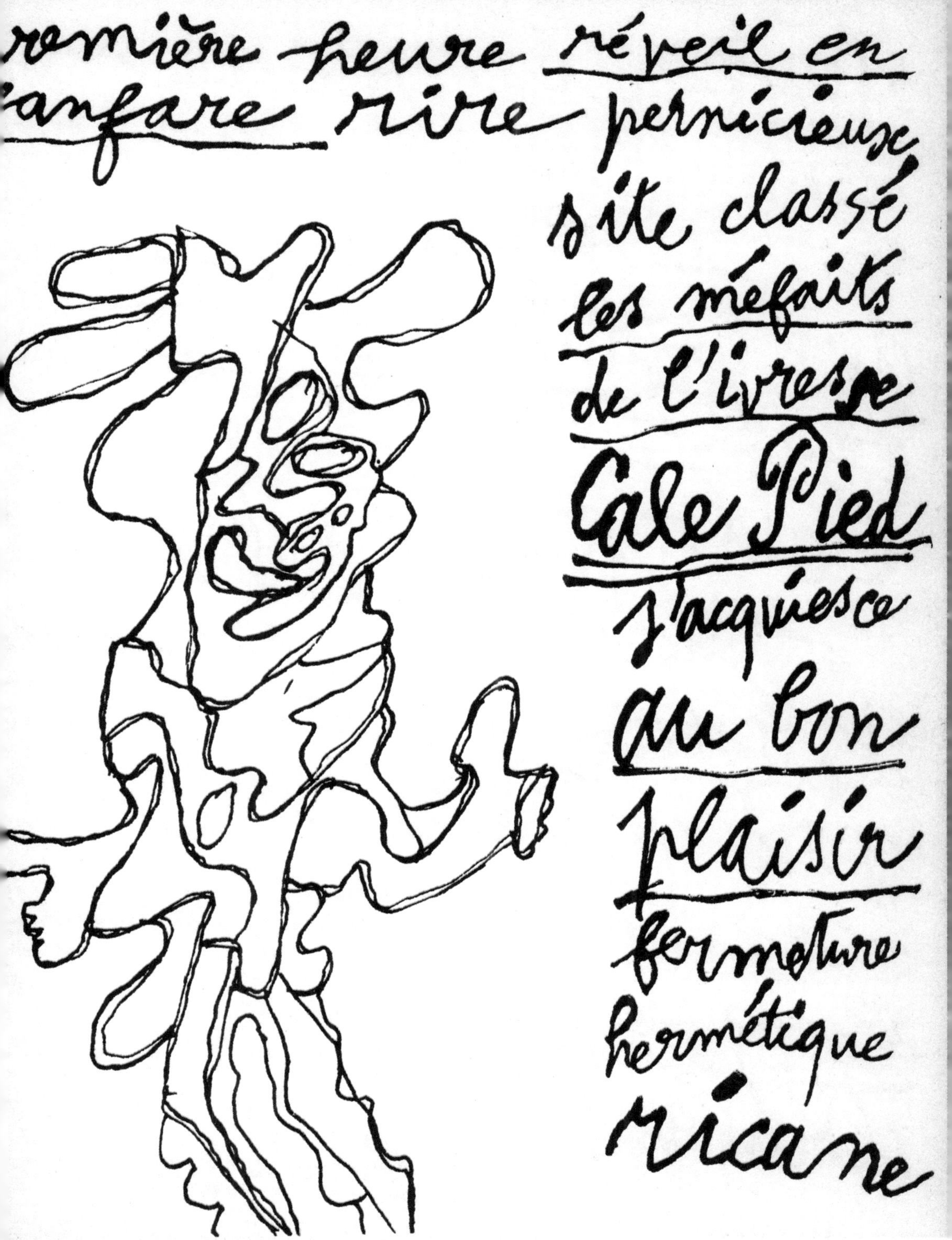

in the first hour *fanfare awakening* **laughter** pernicious **registered site** the ravages of intoxication **FOOT WEDGE** I acknowledge ***At the pleasure of*** hermetic sealing **SNEER**

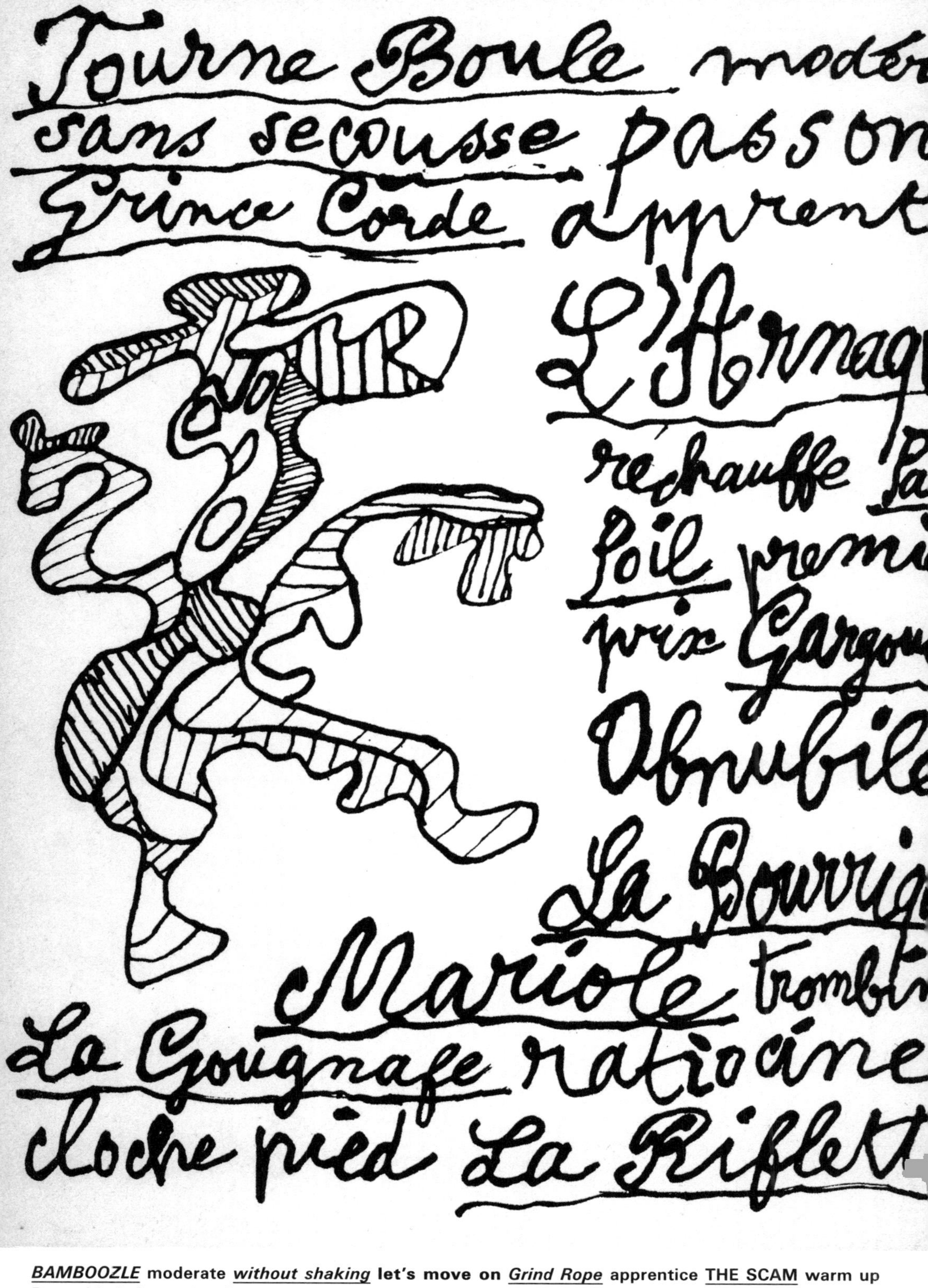

BAMBOOZLE moderate *without shaking* **let's move on** *Grind Rope* apprentice THE SCAM warm up Passed hair first prize Gargoyle OBNUBILATE *LA BOURRIQUE MARIOLE* mug *The Feckless* **quibble** one-legged LA RIFLETTE

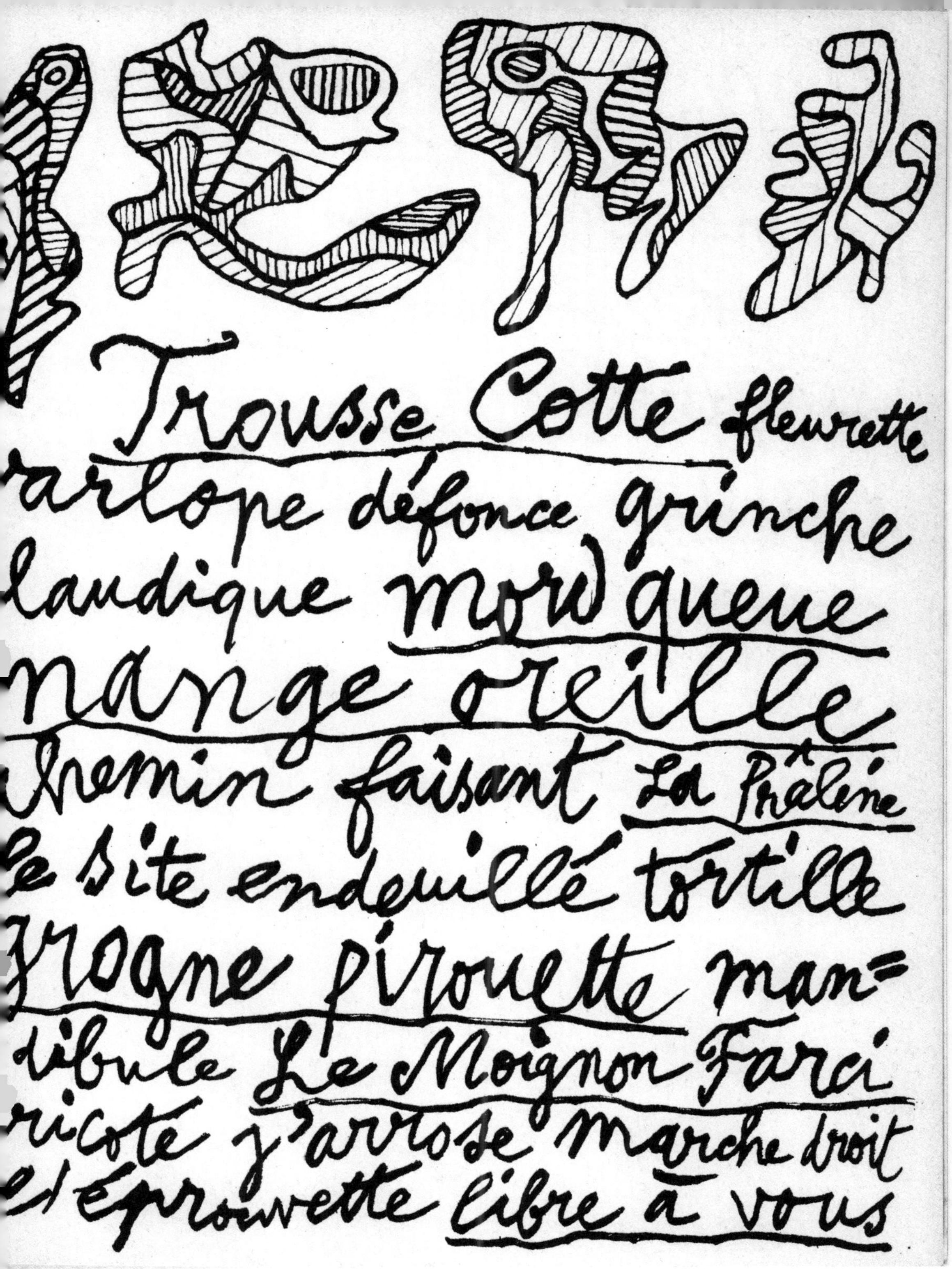

TROUSSE COTTE sweet nothings jointer smash grump limp BITE TAIL EAT EAR along the way *The Prâline* the bereaved site twist and turn GROWL PIROUETTE mandible *The Stuffed Stump* tinker I water straight walk test tube *up to you*

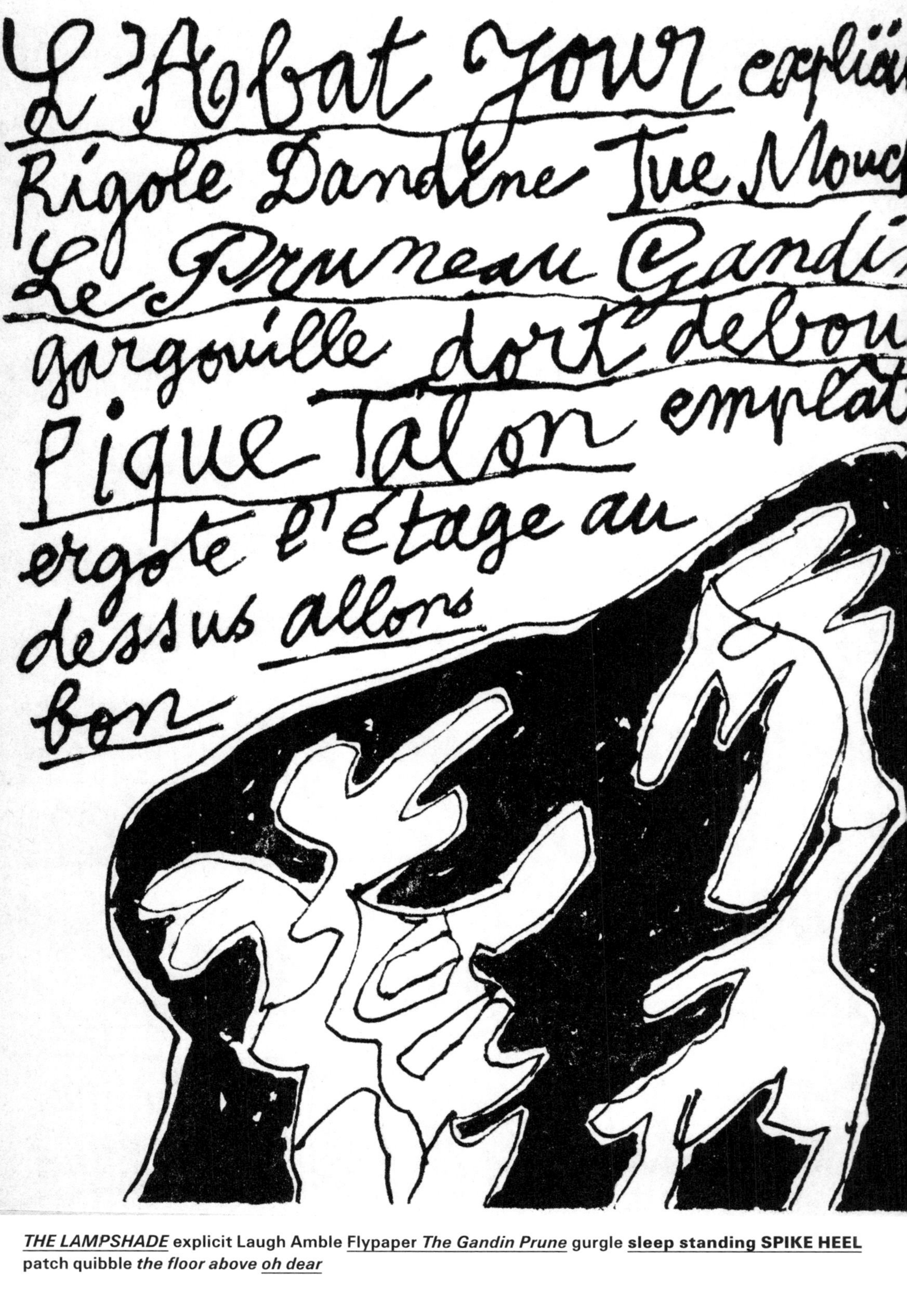

THE LAMPSHADE explicit Laugh Amble Flypaper *The Gandin Prune* gurgle **sleep standing SPIKE HEEL** patch quibble *the floor above oh dear*

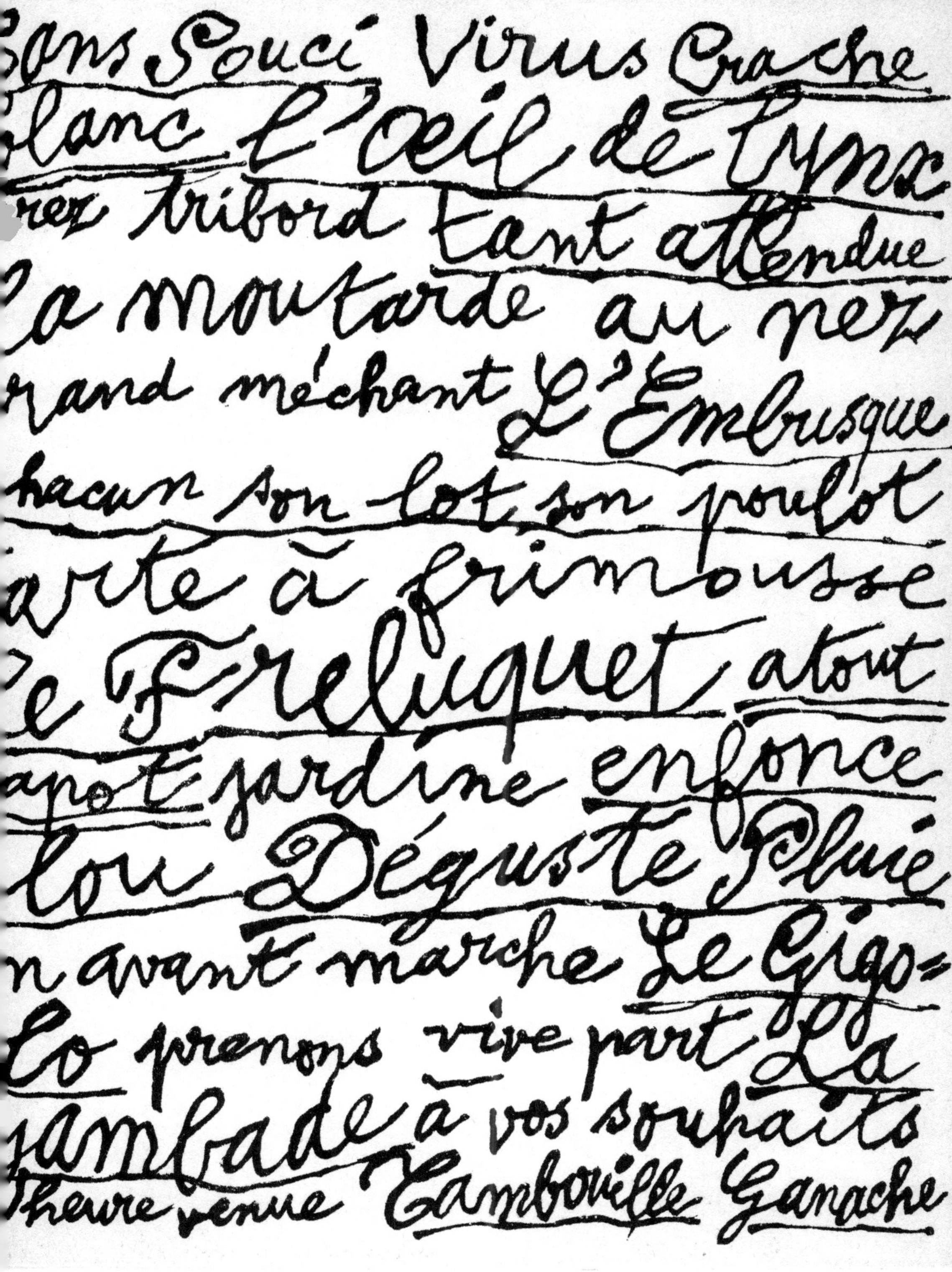
ans Souci Virus Crache
lanc l'oeil de Lynx
rez tribord tant attendue
a moutarde au nez
rand méchant L'Embusque
hacun son lot son poulot
avite à frimousse
e Freluquet atout
apot jardine enfonce
lou Déguste Pluie
n avant marche Le Gigo-
lo prenons vive part La
gambade à vos souhaits
l'heure venue Gamboille Ganache

Sans Souci **Virus** Spit blank THE EYE OF THE LYNX turn to starboard long-awaited lost temper big bad *THE AMBUSH each* his own fate his own little lamb cutie pie **THE WHIPPERSNAPPER** ASSET HOOD garden **hammer home** *TASTE RAIN* forward march *The Gigolo* take lively part THE FRISK **bless you** time has come Grub *Ganache*

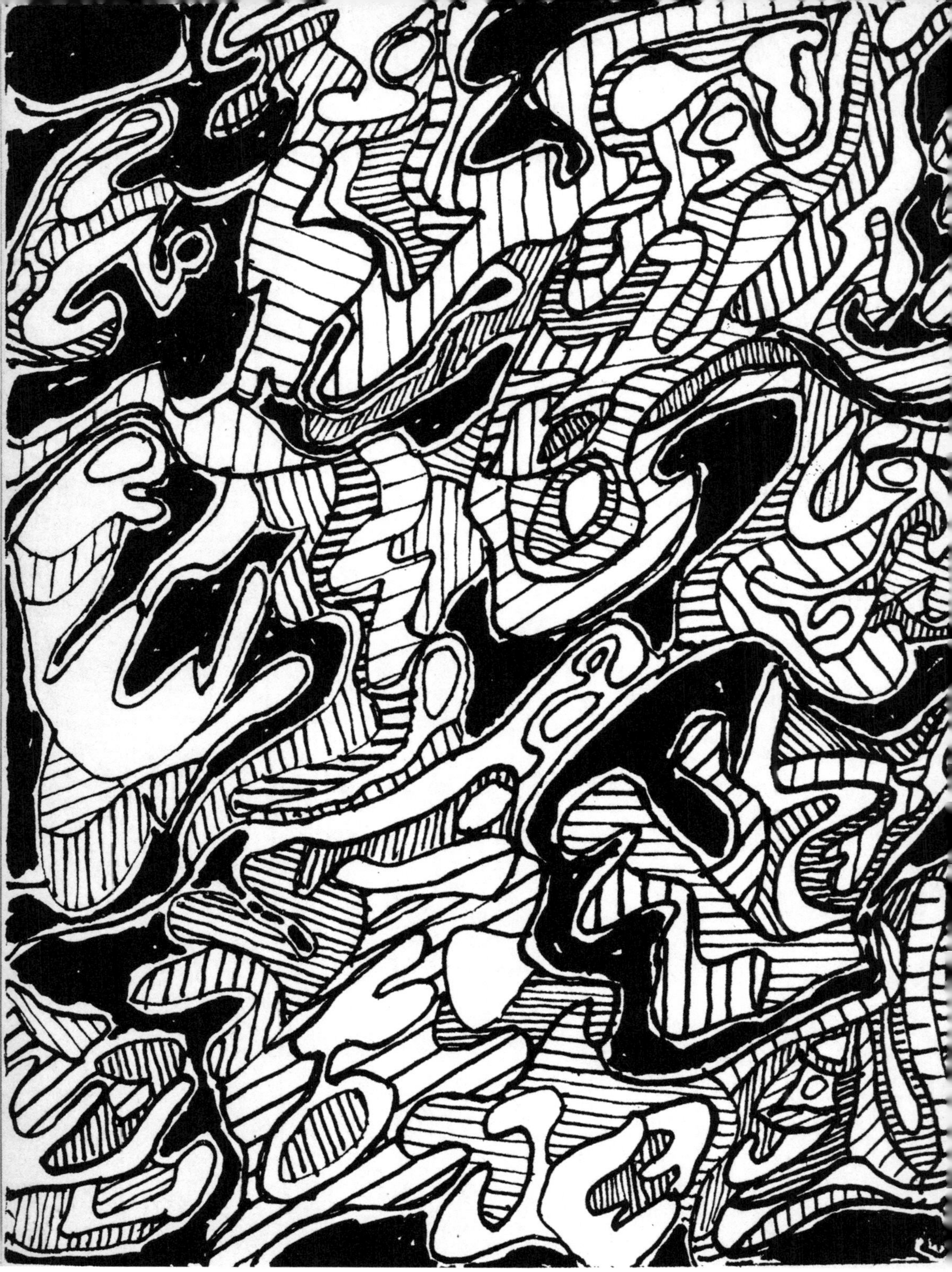

Tiré à 300 exemplaires sur la presse de l'auteur au cours des mois d'été 1963 et édité par Gaston Puel, Veilhes, Lavaur (Tarn)

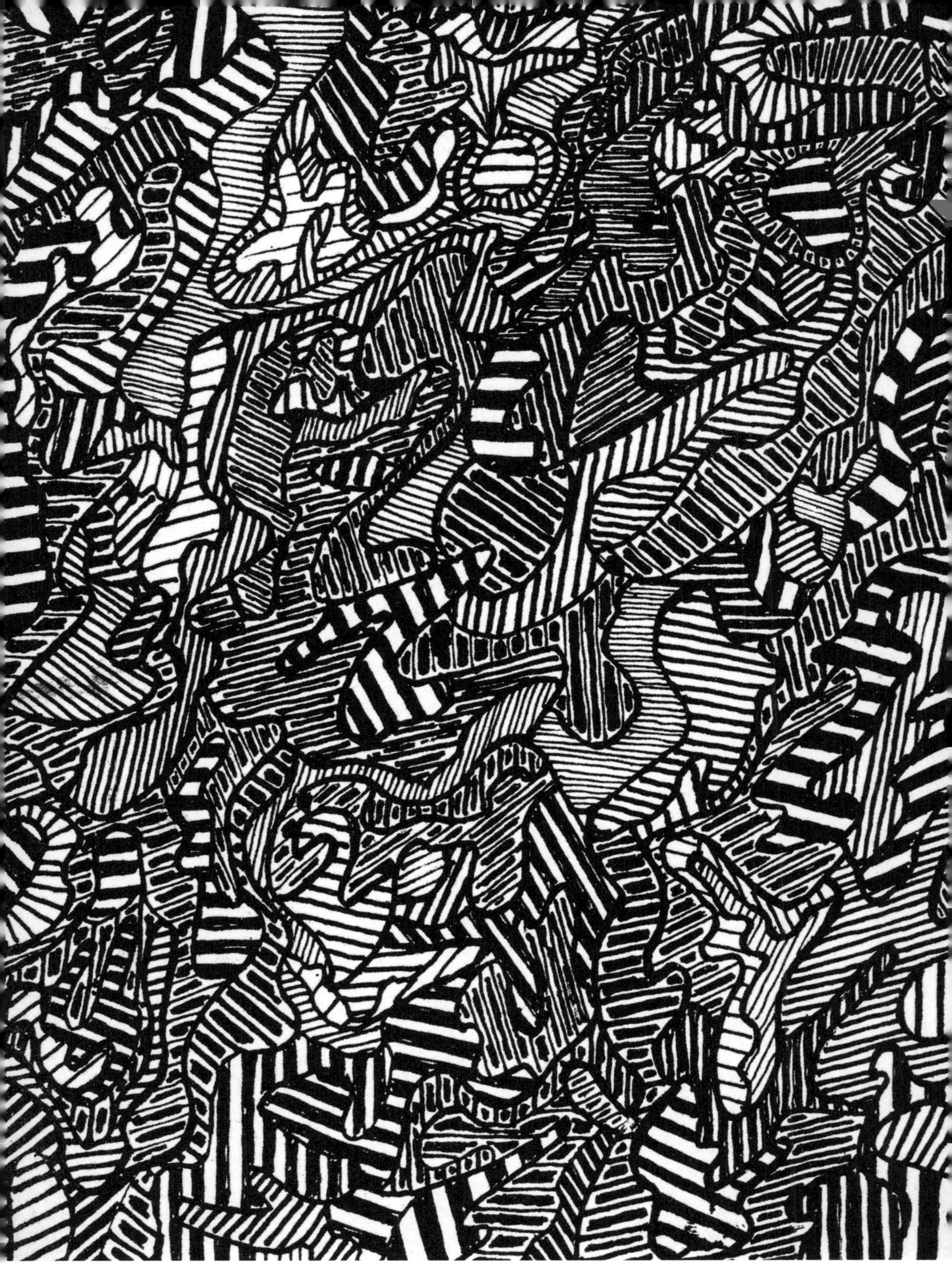

Chapter Four

By Way of Conclusion: Place and Deck

Q: Il semble que l'évocation de ce que vous appelez des "sites"ou des "lieux" a dans vos travaux une place privilégiée.
R: Oui, mais j'aime à leur donner un aspect imprécis, à ce qu'ils ne soient pas caractérisés mais prennent caractère de généralisation, aptes par là à suggérer n'importe quel lieu qui soit tout en suggérant avec force l'idée d'un lieu."

—Jean Dubuffet, 1985

Un site—on pourrait aussi bien dire un lieu—très indéterminé, très général.

—Jean Dubuffet, 1984

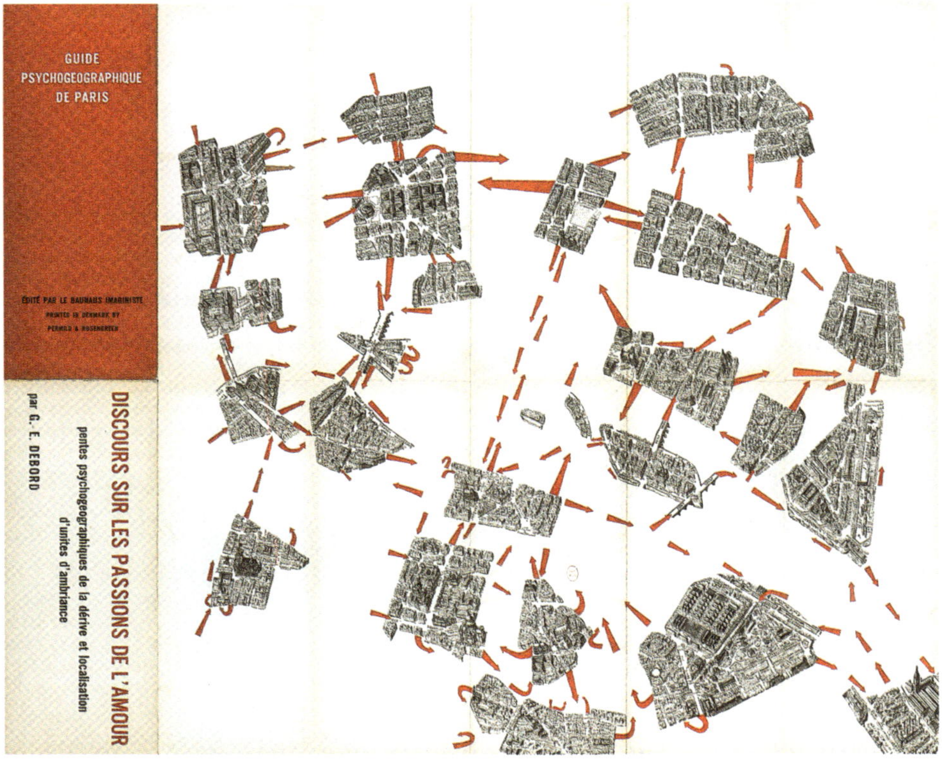

136. G. E. [Guy] Debord with Asger Jorn. Guide psychogéographique de Paris (1957)

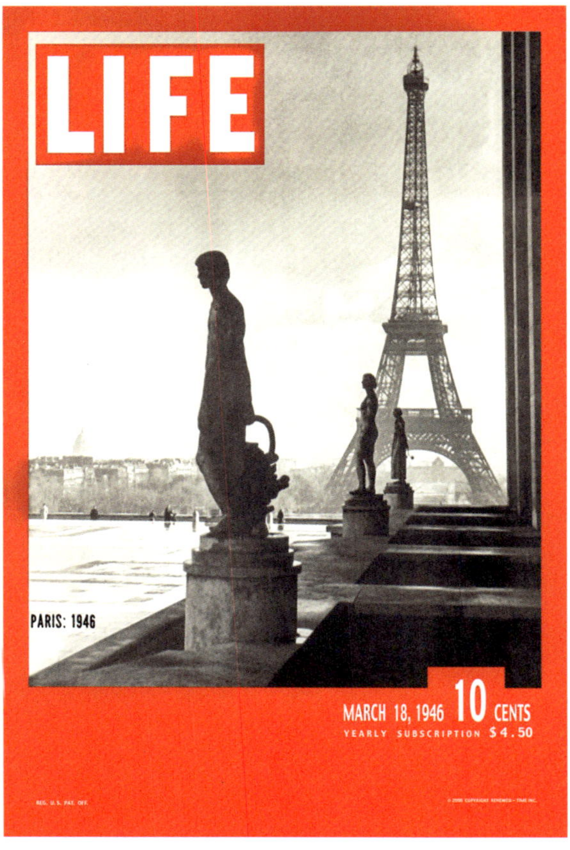

137. Cover of Life magazine, March 18, 1946

In a note concerning "Saint-Ouen—le marché" in his edition of the artist's writings, Hubert Damisch explained that, at the time Dubuffet penned the piece in question, in 1944, he was toying with the idea of writing a guidebook to Paris that "would have mentioned nothing artistic or mysterious, but, on the contrary, only common sites and places devoid of any touristic or archeological interest, which nonetheless appeared to him as very notable."[1] Such a guidebook never saw the light of day, but Damisch's remark suggests some insights into Dubuffet's aesthetics. For a start, it makes plain the affinity between the artist's idea of the *homme du commun*, or "common man," and that of a banal site—literally, a "common place." Something of this affinity emerges, in effect, in "Saint-Ouen" when he describes the earthy colors of man's clothing. Second, the idea of a guidebook cannot fail to call to mind the fascination the city of Paris exerted on the Surrealist artists and poets in the 1920s and 1930s. Whether it was Louis Aragon minutely describing the derelict passage de l'Opéra and the faded, picturesque Parc des Buttes-Chaumont in Le paysan de Paris (Paris Peasant) of 1926 or André Breton, in Nadja (1928), evoking forgotten monuments and sleepy city squares alongside images by Jacques-André Boiffard, Brassaï, and Eugène Atget, the theme of inconspicuous places in Paris ran deep in Surrealist literature and photography.[2] But in 1944, unremarkable sites could also be those in which Parisians gathered for clandestine or other purposes, away from the glittering attractions favored by the Nazi Occupation forces and disseminated in their propaganda images (think only of Hitler posing in front of the Eiffel Tower in June 1940).

Dubuffet's alleged guidebook project would also have contrasted with the kind of tourist imagery Life magazine would circulate in spring 1946, when, to celebrate the Liberation of France, it published a photographic essay about Paris featuring well-known sites and picturesque views (fig. 137).[3] In the years following the war, reconstruction and modernization altered the geography of the city and created new habits of circulation and new places of interest. These would be determined by urban planners who built mass housing developments and decided on systematic divisions of activities and rational flows of people across Paris and its suburbs—but, of course, mental maps and ways of moving around the city were determined by everyone, not just experts and bureaucrats, and when Guy Debord and the Situationists wandered across Paris to identify what they called *unités d'ambiance* (unities of atmosphere), those usually had little to do with the administrative divisions of the city (fig. 136).

The rapid urbanization of the 1960s and 1970s meant that, in France, the percentage of urbanized territory more than doubled in a twenty-year period.[4] In this process, new towns, extensive suburbs, highways, and housing estates appeared across the country along with an architectural vocabulary that included towers, slabs, walkways, and concrete decks. These elements reshuffled the relationship between urbanism and topography, geography, and history—all things that confer significance on a particular location.

If, at its most basic, a place is a location defined by a series of coordinates in space, at its most fundamental it is a condition of human existence. The philosopher Edward Casey argued as much when he stated, at the beginning of his 1997 book The Fate of Place, the premise of his inquiry into the history of the concept: “To be at all—to exist in any way—is to be somewhere, and to be somewhere is to be in some kind of place.”[5] Between these two definitions, geographers have added nuances to what may be conceived of as a “place.”[6] The political geographer John Agnew distinguishes “location” from “locale”—which covers the material conditions in which social interactions take place—and from the “affective attachment that people have to place,” which he calls “sense of place.”[7] For the humanist geographer Yi-Fu Tuan, by contrast, although place is the result of the association of geographic location and human activity, it has a stability that it owes to being free from alterations in the makeup of its observers or participants: “It is in

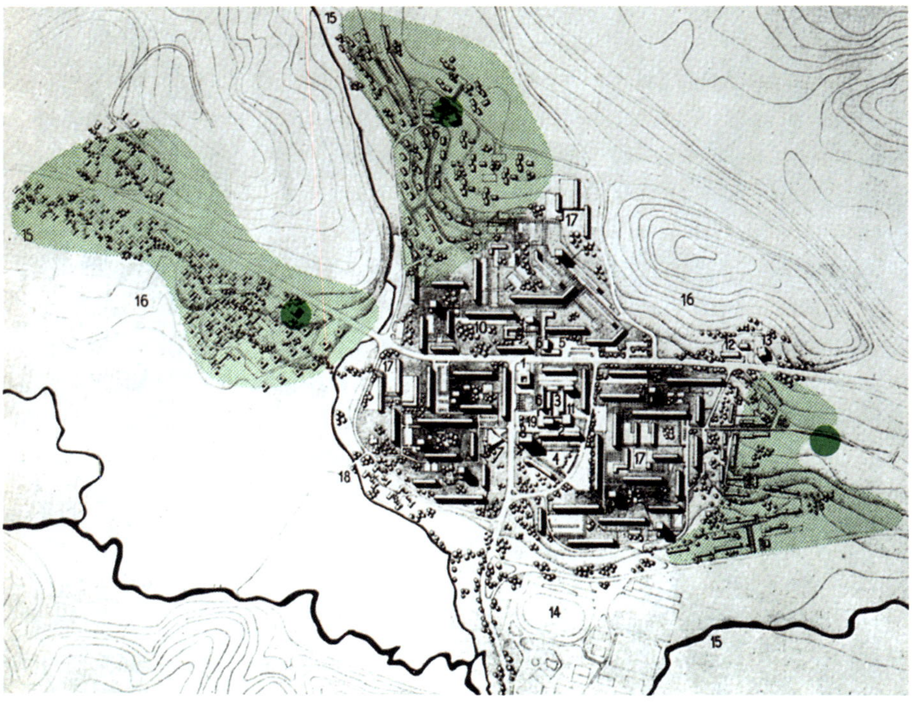

138. Master plan of the *ville nouvelle* of Mourenx, built 1957–61

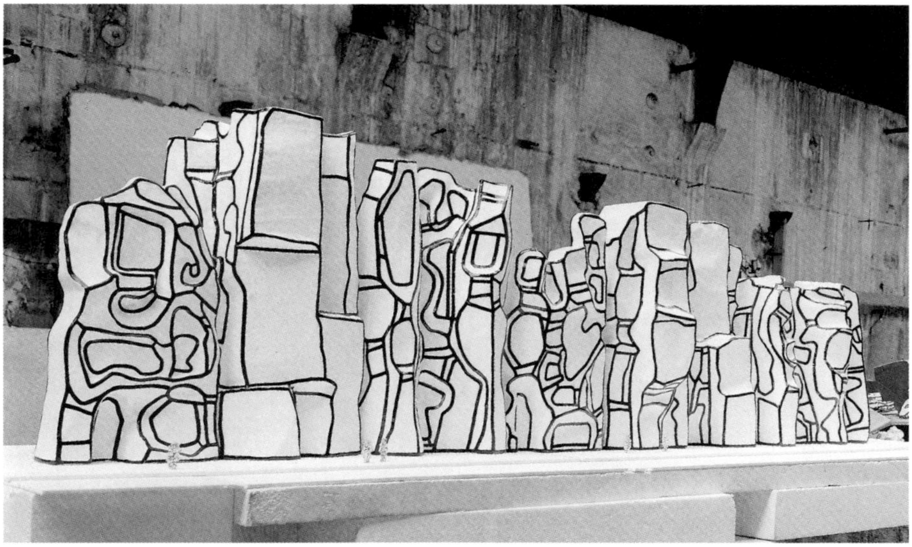

139. Jean Dubuffet. La rue, August 1971–March 1974

the nature of place to appear to have a stable existence independent of the perceiver. A place is the compelling focus of a field: it is a small world, the node at which activities converge."[8]

Although Dubuffet's own way of defining place—or "site," for that matter, as he used the terms interchangeably—was less explicit (the second epigraph of this chapter makes this plain enough), the question of place traverses, under different guises, the artist's entire oeuvre.[9] At the earliest, it appears in the recounting of his beginnings in the 1945 text "Plus modeste." There, the idea of an aesthetic posture is closely linked to that of social and geographic place. In Dubuffet's words, one is either "in the cart" or outside it, *in* the city and *among* people or isolated, and so on.

In contrast with space, which is usually understood as a given, there is no place without a presence, an absence, or a longing for place: place is bound to human experience. Similarly, in painting, the presence of a figure implies that of a background, a place, however undetermined or vaguely sketched out it may be. This simple motif of a figure against a background was, as Damisch contended, Dubuffet's principal subject matter.[10] Often, the artist attempted to muddle the figure-ground organization. In the *hautes pâtes* pictures of his 1940s series Mirobolus, Macadam et Cie, the rough, gritty material incorporated into the paint disturbs the outline of the figures and threatens to absorb them into the background. In the 1960s, during the Hourloupe cycle, Dubuffet achieved a similar effect of equivoque by other pictorial means. There, undulating black lines on a

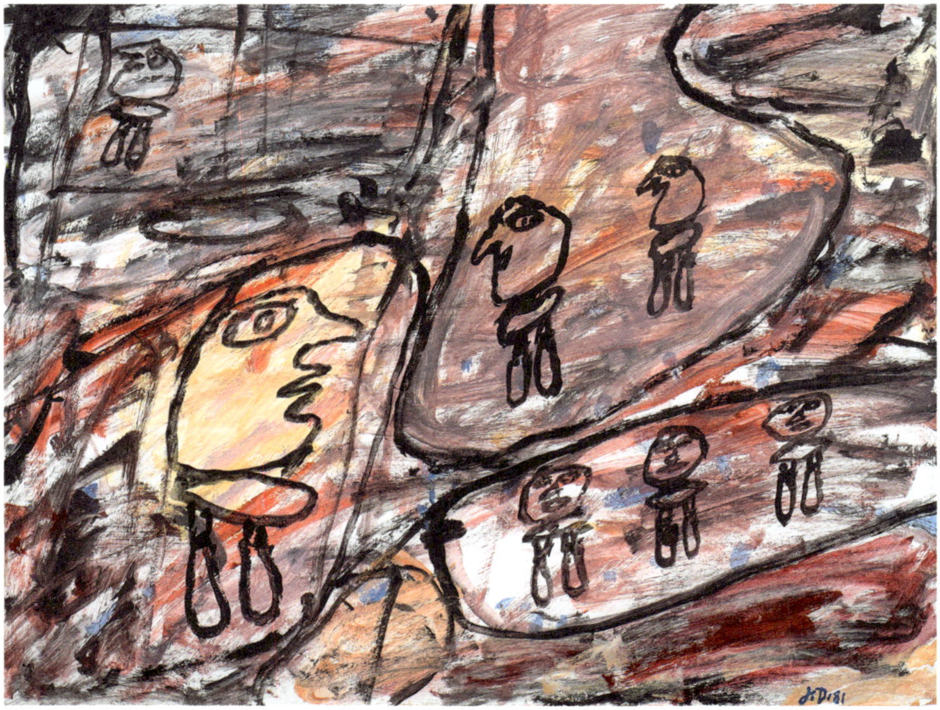

140. Jean Dubuffet. Site avec 7 personnages**, October 18, 1981**

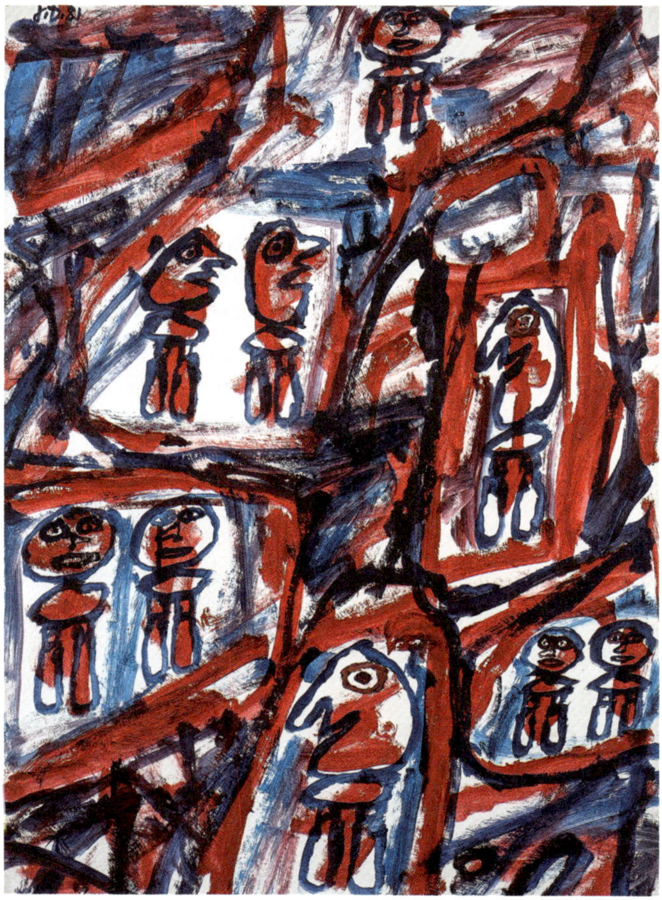

141. Jean Dubuffet. Site avec 9 personnages**, July 25, 1981**

white ground and hatch marks in contrasting colors create optical puzzles in which figures appear and disappear in parts like the Cheshire cat, leaving behind a dancing grin.[11]

In still other works, Dubuffet's focus was less on the figure than on the ground and its delimitation as a place. Consider side by side, for example, two works, one from each end of his career: Vue de Paris of 1943 and Site avec 7 personnages (Site with 7 Figures) of 1981 (figs. 142, 140). In the former, one of several small gouaches depicting the place de l'Estrapade, four figures are shown loitering about the small, triangular plaza nestled between rue de l'Estrapade and rue des Fossés Saint-Jacques at the end of rue Lhomond, where the artist then lived. The location, depicted in a slightly overhanging view, is recognizable thanks to its characteristic shape and blooming paulownias. Site avec 7 personnages, one of no fewer than five hundred pictures in its series, is painted more loosely. With the exception of four bubble-like frames that enclose one, two, or three figures, the surface is almost entirely covered with jagged lines of pale red, with highlights of blue and yellow. Made almost forty years apart, painted in different styles and degrees of simplification, one of these works depicts a specific location in Paris and the other, not, and yet both convey something of a sense of place. In Vue de Paris, that sense is connected to history and topography: the square espouses the natural relief of the land, and the configuration of the streets has a certain history (a quick internet search tells me that the spot takes its name from a torture technique that was practiced there during the Inquisition). In the second painting, place is reduced to a few lines that delimit, within the space of the canvas, areas inhabited by one or multiple figures. The title of the series to which this work belongs, Psycho-sites, suggests that these places might exist in—or for—the mind only.

To read these two pictures side by side in a different way, I could take, as a model, the contrast I mentioned in an earlier chapter between the old Pyrenean village of Navarrenx and the nearby *ville nouvelle* of Mourenx, built purposely to accommodate workers extracting natural gas from the nearby site of Lacq.[12] In his essay about the two neighboring towns, Henri Lefebvre offered a powerful portrait of Navarrenx, a dying village set deep within history and within his own habits: describing its different neighborhoods, he pointed out, "None of them has a separate identity; there are no residential areas separated from the places where people work or enjoy themselves."[13] In Mourenx, by contrast, space was rationalized, and functions were separated: "There are not many traffic lights in Mourenx. But in a sense the place is already nothing but traffic lights: do this, don't do that. . . . Everything which could be has been separated and differentiated: not only specific spheres and types of behavior, but also places and people."[14]

Place, in Mourenx, remained to be invented, after the town was built, ex nihilo, in the name of industrial production. If, like Navarrenx and Mourenx, Dubuffet's two works symbolize two kinds of place, they also suggest the contrast between historically determined places and the mass-produced ones (new towns, housing developments, and so on) that began to dot the country during the Trente Glorieuses.

Dubuffet not only painted figures in different settings but also, as I discussed in chapter 3, planned and occasionally built architectural structures and monuments, often for cities. It was in these projects that he addressed more straightforwardly the issue of place. After all, the main purpose of a monument, in commemorating an event or a person, is to symbolically bring together immaterial history and geographic location so as to create a place of remembrance. And yet, in this instance, Dubuffet challenged place by planning monuments that commemorate nothing—that, as Françoise Choay observed (and it bears quoting again), "mark no collective memory [and] negate natural sites."[15] Comparable to his deliberate effort to disturb the figure-ground distinction and reduce place to little more than a line enclosing a figure, Dubuffet's monuments also unsettle common ideas of place making while—or so he repeatedly claimed, as in the first epigraph to this chapter—"strongly suggesting the idea of place." What interests me here is to what extent Dubuffet's ambiguous thinking about place was triggered by, or perhaps was a commentary on, the reconfiguration of place that occurred through 1960s and 1970s French urbanism. Dubuffet's unrealized architectural projects, such as Rues et immeubles de la ville and Le cirque (The Circus), both of 1973 (figs. 130, 131), and, most of all, the monumental Site scripturaire, which he conceived in 1973–74 for the esplanade of La Défense, are fascinating objects of study in this perspective. To investigate the question of place in Dubuffet's work, then, means to look within the corpus at something that both is impalpable and, at its heart, concerns his very self-definition as an artist, his relationship to the urban environment, and his practice as a whole, all at once.

Painting Places

How, and where, does place appear in painting? The most straightforward answer to this question is in landscape painting, for, as Edward Casey reminds us, places are constituent units of every landscape.[16] Deriving from the Dutch word *landschap*—literally, "shape of the land"—"landscape" was first used in English to define "a vista or 'cut' into the perceived world," and then a painting that represents such a cut.[17] Landscape and place are interdependent: "to be a landscape is to be a *place* already on the road to representation: at the very least it is to be the more or less coherent setting of an embodied point of view."[18] Although Dubuffet frequently used the term *paysage* (landscape) in titles of works throughout his career, only occasionally did he provide a geographic indication or name of a specific place: Place de l'Estrapade (1943), La route d'Étaples (1963), Vue de Paris (Église Saint-Médard) (1943), Paysage du Pas-de-Calais II (1963), La vue sur l'Adret (1961), Faubourg-Montmartre (1962). Naming a place is the first way to appropriate it, as explorers who replaced the phrase *terra incognita* on maps with specific names knew well; thus, in representing places with names, Dubuffet

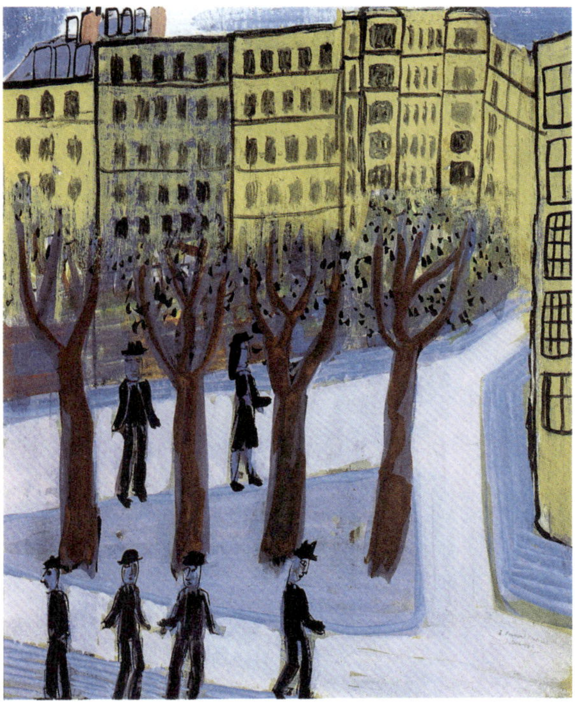

142. Jean Dubuffet. Vue de Paris, April 1943

positioned himself within a long tradition of representation. A place named in a painting or sketch suggests a place that has been seen, scrutinized, and somehow domesticated. In those early Vue de Paris gouaches (figs. 15, 142), Paris seems to have been scaled down to village-like proportions and given a familiarity that brings to mind the rare images of Dubuffet's own home (fig. 143), once described by a critic who visited him in 1976: "Hidden away in a corner of Paris Dubuffet's home off the rue de Vaugirard resembles a secret garden we all possess in memory—a piece of the country concealed in the city."[19]

Most often, however, Dubuffet steered away from intimacy. His painted places veer toward the generic, as far as their titles are concerned, and rather than provoking in the viewer a sense of acquaintance with a place, they disturb expectations. As discussed in the first chapter, Dubuffet, in the large Vue de Paris paintings of 1944—as in the darker, more massive Façades d'immeubles (Building Façades) of 1945—erected high façades that prevent any possibility of a view into the distance and then, as if this were not enough of a rejection of the traditional idea of landscape, created visual ambiguities by which these buildings can also be seen as maps of the city and thereby appeal to a different orientation and a more conceptual reading.

These ambiguities resurfaced when Dubuffet returned to the theme of Paris in the 1961–62 series Paris Circus. While we might initially approach these works as cityscapes, Dubuffet again disrupted the idea of a view in favor of compositions that seem driven by centrifugal and centripetal forces more than by the laws of perspective. The rippling, curved spaces that result place the viewer at the center

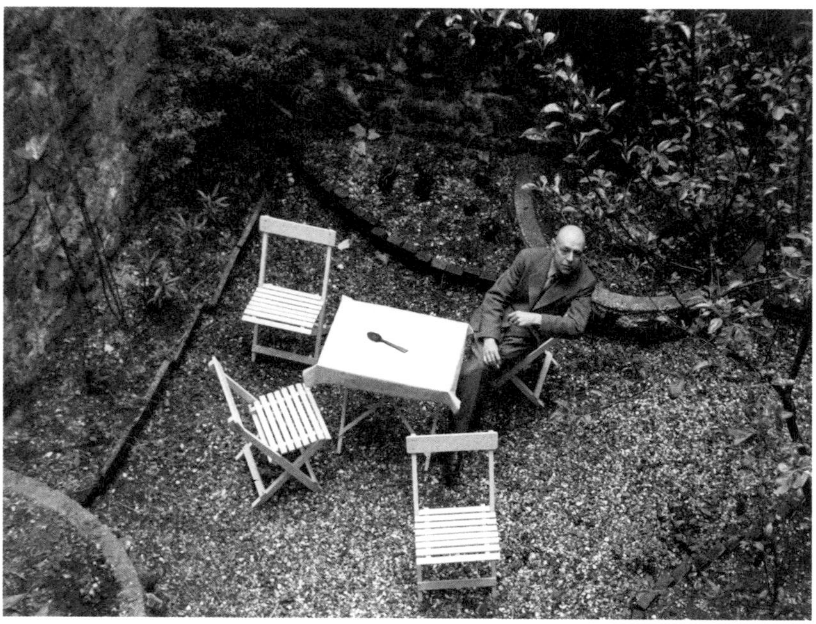

143. Jean Dubuffet seated in his garden, Paris, 1953

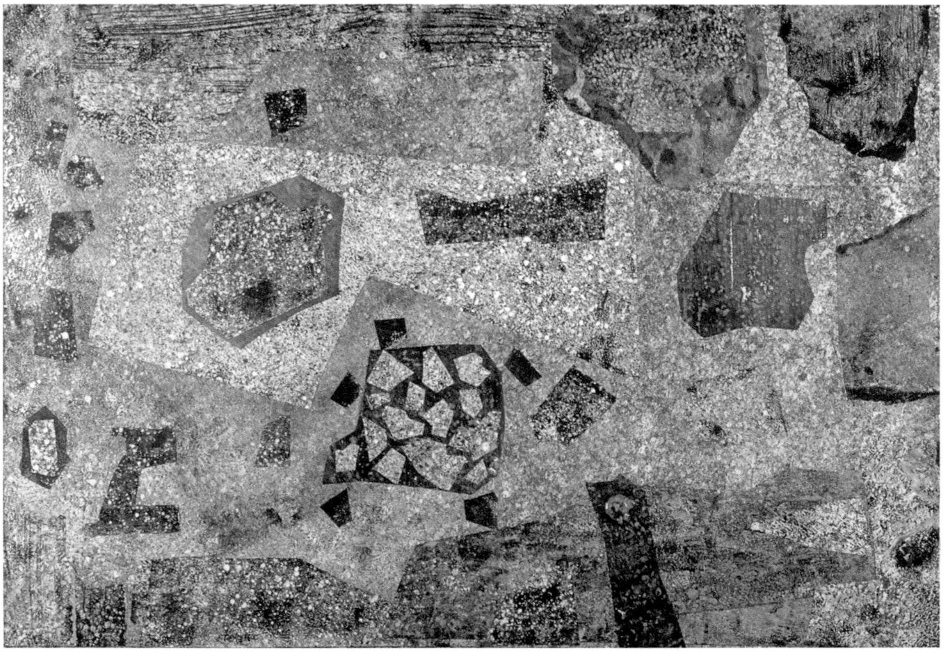

144. Jean Dubuffet. Macadam à la pluie, November 6, 1957

of the image. And, for good measure, most of the names of streets and shops are completely invented. I proposed earlier that Paris Circus stands on the cusp of two epochs—those of postwar reconstruction and 1960s urban expansion—and the same could be said of the idea of place in these paintings. The small shop signs and dinky little buses endow some of the Paris Circus paintings with the quaint, enduring hue of a bygone Paris, and yet the cellular structure of the paintings hints at the generic and the modular, at an industrial coldness to which Dubuffet would give full expression in L'Hourloupe, the cycle into which he delved soon after. With its mix of hackneyed formulas, invented words, and found phrases, Trémolo sur l'œil (1963), the calligraphic text Dubuffet published in the aftermath of Paris Circus (presented here in facsimile and translation on pp. 223–42), conveys in language a sense of estrangement and familiarity comparable to that exuded by the paintings.

Most often, however, Dubuffet's titles are more generic—the word *paysage* appears ubiquitously, for example, to identify unspecific expanses of territory. In some cases, he eschewed the most basic principle of landscape: the intellectual distance implied by one's physical distance from the place depicted. Instead of a view, Dubuffet gives us what appears to be a portion of the Earth, seen in close-up.

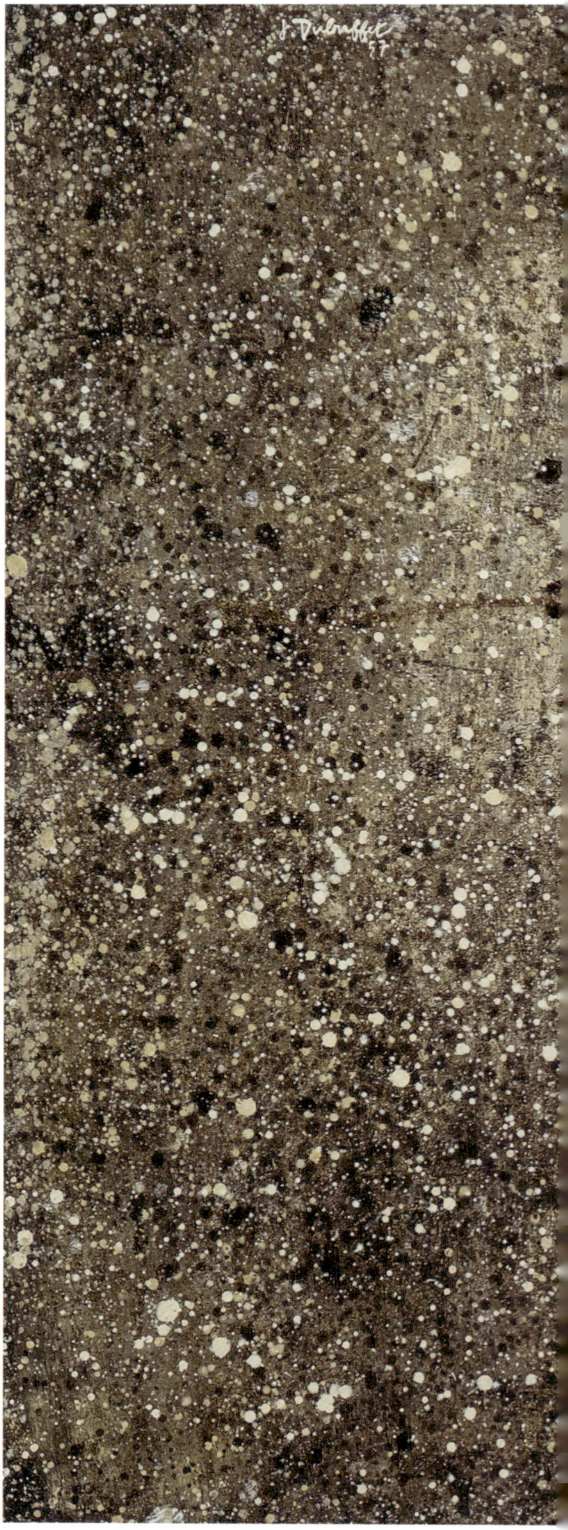
J. Dubuffet 57

145. Jean Dubuffet. <u>Chaussée urbaine mouillée</u>, October 15–26, 1957

He leaves us with land, but no "-scape." *Chaussée urbaine mouillée* (Wet Sidewalk; fig. 145) of 1957 shows a rectangular surface covered in spatters and splashes of an infinite variety of beiges and grays, with whitish highlights. No sense of scale or location is provided, and no context, either: "The very notion of dimension capsizes and abolishes itself," wrote Dubuffet.[20] As with *Chaussée grise* (Gray Sidewalk; fig. 146), also of 1957, which differs in palette and in the shape of the spatters (for which Dubuffet consulted specialized painters' manuals), the closer you look at *Chaussée urbaine mouillée*, the more indistinct it appears. And so it is as well with *Macadam à la pluie* (Rainy Macadam; fig. 144), a *Topographie* of the same year made from assembled pieces of painted paper. All depicting (if we are to trust their titles) fragments of the ground in the city, these works invite close scrutiny and suggest that any unremarkable or unspecified location of any size—such as the ones Dubuffet once aimed to list in his guidebook—can be turned into a "place" if we take care to look down and pay attention to the here and now of our immediate perception.

146. Jean Dubuffet. *Chaussée grise*, November 1957

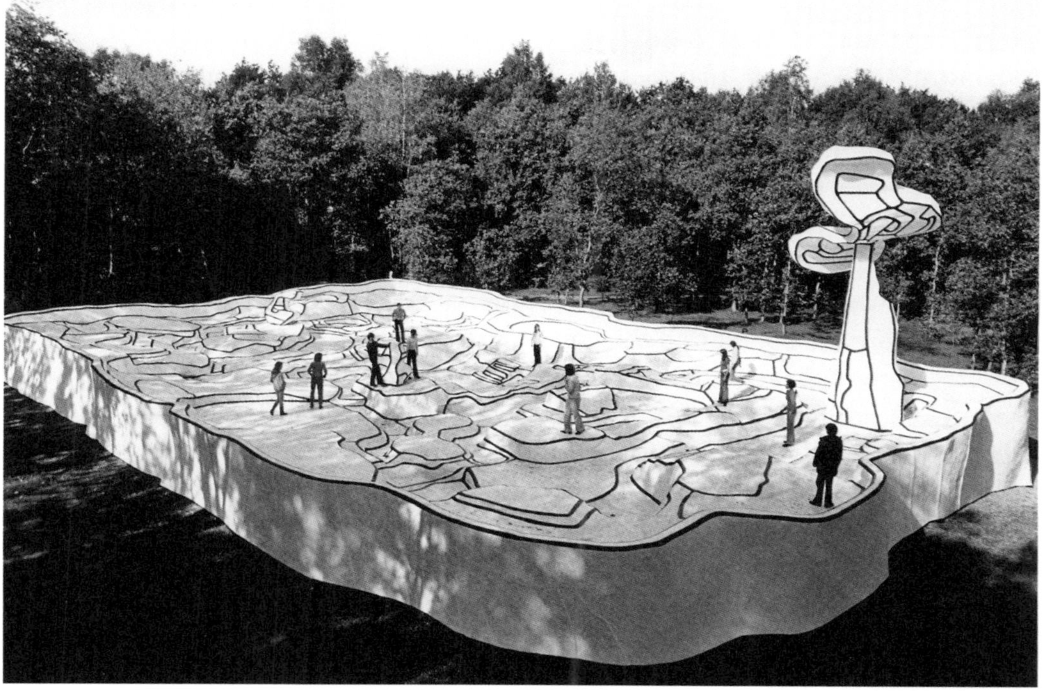

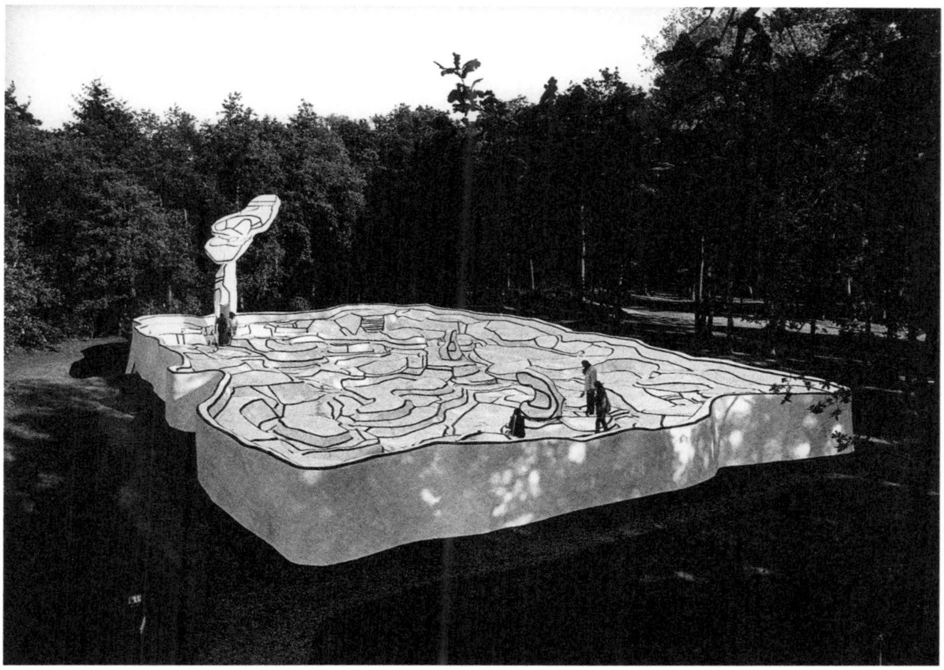

147, 148. Jean Dubuffet (Kurt Wyss, photographer). Jardin d'émail, 1973–74, on the grounds of the Kröller-Müller Museum, Otterlo

Place in the City: Site Scripturaire and Other Architectures

Writing to Rudi Oxenaar, then director of Otterlo's Kröller-Müller Museum, in the garden of which Jardin d'émail was built and inaugurated in 1974, making it the second of Dubuffet's architecture projects to be realized, the artist explained that he had originally conceived his architectural models as staging an ambiguity between two and three dimensions: "I must therefore say that when I was working six years ago on this miniature landscape, it functioned for me half as a painting and half as a model, it was one and the other at the same time."[21]

Whereas I concluded the last chapter by suggesting that Dubuffet aimed less at building than at "inhabiting ideas" and made projects that functioned more like volumetric paintings than livable structures, emphasizing their abstraction, here I would like to proceed differently and begin from the concept of place, then move back into the context of the making of these models, particularly Site scripturaire and several others, to speculate—as the former was canceled before completion—about their relationship to real space and the ways in which Dubuffet envisaged the defining of place.

Le cirque (fig. 130), Petit hôtel particulier, and Rues et immeubles de la ville (fig. 131) can be built in any place and can potentially, to this day, be realized anywhere. But others were developed specifically for particular locations. Such was the case with Site scripturaire, which Dubuffet designed between 1973 and 1974 on commission from the Établissement public d'aménagement de la Défense (EPAD), a public institution created in 1958 to plan and

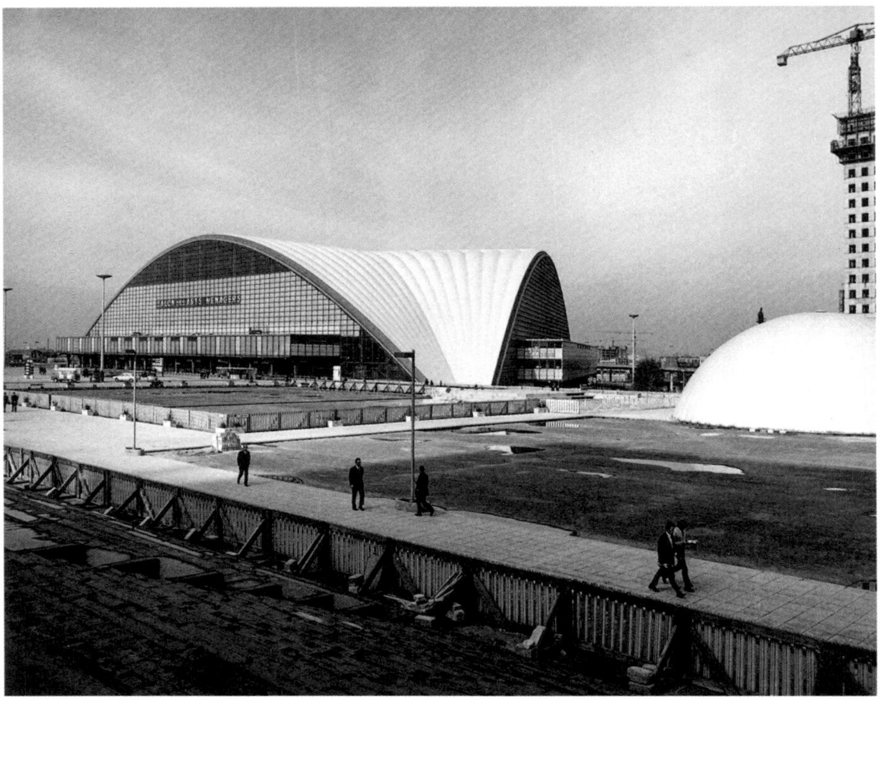

149. Centre des nouvelles industries et technologies (CNIT; built 1956–58), La Défense, near Paris, 1963

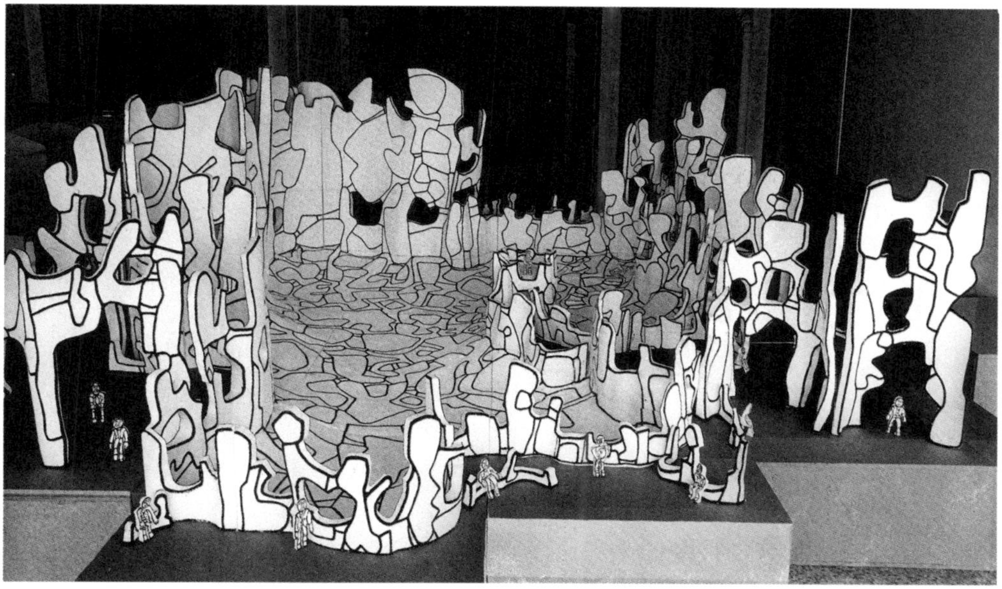

150. Jean Dubuffet. Model of Site scripturaire II for La Défense, January 12–February 17, 1974

organize the new business-focused neighborhood that would cut through three different communes, Nanterre, Puteaux, and Courbevoie, and be called La Défense after a sculptural monument, La défense de Paris, that had been erected in Puteaux in 1883.[22] The technically and formally innovative, clam-shaped Centre des nouvelles industries et technologies (CNIT) was the first building to appear on the site, in the same year EPAD was created (fig. 149). It owed its triangular shape to the outline of the plot of land on which it was built. The principle of a deck covering the central artery of La Défense was determined in 1963 as a way of facilitating underground work on the gas, water, and electricity networks while avoiding disruptive effects on the sidewalks. As the deck became a reality in the years that followed, architects' and planners' dependency on site and plot largely disappeared (even though the official communal divisions remained).[23] High-rises first appeared with the Tour Nobel in 1966.

In 1972, following a consultation with a landscape architecture agency, EPAD launched a series of commissions for works of art to be installed on the concrete esplanade. The selection of Dubuffet was proposed by Germain Viatte, the curator of the artist's 1973 retrospective exhibition at the Grand Palais. Dubuffet secured the assistance of the architect I. M. Pei, with whom he had worked before—on a sculptural project for the entrance of the East Wing of the National Gallery of Art in Washington, DC, which the museum's trustees eventually rejected—and proposed a first version of *Site scripturaire* in November 1973, to which EPAD responded enthusiastically. A second model followed in January–February 1974, accommodating new infrastructure plans for the deck: an elevated "tube" containing a mechanical walkway or "little train" that, in order to be concealed from view, required that the walls of Dubuffet's construction be raised. The artist's second model, six by six meters in footprint (about twenty by twenty feet), showed a closed-off concrete garden with several semidetached archways, viewpoints, and benches around it (fig. 150).[24] The model was projected to be expanded to fifty by sixty meters (about 165 by 195 feet), then situated halfway down the sloping esplanade in an extension of the axis formed by the place de la Concorde and the Arc de Triomphe. This model having been approved, Dubuffet began the long and costly process of casting his original expanded polystyrene model into epoxy. In the meantime, however, the oil crisis of 1973 resulted in budget cuts for EPAD and slowed down its construction projects. In the years that followed, the project gradually fizzled out despite Dubuffet's continued belief that it would be built, until he was finally notified of EPAD's decision to cancel it in 1981.

With its bright white surfaces segmented by undulating black lines, the second model for *Site scripturaire*, pasted into a photomontage (see. pp. 1–2), detaches itself from its environment through a contrast of line and color. Around it is a set of rectilinear low- and high-rises against which its sprawling shape appears almost out of control. Bordered by a rolling, scalloped wall (fig. 152), the irregularly shaped enclosure would be closed off but could, in theory, be walked around and looked at or into, whether standing to peek through an

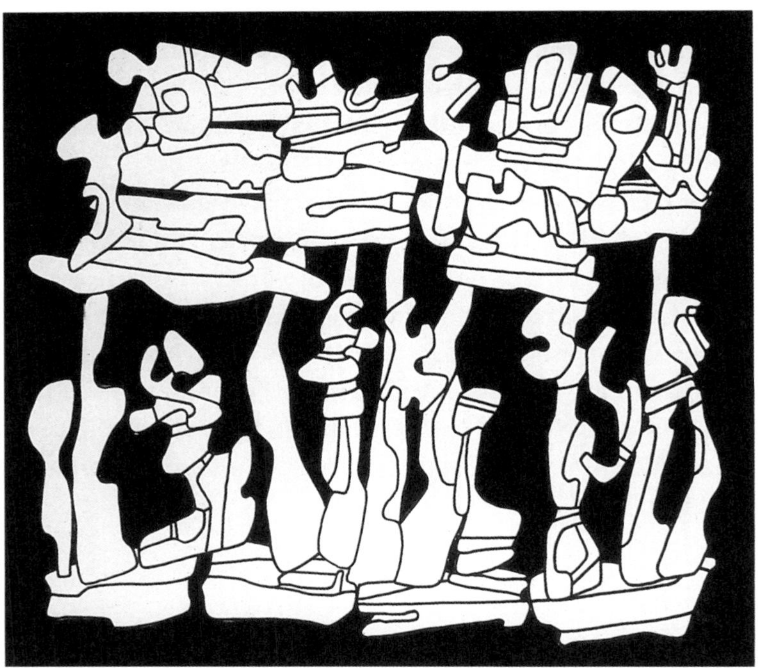

151. Jean Dubuffet. *Arbres portant un château de réminiscences*, December 30, 1970

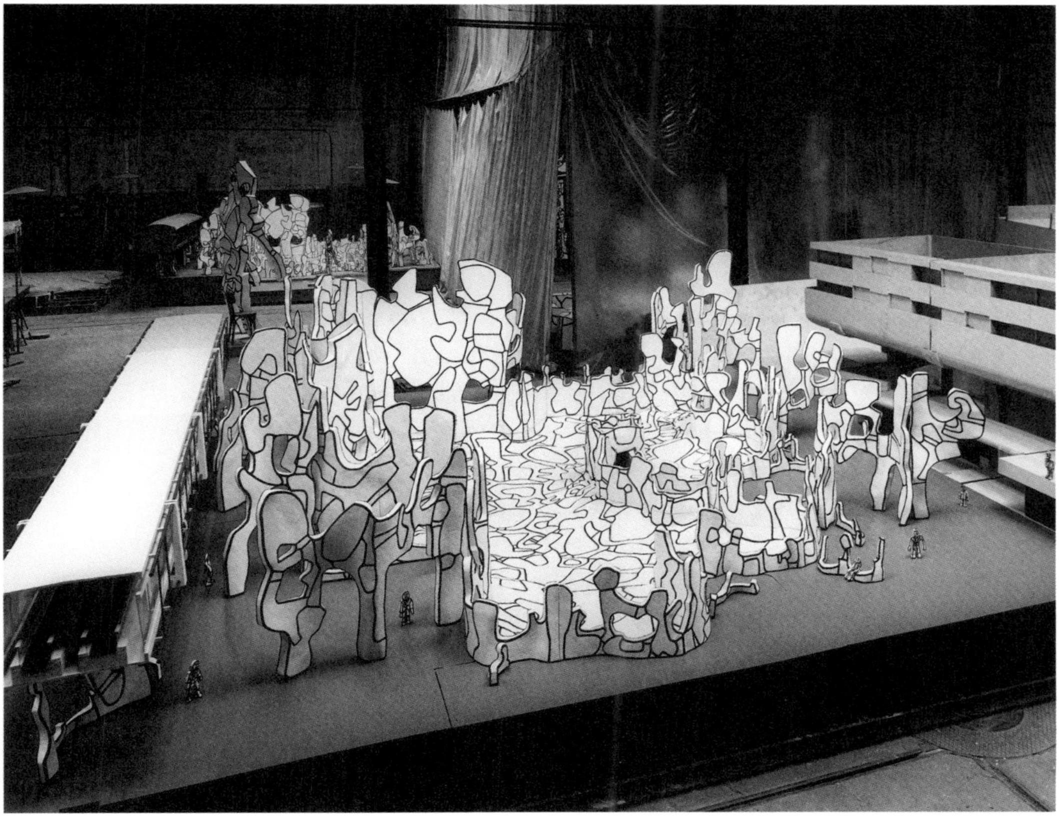

152. Jean Dubuffet. Model of *Site scripturaire II* for La Défense, January 12–February 17, 1974

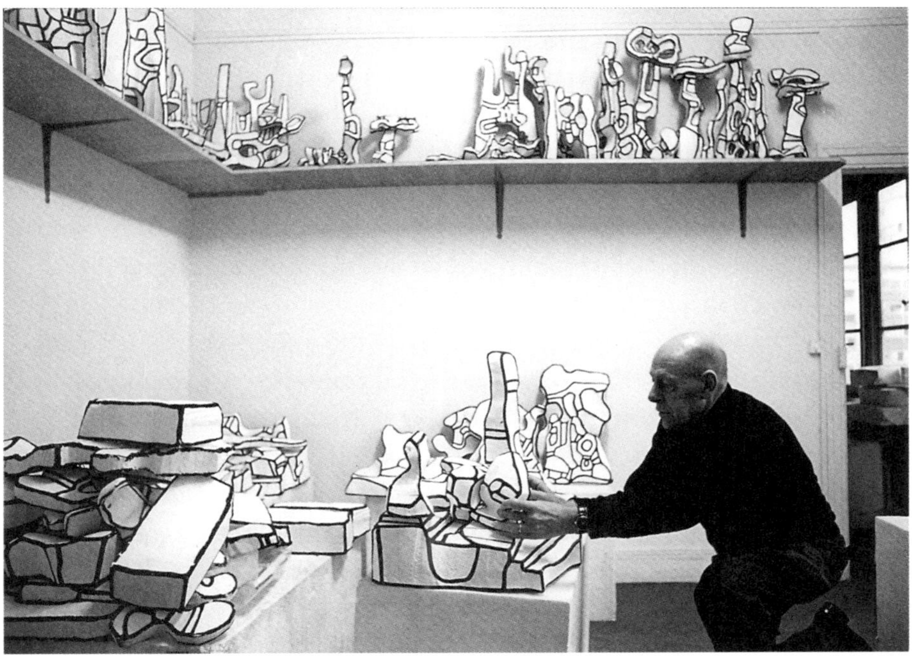

153. Kurt Wyss (photographer). Jean Dubuffet at work in his studio on the rue Labrouste, Paris, 1970

opening in the wall or sitting on a bench.[25] Within the enclosure, the floor was designed to slope gently, leading to a depression in the middle. In other words, Site scripturaire, as envisioned, creates an artificial topography that does not follow that of the deck, mimicking, in that respect, the modernist ideology of the esplanade and its erasure of place but turning it against itself, becoming something "ghostly" and "aberrant," as Dubuffet himself put it.[26]

In her study of Paris urbanism from the 1950s to the mid-1970s, the architectural historian Virginie Lefebvre argued that the concrete deck is more than an architectural motif or a feat of engineering prowess. Literally and metaphorically, it resulted from the desire for a "tabula rasa" with respect to past urbanism and stemmed from a rejection of the street in modern architecture.[27] As early as the 1920s, Le Corbusier called for the disappearance of the street, where ill health proliferates and all-too-frequent intersections prevent the flow of traffic.[28] Later, in 1933, the Athens Charter, written mainly by Le Corbusier, advocated for the independence of the urban project in relation to the site and thus for the negation of topography.[29] The deck exemplifies this new approach to space. It abolishes the connection to the ground, along with its historical dimension and the way streets are formed over time. It is a tabula rasa for a new future.

Approaching the idea of place in Site scripturaire with an ambiguity comparable to that manifested in other works, Dubuffet appears to have mirrored the artificiality of the city with the blatant artificiality of his own construction and the "writing" of black lines. And yet, it was not all about negation. The project recalls the artist's fascination with a range of forms. It extends and sprawls like the foam on the crest of a wave or a cluster of clouds. The difficulty of beholding its circumvallated shape in its entirety and the fact that its central part remains out of reach were reminiscent, for Dubuffet, of the medina in an Arab city, which he often referred to as one of his preferred urban organizations. In a letter to the experimental architect Yona Friedman, the artist extolled the virtues of the Kasbah of Algiers: "One goes from marvel to marvel. Nothing repeats itself. Every forty meters there is a surprise: a sudden constriction; two or three steps; an unanticipated little square. . . . You can see the art of multiplying space, of constituting a whole universe on a small surface. A comforting architecture, stimulating, generating joy."[30] That taste for the Kasbah also appears in other, smaller unrealized projects such as Le cirque, an irregular, broken circle that circumscribes and shelters a plaza, and Rues et immeubles de la ville, whose interlaced walls create a maze of smaller spaces. In this area of his practice, Dubuffet seems to have found another model for affirming the idea of place in his own visual language.

Painting as Place

In the 1975 painting *Esplanade aux passants* (fig. 60), a coarsely outlined landscape is dotted with six figures walking in various directions. There are no buildings or paths, only swift brushstrokes that indicate, here and there, a hint of pictorial depth, a suggestion of a base or grounding of some kind—not that any of these marks ever seems to contain or orient the figures. Several raise their hands, mouths open, as if speaking—although mostly with no visible interlocutor, at least no other figure standing close by. In various spots, darker patches of color suggest shadows, but, like everything else in the picture, they seem to be placed almost at random. Made shortly after Dubuffet finished working on *Site scripturaire*, *Esplanade aux passants* reads to me as a conclusion to the experience of developing a project for the largest and newest esplanade, or deck, in the region—that of La Défense. This is "place" after the invention of the deck—random, without direction, with nothing to orient either us as the viewers or the figures in the painting. The work is part of the series entitled *Lieux abrégés*, paintings representing figures in largely indefinable areas. While some are explicitly about rural spaces, most depict moonlike environments in which male figures dressed in simplified business suits wander aimlessly. The pictures evoke the

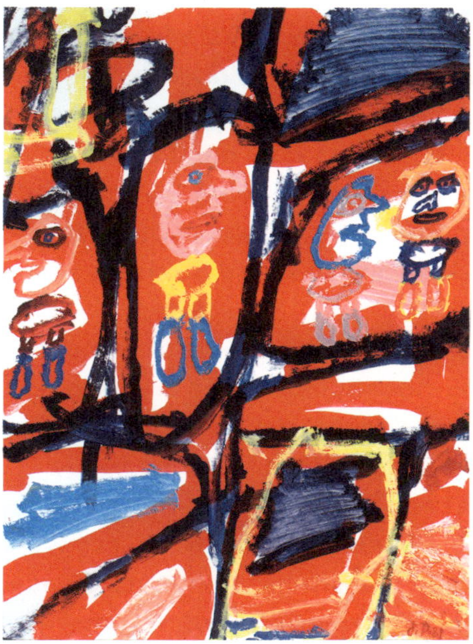

154. Jean Dubuffet. *Site avec 4 personnages*, December 29, 1981

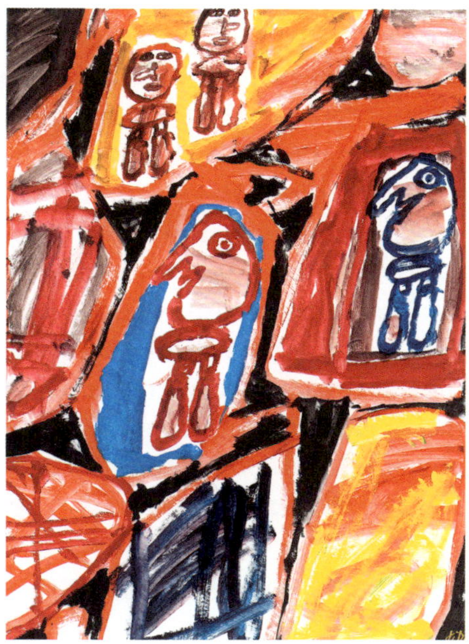

155. Jean Dubuffet. *Site avec 4 personnages*, July 29, 1981

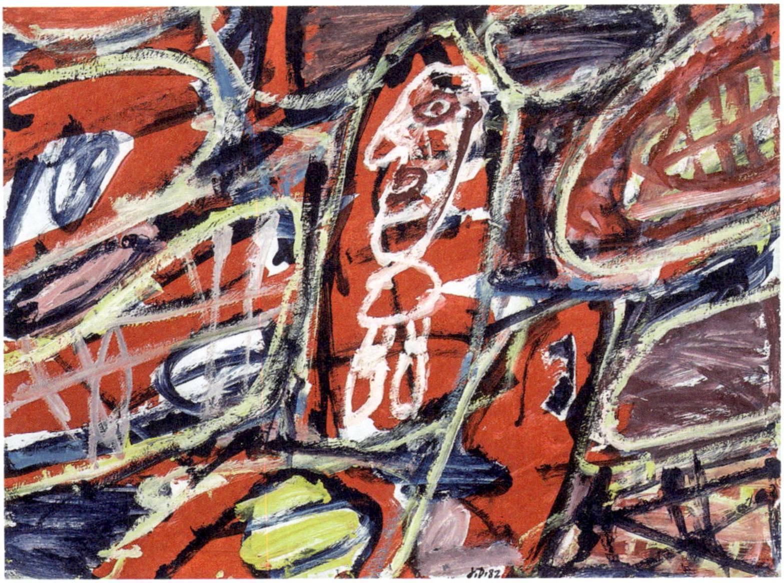

156. Jean Dubuffet. Site avec un personnage, January 21, 1982

kind of postapocalyptic urban space that could erupt after the onset of such futuristic inventions as the walkway and the esplanade. The title, Lieux abrégés, is worth pausing over. It recalls the Lieux momentanés of 1952, simplified landscapes in which Dubuffet relied primarily on extraneous materials added to the paint to react to one another; in parallel, he painted the series Personnages peu corporels (Barely Corporeal Figures), which includes the ghostly L'homme aux cocardes of 1953 (fig. 13). These works elicit phenomenological readings, evoking the quickly shifting field of perception described by the philosopher Maurice Merleau-Ponty, "constantly filled with a play of colors, noises and fleeting tactile sensations which I cannot relate precisely to the context of my clearly perceived world, yet which I nevertheless immediately 'place' in the world, without ever confusing them with my daydreams."[31]

But in the world of Dubuffet, post-Site scripturaire, the smoothness of the paint and the more graphic vocabulary of line drawing and jagged coloring of surfaces suggest another way of apprehending space and defining place within it. In the years that followed the aborted project, Dubuffet worked on the Théâtres de mémoire before returning to a smaller format. He then embarked on several successive series in which the notions of place and site predominate. These are the drawings of the series Sites aux figurines of April–October 1980 and the paintings on paper entitled Partitions of October 1980–January 1981; the five hundred small paintings of Psycho-sites, made between February 1981 and the end of January 1982; and the Site aléatoire paintings of February–December 1982. Despite differences in technique, motif, scale, and palette, these works have in common the presence of one or more figures glued or painted against a background. For the small Sites aux figurines, Dubuffet drew, in felt-tip marker, separate figures and backgrounds covered in hatchings and scrawls, which he then assembled. Such a way of proceeding, separating into different steps the making of an individual picture, evokes the coldness of chain production, and, indeed, the works have less the sensuous appeal of a Chaussée grise than a more distant effect, as if Dubuffet were pushing the idea of representation—in which landscape painting, in the words of Edward Casey, both stands for and stands in for an empirically perceived view—further away. In these last years, Dubuffet claimed more firmly his desire to detach himself from reality. In "Réalisme radical," dated July 9, 1983 (translated here on p. 183), he wrote: "Here I am at the end weary of all instituted images. . . . But having ceased to believe in that embarrassing prosthesis of reality that had been inculcated in me, I must make myself another that suits my use better." Such a statement is anticipated in the text introducing the series Psycho-sites in the thirty-fourth volume of his catalogue raisonné, which the artist had written a year earlier, in May: "It is more ideas of characters

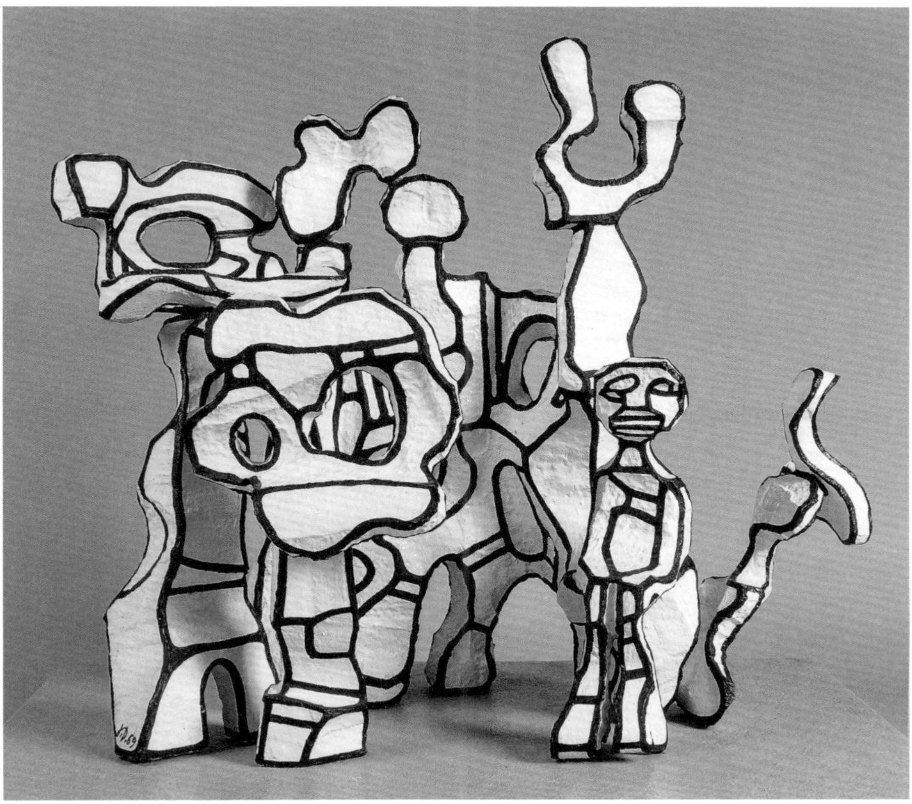

157. Jean Dubuffet. Site à l'homme assis, September 28, 1969

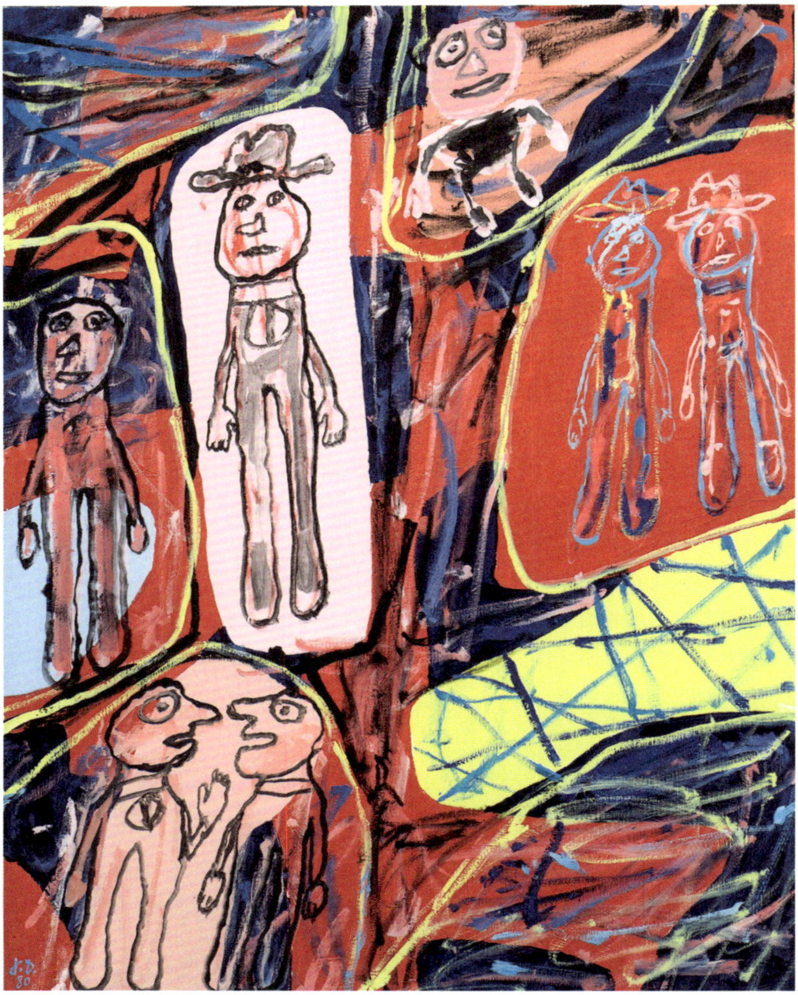

158. Jean Dubuffet. Prestations, December 17, 1980

than people, these ideas of sites."[32] And on the same page: "Rather than a site, it would be better to speak of an idea of a site, somewhat abstract, if you will, nothing more than a notion of place without anything specific."[33] In such a configuration, place might be only an idea, as Dubuffet contended, but I believe, rather, that it shifts from being something represented to something performed. It is performed by us as viewers, who stand in front of these works in which Dubuffet placed absorbed, bewildered, or questioning figures against vague backgrounds, figures that mirror ourselves looking at them and make us aware of our own place—in other words, that help us to create place as we stand or sit before a painting. For the artist who abandons the conventions of representation, place is not *out* there, but *in* there, on the canvas, as he patiently or swiftly outlines a figure before encircling it. The performativity of painting in which Dubuffet engaged throughout his career is reaffirmed in his ultimate series, Non-lieux, laying out the closing of his oeuvre like the closing of a law case.

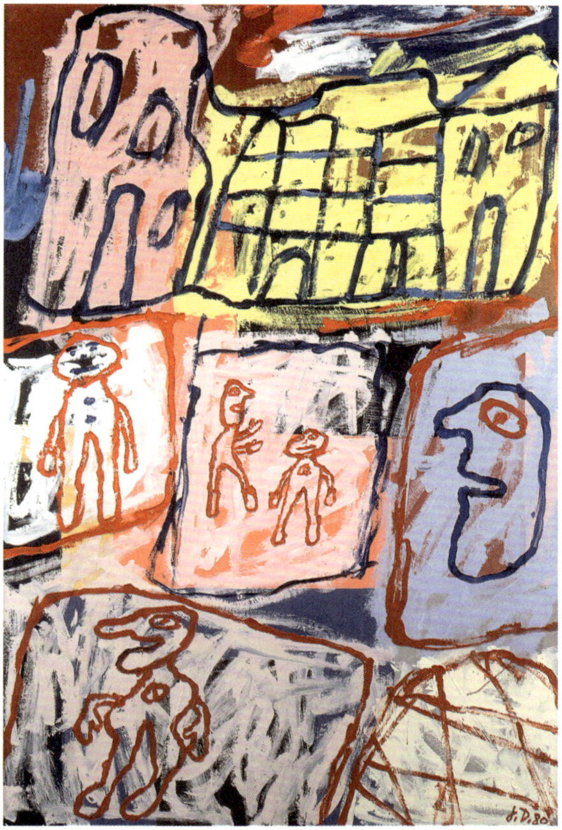

159. Jean Dubuffet. Rencontres en ville, October 27, 1980

As for the city, it played several roles within Dubuffet's imaginary and experience. It was a social and geographic place of production for his work as well as the environment that furnished him with the forms and themes of much of it. In proposing architectural and urban interventions in the texture of the city, Dubuffet became a thinker of the city, largely by reflecting on the way individuals apprehend the space that surrounds them and the possibilities of experiencing a sense of place. He concurrently established and challenged, through monuments and architecture, the idea of permanence that is often associated with place. In this thinking about the city, Dubuffet ultimately extended his painterly speculation about the figure against a ground to the larger scale of urban space. The city becomes a canvas, or *the* canvas—a city where that basic definition of place, as figure on ground, can be endlessly rethought by the artist and re-experienced by his viewers every time they look at one of his paintings on a wall.

Epigraphs: Jean Dubuffet, Bâtons rompus, PES, vol. 3 (1995), 142. "Q: It seems that the evocation of what you call 'sites' or 'places' has a privileged place in your work. A: Yes, but I like to give them an imprecise aspect, so that they are not characterized but have a character of generalization, apt to suggest any place, while strongly suggesting the idea of a place."

Jean Dubuffet, "Présentation" (May 1982), CTJD, vol. 34, Psycho-sites, 1981–1982 (Paris: Minuit, 1984), 7. "A site—one could just as well say a place—very indeterminate, very general."

1 Hubert Damisch, "Note," PES, vol. 1 (1967), 474–75.

2 On the subject of Surrealism and the city, see Ian Walker, City Gorged with Dreams: Surrealism and Documentary Photography in Interwar Paris (Manchester: Manchester University Press, 2002).

3 "Photographic Essay: Paris, Photographs for Life by Edward Clark," Life 20, no. 11 (March 18, 1946).

4 See Michel Winock, Chronique des années soixante (Paris: Seuil, 1987), 121.

5 Edward Casey, The Fate of Place (Berkeley: University of California Press, 1997), ix.

6 See Charles W. J. Withers, "Place and the 'Spatial Turn' in Geography and in History," Journal of the History of Ideas 70, no. 4 (October 2009). See also Tim Cresswell, Place: An Introduction (London: Wiley Blackwell, 2015).

7 John Agnew, Place and Politics (Boston: Allen and Unwin, 1987), cited in Withers, Place and the 'Spatial Turn,' 639–40.

8 Yi-Fu Tuan, "Space and Place: Humanistic Perspective," in Stephen Gale and Gunnar Olsson, eds., Philosophy in Geography (Dordrecht: D. Reidel, 1979), 411.

9 While "site" is usually understood—in geography as well as common parlance—as a geographic location devoid of the theoretical connotations of place, Dubuffet used the terms interchangeably in his writings. Thus, when referring to Dubuffet, I use both terms similarly. Jean Dubuffet, "Présentation," CTJD, vol. 24, Tour aux figures, Amoncellements, Cabinet logologique, 1967–1969 (Paris and Geneva: Weber, 1972), 7.

10 Hubert Damisch, Entrée en matière: Correspondance 1961–1985, Textes 1961–2014, ed. Sophie Berrebi (Paris: La Maison Rouge–Fondation Antoine de Galbert; Zürich: JRP Ringier, 2016), 40.

11 Damisch describes the way in which this contamination of the ground by the figure results, in some cases, in an inversion of ground and figure and points out Dubuffet's refutation, in those works, of the assertion of Gestalt psychology according to which all perception is perception of a figure on a ground. Ibid., 57.

12 See Henri Lefebvre, "Notes on the New Town," in Henri Lefebvre, Introduction to Modernity: Twelve Preludes, September 1959–May 1961, trans. John Moore (London: Verso, 1995), 121.

13 Ibid., 117.

14 Ibid., 119, 120.

15 Françoise Choay, "Les édifices de Jean Dubuffet,'" L'Œil, no. 221 (1973), 16–17.

16 Edward Casey, Representing Place: Landscape Painting and Maps (Minneapolis: University of Minnesota Press, 2002), xv.

17 Ibid., 348.

18 Ibid., xv. Concerning the role of landscape in Dubuffet's oeuvre, see Sophie Berrebi, "Landscape Undone: Jean Dubuffet and the Prehistory of the Picture," in Raphael Bouvier, ed., Jean Dubuffet: Metamorphoses of Landscape (Riehen/Basel: Fondation Beyeler, 2016), 108.

19 John MacGregor, "Art Brut chez Jean Dubuffet," August 21, 1976, PES, vol. 4 (1995), 40.

20 Jean Dubuffet, "Topographies, Texturologies" (April 1959), PES, vol. 2 (1967), 156. Originally published in the catalogue of the exhibition Célébration du sol, Galerie Daniel Cordier, Paris, April 28–June 7, 1959.

21 Dubuffet to Rudi Oxenaar, March 11, 1974, PES, vol. 3 (1995), 364.

22 Prior to the establishment of EPAD, a State decree approving the overall plan of La Défense was passed in 1956. See Lefebvre, Paris—Ville Moderne, 171. La défense de Paris, by Louis-Ernest Barrias, was installed in 1883 in the former carrefour de Courbevoie in Puteaux to commemorate the Franco-Prussian War of 1870.

23 Ibid., 191.

24 The commissioning process of Site scripturaire is explained in detail in Daniel Abadie, Dubuffet as Architect, trans. Elaine Briggs, exh. cat. (Paris: Hazan, 2011), 130–44, from which I draw the main factual elements of my own discussion.

25 In a long letter to I. M. Pei dated November 21, 1973, Dubuffet explained that the chairman of EPAD "and his associates would like the public to be admitted, at least on certain days and at certain times, inside the sculpted garden, wearing protective footwear which would be available for hire"; cited in Abadie, *Dubuffet as Architect*, 132.

26 Ibid. No reference is given for Dubuffet's statement.

27 Ibid., 193.

28 See Françoise Choay, "Mort de la rue," in Marcel Roncayolo, ed., *La ville aujourd'hui: Croissance urbaine et crise du citadin* (Paris: Seuil, 1985), vol. 4 of *Histoire de la France urbaine*, 247, and Françoise Choay, "L'urbanisme en question," introduction to Françoise Choay, ed., *L'urbanisme, utopies et réalités: Une anthologie* (Paris: Seuil, 1965), 35. See also Le Corbusier, *Vers une architecture* (1923), in Choay, *L'urbanisme, utopies et réalités*, 241–42.

29 Choay, "L'urbanisme en question," 34. The Athens Charter, largely written by Le Corbusier, was produced as a result of the fourth installment of the International Congress for Modern Architecture (CIAM), whose subject was the "functional city." See http://www.getty.edu/conservation/publications_resources/research_resources/charters/charter04.html.

30 Dubuffet to Yona Friedman, March 19, 1978. Archives Fondation Dubuffet. My warm thanks to Deborah Couette for bringing this correspondence to my attention.

31 Maurice Merleau-Ponty, *Phenomenology of Perception*, trans. Colin Smith (London: Routledge & Kegan Paul, 1962), xi. First published in 1945 by Gallimard as *Phénoménologie de la perception*.

32 Dubuffet, "Présentation" (May 1982), 7.

33 Ibid.

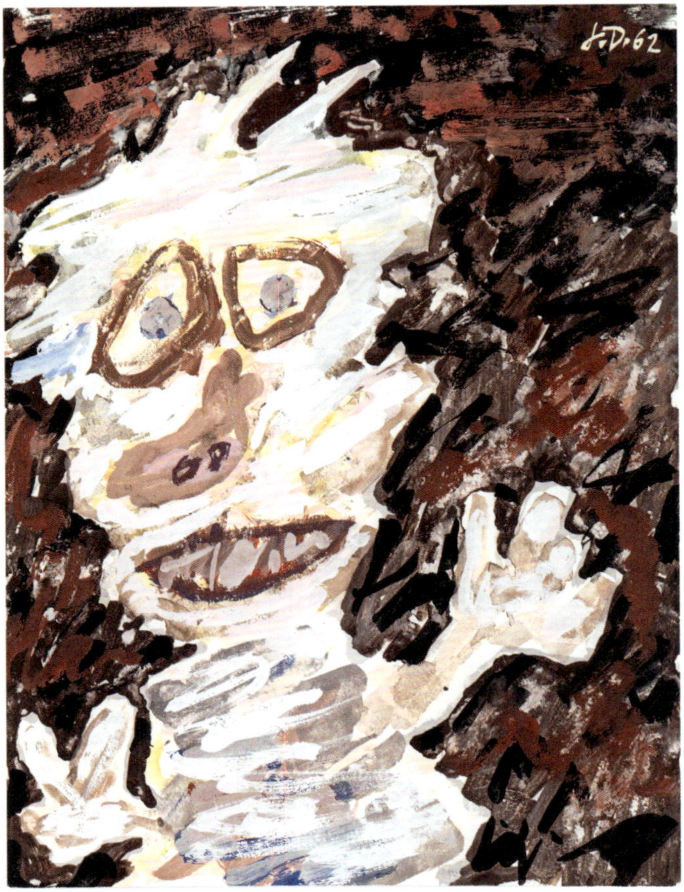

160. Jean Dubuffet. Personnage (buste), March 13, 1962

Acknowledgments

I first extend grateful thanks to Manuela and Iwan Wirth and to James Koch, who invited me to conceive and curate an exhibition on the work of Jean Dubuffet that initiated the research project of which this book, alongside the exhibition, is the result. The idea that the city is central in Dubuffet's art has been a long-standing intuition of mine, and through this project, I have come to see how it provided a model for his work both in its literal transience, often exacerbated by urban development, and in its status as a place where images and encounters, situations and topographies, endlessly form and dissolve. I am very grateful to Hauser & Wirth for giving me the time and space to develop the book and the associated exhibition.

I am enormously indebted to Sophie Webel for her support and generosity throughout the project as well as for her crucial work at the Fondation Dubuffet. I extend additional thanks to Déborah Couette, Léa Yot-Ageron, and Michèle Chakhoff.

Thank you to Hauser & Wirth Publishers—in particular, Michaela Unterdörfer and Kristina Hinrichsen—for their commitment and dedication; to Jennifer Bernstein, for her pristine editing work; and, for the wondrous design of this book, to Linda van Deursen, assisted by Marius Schwarz. My thanks as well to Antonella Casellato at the Pavillon de l'Arsenal, Paris, who was most generous in opening the doors of the center's photography archive and helping me to locate little-known images of exhibitions devoted to the future of Paris and the city itself.

For the exhibition specifically, I wish to thank the entire gallery team for providing such a welcoming and stimulating environment and Julia Wunderlich, in particular, for her fantastic work, in which she was assisted by Carmen Reichmuth and Maria Brassel. I am also grateful to Dieter Thiel for the exceptional design of the exhibition space.

Finally, I thank Marie Baronian, Baptiste Brun, Teri Wehn-Damisch, Bram van Oostveldt, Alfred Pacquement, Carrie Pilto, Alexander van Slobbe, Frédérique Valentin, and Camiel van Winkel for their valuable suggestions and indispensable support during the development of this project and writing of the book.
—SB

Hauser & Wirth and the curator wish to thank all the institutions and generous individuals who made it possible to bring together such an exceptional group of works by Jean Dubuffet:

Acquavella Galleries
Amy Wolf Fine Art
The Baltimore Museum of Art
Brooklyn Museum
Collection d'art Renault
Collection Paul Schärer
Fondation Beyeler
Fondation Dubuffet
Fondation Gandur pour l'Art
Galerie Haas
Indianapolis Museum of Art at Newfields
Jeanne Bucher Jaeger
Katharine Glimcher
Matthew Glimcher
Pace Gallery
Stedelijk Museum Amsterdam
Tate
and all lenders who wish to remain anonymous

Works Cited and Consulted

A

Abadie, Daniel. Dubuffet as Architect. Translated by Elaine Briggs. Exh. cat. Paris: Hazan, 2011.

——. "Réflexion aux couleurs de Jean Dubuffet." In Hubert Damisch, ed., Jean Dubuffet. Paris: Jeu de Paume, Conférences et Colloques, 1992.

B

Bajac, Quentin, and Clément Chéroux. La subversion des images: Surréalisme, photographie, film. Exh. cat. Paris: Centre Pompidou, 2009.

Barthes, Roland. Mythologies. Paris: Seuil, 1957.

Berrebi, Sophie. "The Insider as Outsider: Dubuffet and the United States, 1945–1962." PhD diss., Courtauld Institute of Art, 2003.

——. "Landscape Undone: Jean Dubuffet and the Prehistory of the Picture." In Raphael Bouvier, ed., Jean Dubuffet: Metamorphoses of Landscape, 107–13. Riehen/Basel: Fondation Beyeler, 2016.

——. "L'épingle à nourrice: Dubuffet, image, habit." In Anne Lacoste, Sam Stourzé, and Sophie Webel, eds., Jean Dubuffet: L'outil photographique, 243–51. Arles: Photosynthèse, 2017.

——. "Métromania or the Undersides of Painting." In Christoph Lindner and Andrew Hussey, eds., Paris–Amsterdam Underground: Essays on Cultural Resistance, Subversion, and Diversion, 24–36. Amsterdam: Amsterdam University Press, 2013.

Bertrand Dorléac, Laurence. L'art de la défaite, 1940–1944. Paris: Seuil, 1993.

Boltanski, Luc. Les cadres: La formation d'un groupe social. Paris: Minuit, 1982.

Brassaï. "Du mur des cavernes aux mur d'usine." Minotaure, no. 3–4 (1933), 6–7.

Brun, Baptiste."De l'homme du commun à l'art brut: 'Mise au pire' du primitivisme dans l'œuvre de Jean Dubuffet; Jean Dubuffet et le paradigme primitiviste dans l'immédiat après-guerre, 1944–1951." PhD diss., Université Paris Ouest Nanterre, 2013.

Busbea, Larry. Topologies, The Urban Utopia in France, 1960–1970. Cambridge, MA: MIT Press, 2007.

C

Casey, Edward. The Fate of Place. Berkeley: University of California Press, 1997.

——. Representing Place: Landscape Painting and Maps. Minneapolis: University of Minnesota Press, 2002.

Certeau, Michel de. L'invention du quotidien. Edited by Luce Giard. Paris: Seuil,1980.

——. The Practice of Everyday Life. Translated by Steven F. Rendall. Berkeley: University of California Press, 1984.

Choay, Françoise. Espacements: L'évolution de l'espace urbain en France. Paris: Skira, 1969.

——. "Les édifices de Jean Dubuffet." L'Œil, no. 221 (1973), 16–17.

——, ed. L'urbanisme, utopies et réalités: Une anthologie. Paris: Seuil, 1965.

——. "Mort de la rue." In Marcel Roncayolo, ed., La ville aujourd'hui: Croissance urbaine et crise du citadin. Vol. 4 of Histoire de la France urbaine. Paris: Seuil, 1985.

Cornu, Marcel. La conquête de Paris. Paris: Mercure de France, 1972.

Costes, Laurence. Lire Henri Lefebvre, Le droit à la ville: Vers une sociologie de l'urbain. Paris: Ellipses, 2009.

D

Damisch, Hubert, and Jean Dubuffet. Entrée en matière: Correspondance 1961–1985, Textes 1961–2014. Edited by Sophie Berrebi. Paris: La Maison Rouge–Fondation Antoine de Galbert; Zürich: JRP Ringier, 2016.

Dubois, Jean. Les cadres dans la société de consommation. Paris: Cerf, 1969.

Dubuffet, Jean. Lettres à JB. Paris: Hermann, 1991.

——. Prospectus et tous écrits suivants. Edited by Hubert Damisch. 4 vols. Paris: Gallimard, 1967–95.

Dubuffet, Jean, and Jean Paulhan. Correspondance 1944–1986. Edited by Julien Dieudonné and Marianne Jakobi. Paris: Gallimard, 2003.

Duparc, Christiane. "La folie des grandeurs." Le nouvel Observateur, January 6, 1969.

E

"Édifices." Le nouvel Observateur, December 30, 1968.

Evans, Walker. "The Auto Junkyard." Fortune, April 1962, 132–37. Reprinted in David Campany, ed., Walker Evans: The Magazine Work, 192–97. Göttingen: Steidl, 2014.

F

Fermigier, André. La bataille de Paris: Des Halles à la Pyramide; Chronique d'urbanisme. Paris: Gallimard, 1991.

G Gilardet, Brigitte. Réinventer le musée: François Mathey, un précurseur méconnu (1953–1985). Dijon: Les Presses du réel, 2014.

Gillet, Louis. "L'exposition d'art hollandais au Jeu de Paume." La revue des deux mondes, May 1921, 448. http://www.revuedesdeuxmondes.fr/article-revue/lexposition-dart-hollandais-au-jeu-de-paume/.

Goldwater, Robert. "Dubuffet's Diablerie." View 7, no. 3 (1947), 47–49.

H Haffner, Jeanne. The View from Above: The Science of Social Space. Cambridge, MA: MIT Press, 2013.

Henare, Amiria. "*Nga Aho Tipuna* (Ancestral Threads): Maori Cloaks from New Zealand." In Susanne Küchler and Daniel Miller, eds., Clothing as Material Culture. Oxford: Berg, 2005.

Huxtable, Ada Louise. The Tall Building Artistically Reconsidered: The Search for a Skyscraper Style. Berkeley: University of California Press, 1982.

J Jacob, Max. Correspondance. Vol. 2, Saint-Benoît-sur-Loire 1921–1924. Edited by François Garnier. Paris: Éditions de Paris, 1955.

K Koolhaas, Rem. "What Ever Happened to Urbanism?" (1994). In Office for Metropolitan Architecture, Rem Koolhaas, and Bruce Mau, S, M, L, XL, 961–71. Edited by Jennifer Sigler. Rotterdam: 010, 1995.

L Lampe, Angela. "Une modernité en survol." In Angela Lampe, ed., Vues d'en haut, 32–47. Exh. cat. Metz: Centre Pompidou-Metz, 2013.

Lefebvre, Henri. Le droit à la ville. 3rd edition. Paris: Economica, 2009.

——. The Right to the City. In Henri Lefebvre, Writings on Cities, 63–181. Edited and translated by Eleanor Kofman and Elizabeth Lebas. London: Blackwell, 1996.

Lévi-Strauss, Claude. Le regard éloigné. Paris: Plon, 1983.

Loreau, Max."Présentation" (March 1966). In Catalogue des travaux de Jean Dubuffet, Vol. 20, L'Hourloupe I, 1962–1964, 7–12. Paris: Fondation Dubuffet, 1995.

M Masson, André. Le rebelle du Surréalisme: Écrits. Edited by Françoise Will-Levaillant. Paris: Hermann, 1968.

Mazars, Pierre. "Pas de quartier pour Dubuffet." Le Figaro littéraire, December 16, 1968.

Merleau-Ponty, Maurice. Phenomenology of Perception. Translated by Colin Smith. London: Routledge & Kegan Paul, 1962.

Michel, Jacques. "L'escalade de Jean Dubuffet." Le Monde, January 12, 1969.

Minturn, Kent Mitchell. "Physiognomic Illegibility: Jean Dubuffet's Postwar Portraits." In Jean Dubuffet: Anticultural Positions. Exh. cat. New York: Acquavella, 2016.

Monod-Fontaine, Isabelle. "Chronologie et documents." In Isabelle Monod-Fontaine, ed., Daniel-Henry Kahnweiler: Marchand, éditeur, écrivain, 93–167. Exh. cat. Paris: Centre Georges Pompidou, 1984.

N Nancy, Jean-Luc. La ville au loin. Paris: Mille et une nuits, 1999.

P Paskins, Jacob. Paris under Construction: Building Sites and Urban Transformation in the 1960s. New York: Routledge, Taylor & Francis, 2016.

Perry, Rachel E. "Les messages de Jean Dubuffet." Les Cahiers du MNAM, no. 140 (Summer 2017), 3–33.

Pessis, Céline, Sezin Topçu, and Christophe Bonneuil, eds. Une autre histoire des "Trentes Glorieuses." Paris: La Découverte, 2016.

Picon-Lefèbvre, Virginie. Paris—Ville Moderne: Maine-Montparnasse et la Défense, 1950–1975. Paris: Norma, 2003.

Pluchart, François. "Dubuffet tord le cou à la culture." Combat, August 5, 1968.

R Roger, Alain. Court traité du paysage. Paris: Gallimard, 1997.

Roncayolo, Marcel. "Vivre en ville." In Marcel Roncayolo, ed., La ville aujourd'hui: Croissance urbaine et crise du citadin. Vol. 4 of Histoire de la France urbaine. Paris: Seuil, 1985.

Ross, Kristin. Fast Cars, Clean Bodies: Decolonization and the Reordering of French Culture. Cambridge, MA: MIT Press, 1995.

S Seghers, Pierre. L'homme du commun ou Jean Dubuffet. Paris: Poésie 44, 1944.

Selz, Peter. The Work of Jean Dubuffet. New York: The Museum of Modern Art, 1962.

Semin, Didier. "From Hourloupe to Castille: Dubuffet at Renault." In Ann Hindry, ed., Renault and Art: A Modern Adventure, 71–105. Paris: Hazan, 1999.

Senie, Harriet F. Contemporary Public Sculpture: Tradition, Transformation, and Controversy. New York: Oxford University Press, 1992.

Solier, René de. "Au temps des graffiti, et ensuite." In Jacques Berne, ed., Dubuffet. Paris: L'Herne, 1973.

——. "Court traité des graffiti" [extracts]. Les Cahiers de la Pléiade, no. 1 (April 1946), 52–65.

T Touraine, Alain. La société post-industrielle. Paris: Denoël, 1969.

V Various authors. Selected documents, correspondence, and scrapbooks. Archives Fondation Dubuffet, Paris.

Vitrac, Roger. "Quatrains." Aventure, no. 2 (December 1921), 13–15.

W Wakeman, Rosemary. The Heroic City: Paris, 1946–1958. Chicago: University of Chicago Press, 2009.

Walker, Ian. City Gorged with Dreams: Surrealism and Documentary Photography in Interwar Paris. Manchester: Manchester University Press, 2002.

Winock, Michel. Chronique des années soixante. Paris: Seuil, 1987.

Y Yates, Frances. The Art of Memory. London: Routledge, 1966.

Z Zevi, Bruno. "Tredici progetti per trasformare Parigi." L'Espresso, February 2, 1969.

Ziebinska-Lewandowska, Karolina. Brassaï: Graffiti, le langage des murs. Exh. cat. Paris: Éditions du Centre Pompidou/Xavier Barral, 2016.

List of Illustrations

Works preceded by an asterisk are on view in the exhibition Jean Dubuffet and the City, presented at Hauser & Wirth Zürich June 9–September 1, 2018. Photography credits and copyright information are provided on page 288.

pp. 1–2: Jean Dubuffet (Jean Rabier, photographer). Photomontage of Site scripturaire (1973–74) at its proposed installation site of La Défense, near Paris

* p. 4: Jean Dubuffet. Le citadin (The City Dweller), October 1974. Vinyl paint on canvas, 208 x 130 cm. Collection d'art Renault

pp. 5–6: Kurt Wyss (photographer). Jean Dubuffet in his automobile, 1970

fig. 1: Jean Dubuffet. Dramatisation, January 12, 1978. Acrylic on paper (with 42 cut-out elements), mounted on canvas, 210 x 328 cm. Fondation Dubuffet, Paris

fig. 2: View of Tokyo, ca. 1960

* fig. 3: Jean Dubuffet. Site aléatoire avec deux personnages (Random Site with Two Figures), June 24, 1982. Acrylic on paper (with 2 cut-out elements), mounted on canvas, 67 x 100 cm. Collection Christian Ibrahimchah

fig. 4: Jean Dubuffet and Emilie Carlu (Lili), 1935

fig. 5: Cover of Michel Tapié's Un art autre (Paris: Gabriel Giraud et Fils, 1952)

fig. 6: Distribution of mulled wine at a counter in Les Halles, Paris (Jean Dubuffet standing left of center, in buttoned-up overcoat), January 1, 1942

fig. 7: View of the Tour Montparnasse under construction, Paris, March 14, 1972

fig. 8: Guy Debord. Carte de Paris avant 1957 (Map of Paris before 1957), 1957. Collage on paper, 26.4 x 27 cm

fig. 9: Jacques de la Villeglé. Ex-26, rue du Pont-Neuf, March 11, 1975. Torn posters, mounted on canvas, 80.7 x 115.8 cm. Courtesy Galerie GP & N Vallois, Paris

* fig. 10: Jean Dubuffet. Monument, March 29, 1971. Black marker on cut-out paper, mounted on craft paper, 43.5 x 29 cm. Courtesy Jeanne Bucher Jaeger, Paris

* fig. 11: Jean Dubuffet. Monument à l'homme portant un lionceau (Monument to a Man Carrying a Lion Cub), August 11, 1970. Black marker on cut-out paper, mounted on craft paper, 30 x 21 cm. Courtesy Jeanne Bucher Jaeger, Paris

* fig. 12: Jean Dubuffet. Élégante aux escarpins (Elegant Woman with Court Shoes), January 1946. Oil on canvas, 92 x 73 cm. European collection

* fig. 13: Jean Dubuffet. L'homme aux cocardes, October [n.d.]–November 4, 1952. Oil on canvas, 130 x 95 cm. Private collection, Switzerland

fig. 14: View of place du 18 juin 1940, Paris, March 12, 1971

* fig. 15: Jean Dubuffet. Vue de Paris (View of Paris), April 8, 1943. Gouache on paper, 37 x 30 cm. Private collection

* fig. 16: Jean Dubuffet. Trinité Champs-Élysées, March 25–26, 1961. Oil on canvas, 116 x 89 cm. Fondation Gandur pour l'Art, Geneva

fig. 17: View of the avenue du Maine, Paris, September 1967

fig. 18: Jean Dubuffet. Gambadeuse d'asphalte (Asphalt Saunterer), November 1945. Oil on canvas, 92 x 65 cm. Private collection

* fig. 19: Jean Dubuffet. Rhéteur au mur (Orator at the Wall), March 1945. Oil on canvas, 97.2 x 130.2 cm. The Baltimore Museum of Art: Bequest of Saidie A. May, 1951.293

* fig. 20: Jean Dubuffet. Vire-volte (Spinning Round), May 31, 1961. Oil on canvas, 97 x 130 cm. Tate: Presented by Mrs Cynthia Fraser in memory of her husband, W. Lionel Fraser 1965

* fig. 21: Jean Dubuffet. Deviseurs au journal, July 22–23, 1961. Oil on canvas, 81 x 100 cm. Galerie Haas AG, Zürich

fig. 22: View of place du 18 juin 1940, Paris, March 12, 1971

* fig. 23: Jean Dubuffet. Rue Poisse, February 22, 1963. Oil on canvas, 88.5 x 116 cm. Collection Paul Schärer

fig. 24: View of the Maine-Montparnasse complex under construction, Paris, 1972

fig. 25: Aventure, no. 2 (December 1921). Front cover, table of contents, and interior spread (Roger Vitrac's "Quatrains" illustrated with four woodcuts by Jean Dubuffet)

fig. 26: Jean Dubuffet. Personnage méditant devant une vue de Paris (Figure Meditating in Front of a View of Paris), 1921. Woodcut, 4 x 5.5 cm. Published in Aventure, no. 2 (December 1921). Fondation Dubuffet, Paris

fig. 27: Johannes Vermeer. The Geographer, 1669. Oil on canvas, 53 x 46.6 cm. Städel Museum, Frankfurt am Main

fig. 28: Johannes Vermeer. View of Delft, 1660–61. Oil on canvas, 96.5 x 115.7 cm. Mauritshuis, The Hague

fig. 29: Jean Dubuffet. Vue de Paris (Église Saint-Médard) (View of Paris [Église Saint-Médard]), April 1943. Charcoal on paper, 23.5 x 31.5 cm. From the sketchbook Vues de Paris (p. 12). Fondation Dubuffet, Paris

fig. 30: Jean Dubuffet. Vue de Paris, le petit commerce, February 2, 1944. Oil on canvas, 73 x 92 cm. Private collection, United States

fig. 31: Still from Hôtel du Nord, 1938. Marcel Carné, director; Alexandre Trauner, set designer

fig. 32: Fernand Léger. La ville (The City), 1919. Oil on canvas, 231.1 x 298.4 cm. Philadelphia Museum of Art, A. E. Gallatin Collection, 1952 (1952-61-58)

fig. 33: Jean Dubuffet. Vue de Paris, quartiers résidentiels (View of Paris, Residential Neighborhoods), February 1944. Oil on canvas, 73 x 92 cm

fig. 34: Jean Dubuffet. Paysage vert (Green Landscape), January 1944. Oil on canvas, 65 x 81 cm. Private collection

fig. 35: Jean Dubuffet. Mur aux inscriptions (Wall with Inscriptions), April 1945. Oil on canvas, 99.7 x 81 cm. The Museum of Modern Art, New York, Nina and Gordon Bunshaft Fund

fig. 36: Flyer for La Métromanie ou Les dessous de la capitale exhibition, Galerie Nina Dausset, Paris, 1950. Photolithograph, 33 x 21 cm

fig. 37: View of Demain Paris exhibition, Grand Palais, Paris, March–April 1961

* fig. 38: Jean Dubuffet. Théâtre de la rue (Theater of the Street), January 8–9, 1962. Oil on canvas, 161.3 x 128.3 cm. Collection Paul Schärer

fig. 39: Jean Dubuffet. Rue Turlupet, April 5, 1961. Oil on canvas, 89 x 116 cm. Private collection

fig. 40: View of Demain Paris exhibition, Grand Palais, Paris, March–April 1961

fig. 41: Walker Evans. First spread of "The Auto Junkyard" (pp. 132–33), published in Fortune, April 1962

fig. 42: Jean Dubuffet. L'automobile, fleur de l'industrie (The Automobile, Flower of Industry), June 19–20, 1961. Oil on canvas, 220 x 165 cm. Fondation Louis Vuitton, Paris

fig. 43: Still from Playtime, 1967. Jacques Tati, director; Eugène Roman, set designer

fig. 44: R. W. Yates. Drawn rendition of Giulio Camillo's "memory theater," published in Frances Yates's Art of Memory (London: Routledge, 1966)

* fig. 45: Jean Dubuffet. Les réminiscences associées, September 14, 1977. Acrylic on paper (with 37 cut-out elements), mounted on canvas, 180 x 255 cm. Collection Stedelijk Museum Amsterdam

fig. 46: Jean Dubuffet. Gens et lieux (People and Places), February 2, 1976. Acrylic on paper (with 52 cut-out elements), mounted on canvas, 175 x 194 cm. Private collection

figs. 47–49: Jean Dubuffet. Three sketches for assembling elements of *Gens et lieux* (People and Places), February 2, 1976

fig. 50: Kurt Wyss (photographer). Jean Dubuffet working in his studio on *Garden Party*, part of the series *Théâtres de mémoire*, Paris, June 30, 1976

* fig. 51: Jean Dubuffet. *Autobus Gare Montparnasse (Liqueur des îles)*, early March 1961. Gouache on paper, 67 x 67 cm. Fondation Beyeler, Riehen/Basel, Sammlung Beyeler

fig. 52: Architects at work on the urban master plan for Paris, early 1960s

fig. 53: View of *Demain Paris* exhibition, Grand Palais, Paris, March–April 1961

* fig. 54: Jean Dubuffet. *Maison fondée*, March 27–April 5, 1961. Oil on canvas, 116 x 89 cm. Private collection, Switzerland

* fig. 55: Jean Dubuffet. *Être et paraître* (To Be and to Seem), July 25, 1963. Oil on canvas, 150 x 195 cm. Private collection

* fig. 56: Jean Dubuffet. *Argument et contexte*, March 6, 1977. Acrylic on paper (with 66 cut-out elements), mounted on canvas, 201 x 249 cm. Fondation Beyeler, Riehen/Basel, Sammlung Beyeler

fig. 57: View of *Du Paris des projets au Paris des chantiers* exhibition, Grand Palais, Paris, March–April 1967

* fig. 58: Jean Dubuffet. *Main leste et rescousse* (Nimble Free Hand to the Rescue), December 6, 1964. Vinyl paint on canvas, 150 x 200 cm. Tate: Presented by Galerie Beyeler, Basel, and Galerie Jeanne Bucher, Paris 1966

* fig. 59: Jean Dubuffet. *Mondanité IV*, March 1, 1975. Vinyl paint on paper, mounted on canvas, 64.5 x 92 cm. Private collection

* fig. 60: Jean Dubuffet. *Esplanade aux passants* (Esplanade with Passersby), July 19, 1975. Acrylic on canvas, 133.5 x 165.5 x 5 cm. Indianapolis Museum of Art at Newfields, Gift of Jack H. and Audrey M. Larman, 1988.322

fig. 61: View of *Demain Paris* exhibition, Grand Palais, Paris, March–April 1961

* fig. 62: Jean Dubuffet. *Le passant distrait* (The Distracted Passerby), July 25, 1982. Acrylic on paper (with 1 cut-out element), mounted on paper, 67 x 100 cm. Collection Paul Schärer

* fig. 63: Jean Dubuffet. *La rue* (The Street), November 2, 1980. Oil on canvas, 102 x 140 cm. Fondation Dubuffet, Paris

* fig. 64: Jean Dubuffet. *Scène de rue* (Street Scene), June 23, 1975. Acrylic on paper, mounted on canvas, 102 x 67 cm. Fondation Dubuffet, Paris

fig. 65: Jean Dubuffet. *Monsieur Macadam*, July 1945. Oil and mixed media on canvas, 73 x 60 cm. Private collection

fig. 66: Jean Dubuffet. *Dactylographe* (Typist), October 25, 1944. Lithograph, 26.5 x 16 cm. From the album *Matière et mémoire* (pl. 28). Fondation Dubuffet, Paris

fig. 67: Jean Dubuffet. Four pages from *L'Hourloupe* booklet (clockwise from top left: *Agragule*, *Nautère*, *Poullète*, *Jeandarm*), published in *Le petit Jésus*, no. 10 (summer 1963; original drawings made July 15–25, 1962)

fig. 68: Jean Dubuffet. *Cyclotourisme*, September 13, 1944. Lithograph, 21 x 16 cm. Published on cover of Pierre Seghers's *L'homme du commun* (Paris: Éditions Poésie, 1944)

fig. 69: Invitation card to *Exposition de lithographies de Jean Dubuffet* exhibition, Galerie André, Paris, 1945

* fig. 70: Jean Dubuffet. *Petit hurleur* (Little Howler), March 1944. Oil on canvas, 55 x 46 cm. Private collection

fig. 71: Pablo Picasso. *Femme assise (Dora Maar)* (Seated Woman [Dora Maar]), 1941. Oil on canvas, 99.8 x 80.5 cm. Neue Pinakothek, Munich

fig. 72: Jean Dubuffet. La veuve (The Widow), November 1943. Oil on canvas, 92 x 73 cm. The Metropolitan Museum of Art, New York, The Pierre and Maria-Gaetana Matisse Collection, 2002 (2002.456.2)

fig. 73: Jean Dubuffet. Essayeuse de chapeau, November 1943. Oil on canvas, 60 x 73 cm. Private collection

fig. 74: Pablo Picasso. Nu couché (Reclining Nude), April 4, 1932. Oil on canvas, 130 x 161.7 cm. Musée national Picasso, Paris

fig. 75: Jean Dubuffet. Gambade au sofa, December 1942. Oil on canvas, 50 x 65 cm. Private collection

* fig. 76: Jean Dubuffet. Black Beauty, November 1945. Oil on canvas, 73 x 60 cm. Private collection

fig. 77: Interior spread of catalogue (2nd ed.) for Mirobolus, Macadam et Cie: Hautes pâtes par Jean Dubuffet exhibition, Galerie René Drouin, Paris, May 3–June 1, 1946

fig. 78: Poster for Mirobolus, Macadam et Cie: Hautes pâtes par Jean Dubuffet exhibition, Galerie René Drouin, Paris, May 3–June 1, 1946

fig. 79: Interior spread (pl. 9) of Les murs (Paris: Éditions du Livre, 1950), with poems by Eugène Guillevic and lithographs (1945) by Jean Dubuffet. Fondation Dubuffet, Paris

fig. 80: Brassaï. Untitled, from the series Graffiti, 1945–55. Gelatin silver print, 86.4 x 56.8 cm

* fig. 81: Jean Dubuffet. Époux en visite (Spouses on a Visit), December 12, 1964. Vinyl paint on canvas, 150 x 200 cm. Fondation Gandur pour l'Art, Genève

* fig. 82: Jean Dubuffet. Affluence, March 22–23, 1961. Oil on canvas, 89 x 116 cm. Fondation Dubuffet, Paris

* fig. 83: Jean Dubuffet. Affluence, January 16, 1967. Vinyl paint on canvas, 81 x 100 cm. Fondation Beyeler, Riehen/Basel, Schenkung Collection Renard

* fig. 84: Jean Dubuffet. Mondanité XVIII, March 13, 1975. Vinyl paint on paper, mounted on canvas, 64.5 x 92 cm. Collection Georges and Alain Ibrahimchah

* fig. 85: Jean Dubuffet. Mondanité XXII, March 19, 1975. Vinyl paint on paper, mounted on canvas, 64.5 x 92 cm. Private collection

* fig. 86: Jean Dubuffet. Vertu virtuelle, June 25, 1963. Oil on canvas, 97 x 130 cm. Fondation Beyeler, Riehen/Basel, Sammlung Beyeler

fig. 87: Jean Dubuffet. Archétypes, May 1945. Oil and mixed media on canvas, 100 x 81 cm. Solomon R. Guggenheim Museum, New York

fig. 88: Lucas Cranach the Elder. Adam and Eve, 1538. Oil on wood, 59 x 40.5 cm. Art Museum, University of Toronto, Malcove Collection, Gift by bequest of Dr. Lillian Malcove (M82.147)

fig. 89: Le Corbusier. Le Modulor, 1946. Color print, 15 x 14.6 cm

fig. 90: Jean Dubuffet. Avantage aux cravates (Advantage to the Neckties), March 8, 1978. Acrylic on paper (with 24 cut-out elements), mounted on canvas, 127 x 215 cm. Fondation Dubuffet, Paris

fig. 91: Jean Dubuffet. Promeneur en ville, 1974. Colored pencil and felt-tip pen on paper (with 1 cut-out element), 32.5 x 25 cm. Private collection

fig. 92: Cover of Luc Boltanski's Les cadres: La formation d'un groupe social (Paris: Éditions de Minuit, 1982)

* fig. 93: Jean Dubuffet. Dessin pour un monument (Drawing for a Monument), July 28, 1970. Black marker on cut-out paper, mounted on craft paper, 30 x 21 cm. Courtesy Jeanne Bucher Jaeger, Paris

* fig. 94: Jean Dubuffet. Élément d'architecture contorsionniste IV (Contortionist Architectural Element IV), July 29, 1969. Epoxy resin painted with polyurethane, 50 x 210 x 142 cm. Fondation Dubuffet, Paris

fig. 95: Kurt Wyss (photographer). Jean Dubuffet working on expanded polystyrene elements of La rue (The Street) in his studio, Paris, 1970

fig. 96: Kurt Wyss (photographer). Jean Dubuffet working on model of Site scripturaire II in his studio on the rue Labrouste, Paris, February 2, 1974

fig. 97: Jean Dubuffet (Wolf Slawny, photographer). Tour aux figures, November 1967. Original photomontage (color photographic print cut out and mounted on color photographic print, mounted on cardboard), 33.5 x 26 cm. Fondation Dubuffet, Paris

fig. 98: Jean Dubuffet (Augustin Dumage, photographer). Tour aux figures, 1967. Original photomontage (gelatin silver print cut out and mounted on gelatin silver print, mounted on cardboard), 29 x 39 cm. Fondation Dubuffet, Paris

* fig. 99: Jean Dubuffet. Promenade au jardin (Walk in the Garden), June 21, 1975. Acrylic on paper, mounted on canvas, 102 x 67 cm. Collection Stedelijk Museum Amsterdam

* fig. 100: Jean Dubuffet. Parages fréquentés (Busy Places), October 17, 1979. Acrylic on paper (with 28 cut-out elements), mounted on canvas, 70 x 102 cm. Private collection

* fig. 101: Jean Dubuffet. Carnet de voyage, December 10, 1975. Acrylic on paper (with 39 cut-out elements), mounted on canvas, 150 x 195 cm. Collection Paul Schärer

fig. 102: Jean Dubuffet. Groupe de quatre arbres (Group of Four Trees), April 1971–July 1972. Epoxy resin painted with polyurethane, 11.5 x 12 x 10.5 m. Installed at 1 Chase Manhattan Plaza (28 Liberty Street), New York

* fig. 103: Jean Dubuffet. Habitat urbain, May 28, 1979. Acrylic on paper (with 19 cut-out elements), mounted on canvas, 76 x 70 cm. Collection Paul Schärer

fig. 104: Jean Dubuffet (Augustin Dumage, photographer). Tour aux figures on the esplanade of the Palais de Chaillot (with Eiffel Tower concealed), 1967. Original photomontage (gelatin silver print cut out and mounted on gelatin silver print, mounted on cardboard), 29 x 39 cm. Fondation Dubuffet, Paris

fig. 105: Jean Dubuffet (Augustin Dumage, photographer). Tour aux figures on the esplanade of the Palais de Chaillot (with Eiffel Tower visible), 1967. Original photomontage (gelatin silver print cut out and mounted on gelatin silver print, mounted on cardboard), 29 x 39 cm. Fondation Dubuffet, Paris

fig. 106: Poster by the Association pour la participation du public à l'architecture et à l'urbanisme (A.P.P.A.U.R.): "Non aux bidonvilles, non aux villes bidon: l'urbanisme est un acte politique," May 1968

fig. 107: Jean Dubuffet. Cover of catalogue for Jean Dubuffet: Le Salon d'été et autres exhibition, Musée des arts décoratifs, Paris, March 30–April 30, 1978

figs. 108, 109: Views of Jean Dubuffet: Édifices, projets et maquettes d'architecture exhibition, Musée des arts décoratifs, Paris, December 11, 1968–February 10, 1969

fig. 110: Jean Dubuffet. Cover and interior spread of Dubuffet: Édifices (Paris: Éditions Jeanne Bucher; Basel: Beyeler, 1968)

* fig. 111: Jean Dubuffet. Rue Tournique Bourlique, February 26, 1963. Oil on canvas, 73 x 92 cm. Brooklyn Museum, Bequest of William K. Jacobs, Jr., 1992.107.9

fig. 112: Jean Dubuffet. Machine à écrire I (Typewriter I), June 29, 1964. Oil on canvas, 100 x 81 cm. Private collection

fig. 113: Jean Dubuffet. Cafetière V, December 17, 1965. Vinyl paint on paper, mounted on canvas, 104 x 69 cm. Private collection

fig. 114: Jean Dubuffet. Demeure II (avec seuil et cheminées) (Residence [with Threshold and Fireplace]), March 25, 1966. Vinyl paint on canvas, 146 x 114 cm. Private collection

fig. 115: Jean Dubuffet. Cabinet logologique, August 1967–February 1969. Transfer on polyester, 3.5 x 7 x 6 m. Fondation Dubuffet, Paris

fig. 116: Jean Dubuffet. Closerie Falbala, Périgny-sur-Yerres, built 1971–73. Epoxy resin and concrete painted with polyurethane. Fondation Dubuffet, Paris

figs. 117, 118: Views of Jean Dubuffet: Peintures monumentées exhibition, Galerie Jeanne Bucher, Paris, December 12, 1968–February 8, 1969

fig. 119: Page from scrapbook of press coverage for Jean Dubuffet's exhibitions in the archives of the Fondation Dubuffet, Paris

fig. 120: Cover and interior page of Paris Match ("Paris dans 20 ans" feature), no. 951 (July 1, 1967)

fig. 121: View of Du Paris des projets au Paris des chantiers exhibition, Grand Palais, Paris, March–April 1967

fig. 122: Poster for Du Paris des projets au Paris des chantiers exhibition, Grand Palais, Paris, March–April 1967

fig. 123: Bruno Zevi's article in L'Espresso, February 2, 1969, featuring Jean Dubuffet's Tour aux figures and the Tour Nobel at La Défense, near Paris, from a scrapbook in the archives of the Fondation Dubuffet, Paris

fig. 124 (p. 207): View from the rue de Rennes of the Tour Montparnasse under construction, Paris, February 16, 1972

fig. 125: Jean Dubuffet. Le Gastrovolve, 1968. Reproduced in Dubuffet: Édifices (Paris: Éditions Jeanne Bucher; Basel: Beyeler, 1968)

fig. 126: Aerial view of La Grande Borne, Grigny, built 1967–69. Émile Aillaud, architect

fig. 127: Jean Dubuffet. Groupe de quatre arbres (Group of Four Trees), April 1971–July 1972. Epoxy resin painted with polyurethane, 11.5 x 12 x 10.5 m. Installed at 1 Chase Manhattan Plaza (28 Liberty Street), New York. Fondation Dubuffet, Paris

fig. 128: View of Lever House (built 1948–52), 390 Park Avenue, New York, March 25, 1952. Skidmore, Owings & Merrill (SOM), architects; Gordon Bunshaft, chief designer

fig. 129: View of Lever House (built 1948–52), 390 Park Avenue, New York, 2011. Skidmore, Owings & Merrill (SOM), architects; Gordon Bunshaft, chief designer

* fig. 130: Jean Dubuffet. Le cirque (The Circus), January 2, 1970. Epoxy resin painted with polyurethane, 50.5 x 142 x 114 cm. Fondation Dubuffet, Paris

* fig. 131: Jean Dubuffet. Rues et immeubles de la ville (Streets and Buildings of the City), July 1969. Epoxy resin painted with polyurethane, 50 x 210 x 142 cm. Fondation Dubuffet, Paris

figs. 132–34: Views of Jean Dubuffet: Le Salon d'été et autres exhibition, Musée des arts décoratifs, Paris, March 30–April 30, 1978

fig. 135: Jean Dubuffet. Trémolo sur l'œil, 1962–63. Written and illustrated in black Chinese ink, October 1962; retouched January 1963; transferred to zinc lithographic plates and printed, summer 1963. Illustrated book with 14 photolithographs, 21.5 x 17.2 x 0.6 cm. Edition of 300; published by Gaston Puel, Lavaur

fig. 136: G. E. [Guy] Debord with Asger Jorn. Guide psychogéographique de Paris: Discours sur les passions de l'amour (Copenhagen: Le Bauhaus Imaginiste, 1957)

fig. 137: Cover of Life magazine, March 18, 1946, containing a photographic essay on Paris by Edward Clark

fig. 138: Master plan of the *ville nouvelle* of Mourenx, built 1957–61. René Coulon, architect

* fig. 139: Jean Dubuffet. La rue (The Street), August 1971–March 1974. Epoxy resin painted with polyurethane, 105 x 410 x 70 cm. Fondation Dubuffet, Paris

* fig. 140: Jean Dubuffet. Site avec 7 personnages (Site with 7 Figures), October 18, 1981. Acrylic on paper, mounted on canvas, 50 x 67 cm. Private collection

* fig. 141: Jean Dubuffet. Site avec 9 personnages (Site with 9 Figures), July 25, 1981. Acrylic on paper, mounted on canvas, 67 x 50 cm. Private collection

fig. 142: Jean Dubuffet. Vue de Paris (View of Paris), April 1943. Gouache on paper, 37 x 30 cm. Private collection

fig. 143: Jean Dubuffet seated in the garden of his home on allée Maintenon, rue de Vaugirard, Paris, 1953

fig. 144: Jean Dubuffet. Macadam à la pluie (Rainy Macadam), November 6, 1957. Oil on paper (assemblage), 68 x 100 cm. Private collection

* fig. 145: Jean Dubuffet. Chaussée urbaine mouillée (Wet Sidewalk), October 15–26, 1957. Oil on canvas, 81 x 100 cm. Private collection

* fig. 146: Jean Dubuffet. Chaussée grise (Gray Sidewalk), November 1957. Oil on canvas, 97 x 130 cm. Private collection

figs. 147, 148: Jean Dubuffet (Kurt Wyss, photographer). Jardin d'émail (Enameled Garden), 1973–74. Epoxy resin and concrete painted with polyurethane, length 300 m, width 200 m. Kröller-Müller Museum, Otterlo

fig. 149: View of Centre des nouvelles industries et technologies (CNIT; built 1956–58), La Défense, near Paris, 1963. Robert Édouard Camelot, Jean de Mailly, and Bernard Zehrfuss, with Jean Prouvé, architects

fig. 150: Jean Dubuffet. Model of Site scripturaire II for La Défense, January 12–February 17, 1974. Epoxy resin painted with polyurethane, 160 x 580 x 560 cm. Fondation Dubuffet, Paris

* fig. 151: Jean Dubuffet. Arbres portant un château de réminiscences (Trees Bearing a Castle of Reminiscences), December 30, 1970. Black marker on cut-out paper, mounted on craft paper, 50 x 51 cm. Courtesy Jeanne Bucher Jaeger, Paris

fig. 152: Jean Dubuffet. Model of Site scripturaire II for La Défense, January 12–February 17, 1974. Epoxy resin painted with polyurethane, 160 x 580 x 560 cm. Fondation Dubuffet, Paris

fig. 153: Kurt Wyss (photographer). Jean Dubuffet at work in his studio on the rue Labrouste, Paris, 1970

* fig. 154: Jean Dubuffet. Site avec 4 personnages (Site with 4 Figures), December 29, 1981. Acrylic on paper, mounted on canvas, 67.3 x 50.2 cm. Collection Katharine Glimcher

* fig. 155: Jean Dubuffet. Site avec 4 personnages (Site with 4 Figures), July 29, 1981. Acrylic on paper, mounted on canvas, 67.3 x 50.2 cm. Private collection, courtesy of Pace Gallery

* fig. 156: Jean Dubuffet. Site avec un personnage (Site with One Figure), January 21, 1982. Acrylic on paper, mounted on canvas, 50.2 x 67.3 cm. Collection Matthew Glimcher

* fig. 157: Jean Dubuffet. Site à l'homme assis (Site with Seated Man), September 28, 1969. Polyester resin painted with polyurethane, 60 x 64 x 38 cm. Collection d'art Renault

* fig. 158: Jean Dubuffet. Prestations, December 17, 1980. Acrylic on canvas, 100 x 81 cm, Private collection, New York

* fig. 159: Jean Dubuffet. Rencontres en ville (Encounters in the City), October 27, 1980. Acrylic on paper, mounted on canvas, 102 x 70 cm. Fondation Dubuffet, Paris

* fig. 160: Jean Dubuffet. Personnage (buste) (Figure [Bust]), March 13, 1962. Gouache on paper, 26 x 20.3 cm. Private collection

Index of Names and Places

About the Author

Dr. Sophie Berrebi is an art historian, writer, and curator. Born in Paris and based at the University of Amsterdam, she is the author of The Shape of Evidence: Contemporary Art and the Document (Amsterdam: Valiz, 2015) and the editor of Entrée en matière: Correspondance 1961–1985, Textes 1961–2014, by Hubert Damisch and Jean Dubuffet (Paris: La Maison Rouge–Fondation Antoine de Galbert; Zürich: JRP Ringier, 2016). Most recently, she curated the exhibition Jean Dubuffet: The Deep End at the Stedelijk Museum Amsterdam (2017). She is currently writing a book entitled Elements of Fashion: Icons, Details, Gestures, an investigation into clothes and how they are worn involving visual culture, ethnography, and art history.

Published in conjunction with the exhibition Jean Dubuffet and the City
Curated by Sophie Berrebi
June 9–September 1, 2018
Hauser & Wirth Zürich

Book design and typography
Mevis & van Deursen, with Marius Schwarz

Editing and proofreading
Jennifer Bernstein, Tenacious Editorial

Pre-press by LUP AG, Cologne

Printed by Druckhaus Köthen, Köthen (Anhalt)

Dust jacket: Reprotex
Cover Paper: Munken Lynx, 300g
Paper: Munken Lynx, 120g
Typeface: Univers

On the dust jacket: Jean Dubuffet. La rue (detail), August 1971–March 1974 (see fig. 139, p. 249)

Cataloging-in-Publication Data is available from the Library of Congress.

Available worldwide, excluding Europe, through:

ARTBOOK | D.A.P.
75 Broad Street, Suite 630
New York, NY 10004
Tel 212 627 1999 | Fax 212 627 9484
ISBN: 978-3-906915-11-1

Printed and bound in Germany